Shaka's Children

Stephen Taylor is the author of *The Mighty Nimrod*
(HarperCollins, 1989). He writes for *The Times*.

D1302173

SHAKA'S CHILDREN

A History of the Zulu People

STEPHEN TAYLOR

HarperCollins*Publishers*

To Caroline

HarperCollins*Publishers*
77–85 Fulham Palace Road,
Hammersmith, London W6 8JB

This paperback edition 1995
3 5 7 9 8 6 4 2

First published in Great Britain by
HarperCollins*Publishers* 1994

ISBN 0 00 638468 4

Set in Meridien

Printed and bound in Great Britain by
Caledonian International Book Manufacturing Ltd, Glasgow

I HEARD THE OLD SONG

At first when I heard the old song
I listened bitter, ignorant,
But now in a new voice I make amends.
When your voices murmur in your breasts
Echoing from the depths of old passions,
Carried from the Zulu hills out across the earth,
They call back to me things that are no more,
Faint almost beyond grope of memory
And the long river of my tears.
The song you are chanting, you men of Ngungunyana,
A practised tune for the Vendas of Thobela
Was first sung by the fathers of our fathers
Who dwelt secure in their great homesteads
And through twirling horns of ox and buffalo smoked hemp,
Their women making merry under the trees.
  You strike fire in me, wake me to madness.

Benedict Vilakazi, 1906–47

CONTENTS

ILLUSTRATIONS

LIST OF MAPS

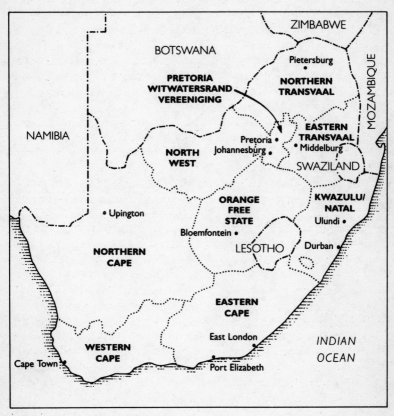

SOUTH AFRICA TODAY

PREFACE

At the end of 1990, I went back to South Africa, having left it more than twenty years earlier to live in Britain. Like many others who had made their homes abroad in the apartheid era, I was drawn back by the drama of political reform in the country of my birth.

Growing up in what used to be called a liberal home in the 1960s, I had learned that it was disrespectful to talk of black people in terms of their tribal background. This seemed only proper in the light of the crude way apartheid categorized people by ethnic group and accorded to each a greater or lesser status. But it was clear, too, that many educated blacks did not like to talk about the African past.

My ideas about ethnic identity were changed gradually over the next two decades, first by travelling in Asia, where I discovered communities in which tribal culture not only flourished but was a matter of pride, and secondly by a period of seven years as a foreign correspondent in Africa, south-east Asia and the south Pacific. In each region, in countries as diverse as Zimbabwe and Afghanistan, Malaysia and Fiji, I found ethnic diversity in abundance, sometimes as a part of a vibrant multiculturalism, sometimes as a force for instability, but everywhere an inescapable part of the landscape.

Inevitably, I found myself observing South Africa in the light of these experiences, following the collapse of apartheid. The Zulu kingdom had been a primary force in shaping the country during the nineteenth century. Now, amid negotiations on a new constitution, it was evident that at least a significant number of Zulus wanted independence restored to them, much like the former Soviet republics following the collapse of communism. Mangosuthu Buthelezi, a traditional chief, and his Inkatha

Freedom Party, stood belligerently in the way of what was being described as the New South Africa. Buthelezi was a mass of paradoxes, a Christian who honoured African tradition and an avowed democrat who yet clearly distrusted the ballot. Urbane and charming, with connections in the boardrooms of Western corporations, he could, in a moment, turn from avuncularity to the language of tribal war. Evidence that he was not to be taken lightly could be seen in the ragtag *impis*, bristling with homemade spears and hubris, cutting a swathe through the townships of the Reef and Natal.

I embarked on this study partly to resolve my own understanding of modern ethnicity. Zulus, by which I mean the Zulu-speaking people, number between seven and eight million and are the largest population group in South Africa. Clearly, their conduct will be critical to peace and progress under the new government. Equally clearly, however, they are a far from homogeneous group. Many Zulu-speakers detest Buthelezi. A significant number would also deny any loyalty to King Goodwill Zwelithini, the eighth Zulu king since Shaka, although the monarchy still commands an involuntary and deep-rooted respect.

In short, Zulu society is infinitely more diverse than the caricature images that colour the common perception of 'tribe'. Western perspectives of Africa have tended to the simplistic: in this respect, there is little to choose between the brute savage whose slavery or salvation was the interest of nineteenth-century Europe and the pathetic figure portrayed in the post-colonial era, the bemused victim, robbed of innocence and land by depraved whites who despoiled an Eden.

It is not only Europeans who reach readily for hackneyed labels. Black South Africans have their own ethnic clichés. Zulus are often held to be backward, largely because of the durability in Zululand of a traditional culture which other ethnic groups congratulate themselves on having left behind. Fear, too, taints the picture. 'A Zulu just likes to fight,' one may hear from other blacks. 'He has to show he is stronger than another man.'

These caricatures are still surprisingly resilient, and there may be a danger that South Africa will become yet another morality play for Western eyes. Faced with the misery elsewhere on the continent – ethnic strife, corruption and famine – many are looking to this profoundly troubled land as Africa's last chance to prove that it can sustain a multi-racial democracy respectful of individual rights, and capable of providing for itself. It is a daunting and unfair responsibility.

At bottom, it was in an attempt to go beyond the clichés that I wrote this book. I hoped to show that the history of one African people, seen through their own oral traditions, their devastating encounter with industrialized man, their experiences of conquest, survival, resistance and assimilation, can shed light on the continent as a whole today. This is obviously not the comprehensive work that one must hope will one day be written by a great Zulu writer in his own language. It can only present some of the personalities and forces that shaped a people in their past and examine the actions that are being taken at what is a critical point for their future.

I make no apology for following the 'biographical approach' to history; leaders and leadership loom large in any traditional society, although I have tried also to set the historical narrative against a backdrop reflecting the lives of ordinary people. Equally, it seems to me that any account that ignores the mythological and mystical aspects of African culture misses half the point. I am aware that in these respects I am rowing against the tide of much modern South African academic thinking.

History and mythology are hard to separate in the life of Shaka, the crucial figure in the Zulu rise. If I have dwelt on him at length it has been in an effort to sift one from the other, and yet still do justice to both. In trying to come to terms with Shaka's exercise of power, I have born in mind David Hedges's admonition that a false image has been produced by 'the concentration on the heroic and terroristic aspects of Zulu history, extended by the need for an exculpatory avenue for the colonising mission'. At the same time, I believe the present tendency to overlook the militaristic and coercive aspects of the Shakan state may be creating an equally distorted impression.

There will be those who feel that in compressing an entire century into a single section, I have failed to do justice to the modern era. However, it becomes more difficult to view Zulu affairs in relative isolation once we enter into the period of South African history following the union of 1910. The subject either required a book to itself or, rather, a treatment which confined itself to tracing the main historical and social strands. This I have attempted to do.

Few African people have been more chronicled than the Zulu, and this volume owes an immense debt to the research done in recent years by specialists such as Jeff Guy, Norman Etherington, Shula Marks, John Laband, Carolyn Hamilton, Colin Webb and John Wright. Above all, however, it draws on an extraordinary archive, a treasure trove of Zulu oral history collected at the turn of the century by a colonial official, James Stuart.

Stuart was a fluent Zulu-speaker who, over twenty years in the course of his duties as a travelling magistrate and in his spare time, filled more than a hundred notebooks with the testimony of almost 200 informants, many of them tribal elders alive in Shaka's day. The archive is a unique contribution to South African historiography. Stuart did much more than just obtain information from his subjects about history, customs, language and oral literature; he engaged them in debate on philosophical and spiritual matters. He met his informants as equals, and many unburdened themselves to him of their resentment and bewilderment at the white man's treatment. The results have the power not just to inform, but to move.

Stuart intended to turn his work into a Zulu history. He started a biography of Shaka, which was abandoned, and then went on to produce four Zulu-language readers, based on historical episodes, which are still fondly remembered by many acquainted with them. He died far from his native land, in England in the winter of 1942, with his richest work unknown and unpublished. Fortunately, this material passed to the Killie Campbell Africana Library in Durban, the source of so much valuable documentation on the history of south-east Africa. Since 1976, Stuart's papers have been gradually published by the University of Natal Press in four volumes, *The James Stuart Archive*, edited by Colin Webb and John Wright. A fifth volume has been delayed by Webb's death, in 1992. Already, however, the set has established itself as an enduring memorial to a remarkable South African.

❊

A great many people assisted me with information, advice and hospitality during my research and sometimes simply with their company during my travels. For insights into Zulu customs and ways, I must single out for thanks King Goodwill Zwelithini and two other members of the royal family, Prince Vincent Zulu and Prince Clement Zulu. My understanding was helped by three non-Zulus, each of whom has spent a lifetime in the region and has a deep knowledge of and respect for its people: Arnold Colenbrander of Eshowe, Ian Player of Howick and Sighart Bourquin of Durban. Each of these gentlemen was remarkably tolerant of my ignorance and free with his hospitality.

On the academic side, I would like to thank Paul Forsyth, John Laband and Paulus Zulu of the University of Natal; Simon Maphalala of the History department at the University of Zululand; Hariet Ngubane, Professor of Anthropology, and Hermann Gili-omee, Professor of Political Studies, at the University of Cape Town; and John Aitcheson of the Centre for Adult Studies at the University of Natal. All gave of their time to answer my questions, or provided help with documents. I am particularly indebted to two other academics: Tom Karis of the City University of New York generously showed me a draft of his chapter on Buthelezi and Inkatha before its publication in *From Protest to Challenge: A Documentary History of African Politics*, Vol. 5 (with Gail Gerhart) by Oxford University Press; and Christopher Saunders, Professor of History at the University of Cape Town, read my manuscript and offered constructive criticism.

On the political side, Rowley Arenstein, who suffered many years of house arrest and banning, told me much about the ANC and South African Communist Party in Natal in the 1950s. Gavin Woods of the Inkatha Institute was helpful in ways that had nothing to do with his political responsibilities. Oscar Dhlomo, formerly secretary-general of Inkatha, provided information and insights which were more independent than I could have expected. Peter Gastrow, MP, and his wife, Sheila, gave information and insights to a critical period in Natal during the 1980s. A number of active politicians granted interviews, including Chief Buthelezi and Harry Gwala, ANC chairman in the Natal Midlands.

The church and the press have been closely involved in monitoring the political violence of recent years, and for their knowledge and advice I should like to thank Bishop Stanley Mogoba, the Methodist Bishop of South Africa; Peter Kerchoff of the Pieter-maritzburg Agency for Christian Social Awareness; and Khaba Mkhize, editor of the *Natal Echo*.

Finally, Bobby Eldridge and Stacie Gibson of the Killie Campbell Africana Library in Durban, the staff of the South African Library in Cape Town and those of the School of Oriental and African Studies in London were as considerate and helpful as such dedicated people almost always are.

It is common for an author, while acknowledging help, to absolve everyone else of any responsibility for the final result. In the present case, it is perhaps necessary to emphasize the point. Some of those who have spoken to me will disagree strongly with my interpretations and conclusions. It could not be otherwise when Zulu history writing has become a subject of such intense – indeed, often ideological – debate. Nobody should be tainted by association with anything I have written.

Three friends read the manuscript and offered comments. One was my father, Sam, who had it read to him in his blindness by my mother, but died before it could be published. The encouragement of Michael Holman, Africa editor of the *Financial Times*, meant more than I can say. Once again, however, I have to acknowledge my greatest debt of all to Tom Fort, who gave detailed criticism on style and, by comment and discussion, helped immeasurably in the distillation of my own thoughts; only he and I know how valuable his contribution was.

Finally, the whole enterprise would have been impossible without my family, my wife Caroline, and children, Wilfred and Juliette, who were uprooted from home and schools and transported across the world for more than a year, enabling me to do the research and fieldwork. They never complained and, moreover, sustained me through what often seemed an impossible task by their generosity of spirit, tolerance and, above all, love.

Stephen Taylor
June 1994

SHAKA'S CHILDREN

A History of the Zulu People

PROLOGUE

THE SHAPING OF AN ICON

The invasion was so slow that most did not even notice it. By the time war came to the People of Heaven, the enemy was already within. He had penetrated to the nation's core, to its campfires, its councils and its hearths. He wandered the land without risk or restriction. He advised the king and was held in awe by the multitude. So influential was he, it seemed unthinkable that many still living could remember a time when his existence was unknown. He was a source of riches, magic and power. Perhaps this should have been warning enough, but the truth was that by the final quarter of the nineteenth century the Englishman was no longer recognised by the Zulu as a foe.

Across the world, the perception was of a different order of things. The very name People of Heaven would have evoked grim mirth had it been known. In London, the talk was of a savage power, overweening in its pride, baying at the frontier of empire. There was, it was certain, no more brutal tyranny anywhere in Africa. If England had been slow to appreciate the danger to colonial civilization from this barbarian horde, it had certainly done so by 1879. In the imperial gallery of ethnic prototypes – from the dashing Pathans and swaggering Sikhs on the North-West Frontier, to their mettlesome counterparts in the antipodes, the Maoris and Fijians of the south Pacific – the warrior was held to have reached his apotheosis in the people known variously as Zooloos, Zoolahs or Zulus.

The popular image of this figure was the stuff of nightmares: a regimented and celibate man-killer, without fear or pity, he was said to roam southern Africa in swarms akin to the wild creatures there. He went naked but for a bare covering of skins and feathers, carrying a cow-hide shield the size of an ordinary mortal and a short stabbing spear that was as effective in his hands as the *gladius* of the Roman legions. He lived for conquest and plunder. In short, he represented the elemental brute in Africa that Europeans had decided it was their duty to tame.

At the beginning of the nineteenth century the British gaze was fixed on India, where it had been drawn by rivalry with imperial France. The explorations of Mungo Park and James Bruce had caused a flicker of British interest in Africa, but the continent was *terra incognita* south of the Equator, apart from the farthest tip where a small population of Dutch, German and French origin had clung for more than 150 years, neglected by their motherlands and ignored by the rest of Europe. Briefly, Napoleon's ambition roused Britain to an appreciation of the Cape's strategic value as a trade route to India, sufficient to prise it from a feeble Dutch grip. Then, Bonaparte defeated, the British turned east again, to the pickings from French and Dutch decline. When, in 1820, George III died mad in the sixtieth year of his reign, the European population of the Cape Colony numbered no more than fifteen thousand. That same year the first group of British settlers in Africa, some four thousand farmers and tradesmen, was landed.

The colony was, very roughly, an oblong some 500 miles across and 200 miles high, bounded by ocean to the west and south and by rivers in the north and east. Of the land beyond, the colonists were largely ignorant and distinctly wary. Much the same could be said of their attitude towards the native inhabitants.

Southern Africa's indigenous peoples were the product of a process of migration and conquest that had been in progress for millennia. Two distinct ethnic groups inhabited the southern end of the continent, the Khoisan (more generally known as Hottentots and Bushmen) and the Bantu. It was the Khoisan who were encountered first by the Europeans. The Dutch East India Company's settlers, transported across the world in 1652 to the storm-battered tip of an unknown continent, had come from Europe's wealthiest civilization. They found a slight, yellow-skinned people, whose odd appearance was matched by their speech, a rapid-fire string of implosive consonants or clicks. The ability of these pastoralists and hunter–gatherers to flourish in the meanest of environments was overlooked by the newcomers, who saw only the incarnation of primitive brutishness. Jan van Riebeeck, founder of the white settlement in Table Bay, whose previous diplomatic experience had been among Orientals, thought the Khoisan 'black stinking dogs' and 'dull, stupid and odorous'. Such attitudes, backed up by firearms and supplemented by the introduction of alien diseases like smallpox, led to the rapid disintegration of the Khoisan. Much subsequent history was founded on the lesson learned from this experience: European had encountered African and had found him not only inferior but vulnerable.

With psychological constraints on expansion and conquest lifted, the first colonists started looking to the limitless terrain to the north and east, where dwelt the subcontinent's second indigenous group, the Bantu. On the colony's eastern frontier, demarcated by the Fish River, the interaction between black and white that has dominated South African history began in earnest.

From the earliest encounters, it was apparent that the sturdy Bantu would prove an altogether more formidable obstacle to expansion than the Khoisan. From 1779, conflict over land and cattle flickered constantly on the eastern frontier between Dutch freebooters, nomads known as *trekboers*, and the Bantu. In the beginning, however, these troubles meant little at the Cape. To the colonists, the territory between the Fish River and the Portuguese entrepôt of Delagoa Bay was a forbidding wilderness, a blank on the map known simply as Kaffraria, its inhabitants a homogeneous black mass known as Kaffirs, the 'infidels', so termed by early Arab traders on the east coast. The first, disastrous, attempt to fill this gap was made in 1808 when an expedition led by two Englishmen, Robert Cowan, a surgeon, and Captain Goddard Donovan, was despatched to find an overland route from Table Bay to Delagoa Bay. The party made its way to the colony's north-eastern border, then struck east into the bush and disappeared for ever.

The seaboard from the Cape up to Delagoa Bay, a distance of more than 1,200 miles along a storm-blown coast, was better known, but the wreck of many an East Indiaman served to deepen the shadow that the colonists perceived over Kaffraria. Those few survivors who emerged from the wilderness had harrowing stories to tell of hardship and hostile tribes. Most traumatic of all, so far as the Cape was concerned, was the fate of the frigate *Grosvenor* which, bound for England from India in 1782, sank while still about 800 miles up the east coast from Table Bay. Although 123 people, including a number of women and children, were brought safely to land, their ordeal had just begun. Only sixteen men and two women reached the colony, bearing harrowing tales of suffering and persecution at the hands of Kaffirs. Years later half-caste communities were discovered in Kaffraria, but no further trace of the *Grosvenor* or any other survivors was ever found.

Although the Cowan party's disappearance had put a damper on government-sponsored exploration, the arrival at the Cape of the first organized settlement from Britain in 1820 stimulated a sudden interest in the eastern seaboard. The British government wanted a survey of the coast; the emergent merchant class at the Cape was looking for adventurers to open up trade. On the back of these twin needs was founded a series of seafaring enterprises that would finally bring Englishmen into contact with the most powerful tribal society in southern Africa.

In August 1822, two rather dilapidated Royal Navy vessels commanded by Captain William Owen set sail from the Cape. Owen's orders were to chart the coast to Delagoa Bay but the political information with which he returned was no less important. From the Portuguese and Bantu whom he interrogated, Owen learned of a rising force in the interior, a 'tribe of warlike Kaffers, called Zoolos, but by the Portuguese Vatwas'. Owen had, in fact, encountered the outer shockwaves of an upheaval which had its epicentre far to the west; the effect was still enough to impress the explorers. Even more interesting were accounts of the Zulu chief, an all-powerful warrior king whose name was to have as many transliterated versions as that of his people, but which likewise had the benefit of clarity and brevity and which, unlike many other native names, came easily off the tongue – whether as Tshaka, Shaka or Chaka.

The men who established the first European contacts with the Zulu kingdom were buccaneers and wanderers, naval officers and teenage adventurers, eccentrics and itinerants, all with an eye for the main chance and a few not above profitable skulduggery. They were the pioneers of Natal. Like most pioneers they were idealized by following generations, and like most they have suffered the backlash of revisionism. While one's inclination is to allow that they were neither heroes nor villains, but simply men of their time and place, it must be said that they were a particularly venal band.

The first one on the scene after Owen was much the most attractive – Henry Fynn, a resourceful young fellow with medical, linguistic and seafaring experience, who quickly took to African life and was destined for an important place in Shaka's kingdom. Then there were the mariners, Lieutenants James King and Francis Farewell, Royal Navy men in the Kidd tradition who established the Port Natal trading post on the basis of a spurious land grant from Shaka. After them came a Jewish boy from Kent, Nathaniel Isaacs, still only seventeen when he arrived at Port Natal and with a career as a West African slave-trader ahead of him. All had close dealings with the Zulu kingdom from 1824 onwards and were responsible for shaping images of it that still have influence.

An exercise of the imagination is also needed to unravel the traders' portrayals of Shaka. What is most striking is how quickly he was transformed in their reports from benefactor to beast. For two years after the first encounter with the Zulu king, trader despatches to the Cape extolled the potential for doing business with a powerful monarch, well disposed towards the British, ruling his orderly, well-mannered people with a firm but judicious hand. These were profitable years for the traders, as Shaka had within his gift the bounty of land and nature between the Pongolo and Mzimkulu rivers, roughly the area known since as Natal and Zululand. Port Natal soon outstripped Delagoa Bay as the regional headquarters of the ivory trade, and, as demand for Africa's white gold increased in Europe, so did its impact on the tribal societies which supplied it. At Shaka's capital, kwaBulawayo, 120 miles to the north-west, the traders were made welcome with food and beer. After the conclusion of business, which involved the exchange of ivory for beads, brass and trinkets, they were sent on their way with a few head of cattle as a token of friendship to feed them on the journey home.

A British naval officer calling at Port Natal in 1825 found the traders 'living on the best of terms with the natives and under the protection of King Chaka, who professes great respect for white people'. In an article published in the Cape in April 1826, the Zulus were described as 'harmless' and behaving 'extremely well'. Not long afterwards, James King reported that Shaka was obliging, charming and pleasant, stern in public but good-humoured in private, benevolent and hospitable. Such reports persuaded public opinion at the Cape that this amiable monarch was the sort of man the colony could do business with. That the Zulu king had been responsible for devastating large areas of independent Kaffraria was by now widely known, but the occasional reports of his barbarity, of tribes slaughtered and dispersed, were quickly pooh-poohed. Certainly he could be no threat to the Cape. Indeed, so civilized was his conduct toward whites that in one Cape newspaper it was suggested that he must be of European extraction.[1]

Shaka's good reputation did not long survive his assassination by his brother Dingane in 1828. The change was signalled in a newspaper article by King who, in an extraordinary *volte face*, contradicted everything he had said before and set the tone for what was to follow:

History, perhaps, does not furnish an instance of a more despotic and cruel monster than Chaka. His subjects fall at his nod.[2]

The rapid transformation of Shaka the Good to Shaka the Terrible had begun, and with it was transformed the portrayal of the Zulu people as a whole. King's theme was taken up in the first book to bring Shaka and the Zulu to the attention of an English readership, George Thompson's *Travels and Adventures in Southern Africa*, published in 1827. Thompson never visited Zululand himself, but his description of Shaka as a tyrant who had established 'a barbaric kingdom of large extent, which he governs upon a system of military despotism' was naturally accepted. The Zulu monarchy was contrasted by Thompson with 'the loose patriarchal polity generally prevalent among the other Kaffir tribes', such as the Xhosa.

From other accounts of the period emerged, full-blown, the 'black Attila' of popular history. Owen's journals, published in England in 1833, five years after Shaka's death, described depopulation 'carried on with savage rapidity by the merciless and destructive conquests' of a 'tyrannical monster'. In an appendix to this two-volume work, Farewell now joined in the general lambasting of his former benefactor. His opening sentence reads: 'Chaka is one of the most monstrous characters that ever existed; Attila himself was hardly his fellow.'

But of all the gore-drenched portraits of the first Zulu king none surpasses that of Nathaniel Isaacs' *Travels and Adventures in Eastern Africa*, published in 1836. Having failed to make his fortune as an ivory trader, Isaacs set about writing a bestseller with the help of a publisher's hack. In grandiloquent prose, he set a benchmark for a style of melodramatic travel adventure which became popular in the Victorian era, combining lurid accounts of strange lands, exotic creatures and savage peoples. The narrative shudders with scarcely concealed relish:

Chaka seems to have inherited no redeeming quality; in war he was an insatiable and exterminating savage, in peace an unrelenting and ferocious despot ... The world has heard of monsters – Rome had her Nero, the Huns their Attila, and Syracuse her Dionysius; the East has likewise produced her tyrants; but for ferocity, Chaka has exceeded them all.[3]

There is very much more in the same vein: of Shaka's warriors, forced into celibacy to heighten their bloodlust; of the many hundred bare-breasted women of the king's seraglio, and the summary executions of those who were tempted to infiltrate it; and of massacres ordered by the grief-crazed tyrant on the death of his mother, Nandi. For good measure, Isaacs hinted coyly at lascivious doings at court, the 'sensual depravity' of Zulu women and the 'native concubines' taken by white traders at their camp by the lagoon.

No wonder Isaacs' *Travels* did so well. It is a rollicking read, even today, notwithstanding acres of humbug and its tortuous style. Unfortunately, however, it was also extremely influential. In the absence of other firsthand accounts, Isaacs was for a long time the standard work on the Zulu and was imitated, copied and plagiarized. The effect was malign. Among administrators and colonists, and in England, an impression gained currency that the Zulu kingdom was predisposed towards conquest, its society inherently savage, and every warrior a berserker; that, moreover, when not at war, the Zulu were occupied with witchcraft and all manner of black arts.

Two years after its publication, to the savagery of Shaka was added the treachery of his successor, Dingane. The massacre of hundreds of migrant Afrikaners led by Piet Retief was reported by *The Times* as having taken place in 'circumstances of the most appalling barbarity'. The mould was now set.

Not all early reports of the Zulu were hostile, but the pious sympathy and hearty manliness of the missionaries and hunters who followed the traders proved no better starting points from which to interpret African society. A poem entitled 'The Caffer', published in an English anthology in the year of Shaka's death is fairly characteristic of the missionary perspective.

> Lo! where he crouches by the Kloof's dark side,
> Eyeing the farmer's lowing herds afar;
> Impatient watching, till the evening star
> Lead forth the twilight dim, that he may glide
> Like panther to the prey. With freeborn pride
> He scorns the herdsman, nor regards the scar
> Of recent wound – but burnishes for war
> His assagai [sic] and targe of buffalo hide.
> He is a robber? – True; it is a strife
> Between the black-skinned bandit and the white.
> A savage ? – Yes; though loth to aim at life,
> Evil for evil fierce he doth requite.
> A heathen ? – Teach him, then, thy better creed,
> Christian! if thou deserv'st that name indeed.[4]

It was not long before the Victorians saw this literary caricature of the black-skinned heathen turned into a flesh and blood one. In 1853, a decade after a successful British tour by George Catlin's circus of North American Indians, a Natal merchant took a troupe of thirteen Zulus to London. At St George's Gallery in Piccadilly they appeared before audiences that included Charles Dickens, and gave a command performance for the young Queen and her consort at Buckingham Palace before setting out for the provinces and the continent. A reporter from *The Times* described the show:

Now the Kafirs are seen at their meal, feeding themselves with enormous spoons, and expressing their satisfaction with a wild chant. Now the witch-finder commences his operations to discover the culprit whose magic has brought sickness into the tribe, and becomes perfectly rabid through his own incantations. Now there is a wedding ceremony, now a hunt, now a military expedition, all with characteristic dances; and the whole ends with a conflict between rival tribes.[5]

Black Africa, it was plain to most Victorians, had produced no civilization of any note, no written culture, and its customs, when not merely primitive, were repulsive. Its backwardness and suffering were entirely beyond the understanding of a people in thrall to the revolutions of industry and science, and produced one of two responses: at best, a high-minded idealism which overcame the slave trade and sacrificed itself in noble causes; at worst, a coarse, exploitative contempt that took its cue equally from the pseudo-Darwinism of the public house and the Mayfair salon. The novelist, Anthony Trollope, who toured South Africa in 1877 and wrote a perceptive and sympathetic account of the country, was rare among English visitors in perceiving the Zulu with a simple and direct humanity that had nothing to do with their land or their souls. He wrote prophetically: 'I have no fears myself that Natal will be overrun by hostile Zulus; – but much fear that Zulu-land should be overrun by hostile Britons.'[6]

If the image of the bestial savage was built around the legend of Shaka, the Anglo-Zulu war was the making of the brute's noble *doppelgänger*. Persuaded of the need to break the barbarian power on the Cape's frontier, Britain went to war in 1879 with little on its side besides the Gatling gun and was shamed, not by the astonishing defeat of Isandlwana, but by the manner in which the enemy defended his home. Imperial soldiers recognized a noble foe, savage or not, and the Zulu way of giving battle – charging across open ground in massed ranks, armed with *assegai* and cow-hide shields, in the face of withering fire – was the very stuff of raw courage. With their splendid appearance, burnished black bodies draped in animal skins and ostrich plumes, they were, as Jan Morris has noted, the most spectacular of all the theatrical enemies the British Empire felt itself obliged to fight. On the mounds of Zulu dead, some eight thousand of them, there arose a new paradigm for the warrior nation.

Britain had her own dead, almost seven hundred at Isandlwana alone. The imperturbable Disraeli, for once caught off-balance, was at a loss to explain the disaster to the House and took to his bed. *The Times*, phlegmatic as always, noted that the Zulus had turned out to be even more formidable than expected, not only disciplined and brave, but able as well to muster a large force. Correspondents and artists were hastily despatched to Zululand, among them Melton Prior, who reached the battlefield of Ulundi in time to record the immolation of the kingdom. Prior's hasty but deft sketches for the *Illustrated London News* were the first widely circulated images of

Zulu warriors and had an immediate impact, providing a model for a generation of *Boys' Own* imitators.

It helped the cause of the noble savage that the Zulu had finally found a passionate and eloquent champion. The Bishop of Natal, John Colenso, a Cornishman of slight frame and bright, bird-like eyes, might not have seemed an ideal choice for the job; Zulu scepticism for the Word had so challenged his own faith in the Old Testament that he had been pronounced a heretic by his provincial bishop in Cape Town. But Colenso, whatever his shortcomings in orthodoxy, was an inspired preacher and an indefatigable and compelling moral force. His campaigning was crucial in revising public opinion about the justness of the war, and in stirring British conscience over the imprisonment of the defeated king, Cetshwayo, and securing his freedom.

The image of the bestial savage was finally laid to rest by the arrival in England of Cetshwayo himself. A big, handsome man of regal bearing, Cetshwayo visited the enemy capital three years after the war and proceeded to charm the English. Nothing that was known about the Zulu king had prepared public opinion for this courteous and dignified figure.

Of course, it is easy to hold a foe in high esteem when he is defeated, and it was clear by now that the Zulu were a ruined people. At the same time, another ardent advocate of the Zulu had emerged in the popular author, Henry Rider Haggard. In four years as a colonial official in Natal before the war, Haggard had soaked up the African landscape and drunk deeply of Zulu history and lore. These, and a fecund imagination, supplied him with the raw material for the spectacularly successful African romances that started to flow from his pen with *King Solomon's Mines* in 1885. The character of Umslopogaas, Haggard's idealized Zulu warrior, became as popular with his readers as the hunter Allan Quatermain. The teenage Winston Churchill was avid for more Quatermain adventures.

More importantly, Haggard set a precedent as a fiction writer trying seriously to understand an African society. From his study of the Zulu, Haggard found that 'in all the essential qualities of mind and body they very much resemble white men, with the exception that they are, as a race, quicker witted, more honest, and braver than the ordinary run of white men.' He was the first author to write a popular fiction peopled entirely by blacks – *Nada the Lily*, a reworking of the Shakan legend. As in the Zulu trilogy that followed it, Haggard took liberties with historical fact, but his grasp of culture was sure and, as the historian Norman Etherington has pointed out, he succeeded at his best in showing the Zulu as neither beastly nor noble but, at last, as people of 'wonderful ordinariness', no small achievement in a race-obsessed age. At one point Haggard has Quatermain reflect:

When you come to add it up there's very little different in all main and essential matters between the savage and yourself. By what right do we call people like the Zulu savages? They have an ancient and elaborate law, and a system of morality in some ways as high as our own, and certainly more generally obeyed. A clever man or woman among the people we call savages is in all essentials very much the same as a clever man or woman anywhere else.[7]

Interest in 'tribals', romantic or not, faded as the trumpets bade farewell to empire. Ethnic identities generally became blurred. Independent African states emerged with names that gave no hint of their pre-colonial tribal composition. In cases where 'tribalism' surfaced as a political factor, it was usually perfunctorily reported and quickly forgotten. Academics could argue, and did, that where ethnic tensions existed, they were a legacy of colonial divide-and-rule policies. Apartheid reinforced the process. The more South African governments emphasized the differences between races, the more well-intentioned people everywhere became convinced that there were none. Even to talk of the Xhosa, the Zulu or any other ethnic community was somehow to pander to prejudice. Such was the international revulsion at Afrikaner nationalism that South African affairs became a morality play in which it appeared to many that only apartheid stood in the way of a harmonious, multi-racial solution where minorities simply faded into the background.

In Britain, meanwhile, generations grew up barely aware that the Zulu even existed. Brief flurries of interest accompanied the release of the adventure film *Zulu* in 1964 and the centenary of the Anglo-Zulu war in 1979, but as in an old cowboys 'n Indians movie, interest was focused on the red-coated and be-whiskered victors, while the vanquished were so many shrieking extras.

In recent times, the caricatures of the past have been revived in headlines and news coverage of South Africa's transition from apartheid to democracy. Amid the violence which has lacerated the black townships, television images send a half-heard echo of history resounding down the years. These scenes indicate to many that the Zulu are on the march again. Chief Mangosuthu Buthelezi, the Inkatha leader, does nothing to dispel this idea, invoking Shaka's name as a symbol of his own political muscle and proclaiming that the Zulus are still a nation and will not submit to the designs of others.

In South Africa, foreign-made images have for centuries overlooked and obscured the richness that is part of any people's past. In presuming to try to flesh out some of the missing elements, I run the same dangers as those who have gone before: of selective interpretation, cultural condescension, misunderstanding and plain incomprehension. But the materials are there for the job, in the rich seam of oral tradition by which Africans have ever known their history. There is a Zulu voice, and it is time that it was heard.

PART 1

RISE – UP TO 1828

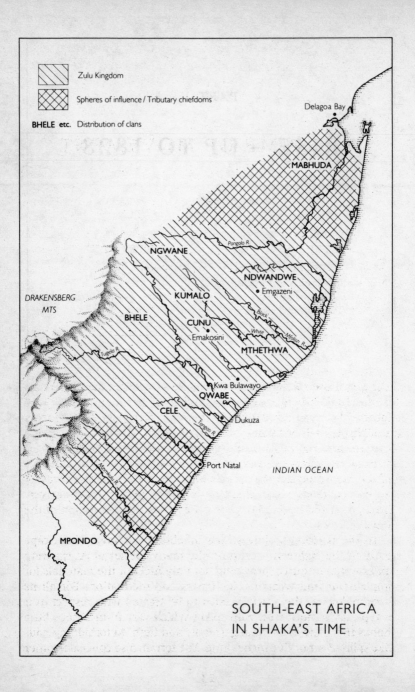

SOUTH-EAST AFRICA
IN SHAKA'S TIME

1

THE TIME OF MOVEMENT

We are the people who came down from the
mountains in a grain basket.

Zulu proverb

The green and rolling land that tumbles away from the mountains
of the Drakensberg east to the Indian Ocean is unusually well
forested for southern Africa. To these hillsides cling delicate trees
and shrubs, a lacy filigree of foliage known as mist forest which
clusters around ravines and gorges down which hundreds of
streams and rivers course to the sea. Gradually, the great knuckles
of the landscape start to subside and the mist forest gives way to
lesser woodlands and thickets. Here, on the gentler slopes of river-
ine upland and lowland, is found the acacia, most common of the
region's trees.

To the pastoral society which inhabited this lovely landscape
early in the eighteenth century, the many species of acacia were
an essential resource, providing not only fuel but the materials for
implements and weapons, for fences and medication. For all its
uses, however, the acacia needed to be treated with respect as it
is typically a thorn tree, with spikes which vary from vicious little
hooks that claw and tear at garments and flesh, to forbidding nail-
like spikes four or five inches long. The terrain also concealed other

sharp surprises. Underfoot was found a species of prostrate herb from the stems of which grew clusters of hard little thorns about a centimetre in length, one of which is always uppermost. Thorns of the plant, *tribulis terrestris*, were known as *nkunzana* by the people of these parts, who shod themselves with ox-hide sandals when setting out beyond their own settlements, as when warriors of one clan were involved in a trial of strength with another.

These clashes, to settle a dispute over land or cattle, were frequent but rarely very bloody. Warrior groups would square up to one another and, watched and encouraged by their womenfolk from a convenient vantage point, proceed to hurl first insults – often of a sexual nature – and then spears at one another. Sometimes, in more serious disputes, the combatants would close in with spears and clubs, and then casualties would increase and prisoners might be taken. But after some parlaying, the captives would be returned, a tribute of cattle exacted and the quarrel would be patched up for the time being. This is the substance of oral tradition, and if it has a whiff of old men's idealized recollections, it is still consistent with what we know of this society in the early eighteenth century, a multiplicity of clans, fractious but at the same time tolerant, blessed with resources and indulgent towards children.

In just a few decades, however, much changed. Warfare was no longer a tournament or a test of honour. Born and sustained in isolation from the movements that had shaped the modern world, one of the last primeval societies had finally encountered the twin agencies of colonial transformation – trade and firearms. A maelstrom was developing which would eddy out with devastating impact on southern Africa.

At the epicentre of the turmoil, a young warrior, in a gesture of revolutionary intent, discarded his sandals, declaring them an effete hindrance to the mobility needed by a fighting man. Conservative elders objected but a new era was at hand. Agile, powerful and apparently impervious to the *nkunzana*, the young warrior proved his point by his prowess. On the battlefield he rapidly won a reputation as a fearsome adversary. As his star waxed, so did his insistence that men should go barefoot to battle. Finally, having gained the chieftainship of his own clan, he summoned his warriors to a parade ground over which *nkunzanas* had been scattered and ordered them to stamp the hard little spikes into the dust. Those who hesitated or held back, he said, would be killed. A half-dozen or so men failed to heed his words. They were swiftly despatched with clubs. The remainder then chanted and stamped their way around the ground until there were no *nkunzanas* to be seen. Thenceforth, Shaka's Zulu warriors went to war as he had done, barefoot.

The stamping of the thorns speaks across almost two centuries as a seminal episode in the rise of the Zulu and the shaping of what one can only call a Zulu psyche. Shaka's ways of winning obedience and instilling discipline were as effective as they were ferocious. Allied to his political vision, a gift for inspiring men and a sure grasp of charismatic demagogy, they made him a nation builder comparable with Bismarck or Garibaldi, the crucial figure of Zulu history and a pan-Africanist hero. Within a decade his following had expanded a thousandfold. Where he found hundreds of squabbling clans, his successors ruled over a people bound together by language, culture and a successful system of political patronage.

What Shaka did best, however, was to channel the instinct of male ascendancy. Militarism runs as a thread through Zulu history. It will not be denied, and it is not easy to escape from the two most common responses to it: attraction to the dark magnificence that clings to the warrior past; or revulsion at the modern violence with which it is associated. It does not help that the two seem inseparable.

Yet, paradoxically, patience, generosity and a tolerance of human failing are just as strong strands of the same social fabric. Early travellers commented upon these qualities among the Zulu, noting also their love of laughter, their dignity, stoicism and honesty. While many later arrivals, the white settlers in Natal, took refuge in prejudice, others saw in the native peoples an inherent nobility. In our age such judgments are regarded as facile, patronizing and even racist, for if one ethnic group can be found fine and noble, it follows that another must be less fine and less noble. Nevertheless, for all the effects of conquest, urbanization, apartheid and political conflict, today's traveller among the Zulu-speaking people is likely to be struck by the same virtues noted by those early visitors.

What are we to make of these seeming contradictions? In

addressing this question, one is brought back again and again to the Shakan revolution. But therein lies a problem: the reputations of all great historical leaders are at least part myth; in the case of the first Zulu king, oral history made the mythical element especially potent. This remains the case. One of the most acerbic historical debates to be heard in South African academies these days concerns the character, aims and achievements of Shaka.[1]

In embarking on our chronicle, therefore, it is proper to note that just over two hundred years ago the Zulu were among the least significant of their kind, a clan of probably fewer than two thousand people, no more acquainted with warfare than any other, and less than most. In the circumstances of their rise lies, perhaps, a reconciliation of these paradoxes.

South Africa's twenty-five million or so black people are descended from one of the most successful colonial movements in the world's history, a great migration which led to the occupation of almost the entire continent south of the Equator within a few hundred years. The Zulu emerged from a small branch of the main migratory trunk. These facts can be stated with confidence. Much else concerning the origins of black South Africans is wrapped in almost equal parts of mystery and controversy.

Early in the first millennium AD, transient hunters from the north established in present-day Zaire a bridgehead comparable with those founded by European settlers in North America or at the Cape of Good Hope. Here was fashioned, in a basin of prosperity, a Bantu language and a society which improved techniques of food cultivation and stock-raising. From this nucleus, the tide swept out during the millennium, first west and east, reaching the coasts of the Atlantic and Indian Oceans, before turning north and south. In the view of the historian, Roland Oliver, 'We should think of the southward expansion of the Bantu as a cumulative process, in which the surplus population generated in the favourable conditions at the heart of the Bantu world was constantly pushed out towards the perimeter in an unending sequence of migration, conquest and absorption.'[2] There are premonitions here of the Zulu rise, although the Bantu genius was for cultivation and metallurgy, through which they constantly attracted new adherents, rather than for warfare. It is now generally accepted that the migration coincided with the spread of the Iron Age. Such was its speed and success that Bantu languages retain many common roots today, although spread over a vast area from Cameroon to the Cape, and comprising more than three hundred tongues including the nine main Bantu language groups of South Africa – Zulu, Xhosa, Tswana, Pedi, Sotho, Tsonga, Swazi, Venda and Ndebele.

The Bantu were a tall, finely made people, particularly powerful in the haunches and legs, robust in health thanks to their agricultural skills, and with a skin pigment that varied from dark copper to near black. The stone-age peoples whom they encountered and absorbed as they spread southwards over central Africa were short and slight, with a colouring that was yellow rather than black, and with prominent fat-storing buttocks which bore testimony to an irregular diet. Dominant among them were the Khoikhoi, who were once found all the way from the Cape to Angola and eastwards to Tanzania. As the Khoikhoi gave way, the Bantu set up loosely established settlements around which they cultivated sorghum and millet, and grazed livestock. By the fourth century they had spread over much of present-day Zimbabwe, Zambia and Malawi and, although the archaeological research has not been done to confirm it, had almost certainly reached the coastal plain of Mozambique as well. Arab geographers record that by the end of the first millennium an export trade in ivory was being conducted from the vicinity of modern Beira in Mozambique. With the rise of commerce over the next century or so, the first sign of a Bantu state is glimpsed at Great Zimbabwe on the plateau to the west. This stone metropolis was trading gold at the coast by the fourteenth century, while another centre of power, the Monomatapa dynasty, arose on the Zambesi.

Myths about the Bantu migration abound, often because of racial axe-grinding. Great Zimbabwe was long held by Rhodesian administrators to have been built by Arab or Phoenician traders, on the ground that blacks could not have been capable of such fine stonework. In South Africa, the fiction was maintained by apartheid ideologues, in the face of all contradictory evidence, that the Bantu were recent arrivals whose southward momentum towards the Cape was actually in progress when they encountered, and were checked by, white expansion from the colony in the eighteenth century. As simultaneous migrants, it was argued, the European and Bantu had only equal claims to the country. Although this lie has long since been nailed, many of the mysteries of the Bantu migration in South Africa remain unresolved.

Stone-age man lived within the boundaries of modern South Africa for more than 120,000 years. These early inhabitants were the ancestors of the hunter–gatherer San and Khoi encountered by Dutch settlers at the Cape in 1652. Iron-age people, probably negroid, were scattered across the subcontinent from around 3,000 BC. The first distinctly Bantu people seem to have arrived in the fifth century after a long, slow migration that passed through modern Zambia, crossed the Limpopo and fanned down via the coastal plain of Mozambique to present-day Natal. Later waves crossed the Limpopo but remained on the high plains. Within an area that includes Transvaal, Orange Free State and eastern Botswana, a myriad of groups swirled and eddied between AD 1000 and AD 1500, overlaying and infiltrating one another. Somewhere around the eleventh century, a particularly large group descended from this high plateau to the coast and settled on the great swathe of territory lying between the Drakensberg mountains and the Indian Ocean. They were cattle-owners, and this, along with archaeological evidence on their laws and totems, has led scholars to speculate that they came from the highlands of East Africa.[3] These were the ancestors of the people known as the Nguni. Amid the relentless search for political correctness that accompanies much South African scholarship in history and anthropology, the term Nguni shows signs of falling into disfavour and is no guide to cultural uniformity. But it remains useful to define the country's largest language group. Today the descendants of the Nguni include about eight million Zulu-speakers and six million Xhosa-speakers.

The south-eastern edge of Africa is a bold, green, gnarled land, slashed by gorges and topped by hills, over which clouds may appear in a matter of minutes and turn a bright, steamy pastoral into thunderous deluge. To the north, numerous rivers take their rise in the Drakensberg mountains and course down through forested hills to the sea. Here, along the coastal plain, was a natural Eden, where herds of the great African browsers, the elephant and the buffalo, wandered with antelope and their natural predators.

In the midst of this blessed region lies an area about four times the size of Wales, bound in the north by one river, the Pongolo, in the south by another, the Mzimkulu, and bisected by a third greater than either, the Tugela. Besides the mountains and rivers, no other feature separates this area from those to the north or south, but its history sets it apart. It is here that our chronicle is set.

Among the eight million or so South Africans whose language proclaims them to be Zulu, there is no single ethnic forebear. For centuries these people defined their identities by a variety of means: for example, as Mbo, lowlanders who used pits to store their grain and were held to be the oldest inhabitants; or as Ntungwa, uplanders who used grain baskets, and had crossed over from the Drakensberg at a later date. Numerous efforts have been made, since the time of Alfred Bryant, a missionary and the father of Zulu ethnology, to shape the mass of conflicting testimony into a catalogue of Zulu sub-groups, but the oral traditions remain defiantly unresponsive to such neat packaging. What we are left with is that midway through the second millennium, the society of the Pongolo-Mzimkulu region consisted of hundreds of lineage groups, each identifying itself by descent from a common ancestor.

The basic unit was the kraal, a patriarchal and polygamous colony consisting of a man, his wives, their children and, perhaps, a network of dependent relatives, along with their livestock. Brothers of the kraal head and their families sometimes augmented the group, but most homesteads consisted of fewer than a dozen huts, built in a circle to surround the cattle pen. Similar homesteads of people from the same lineage would be found some distance up the valley, or on the other side of the river, and an informal hierarchy of clan heads, the *abanumzana*, would regulate matters affecting all members of the lineage, such as grazing rights. These elders were also living representatives of the ancestors and, as such, high priests who would intercede with the spirit world to ward off disaster and celebrate the new harvest.

Blessed by rich and well-watered soils on the one hand, the region is afflicted on the other by oppressive heat and humidity, against which the people living here devised a shelter both attractive and effective. A beehive-shaped shell of wattle saplings covered with thatch made an insulated hut which was a sanctuary from the hot summer winds and yet is warm in the winter frosts that fall on high ground. At one end of the hut was a small opening, through which the occupant crept on all fours; the opposite end was a shrine where the spirits of departed relatives dwelt and utensils were kept. At the highest point, a man might stand upright, but the hut was essentially a place for rest. The floor, made of clay and polished to a hard finish with cattle dung, was a deliciously cool place to recline at the end of the day.

The kraal head expected and received complete obedience from his small community. A woman deferred not only to her husband but also to his male relatives, in particular his father and his brothers. His children held him in awe. Between a mother and her children a special devotion developed. This bond was central to a woman's existence. Sharing, as she did, her man with other women, it might be the only emotional sustenance on which she could draw in a life in which the physical burdens were heavy. For, in addition to her household duties, agriculture was also woman's business.

Man's business was husbanding the society's treasure, its cattle. Almost all activity was regulated by this single animal. Cattle were more than a source of essentials, such as meat and leather, or of luxuries, like milk and curds. They were more, even, than symbols of wealth and status. Cattle were the focus of the entire social order, regulating the institution of marriage. They were a source of conflict and the means of peacemaking. In many lineages, the cattle enclosure was the focus of ritual ceremonies and, although they were not exactly worshipped, they did take on a religious significance in their nearness to the Nguni soul. A pervading characteristic of the monarchs of the Zulu-speaking world, from Dingane and Cetshwayo to their distant brethren of the Ndebele, Mzilikazi and Lobengula, is the profound, almost spiritual, pleasure they derived from surveying and wandering among their herds.

The nomadic Bantu, lacking institutions to enforce control, had been egalitarians. On the coastal belt, as elsewhere, their descendants gradually lost their freedom as they gained in political sophistication. The lineage system prospered on these well-watered and fertile soils, and as the herds in the cattle enclosures grew, the kraal head was encouraged to take further wives through the custom of bride barter known as *lobola*. Control of livestock gave him authority over his children well into adulthood, as sons needed cattle to acquire their own wives. Meanwhile, as in most polygamous societies, the rules of inheritance were elastic, giving rise to frequent succession disputes and breakaways. In this inherently fissiparous society, successful clan heads were able to attract adherents who became a force to be marshalled for labour and, eventually, military purposes. The anthropologist Max Gluckman has given a penetrating insight into the dynamics of social organization:

As a group increased in numbers, a lineage might split off to become independent, or a quarrel would lead to a split in a tribe, and two tribes would be formed. Refugees from one tribe who were discontented might pay allegiance to the chiefs of another tribe with a reputation for generosity and justice. Thus chief was balanced against chief, for the unsatisfactory chief lost followers to a more popular neighbour.[4]

Among the early casualties of the gradual aggregation of Nguni power were the original inhabitants of the coastal belt, the San hunter–gatherers – more commonly known as Bushmen – who retreated to the mountain fastness of the Drakensberg. Within a few hundred years they were extinct here, as in the Cape. The San's sole poignant legacy to modern South Africa are some exquisite rock paintings and the range of implosive consonants that continue to echo through the Nguni languages.

From archaeological evidence and mariners' records, it is possible to discern by the seventeenth century a patchwork of hundreds of clans, living under chiefs in the land that was to be called Zululand. A Portuguese sailor in 1647 described the area as 'a very thickly populated plain studded with kraals and covered with cattle'.[5] A consistent feature of these reports is the peaceful, generous society they portray. One shipwrecked crew 'found the people everywhere both friendly and hospitable'.[6] Another reported that they 'vied with each other in offering the white sailors food and drink and their habitations for lodging'. They were 'orderly and obedient to their chiefs'.[7] A somewhat later arrival marvelled at 'the most cheerful and happy people of which I have had any experience':

That the stranger is well provided with food is always with them a matter of first consideration. The greatest stranger, if even but passing by a village when any of the inhabitants happens to be at their meals, sits down uninvited, holds out his hand, and it is immediately filled, even should it extend to depriving themselves.[8]

31

The tongue of these people, then as now, is one of mellifluous beauty, a language dark and masculine but capable nevertheless of being rendered with a soft sensuousness, with the unique delicate clicks of the San, which are neither vowel nor consonant but a bit of both, and deeply rounded vowels, in which the 'u' is sounded something like the hooting of an owl, set among the dark hum of the predominant consonants, the 'm's and 'n's. The effect can be tested by repeating a warming Nguni proverb: 'Umuntu ungumuntu ngabantu' ('Man becomes human through other humans'). It is a language expressive of the poetic imagery in Zulu oral literature, as in the description of the crocodile as, 'the cruel one, whose teeth laugh when killing'. It is also a language richly suited to the epics of fireside storytelling typical of Bantu society and to a folklore which keeps alive the oral literature of centuries. Proverbs are essential to this tradition of homespun philosophy. One of them runs 'Akukho mful' ungahlokomi', literally, 'There is no river without noise', meaning no situation is without its drawbacks.

Perhaps the most precious possession of the Bantu was also the one which it is hardest for industrialized man to grasp: his spiritual life. Like other oral societies, such as the American Indians and the Australian Aborigines, he was in touch with the inner core defined by the psychoanalyst Carl Gustav Jung as the subconscious. The concept of the subconscious is easily scorned by our own scientific, rational and egocentric awareness, which has caused us to lose touch with it. However, many of the outsiders who have experienced African society most intimately, including Jung himself, bear powerful witness to this intuitive, non-rational self – the natural psychic condition – being the state of the Bantu. For a moment let us try to suspend disbelief or cynicism, and imagine that state.

Man saw himself not as an individual but an element of a communal whole, a concept which embraced not just his society but the environment upon which he depended. An individual's interests were submerged in those of the community, and the fate of both was in the hands of ancestral spirits. From this ethos stemmed the phenomenon of a collective unconscious. The spirits, or dlozi, revealed themselves through dreams which, although they might be sent to individuals, were to be shared with the community as messages that might affect the common destiny. These spirits were not remote, but real and immediate, dwelling as they did at one end of a family's hut.

The broad effect of this creed was to make individual conduct selfless. By being at least notionally in touch with his subconscious, man's intuitive and elemental instincts were strong. Above all, perhaps, he had no compulsion to rationalize, or answer the unanswerable; his psyche was rarely troubled by events that lay beyond his control. Equally, his affiliation to a group consciousness made him responsive to strong leadership. For all the subsequent impact of colonialism and urbanization, these attitudes survived in many Bantu. Jung believed that of all peoples, the inhabitants of sub-Saharan Africa were closest to the original universality of the human spirit, a wholeness known to the Zulus as *ubuntu*.

Dreams run as a constant strand through Bantu mythology, and the dream force also remains a factor in the psychological make-up of many black South Africans. The conservationist, Ian Player, himself a Jungian, recalls a conversation with the author, Credo Mutwa, early in 1984, when the turbulent African townships had been quiescent for seven years. 'What are the people dreaming?' Player asked. Mutwa looked troubled and replied: 'They are dreaming of smoke and fire.'[9] Soon afterwards, Soweto erupted again as it had in 1976, ushering in the final demise of the apartheid era.

Language and belief came together in the highest form of Bantu oral literature, a form of declamatory epic known as *isibongo*, or praise-poem. Arising from myths and legends about clan ancestors and past heroes, *isibongo* extolled the virtues and, more surprisingly, sometimes the failings, of chiefs and clans. James Stuart, that indefatigable compiler of Zulu lore whose researches have made a vital contribution to this volume, collected hundreds of praise-poems. Many record events beyond recall or present comprehension, but others offer valuable information on how tribes and individuals saw themselves, and wanted to be seen.

In one lyrical *isibongo*, for example, the Ngwane clan described themselves as 'mighty milkers who milk with the suction of a yearling'. An *isibongo* of the Sibiya clan – 'those who fence their cattle kraals with cattle while others use branches' – seems to have alluded to their prosperity, while a small but war-like group, the Zibisi, were 'those who are red-mouthed from the lapping of blood'. Other clans, too, celebrated their martial prowess.

Such clues are helpful antidotes to sentimentalized versions of

African history which portray clan life as a pure and untroubled Elysium before the coming of the white man. As we have seen, the Nguni lived in a land blessed with resources and with few external stresses. Theirs was a generous and enfolding society. But there is plenty of evidence that it was also familiar with violence.

Political volatility was increasing as settlements expanded and the authority of individual chiefs, or *nkosi*, grew. Most clans remained independent but, by the beginning of the eighteenth century certainly, tribal alliances and power blocs had emerged. Portuguese travellers reported how groups of lesser chiefs, each ruling over a territory, deferred to a great *nkosi* in important matters. Although wars of conquest were still unknown, a strong chief might subordinate others through control of resources, asserting his paramountcy by demanding tribute in cattle from his neighbours and raiding recalcitrants.

At this stage, however, the main challenge to a chief was likely to come from within, rather than without. With imperfect means of control, and, in all likelihood, numerous offspring ready to lay claim to the succession, weak rulers quickly fell. Thus, on the one hand, chiefs would act quite ruthlessly to snuff out any incipient threat: the over-ambitious son was likely to be dragged away by the *nkosi*'s henchmen and clubbed or stabbed. On the other hand, chiefs had to wield their authority with care if they were to retain their followers' support, and any decision that bore on the clan would be put to the *abanumzana*, the kraal heads, meeting in council. An unpopular leader risked not only overthrow but abandonment by his people for another – being left, in an ancient idiom, as 'chief of the pumpkins'.

It is not clear at what point religious belief started to be turned to the ends of power, but in this long period of political evolution other members of an emergent hierarchy, the healers and seers, were frequently co-opted by the chiefs. Somewhere along the line, the *nkosi* became not just the civil and military head of his people, but their spiritual head as well. Rulers came to be seen by their subjects as divine. A link was established between the health of the chief and the health of his people. The corollary was that the customs and rituals which sustained the health of the *nkosi* and the group became cultural imperatives; those which threatened it, taboos.

No doubt Bantu political evolution, with all the attendant

turmoil, would have continued apace anyway. But from the middle of the eighteenth century, forces beyond the control of the coastal clans pressed in with ever more disruptive effect. Maize is believed to have been introduced to the east coast of southern Africa by the Portuguese; it took some time to spread, but was then quickly accepted by the Nguni and overtook cultivation of their traditional cereal, sorghum. The upshot was a population explosion that gradually introduced a new friction into inter-clan relations: rivalry for pasture.

Another event, little understood at the time, ended the clans' isolation from the wider world, with even more destructive consequences. To the north, beyond the Pongolo river that roughly marks the border of modern Zululand, dwelt the Tsonga-speaking peoples, descendants of the first Bantu migrants to reach southern Africa. Here a clan under the leadership of an *nkosi* named Mabhudu had risen to an unprecedented state of organization and power on the fringes of the Portuguese settlement at Delagoa Bay. To the coastal people, it was evident that Mabhudu's ascendancy was in a mysterious way connected with an animal for which they had little use. *Ndlovu* was the elephant, the giant pachyderm of Africa, dangerous and difficult to hunt, like the buffalo and hippopotamus, and best trapped in large, camouflaged game pits. Mabhudu's people, however, had been organized into groups to kill *ndlovu* in great numbers, not for meat but for their tusks. Other chiefs were pressed into raising stocks of the tusks which, when carried by armies of bearers to Delagoa Bay, could be exchanged for treasures: rings of brass and copper, and brightly coloured cloth and beads.[10]

Trade had been going on along Africa's east coast for centuries but, although it had given rise to substantial kingdoms in Zimbabwe and Mozambique, it had made little impact in the southeast. Almost as alien as the process itself were those who had introduced it. Contacts with these pale apparitions who came from the sea had been scant and sporadic, but it was well enough known that they possessed great power. This stemmed not just from the abundance of their treasure, nor their mastery of the sea, which the coastal people avoided whenever possible, nor even perhaps their weapons, which could issue death unseen and from a distance. It was all these things and more. From out of the void filtered other tales of these people which made them seem even more frightening. In time, they would come to be known as *abelungu*, white men. At first, however, they were called *izilwane*, wild beasts.

✸

It was a disease which induced whites to settle on the southern tip of Africa. Portuguese navigational genius had found a route to India in 1497, when Vasco da Gama rounded the Cape and, finding a green and rocky coast on Christmas Day, named it Natal for the birth date of the Saviour. The Dutch, British and French followed in da Gama's wake to the East Indies, but the spice wealth was dearly bought as the mariners' plague, scurvy, often took off more than half a ship's crew. European trader barons recognized that to secure their investment, refuelling stations to supply life-saving vegetables and meat would have to be established in Africa.

Although it was a Portuguese navigator, Bartholomeu Diaz, who invested the Cape with the aspect of Good Hope – he called it *Boa Esperanca* in the belief that it would lead to the Indies – the spot did not enjoy a happy reputation in Europe. In 1510, Francesco de Almeida, a Portuguese naval commander, was returning from piracy and adventure in the Indian Ocean when he landed just north of the Cape in Table Bay and, trying to plunder a Khoikhoi settlement nearby, got more than he bargained for. Almeida and many of his companions were slaughtered on the beach as they attempted to regain their ships. The south-east coast of Africa also had a justified notoriety for its storminess, and the Portuguese opted for the calmer east coast on which to site their settlements, at Sofala and the island of Mocambique. Only in 1652 was a settlement established at the Cape by the Dutch East India Company. By then, the Portuguese influence had been felt with dramatic effect on the east coast.

It is not hard to imagine how the seafarers acquired the name *izilwane*. Contacts with the whites were limited to the occasions when one of their wooden shells was washed up on the shore and yielded up its occupants with their magical weapons and other astonishing objects of wood and metal. From 1552, dozens of vessels, mainly Portuguese but also Dutch and British, were wrecked off southern Africa. A few hundred crewmen succeeded in making their way back to European settlements. Many more perished in the wilderness or found a strange new existence among the natives. One Portuguese mariner, discovered living on the coast some forty years after being shipwrecked, had a wife and children and declined to leave his idyll. 'He spoke only the African language, having forgotten everything else, his God included,' wrote a would-be rescuer.[11]

The Portuguese settlement nearest to Nguni territory was Delagoa Bay, which lay only some three or four days' journey to the north. But for almost two hundred years after it was first explored by Lourenco Marque and Antonio Caldeira in 1554, the bay was only sporadically inhabited and played a small part in the Portuguese trade in slaves and ivory, which was concentrated at Mocambique and Sofala, many hundreds of miles to the north. Then, from the mid-eighteenth century, European interest in Delagoa Bay quickened – not just among the Portuguese, but the British, French and Dutch. Between 1770 and 1780, the exchange rate for ivory at the bay doubled. On the back of his treasury – beads, brass and cloth – Mabhudu built up a system of patronage and coercion powerful enough to establish him as south-east Africa's first great ruler.

Rivals were not far behind. Mabhudu's paramountcy sent waves of turbulence eddying out from Delagoa Bay, to where other large clans were organizing and starting to jostle one another. Alliances were forged between chiefs to control trade and the routes by which goods were transported. Between the Pongolo and Mzimkulu rivers, among the clans to emerge as most powerful was the Qwabe, who traced their origins to a much-revered ancestor, Malandela, and dwelt in the fine rolling coastal country north of the Tugela. Here, they rose to affluence on the strength of their maize production, which was bartered for cattle. The Qwabe were starting to assert their authority over two other large neighbouring clans, the Cele and the Tuli. However, at this stage the two dominant clans south of Delagoa Bay were the Mthethwa and the Ndwandwe. Each was ruled by a remarkable man, the Mthethwa by Dingiswayo, whose name in oral literature is synonymous with wisdom and benevolence, the Ndwandwe by a ruthless tough named Zwide. In the idiom of the *isibongo*, Dingiswayo was the lion and Zwide the crocodile.

Whatever the difference in their personalities and methods, Dingiswayo and Zwide had much in common. In building military organizations, they recruited young men by age group into bands known as *amabutho*, whose members passed through adulthood

rituals together and in the process came to share a strong communal identity. *Amabutho* were deployed to hunt elephant and to
carry out cattle raids. Weaker clans were brought into alliances as
the rival blocs sought to widen their power bases, Dingiswayo
through a judicious blend of diplomacy and force, Zwide by ferocious conquest. Other big clans joined in enlisting age-based
groups of men, including the Qwabe and the Cele. Here can be
glimpsed, in embryonic form, the regimental system which would
in time make up the most powerful of African armies.[12]

As turmoil swept the land, Nguni cosmological certainties
wavered. Alarm was heard in the councils of the *nkosi* and at
firesides. The sinister face of a psyche rooted in intuition and mysti-
cism showed itself: superstition gained ground, as did established
beliefs in sorcery and evil spirits. Blame for all ills was showered
upon *abathakathi*, living people possessed by malign forces that
turned them into wizards. In this time of troubles, witchcraft
became the most terrible of crimes, punishable only by death and
usually by a most terrible method – impalement on sharp stakes
driven up through the anus. Thus did a chief's *issanusi*, the
mediums who conducted ceremonies at which wizards were
'smelled out' and denounced, acquire a dreadful authority.

The long idyll was over. At the end of the eighteenth century,
south-east Africa was on a cusp of history. What none could have
foreseen was that the new era would be shaped by a clan so puny
and insignificant that its members were often insulted by their
neighbours as, 'you who came from the dog's penis'. In fact, the
clan shared with the Qwabe descent from the illustrious patriarch,
Malandela. But it took its name from his second son, who was
called Heaven, or Zulu.

2

SHAKA ZULU

Ah, let us come together Zulus
And dance, unfettered, in his honour! –
For we shall never fail him or allow him
To be defamed by any foreign breeds.
So let us dance or use our eager pens
In praise of all the victories
Of him they spoke of as 'The Hoe' –
Of Shaka, the mightiest Hoe of all!
Let us tell how tribes once reeled and fell,
Their blood congealed with shock and terror.

B.W. Vilakazi,
Zulu Horizons,
1945

Unlike Napoleon, with whom he has been frequently compared,
there is no certainty about the year of the first Zulu king's birth.
In all likelihood, however, it was 1787, when the young Bonaparte
was a military student and the French monarchy was in its death
throes. In most other biographical respects we are on firmer
ground: indeed, South Africa's most remarkable black leader seems
to epitomize the formula of the great man produced by a scarred
cradle. The child of an unhappy union, a bastard and an outcast
who was bullied in his youth, he turned tormented energy first

to military and then to political achievement. Here, in a father's rejection and a domineering mother, in childhood traumas and adolescent yearnings for status, lie the forces that have shaped revolutionary leaders across cultures and down the ages. Among all the myths, fantasies and outright distortions that hide the real man, these prosaic facts are fundamental to the life of Shaka ka Senzangakona ka Jama ka Punga ka Mageba ka Zulu.

The excesses of Shaka's personality have contributed greatly to the misapprehensions about him. That he was capable of monstrous cruelty cannot be in doubt: it is fairly clear that towards the end of his life he was drunk with power, and perhaps a little mad. However, one-dimensional accounts of his barbarism overlook as much as they reveal. Matters have not been improved by the sheer lack of first-hand information. Only three of the literate men to have known him left memoirs, and one of these had good reason to besmirch him as thoroughly as possible. On to this lurid outline further myths were embroidered over the years and have made of the first Zulu king a comic-strip figure, a sword-and-sorcery caricature located somewhere between Edgar Rice Burroughs' Tarzan and Robert Howard's Conan the Barbarian.

Given such malleable biographical materials, it is scarcely surprising that Shaka's career has come in the one hundred and sixty or so years since his death to represent so many things to different men. To early white colonialists, he appeared through the pages of Nathaniel Isaacs' self-serving memoir *Travels and Adventures in Eastern Africa* as the gore-drenched savage of nightmare; a later generation found much to admire in him, as the incarnation of the Arthurian warrior king in E.A. Ritter's *Shaka Zulu*, published in 1955 and scarcely out of print since. To Zulu nationalists, like the poet Benedict Vilakazi whose work is quoted above, Shaka, the king of the mightiest force produced in South Africa, manifested past glories and was a model for the modern warrior who would one day liberate his people; the many Zulu treatments of Shaka's life include one by John Dube, a founder of the African National Congress. Among other South African blacks, through the haze of folklore, Shaka's name could conjure up awe and even dread, while also inspiring confidence and pride because of an African leader before whom white men quailed. One of the landmarks of black South African literature is *Chaka*, by the Sotho writer Thomas Mafolo, written in 1908.

Other strands, too, have been picked out of the tapestry of Shakan legend. For African nationalists who aimed at unifying the continent against European dominance in the post-colonial era, Shaka was the great amalgamator – 'the father of modern pan-Africanism', as Jordan Ngubane, the South African writer and politician called him. As such, he was as much revered in Francophone west Africa as in his own land, appearing prominently in the literatures of Mali, Guinea and Nigeria. Leopold Senghor, the first president of Senegal, celebrated him in a dramatic poem.[1]

Shaka is a protean figure. Quite possibly, as Professor Norman Etherington has remarked, he is beyond the reach of historians. But he is patently not yet out of the reach of polemicists and politicians. In coming to grips with the Shakan period, let us turn to those nearest to it, and listen to the two hundred or so informants whose memories and knowledge make up the Stuart archive of oral history.

No attempt has so far been made here to classify the people known as the north Nguni, who lived between the Pongolo and Mzimkulu rivers, the area covered roughly by the modern area of Natal and Zululand. Much of the long-accepted scholarship on the subject is undergoing revision and to attempt a new categorization is beyond the scope of this work. It may, in fact, be one of those objectives that will continue to defy academics. Migrant groups had been crossing one another's paths for centuries, acquiring a linguistic inflexion here, imparting a style of pottery there, scrambling the clues, and leaving a trail of red herrings to baffle and mislead the historian and anthropologist.

What can be said is that the one hundred and fifty or so clans fell into one of four great groups: the Nguni, the Mbo, the Lala and the Ntungwa. The Lala may have been the first to have come on to the scene, the Ntungwa the last. Status attached more to some groups than others: at the top of the pecking order were the Nguni, who claimed to have come from ancient and revered stock. Those regarded as Lala, on the other hand, were known as 'those from down country' and tended to be looked down upon. The Ntungwa may have had links with the Sotho-speakers across the Drakensberg, and in tribal lore were said to have come down from the mountains 'in a grain basket'. The small Zulu clan was almost

41

certainly a member of this Ntungwa group and, with the Qwabe, were thus comparative latecomers to the coastal belt.[2]

Notions of class were quite pervasive, fed by the divisions and jealousies inherent in so fragmented a society. Clan chiefs recognized no authority other than their own, unless it was of a more powerful neighbour, and advanced their own claims to status while frequently deriding others as *amankengana*, inferior outsiders. But class did not carry with it any wider privilege or authority and in the developing struggle for power at the end of the eighteenth century the old order was in the process of being stood on its head. Although a Lala clan, the Mthethwa were the most powerful regional grouping, attracting allies and subjects because of their dominance in trade with the Portuguese at Delagoa Bay, where ivory and leather were bartered for metals and beads. Clans which had pledged allegiance to the Mthethwa included the Zulu, whose chief was Senzangakona.

Senzangakona's domain lay south of the Mthethwa, among the hills between the middle reaches of the White Mfolozi and Mhlatuze rivers. From the time of Malandela, the tribal Moses, who had brought his people to the region, the Zulu chiefs had founded their kraals here, and flourished in untroubled obscurity. Malandela's youngest son Zulu gave the clan its name; he had been succeeded by Mageba, he by Punga, he by Ndaba and he by Jama. It was the custom for a man to add after his own name a roll-call of his ancestors, back to the clan founder, so the full name of Shaka's father was Senzangakona ka (son of) Jama ka Ndaba ka Punga ka Mageba ka Zulu. These former *nkosi* were buried in a valley known as the Emakosini, the Place of the Chiefs, where at times of crisis such as drought, Zulu clan members would be summoned to praise and seek the favour of their ancestors. The custom has continued, and the Emakosini valley, situated in lovely, gently undulating countryside south of the White Mfolozi, remains a sacred place.

From the oral evidence, Senzangakona was a rather feckless character, too fond of the *isigodlo* – the enclosure where a chief's wives dwelt – to have been a strong leader. While Shaka created a personality cult around his mother, the father who rejected him was largely dismissed from oral history. His part in Shaka's early life is, however, well known. While still in his early twenties, and unmarried, Senzangakona was herding cattle with a group of fellows in the district of the Langeni clan. The chief, Mbengi, had a headstrong and wilful daughter named Nandi. According to one well-connected informant, it was Nandi who took the lead in their courtship, singling out Senzangakona and stealing away to a hut where he was spending the night.

Tribal custom saw nothing unnatural in congress between young people, who were allowed to enjoy sexual play from adolescence onwards. This ranged from mutual stimulation to a form of external intercourse known as *hlobonga*.[3] Both parties were free to enjoy themselves, but were expected to retain self-control. Above all, a girl's virginity was not to be lost, and she was not to fall pregnant. These matters were female responsibilities, and girls were instructed in techniques of *hlobonga*, which involved squeezing their thighs together, both to give their partners pleasure, and to prevent penetration. On the night Nandi visited Senzangakona, something went wrong. Perhaps, in the Zulu idiom, *kwehl' itonsi* – 'a drop descended'.

Faced with disgrace, Nandi tried to conceal her pregnancy, complaining as her stomach started to swell that she was suffering from an intestinal complaint known as *itshaka* after the beetle which supposedly caused it. However, the ruse could not be sustained indefinitely and eventually she named Senzangakona as her lover. Precisely what followed is uncertain, but the effects were undoubtedly painful and humiliating for the young mother and her baby. She seems to have left her own people and spent some time at the kraal of the young Zulu chief, but it is unlikely that he *lobola'd* cattle for her, or that they were ever married in the accepted sense, although she bore him another child, a daughter.[4] The assertive Nandi was probably just too much of a handful for Senzangakona. Not long after the birth of Shaka, so named after the beetle for which he had been mistaken, she was back among the Langeni, supposedly having been expelled by Senzangakona for her violent temper.

Nandi's shame had been doubled. Not only had she fallen pregnant out of wedlock, but she had failed to hold on to her lover. She took up with another man, a commoner named Gendayana, by whom she had a second son, Ngwadi. She also acquired a reputation for promiscuity, as a praise-poem of the time shows. This was fatal in a culture where tolerance of physical needs was tempered by a keen sense of sexual propriety. Although a chief's daughter, Nandi was shown no mercy by the Langeni. As an *izirobo*, a deflowered girl, she was treated with contempt; a contemporary verse mocked her supposed inability to keep her thighs together in the *hlobonga* manner when her favours were sought. Shaka, an *mlandwana* or illegitimate child, was bullied and teased.

It is easy to imagine childhood, in the pastoral, enfolding and prosperous society of the southern Africa savannah, as an Elysium. For Shaka, it was wretched. Boys were responsible for herding and milking; Shaka was put in charge of a cow which was notorious for goring and almost impossible to milk. In a child's game in which stones were used to represent bulls, Shaka's stones were taken by bigger boys. His fellows played tricks on him. Years later, he recalled being urged to reach into a hole in the ground because there was a bird's egg there, only to put his hand into a pile of faeces. The roots of his troubled sexuality lay in this period too; his genitals were poorly developed and older boys jeered at him as 'the one with the little half-cocked penis'.[5] Knowledge that he was actually the son of a chief only added to his misery and bitterness.

Fanciful it may be, but there is something almost Shakespearean in all this. Ambitious and strong-minded, Nandi is a figure reminiscent of the most compelling of the playwright's women, a Lady Macbeth or, better still, a Volumnia, plotting the career of the warrior son she called *Mlilwana*, or Blazing Little Fire. Under her tutelage, Shaka developed much like a young Coriolanus, resentful, arrogant, dismissive of the common herd. The relationship of mother and son, each harbouring a sense of grievance and forced by their outcast status to turn to each other for emotional support, was seminal to the rise from obscurity of Senzangakona's clan.

The boy Shaka grew up amid the hilly country around present-day Eshowe, about a day's journey from his father's kraal. Senzangakona, by now installed as Zulu chief, was married with a number of wives, including his favourite, a legendary beauty named Bibi ka Nkobe, by whom he had a son, Sigujana. Besides Shaka, Senzangakona had at least nine other sons, three of whom appear prominently in this story, Dingane, Mpande and Mhlangana. His first-born, however, he at best ignored, at worst saw as a threat. As we have seen, succession disputes were the bane of dynastic stability and it was not uncommon for chiefs to do away with sons who were thought to have ambitions which might disturb the *status quo*. Whether or not, as some sources maintain, Senzangakona actually took steps to have Shaka killed, the risk was sufficient for the teenage boy to be sent by Nandi to relatives among the powerful Qwabe people.

The Qwabe shared with the Zulu a common ancestor, Malandela, but Shaka was no happier there than he had been with the Langeni. Demanding to be treated as a chief's son, he seethed when his hosts refused to serve him curds in a cooling earthenware pot, as was the privilege of status, instead pouring the refreshment into his hands as though he were a commoner. Moreover, as members of a Nguni clan, which the Qwabe claimed with little justification to be, his new companions taunted Shaka with his social inferiority, as 'this little Ntungwa'. The barb of discrimination deepened his rage and sense of isolation.

Shaka's youthful fury at the world started to find expression in rebellion. He antagonized the relatives among whom he was living and quarrelled with his peers. Powerfully built, he could assert himself painfully in the stick-fighting contests that were a traditional sport of youth. Whether because of his pugnacity, or because of a new threat to his safety from Senzangakona, he did not remain long among the Qwabe. Nandi, seeking a new asylum for her son, settled fatefully on her mother's people, the Mthethwa. Here, finally, Shaka found respite from his demons and a channel for his talents.

The year would have been around 1802. The Mthethwa, under their able chief, Dingiswayo, were a fast-rising power between the Mhlatuze and Black Mfolozi rivers, but a number of other clans were able to challenge their paramountcy, and at least one was their superior. To the north, the Ndwandwe under the fearsome Zwide had risen as an ally of the Delagoa chief Mabhudu, and were now the most formidable force in south-east Africa. To the north-west lived the Ngwane, to the west the Tembu and Cunu, and to the south, the Qwabe. These embryonic tribal states were in various stages of military development and political aggregation. In this enchanting corner of southern Africa was developing a maelstrom that would shape the subcontinent more decisively than any event since the arrival of the white man.

Well-connected though they were, the Zulu teenager and his Langeni mother were accorded no special treatment by the Mthethwa, and were not even found a place at the main kraal, the *umuzi* of the elderly *nkosi*, Jobe. Instead, they went to the kraal of one of his headmen, Ngomane, where they were to live for some years. This man was to be Shaka's first mentor, an unobtrusive but constant presence throughout his life, from whom he drew support and advice – the nearest thing he had to a father.

But for the decade he spent among the Mthethwa and his association with the chief who succeeded Jobe, it is unlikely that Shaka would have left such a mark on history. Like Shaka, the new *nkosi* had been an outcast. Dingiswayo – an adopted name meaning 'one in distress' – was born Godongwana but was forced to flee his father's *umuzi* as a suspected usurper and spent years away from home, a rare and broadening experience. The view was long advanced by historians that during his absence Dingiswayo visited the Cape where he observed the whites' military organization and so learned how to gain the upper hand on his rivals. This clearly rings false, but it does seem that when he returned home to claim his birthright, Dingiswayo knew about firearms, and may even have brought a gun with him -- along with a vision of a great Bantu nation united under a single leader.

Dingiswayo seems to have had a generous spirit as well as imagination and a gift for organization. Alfred Bryant,[6] who was fond of historical allusions, likened him to Alfred the Great. Here was a model for the turbulent Shaka. Emerging from his teens, the young man passed into one of the groups known as *amabutho*, in which men served their chief, partly as labourers and, increasingly, as warriors. This regimental system, which was to be critical in the creation of the Zulu state, arose from the practice of separating groups of boys aged between sixteen and eighteen from the main body of the clan in ritual circumcision lodges. Dingiswayo may have been the first to see how such a pool of youthful energy could be channelled, but others were not long in following. Among his rivals, Zwide of the Ndwandwe, Matiwane of the Ngwane, and Pakatwayo of the Qwabe, all had age regiments at this time. The *amabutho* system, often attributed to Shaka, thus came well before him, although it was Shaka who honed it into a means of waging total war, and of controlling the labour and sexual reproduction of his subjects.

Shaka rose quickly within his new regiment, the iziCwe, where his innate aggression and pent-up frustration found a natural outlet. Perhaps in these years as a member of a tightly knit unit he also felt some stirrings of companionship. The conventional portrait of a man who, when not simmering in a state of unbridled ferocity, was a solitary dreamer capable of warmth only towards his mother, starts hereabouts to appear incomplete. Nandi did indeed remain unhealthily the linchpin of his emotions, but there is evidence that Shaka formed the sort of friendships common among men-at-arms, and there is no doubt that his ability to inspire his fellows was based on a great deal more than mere fear. Dingiswayo recognized as much and made him *induna* of the iziCwe, an act of patronage that sealed their destinies. The shrewd Mthethwa chief gained a protégé who, despite his illegitimacy, was descended from the Zulu chief, Senzangakona. Meanwhile, Shaka's star continued to rise, his exploits inspiring verses from the praise-singers that established him as a Mthethwa hero. One early *isibongo* runs:

> Shaka who always escapes from a conflict unhurt,
> He who thunders though in repose,
> The stabber who surpasses all others.[7]

Accounts of Shaka's prowess on the battlefield have more than a touch of the apocryphal about them. In particular, tales of his early career, of mortal struggles with wild animals and men possessed by demons, are in the classical tradition of myth and legend. One well-known example is the story of how he overcame a madman who was terrorizing the Mthethwa and stealing cattle; the insane were held in awe, being thought to have supernatural powers. In this version, the story was told to Stuart by Mkebeni ka Dabulamanzi, a great-grandson of Senzangakona:

Shaka heard some of Dingiswayo's people talking about the madman. He asked: 'Why hasn't he been killed?' They replied: 'He has overcome everyone.' Shaka said: 'If the king would give me four companies of men, I should kill him.'

[The people and Dingiswayo resisted, but Shaka would not give up, so eventually a party of warriors was raised and set out apprehensively with him at their head.]

When the madman saw them he took up his shield and his assegais and went towards them. He had on his finery, in the form of bird plumes, sewn to long threads, hanging down over his whole body; he flourished his shield as he went. Shaka commanded: 'Do not run away.' But as the madman approached the warriors ran away. Shaka went forward and confronted the madman. Their shields clashed together like the clashing of bateleur eagles. Shaka stabbed the madman and beat him to the ground. The Mthethwa warriors came up and stabbed him as he lay. Shaka gave a loud whistle, and thus became 'the whistler, the lion'. He was so praised when he returned the cattle of the Mthethwa country, those which had been robbed by the madman. They collected cattle and goats and sheep from all the ridges. Their dust obscured the sun.[8]

Shaka's deeds in more conventional battles have no doubt also gained in the retelling as Dingiswayo was more diplomat than conqueror and the campaigns in which the iziCwe would have been sent to draw new allies into the *pax Mthethwa*, or extract cattle from vassal chiefs, seldom required a great deal of bloodshed. Allowing for exaggeration, however, Shaka must still have been a formidable warrior. Suited by temperament and physique to fighting, he was also fearless, innovative and utterly implacable. Dingiswayo's moderate methods, he was quick to recognize, would not win the kingdom he sought. While still *induna* of the iziCwe he is said to have surveyed the regiment and said: 'Wo! If these men were mine I would cut a single assegai for each of them. I do not want them to bear wounds behind. A good man should have his wounds on his chest.'[9] Foes, in Shaka's eyes, were to be overawed, then destroyed. Anything that helped make the fighter more fearsome and more mobile was to be encouraged. Anything that inhibited or restricted him was to be suppressed. Many years later one old warrior summed up Shaka's way of waging war:

In the fights that took place in former days, the men would hurl assegais at one another. They did not approach closely. If one side was defeated and a man was left exhausted he would say, 'I am defenceless!' He would be taken captive but never killed. When the fighting was over his family would come and ransom him with a beast . . . Women were not killed in war, nor was a man who was running away, for he was like a woman. Only a man who was fighting was stabbed. The practice of stabbing a man who was running away, or one who was left wounded was begun by Shaka. Small boys, children, used not to be killed. The practice of killing even women was one begun by Shaka. Chiefs are responsible for acts of madness.[10]

Shaka's appearance has been a matter of much speculation, and further heroic embroidery. Zulu sources agree that he was powerfully made, with the heavy haunches – produced by a meat and cereal diet – associated with privilege in Bantu society, and that his skin had an especially dark tint. He was extremely strong and, it was said, could lift a cow off the ground by its back legs. But there his resemblance to the perfect physical specimen depicted by Ritter and many others ended. He was not unusually tall, and certainly not the giant of legend. And he was ugly.

The only portrait of him is not much help. James King, an early white visitor, was an adventurer not an artist, and his well-known sketch, executed around 1825, of Shaka holding an outsize shield and assegai, is largely a product of memory, if not imagination. Shaka himself had no illusions about his appearance, and used to joke with his great friend, Magaye ka Dibandhlela, that he could not afford to have him killed as the people would say it was because he was handsome while Shaka was ugly. In what way his features were unattractive is unclear, but he is said by some sources to have had a protruding forehead and buck teeth. Perhaps because of this slight deformity, his speech was impeded; it appears that the great warrior was afflicted with either a lisp or a stutter.[11]

Of his purposefulness, there could be no doubt. He had none of the fatalism that has often been the African's best comfort against disaster, and the worst enemy of his progress. Shaka knew that he would have to create his own destiny and appears never to have doubted that he would succeed. As he passed through early manhood, one sign of the single-mindedness that set him apart was his avoidance of women. The shadow of Nandi in the background was doubtless inhibiting, but there were other reasons too. Ngomane, his old adviser, is said to have once urged him to father children, and he to have replied: 'Would they hold to me? They would achieve their own notability and turn against me.'[12] Ruthlessness went hand in glove with determination. On another occasion he said: 'A chief is not made, he makes himself. It is the calf which is picked out and has its place assigned to it.'[13]

Other ambitious men were already assigning places to themselves. By the second decade of the nineteenth century the struggle for paramountcy in south-east Africa was approaching a phase as critical in its way as that taking place across the world in Europe. Increasingly, Dingiswayo was being seen as a threat to the supremacy of the Ndwandwe power to the north under Zwide. Early in his chieftaincy, Dingiswayo had concluded a trade and military alliance with the Delagoa Bay chiefs, undermining Zwide's control over trade. Having married one of Dingiswayo's sisters, Zwide was perhaps reluctant to bring matters to an early head. But a number of new factors added pungency to the rivalry that now simmered like a stew in a three-legged cooking pot over a fire. Competition for both livestock and pasture was intensifying, stimulated by population growth and the *amabutho* system, which made heavy demands on a chief's ability to keep his leading men sweet with rewards of cattle. A seven-year drought had just ended and an even longer one was not far off.

Shaka was by now nearing his thirtieth year and Dingiswayo's foresight in adopting him as a protégé was soon to be born out. The crucial point occurred after Senzangakona visited the Mthethwa court to select a new wife. There, as a trusted if insubstantial ally, he was welcomed by Dingiswayo and invited to pay a return visit for a festive dance. On this occasion he met for the first time in many years his first-born son. There are a number of detailed accounts of what followed. One of the most vivid comes from Jantshi ka Nongila, the son of one of Shaka's spies and as a result a source of special value:

When dancing had been going on some time, Dingiswayo came forward and said, 'Where is the hoe that surpasses other hoes?' He sang out [Shaka's] praises. Shaka then came out of the cattle pen carrying his war shield of one colour. It had pieces of skins of various wild animals placed in those holes in the shield caused by assegai thrusts . . . Shaka ran round in circles and eventually ended off in front of Senzangakona where he stood still. He then said, 'Father, give me an assegai, and I shall fight great battles for you!' His father directed assegais to be fetched from the huts. Senzangakona said, 'Take one yourself.' Shaka replied, 'No, let it come from your hand.' Senzangakona thereupon felt a number and, deciding on one, gave it to Shaka.[14]

This apparent reconciliation – which also involved Senzangakona's other sons, including his chosen heir, Sigujana – concealed deeper currents of vengeance and guilt. It is part of Zulu lore that later the same night Shaka, with Dingiswayo's connivance, climbed on to the roof of his father's hut where he washed himself with magic potions which dripped through the thatch on to Senzangakona. Overcome with fear, the aging satyr then fell mortally ill and, soon after returning home, died.

Whatever the reality of Shaka's last encounter with his father, its aftermath was prosaic. When news of Senzangakona's death reached the Mthethwa court, Shaka set off with Dingiswayo's blessing and the iziCwe regiment for the land from which he had been so long exiled. With him, too, went his young half-brother, Ngwadi. The succession dispute on this occasion was brief: Sigujana was impaled in a stream beside his kraal; Ngwadi did the deed, not because Shaka was unwilling himself, but because a taboo stood in the way of an assassin becoming a chief.

Senzangakona's maiden sister, Mkabayi, an influential matri-arch, pronounced Shaka an acceptable successor. The old chief's surviving sons, including Mhlangana, Dingane and Mpande, hastily gave assurances of allegiance. The Zulu ascent had begun.

The Zulus' new ruler wasted little time before moving the chiefly *umuzi*. In abandoning Senzangakona's Nobamba kraal in the Emakosini valley, among the spirits of the clan ancestors and set-ting forth to found a new home two days' journey away, across the Mhlatuze river, Shaka could be seen as turning his back on his childhood misery, or even making a revolutionary gesture. However, strategic considerations were at least as likely to have been uppermost in his mind. The new *umuzi* bordered the Mthethwa country. Here, on a high ridge overlooking the hills that roll away to the Indian Ocean, Shaka founded the kraal which with uncharacteristic self-pity he called kwaBulawayo – 'the place of him who was killed, with afflictions'.

The Zulu clan is estimated at this time to have numbered no more than a couple of thousand people. No development had taken place under the dead hand of Senzangakona and the tribe had little wealth and less military organization. Shaka's transformation started with the military and the formation of the first four make-shift Zulu *amabutho*. Before this rudimentary army, he laid down the creed he had brought from the iziCwe: the assegai was not an arrow but a sword, to be used in concert with a large cowhide shield in close-quarters combat; sandals were to be discarded as they restricted mobility; units were to maintain orderly move-ments in close formation. Any man who disobeyed these orders, who lost his assegai or who fled, would be put to death. One old warrior later recalled:

Shaka proclaimed that only one assegai was to be carried by each warrior. He said there was to be no throwing but every warrior was to stab at close quarters. All his troops carried one assegai, the *isijula*, with a nine-inch blade and about a fourteen-inch haft. Should a man break his assegai when in conflict, he was to grip the other with his arms and fight for the one carried by his assailant.[15]

These tactics were deployed as Shaka set about demonstrating to his neighbours the mettle of the new Zulu ruler. First to feel the bite of the stabbing spear were the Buthelezi, a clan which had been a tributary of the Zulus in Jama's time but had broken away from the feeble paramountcy of Senzangakona and now, under their chief Pungashe, could turn out a far more formidable force than the Zulus. Or so it had seemed. When the two sides met, Shaka's warriors raced in at the astonished Buthelezi who did not need to take many casualties before fleeing the field. Shaka was intent on making a demonstration, however. The Zulus proceeded to the Buthelezi kraal, firing huts and slaughtering women and children.

Next Shaka turned to another neighbouring clan, his mother's people, the Langeni, of whom he had such bitter memories. Whether it was to satisfy a desire for revenge, or to drive home his message, the effect of another sanguinary example was the same: the butchery of the Langeni elders was never forgotten. After this, other chiefdoms between the Mfolozi and Mhlatuze rivers joined the Buthelezi and Langeni in pledging their allegiance. The Ntombela, the Biyela and the Mpungose had been served notice that their new overlord was not to be trifled with.

Despite these well-known conquests, it does not do to over-emphasize militarism at this early stage of the Shakan revolution. Creating the much-vaunted Zulu fighting machine took years and initially met with resistance from elderly *izinduna* in what was an innately conservative society. For all his fast-rising star, Shaka was still a vassal of Dingiswayo and needed to act with circumspection. Ultimately, the means by which he set himself apart from other regionally powerful *nkosi* was a genius not for the tactics of battle but for something far more profound.

Shaka's security throughout his twelve-year rule was never assured, as two assassination attempts, the second successful, demonstrate. A system so familiar with succession disputes had no great problem with usurpers, but outsider usurpers were a different matter. Staying on top now, he perceived, would mean disposing of the old order and starting afresh; it meant attracting new adherents as fast as they could be found, not just the high and mighty but the meek and lowly; it meant making allies wherever he could find them and disposing of anyone who might conceivably be a threat.

Above all, it meant imbuing those who would follow him with a new spirit, one that offered membership of a wider family than that of the clan. Shaka himself is unlikely to have felt any strong sense of clan loyalty. He had lived among the Zulu, the Langeni, the Qwabe and the Mthethwa before returning to the Zulu, and had never been a true part of any one of them. As a result, he could grasp better than most the concept of nationhood, of one people ruled by a king. There were many others like him, migrants, exiles and refugees who had been grafted on to clan groups, temporarily or permanently. The basis of linguistic unity already existed, all the clans of the coastal corridor speaking dialects of a basic Nguni tongue. A large degree of cultural uniformity could be imposed by a strong-willed leader. But it would take more than willpower to make a nation. It would require a shrewd sense of when to use terror as a political tool and when mercy; it would take a grasp of what it is that ordinary men and women want for themselves – and when to let them have it; and it would most certainly take a wonderful instinct for how to inspire and manipulate them by all means of propaganda and mass delusion.

All these qualities of statecraft Shaka demonstrated in the twelve years of his reign. Alfred Bryant's ground-breaking work on the history of Natal and Zululand was carried out more than fifty years ago and is unfashionable with modern South African academics, but his tribute still sums up much of the greatness of the founder of the Zulu state :

Strange, but true, this Shaka was as sublime a moral teacher as martial genius. Submission to authority, obedience to the law, respect for superiors, order and self-restraint, fearlessness and self-sacrifice, constant work and civic duty – in a word all the noblest disciplines of life were the very foundation-stones upon which he built his nation. So rigorously enforced was the lifelong practice of all these excellencies, that he left them all a spontaneous habit, a second nature, amongst his people.[16]

When Shaka succeeded his father he may have expected that he would have some years at least to consolidate his position under Dingiswayo's patronage. Instead, within the year, he was catapulted into even more vulnerable prominence by his mentor's death.

By 1817 the ferocious Zwide considered he had stalked his Mthethwa rival for long enough. Dingiswayo was now summoned to battle. It is unlikely that he would have set forth against so formidable a foe without seeking Shaka's support but, although a request was probably made, it came too late. Some say that Shaka betrayed his mentor by deliberately holding back his forces. More widespread in the oral traditions is the belief that Zwide obtained ascendancy by magic, sending to Dingiswayo a woman who had orders to obtain some of his semen in a snuff-box. After an act of *hlobonga* she returned to Zwide with a sample to be doctored by a *sangoma*, and in the battle that followed Dingiswayo was separated from his warriors, captured and put to death.

The defeat of the Mthethwa was a turning point. Zwide was left unchallenged between the Pongolo and Tugela rivers, the area of modern Zululand. The *pax Mthethwa* rapidly disintegrated as chiefs took the opportunity of Dingiswayo's death to reclaim their independence. Shaka, whose own little empire had been growing so satisfactorily under the Mthethwa wing, was now left exposed between the Ndwandwe in the north and the Qwabe under their chief Pakatwayo in the south. Considering all this from the hillside of kwaBulawayo, Shaka is bound to have reflected that, in the end, the methods of Zwide had triumphed over those of Dingiswayo. The lion had been laid low by the crocodile.

As a turning point, the consequences went beyond the fortunes of leaders. The tide that had so long been swelling on the coastal plain was about to crash over the Drakensberg on to the territories beyond, swamping the Bantu people in its wake. It was a calamity that reshaped the subcontinent, and indeed the lands to the north, as far as the Great Lakes of the Rift Valley. It would leave wounds that fester even now in South Africa.

3

SURVIVAL AND CONQUEST

After Dingiswayo's death, disturbances broke out in
every direction. Men were sent in one way, only to
be sent in another. Presently the whole country was
upside down, and it continued so until subdued by
Shaka. All the nations *konza'd* Shaka, for he had
killed their chiefs and eaten up their cattle and taken
their people.[1]

Ndhlovu ka Timuni, Zulu *induna*,
November 1902

George McCall Theal, the father of South African historiography,
estimated in 1910 that two million people had perished in Shaka's
conquests. How Theal arrived at this impressive figure is not clear,
but it squared neatly with what was known of 'the black Attila'.
Historians of the day sometimes had difficulty distinguishing one
group of black marauders from another, and as the great nineteenth-century conflagration in tribal society known as the *mfecane*
had emanated from the region known as Zululand, it was accepted
that Shaka was responsible. So one more of the many enduring
myths of South African history became established.

Shaka, certainly, was second to none in using terror and conquest as political weapons. However, diplomacy and propaganda
were, of necessity, as important elements of his armoury as

warfare, and for the decade after taking over the Zulu chieftaincy in 1816 his policy was primarily defensive. The source of his concern, and of much of the instability often attributed to Shaka, was Zwide.

Predatory and cunning – and one of the very few leading men of his generation to die, as it were, in his bed – the Ndwandwe *nkosi* Zwide is among the most neglected figures in South Africa's history (as yet the five-volume *Dictionary of South African Biography* has accorded him no entry at all). We know little about him, although he, like Shaka, had a domineering mother, the sorceress Ntombazi, a sort of Morgan le Fay of oral literature. Zulu accounts of his treacherousness should perhaps be treated with the same caution as Tudor propaganda about Richard Plantagenet; he was capable of attracting as an ally an even more remarkable man than himself, the Kumalo chief Mzilikazi, who later transferred his allegiance to Shaka before breaking away to found the Ndebele state. Of Zwide's cataclysmic impact, however, there is no doubt.

The trigger for his sudden onslaught on his neighbours in 1817 appears to have been a desire to break Dingiswayo's hold over trade with the Portuguese at Delagoa Bay. It is also possible that the rapid organization of other large clans, such as the Ngwane and Qwabe, was for the first time putting a strain on the region's capacity to sustain a burgeoning population.

Zwide began with a strike north at the Ngwane of Sobhuza, who fled with a core of followers and, picking up adherents on the way, settled west of the Lubombo mountains where he laid the foundations of modern Swaziland. Zwide then turned his attention to another Ngwane chief, Matiwane. He was driven west into the foothills of the Drakensberg where, armed with the methods learned in a hard school, he started lording it over another large tribal group, the Hlubi. This started a domino effect which spilled over the Drakensberg into the Bantu peoples of the Highveld. Having put Mtimkulu of the Hlubi to death, Matiwane swept on, defeating Sikonyela of the Tlokwa and succeeding in imposing himself on the redoubtable Sotho chief, Moshesh. Meanwhile, Zwide had reached the zenith in his fortunes with the defeat of Dingiswayo.

Thus began the *mfecane*, an era of mass migration and turmoil which led to the emergence of new tribal states across the subcontinent and as far north as the Great Rift Valley. In addition to South Africa, modern nations within whose boundaries the *mfecane* was felt include Swaziland, Lesotho, Zimbabwe, Mozambique, Zambia, Malawi and Tanzania.[2]

It was no time for faint hearts. The new warlords sought to instil awe among their followers, respect among their allies and to strike fear into their foes. Zwide – 'the one who crouches over people so that they may be killed' – made it known that his mother's hut was decorated with Dingiswayo's skull. Matiwane revelled in the *isibongo* of 'the gwalagwala bird who reddens his mouth by drinking the blood of men'.

At this stage, Shaka's concern was solely with survival. It could only be a matter of time before the rampant Zwide attacked the Zulu and Shaka was sorely in need of a major ally. He turned to the Qwabe, who were descended with the Zulu from Malandela and had become the main military power to the south, as the Ndwandwe were supreme to the north. It was an audacious proposition: the Qwabe saw themselves as the aristocrats of the region, with an especially rich body of folklore and tradition, and Shaka's overture had been sent to the *nkosi* Pakatwayo, with whom he had quarrelled during his sojourn among the Qwabe. Remembering the pathetic little boy who had been bullied by his fellows, Pakatwayo responded rashly – insulting the size of both the Zulu army and Shaka's genitals. 'Where did he get an *impi* from?' he jeered. 'Is the *impi* like the rain? It is nothing but a little string of beads that doesn't even reach to the ears.' Shaka he referred to contemptuously as 'the little Ntungwa who wears as a penis-cover the fruit shell used for snuffboxes.'[3]

Whatever his earlier intentions, Shaka now had no alternative but combat. Jantshi ka Nongila recalled:

Shaka at once called his *impi* together and said to them, 'I have been insulted by the Qwabe. Take up your arms and assemble here.' The next day his army was drawn up, given its orders, and despatched. Shaka himself went with it. He looked on at the fight. Pakatwayo's *impi* was quickly overcome. Afterwards Pakatwayo was found seated on the ground with his head buried in his folded arms. Pakatwayo looked up and, as he saw Shaka, was seized with fear. Shaka then said, 'Take him home.' Pakatwayo was then carried off to his kraal by the *impi*, which chanted war songs as it went.

On the day following the battle it was found that Pakatwayo was dead, having apparently been killed by fear alone.[4]

Shaka's defeat of Pakatwayo was a vital step in his rise. The new Qwabe chief, Nqeto, at once saw the wisdom of alliance with this formidable newcomer. As the senior partner, Shaka gained a large new source of manpower, and the support of important chiefs. The most notable of these was Zulu ka Nogandaya, also known as Komfiya, who was destined to be one of his most renowned and faithful generals. When Komfiya and three other Qwabe *izinduna* arrived at kwaBulawayo to *konza*, or pledge their allegiance, Shaka turned to the assembly and said: 'Halala! Celebrate, Zulu people, for I am chosen as a husband!'[5]

As well as substance, the Qwabe brought *éclat* to Shaka's growing fiefdom. He had rejoined his house with 'the great reed-bed of the Mhlatuze', as one *isibongo* described the Qwabe, and could claim now to have healed the ancient rift between the sons of Malandela. At the same time, he assumed a Qwabe conceit that their lineages were pure Nguni, implying great antiquity. Neither Zulu nor Qwabe was entitled to it, both being later arrivals of the Ntungwa group. But tradition and prestige, the African equivalent of class, were ever malleable materials in Shaka's hands.

Pakatwayo's defeat also illuminates Shaka's gift for propaganda. Through *isibongo* and the stories of the fireside, an image was being fostered of a mighty new *nkosi*, one invincible in arms and so powerful in magic that he had frightened the Qwabe chief to death. 'He got his power from the Almighty,' averred one awed *induna*. 'His cunning was superhuman.'[6]

The spread of Shaka's reputation strengthened his hand in forging alliances, as other clans were coerced or cajoled into the rapidly expanding Zulu fold. One new ally was to be particularly important: Zihlandlo, chief of the Mbo, became one of the few people Shaka really trusted. Then the Mthethwa, who had appeared likely to disintegrate after the Ndwandwe defeat, accepted a successor nominated by Shaka. Within a year of Dingiswayo's death, Shaka had surpassed his mentor.

Victory over the Qwabe hastened the inevitable Ndwandwe attack. In the first of two battles, in mid-1818, the armies of Zwide and Shaka met at a place known as Gqokli hill. In his influential but semi-fictional biography, *Shaka Zulu*, E.A. Ritter turned this encounter into an epic of African warfare in which some 1500 Zulu and 7500 Ndwandwe died. As with many of the figures bandied about in connection with Zulu warfare, this is pure fancy.

Stuart's sources are uncharacteristically mute on the subject of Gqokli hill and the action was probably no more than a limited defence of high ground with an indecisive outcome. One account actually describes Gqokli hill as a Zulu defeat, on the ground that the Ndwandwe made off with some of their foes' livestock.

Critically, however, Shaka had gained a breathing space. In the period that followed, the tenets of the Zulu military system were welded into place. Recruits from his new vassals were incorporated into Shaka's four regiments and a fifth was formed. Discipline was stiffened. It was not just the warrior who lost his assegai who might be executed; any sign of cowardice would be so punished. Shaka had always drilled into his men the doctrine that a warrior should take his wounds on the chest. During the Ndwandwe campaigns a wound in the back became a death sentence. Men picked out for execution would be brought before the assembled *impi* and Shaka would order: 'Let him feel the assegai.' The victim's arm would be raised and the assegai tip pressed up against his armpit. Then, with a sudden thrust, it was driven in at the heart.[7]

As the Zulu military system gained in strength it became quite common for one or two men to be selected at random in the absence of any cowards, and executed along the lines of the Voltairean maxim, *'pour encourager les autres'*. At this early stage, however, every warrior was an asset and Shaka's methods of stimulating *esprit de corps* were more conventional. The wearing of regalia was encouraged, and individuals who had pleased Shaka were rewarded with brass decorations. The warrior's panoply included the skins of genet and monkey worn around the waist and the tails of cows fastened like tassles at the knees, while regiments were assigned shield colourings to distinguish them. As regalia gained in importance, so did certain plumes and skins, such as that of the otter which was especially prized for headbands. The feather of the blue crane could be worn only by Shaka.

Shaka also introduced another custom, one which, as the writer Jordan Ngubane has pointed out, was to help shape the character of the Zulu military system and evidently helped instil the discipline and pride on which it thrived. This was the practice known as *uxoxa impi*, or 'to talk about war', in which warriors discussed in fireside forum their *ibutho*'s deeds, praising one another's prowess and denouncing cowards. The custom gave even the humblest soldier the feeling of involvement in the performance of his regiment, while exposure of a man's personality to the scrutiny of his fellows inspired the standards of bravery that enabled men sixty years later to hurl themselves, again and again, against the Gatling gun and Martini-Henry rifle.

To dance, or *giya*, was an essential part of the rituals of war. Before setting out, regiments gathered at the cattle enclosure and warriors who had already won honour would be called on, with a few lines from their praise-poem, to *giya* – 'Dance, Ndengezi who rushes like a lion!' Then the man would race out and fling himself into a furious and abandoned dance to the praise of his comrades. The *giya* was 'to sharpen the heroes', as one old warrior, Mtshapi ka Noradu, put it to Stuart:

Praises would cause a person to become roused. He would remember his praises when the battle was on, feeling he would be worthless if he did not fight fiercely. For it was one's praises that displayed one's popularity.

When a man was not praised, when he did not *giya*, when he did not work himself into a frenzy, as one who was no longer a fierce fighter, his meat would be soaked in water.[8]

From his small original base, Shaka was gradually shaping not only a formidable army but a militarized society which conformed in every respect with the great armed forces across the ages, as defined by the military historian, John Keegan:

Pride in a distinctive (and distinctly masculine) way of life, concern to enjoy the good opinion of comrades, satisfaction in the largely symbolic tokens of professional success, hope of promotion, and expectation of a comfortable and honourable retirement.[9]

In early writings on the Zulu, Shaka is routinely described as a master tactician. It is time that this idea was dispelled. There was in any case little room for tactical manoeuvre in African warfare. The so-called bull's head formation – in which the main body of the *impi*, the 'head', met the foe while the 'horns' streamed ahead on either side and enveloped him – was an earlier innovation. So was the regimental system, with which he is also sometimes credited. Although both these features were refined by Shaka, his talents, as we see here, were rather those of the great inspirational military leaders – a personality which imposed itself on any situation, and a flair for extracting the best from fighting men. To borrow Donald Morris's eloquent tribute to General Redvers Buller, he was one of that small and fabled band of leaders men cheerfully follow to hell.

In about 1819, four years after Waterloo, a campaign was fought between Zulu and Ndwandwe which had scarcely less momentous consequences for southern Africa than Napoleon's defeat did in Europe. Unlike the first Ndwandwe invasion, Zulu oral literature is rich in accounts of it and the following, drawn from several of Stuart's sources, is typical.[10]

Hearing from his spies that Zwide was preparing to launch another invasion of the Zulu lands, Shaka despatched his most powerful 'war doctors' or *izangoma* to the great Ndwandwe kraal of Emgazeni, near present-day Nongoma, to cast medicines in the waters from which Zwide drank. The Zulu meanwhile made their own preparations: the outlying territory up to the Ndwandwe country was stripped of cattle and crops; kraals were abandoned and their inhabitants fell back towards Shaka's capital; every available man was drafted into the five *ibutho*: the amaWombe, the inTontela, the umGamule, the uFasimba, which was Shaka's favourite, the imGamanqa, the newest with their distinctive red and black hide shields, and the nucleus of a sixth, the uDlangezwa. When scouts brought news that the Ndwandwe were on the move, a decoy was sent out. About forty miles north-west of kwaBulawayo, they encountered the Ndwandwe *impi*.

The Zulu strategy was to avoid open battle at this stage and draw the foe on until he exhausted himself. After two or three days of marching, Ndwandwe warriors were tiring and rations of maize bread were running low as they passed through the bare country. But the charms and spells cast by Shaka's war doctors now took hold and the Ndwandwe, being bewitched, followed the decoy that harassed and harried them. At night the Zulu infiltrated the enemy's camps, and although no great number of casualties was inflicted, the Ndwandwe believed they were being tormented by spirits and became further demoralized.

Skirmishing as they went, the two forces crossed the Mhlatuze river, bypassed the Nkandla forest and the surrounding hills, and almost reached the Tugela river before the Zulu decoy doubled back towards the Mhlatuze where Shaka had assembled the main body of his force.

Shaka addressed his men on the river banks. The *ibutho* were drawn up in their finery, in kilts of monkey, civet or genet fur, plumage bobbing at their heads, cow-tail fringes tied at their legs, war shields on arm and stabbing spears in hand. Shaka, carrying his own distinctive white shield with a black blaze in the centre, roused them with a call: 'The enemy are in our homes. Let us loose at him.'

Suddenly, unnervingly, Shaka's blue crane plume fell from his headdress to the ground where it stuck upright. The assembly was dismayed but with the touch possessed only by the greatest commanders, he turned the evil omen to his advantage. As an alarmed attendant stepped forward to pick up the feather, Shaka commanded: 'Leave it! It is Zwide who will fall.' Given this assurance that the feather had dropped at his design, the *impi*'s morale rose.[11]

Morale was something the Zulu sorely needed. No reliable figures exist for the size of the two armies, but the Ndwandwe were clearly far superior in numbers and, although fatigued by their march, must have been confident under their renowned general Soshangane and his deputy, Zwangendaba. On the banks of the Mhlatuze, however, the true mettle of Shaka's stabbing spear proved itself once and for all. While the Zulu were by now steeled in hand-to-hand combat, the Ndwandwe still expected to break up an enemy force under showers of assegais and then move in on the disintegrating components.

Of the battle itself there is conflicting testimony. It is said that fighting started soon after dawn and continued until nightfall, but it is unlikely that a battle fought at hand-to-hand intensity could have lasted so long without pause or regrouping. Among those who distinguished themselves on the Zulu side were Nomzane, 'who does not fight but to destroy', and two *izinduna* of the inTontela, Ndlela and Hlati. But the hero of the hour was Komfiya the Qwabe, who was fighting with the new umGamanqa regiment. Komfiya, a man of particularly dark colouring and stocky build, with immensely powerful shoulders, was wounded in the arm. Unable to hold a shield, he battled on ferociously with just his assegai, killing a number of Ndwandwe. Shaka was so impressed that he declared that he had been able to tell from the clamour where Komfiya was fighting, and conferred on him an *isibongo* that he himself had won among the Mthethwa, 'the heavens which thundered in the open where there are no mimosas or acacias'. This mighty fellow survived to fight in most of Shaka's campaigns and lived into his eighties, having forty-five wives and fathering many sons. One of them, an early convert to Christianity, recalled him as an awesome figure. 'When he danced no one dared to perform after him, for he would beat him about the head for his pains.'[12]

The toll of the battle was heavy and the outcome decisive. By the end of the day Ndwandwe and Zulu bodies lay across one another on either side of the Mhlatuze but it was the Ndwandwe who were vanquished. Four of Zwide's sons were among the dead. A Zulu *impi* pursued the retreating army, and this time there was no question of reaching an accommodation with the defeated. Zwide's capital, Emgazeni, was razed and the civilian population slaughtered.

The defeat of Zwide was a turning point. So recently fighting for his survival, Shaka was left master between the Mfolozi and Tugela rivers. Zwide abandoned Emgazeni and moved his kraal north of the Pongolo river. He remained a formidable presence, but never again would he challenge Shaka on his own ground. From this point we can discern the outlines of the Zulu kingdom starting to emerge from a loose federation of vassal clans. Although the British at the Cape had not yet heard of him, Shaka's acquisition of the trade monopoly with Delagoa Bay, previously held by Dingiswayo and Zwide, quickly brought him to the attention of the Portuguese.

Ndwandwe decline had fateful consequences elsewhere too. Zwide's conquests had already caused the Ngwane and the Hlubi to flee across the Drakensberg and collide with the Tlokwa and Sotho. Now his defeat triggered further upheavals. Soshangane, the beaten general, broke away from Zwide, set out in the direction of Delagoa Bay and, in the west of modern Mozambique, founded the Shangane state. His journey was a mere jaunt compared with that of his former comrade-in-arms, Zwangendaba, who led another Ndwandwe faction on an epic northward trek. Running against the tide of previous Bantu migrations, they crossed the Limpopo river, continued on over the Zambesi to the west of Lake Malawi, following the Rift Valley that bisects central Africa, and at the end of a march of well over 2000 miles settled in what is now Tanzania, where they are known as the Angoni.

The Kumalo leader, Mzilikazi, had been an Ndwandwe protégé and for some time after Zwide's defeat he submitted to Shaka. Then he broke away and followed the by now well-trodden route north, conquering and absorbing adherents from the Pedi, Phuthing and Sotho peoples. He settled near what is now Pretoria, only to be uprooted twenty years later when an even more powerful force of invaders was borne on to the scene on horseback and in columns of ox-wagons. The indomitable Mzilikazi thereupon decamped to the north of the Limpopo where, in present day Zimbabwe, he founded the Ndebele kingdom.

The devastating fission of peoples on the Highveld was meanwhile being repeated across the Tugela. Having established his paramountcy between the Mfolozi and Tugela, the area generally known as Zululand, Shaka had shifted his attention south, and to the area now called Natal. A policy of defence turned to one of conquest, driven largely by a need for cattle to sustain the growing machinery of state.

There could be no neutrals. Chiefs who bent the knee and konza'd Shaka, would be grafted on to the growing Zulu family; they could retain local authority while giving up to Shaka their men as warriors and their cattle as tribute. Their daughters were submitted to be used by Shaka in creating marriage alliances with other clans. Chiefs who resisted were 'eaten up' – killed and replaced by pliant subordinates – or 'driven out'. If the latter, they fled into territories in which they became involved in conflict over resources with the resident tenants. Tribes cannoned into one another and splintered. Some ceased to exist, others were reformed under new leaders.[13]

The troubles of the peoples south of the Tugela in the years of Shaka's conquests, between 1820 and 1824, would have been great anyway. But their suffering was compounded by drought. As cattle and crops became the spoils of marauding warriors, shortage turned to famine. Starvation spread and a land of almost profligate abundance became a wilderness. Cannibal bands roamed this desolate landscape, and refugees took shelter in caves and forests. More perished from starvation than at the point of the assegai, and although estimates of the number who died can be no more than guesswork, the horror of that time was burned into the collective consciousness of those who endured it, and their descendants.[14]

Not all Shaka's opponents were defeated militarily. A description of the process by which each tribe was subdued would make tedious reading, and one example must suffice as illustration. The Tembu were a large clan who had once lived within the same region as the Zulu. Their chief, Ngoza, had been unwilling to submit to Shaka and moved off to the south. An *impi* sent to bring him to heel was instead sent packing, but rather than hold his ground, Ngoza fled further south, cutting a blackened swathe through the kraals of Natal as he passed. Once across the Mzimkulu river, the Tembu were some two hundred miles south of kwaBulawayo, and beyond the normal range of Zulu operations. Here Ngoza was in the domain of the Mpondo chief, Faku. The two reached a brief accommodation, but Ngoza proved himself a difficult neighbour and was killed. Some Tembu submitted to local chiefs, while others retraced their steps to Zululand, where Shaka received them, according to one account, with words of praise:

Heleleyi! These are now our people. I am happy that I have found the Tembu, who fought against me, and drove me in retreat until I vomited with exhaustion. They followed their chief and destroyed many nations. Never did they desert their chief; always they remained loyal to him. To me too they will remain loyal. Let them suffer no longer. Let them join my house.[15]

By 1824 resistance had ceased. Shaka had consolidated his rule over the Pongolo–Tugela region, and extended it southwards through large tributary chiefdoms – the Tuli and Cele as well as the Tembu – as far as the Tongati river.[16] In modern geographical terms, the Shakan state covered roughly two thirds of the province of Natal. In addition, the Zulu sphere of influence extended to the north to Delagoa Bay and, in the south, to Faku's domain in the Transkei. Only logistics and the limitations of infantry now constrained Shaka. In less than a decade, he had established the mould of an enduring society. The vision had been Dingiswayo's. 'It was not the intention,' he had said, 'of those who first came into the world that there should be several kings equal in power, but that there should be one great king to exercise control over the little ones.'[17] His dream had now been realized by his protégé.

❋

Shaka's kingdom extended over an area of roughly 18,000 square miles, and was estimated by Alfred Bryant, the missionary and Zulu linguist, to have had a population of about 100,000 people. Within this area, each *nkosi* ruled at Shaka's pleasure, and every man's life was at his disposal. No threat to the state existed from within or without. It was not, however, a homogeneous society. KwaBulawayo was the centre of the empire and, by 1820, a sight to strike awe into any visiting tributary or envoy. The approach from both north and south was across hilly country, bisected by streams and rivers. A series of outlying kraals and vast cattle herds over the last ten miles or so signalled the journey's end. Then, on a high ridge, a grand vista of green hills opened up with, on the one side, the river beloved of Zulu poets, the Mhlatuze, and, on the other, Shaka's great kraal, a stockade about two miles in circumference swarming with life.

The royal kraal was a vast civic fortress, surrounded by a barrier of branches about ten feet high. Inside lay a circle of thousands of beehive-shaped huts, and within that a cattle enclosure – symbolically and emotionally at the heart of the nation. This formation dated from a time when clans placed themselves between their wealth and potential raiders. The military aspect was evident, too, in the frequent drilling of warriors. Shaka is reputed to have had little time for conversation other than about war, and spent much of his time putting the *amabutho* through their paces on the hills around kwaBulawayo. But domesticity was to be found as well, among the huts which were the domain of the women and their children. Pride in homemaking and cleanliness were intrinsic to the Zulu character, and great care was taken in the construction of the wattle frame and thatch dome huts, called *indlu*, and in keeping the hard-beaten floor of clay and cow-dung in a state of polished glossiness. *Indlu* of lesser households were at the lower end of the kraal, followed by those of the *izinduna* and their families, while at the top end was the royal household itself, including the quarters known as the *umdlunkulu*, where dwelt the hundreds of women of the seraglio, and the series of huts called the *isigodlo* in which Shaka gave audiences, ate, dressed and slept.

In another valley, just a few miles off, Shaka's mother, Nandi, had her own kraal, where she lived with her mother. By all accounts the headstrong young woman had become a prematurely aged virago, whose reputation inspired scarcely less dread than that of her son. Her one human longing seems to have been for the grandchild which, as we shall see, Shaka was determined to deny her.

Shaka had taken the unusual and risky course of allowing his half-brothers to live after usurping their sibling, Sigujana, but at this point they gave the impression of accepting his authority entirely. Dingane, a brooding, taciturn figure known as 'the Silent One', was tall and powerfully built as a young man, but had his father's weakness for sensuality and was turning to fat. Mhlangana was his inseparable companion and a far more imposing figure. Mpande was overweight and gave the misleading impression of being half-witted; he would outlive them all. However, only with Ngwadi, his fourth half-brother and Nandi's other son, were Shaka's relations warm. Ngwadi was the one most like him, a warrior born. The brothers' homesteads were scattered around the country, each being attached to an *ikhanda*, a military kraal for the warriors of a particular *ibutho*.

One other member of the royal family stands out. This was Mkabayi, Senzangakona's sister, and, like Nandi, one of those redoubtable women who are the frequent counterpoint of male dominance in Zulu society. She had supported Shaka's succession and, perhaps in recognition, was installed as head of an important new kraal in an area of questionable loyalty in the far north of the kingdom. So successful was she that this northern Qulusi section became renowned as almost fanatically devoted to the royal house. Mkabayi's influence waxed accordingly, and in a line of her *isibongo* she was known as 'the opener of all the main gates, that people might enter'.[18]

The Zulu house now had within its domain hundreds of clans, living in three geo-political divisions and distinguished by differences in custom, law and dialect. The first tier consisted of an aristocracy of clans between the Mfolozi and Mhlatuze rivers – the Qwabe, Mpungose, Biyela, Ntombela, Sibiya and Buthelezi among others – with kinship and traditional ties to the Zulu. A second tier of clans which had been incorporated into the state during its early expansion, dwelt south of the Mhlatuze as far as the Tugela, and north of the Mfolozi to the Mkuze. Under the Shakan system these clans obtained similar rights to the inner circle. With few exceptions, members of both groups called themselves Ntungwa. This much-debated term, meaning those who came to Zululand in a grain basket, in time came to imply status, and set apart the peoples of Zululand from the third tier, those living south of the Tugela who had been conquered between 1820 and 1824.

The Tugela was the Rhine of south-east Africa, a formidable natural frontier, impassable for months after the summer rains, which had limited patterns of migration over generations. Clans living south of the Tugela had thus evolved largely in isolation from those north of it. Differences of custom across this divide were quite sharp. But the distinction by which the trans-Tugela people were most immediately recognizable was linguistic. The implosive consonants of the Zulu language sounded softer in their enunciation because, it was said, their tongues lay *lala* (flat) in their mouths, and they were known as *amaLala*, or Lala.

For all his farsightedness, Shaka's vision of nationhood never fully embraced the Lala. According to a popular prejudice, 'Shaka said they had dirty habits and did not distinguish between good and bad. They did not pay respect to chiefs, nor wash, nor keep neat.'[19] An earthier tradition has it that, 'the Lala farted on the mimosa tree, and it dried up.'[20] The terms Ntungwa and Lala became labels of privilege and servitude. 'True' Zulu lived north of the Tugela. With the exception of a few chosen clans, those on the other side were never really part of the kingdom. In Natal, as one elder later put it, 'Shaka established colonies like Europeans.'[21] For their part, Natal clans knew the era of Shaka's conquests as the *izwekufa*, the 'destruction of the nation'.[22]

The legacy endures. During the twentieth-century European domination of Zululand and Natal a division has been perpetuated along the Tugela. Just as whites regarded blacks as inferiors, so many Zulus living in the heartland of the kingdom have looked down on Zulu-speakers south of the Tugela and applied to them terms sometimes tinged with insult – *iziyendane*, or tributary peoples – and sometimes overtly contemptuous – *amakafula*, or 'kaffir'[23]. This north–south divide remains a combustible element in the region to this day, and even something of a line marking political affiliations.

✻

Shaka's consolidation of his kingdom – in a form durable enough to have survived an incompetent successor, infiltration by a power- ful foe, invasion, civil war and subjugation – tends to be overshadowed by his rapid descent into tyranny, and possibly psychosis, and the ghastly excesses of his final years. But it deserves to be remembered as a crowning feat of African statecraft. The process involved a complete restructuring of the established order, in which the old patchwork was replaced by a powerful central authority served by a series of regional overlords.

It started with the emasculation of the *amakosi*. A chief's authority to enlist warriors was abolished and he was forbidden to have his traditional praises declaimed by his *imbongi*, or court poet. Another potent blow at the kinship system was the abolition of each clan's celebration of the first-fruits harvest festival. This broke the chief's authority as a religious leader who interceded with the ancestors on his clan's behalf. Even the chief's right to sit in judgment on cases brought by his people was done away with. In the words of Ndukwana ka Mgengwana, a Mthethwa elder, most chiefs 'became mere *abanumzana* (headmen) of the king'.

Into this vacuum of authority, Shaka inserted a new rank of regional super-chiefs, known as *izikhulu*, composed of important clan heads on whom he could depend. These included Nqeto of the Qwabe, Zihlandlo of the Mbo, Magaye of the Cele and Myandeya of the Mthethwa.[24] Mapitha ka Sojiyisa, a cousin of Shaka's, was appointed governor of the sensitive region north of the Mfolozi, where concern still centred on the Ndwandwe.

Shaka was as assiduous in cultivating his spiritual as his temporal credentials. He had always been quick to adopt any rival praise-song to which he had taken a liking – indeed the great chorused salute of '*Bayete*!' by which the Zulu have ever since hailed their king is believed to have been expropriated from Zwide.[25] Now Shaka alone conducted the first-fruits *umkhosi* ceremony. This attempt to use the most important Nguni festival to establish the primacy of the Zulu ancestors over those of all other clans was not particularly successful. Still, the great annual gathering, usually held in the high summer month of December, became in time a potent celebration of nationhood, when new *amabutho* were raised.

Rivals in the spiritual arts were not tolerated. The *izangoma* – diviners who 'smelled out' *abathakathi*, people possessed by evil spirits – wielded a fearful power, and it may be that Shaka had decided anyway to curb them. A bloody purge was recounted by Baleka ka Mpitikazi, a Qwabe woman:

Shaka took the blood of a beast and sprinkled it in the doorway of his *isigodlo* (private enclosure) during the night, without being seen by anyone. At dawn the next day he reported the matter to his *izinduna*, saying 'Look at the evil omen that has befallen me! Here is blood! Let all the *izangoma* be gathered, all the people of the land.'

All the *izangoma* were gathered. They came and were told to *bula* (smell out the one responsible) at once. The Zulu people assembled. The *izangoma* then *bula*'d. One would *bula* and smell out a person, then another would do the same, until only two remained. One of them got up and *bula*'d and said: 'I do not see that this was done by a *thatkathi* I say that it was done only by the heavens above' (a pun on the word Zulu, or heaven, in this case meaning Shaka). The last *izangoma* said the same thing.

Shaka then ordered all the *izangoma* to be killed, except for those two. For they saw it was no *thakathi* that had done the pouring; it had been done by the king.[26]

A broadly based society could be achieved only through breaking down the customs and taboos particular to individual clans. In Ndukwana's words: 'Only the Zulus retained their old laws. Other tribes were made to relinquish many old customs.' Conspicuous among the codes imposed by this exercise in cultural imperialism was the universal abolition of circumcision among young men, and its substitution with a kind of badge of maturity, a fibrous headband known as the *isicoco* awarded to men who had proved themselves as warriors and earned the privilege of taking a wife. This shrewd innovation did away with a ritual which was costly in labour – lost while youths were isolated in circumcision schools – and replaced it with a reward system for men who had already devoted their most productive years to the nation.[27]

Language was another unifying force. Zulu usage attained a greater degree of standardization as new words and concepts related to the nation were introduced. The rich imagery of the Zulu tongue – 'a language so perfect' (in the words of Henry Fynn, the early trader and one of the white men who knew it best) 'as to be capable of conveying every idea of the mind, with the exception of the terms used in arts and science' – performed valuable service for the new regime. The very fact that groups such as the Lala were recognized by their pronunciation as being outsiders was an inducement to speak the 'pure' Zulu of the kingdom.

Of all the features of the new regime, however, the most striking was the politics of sex. The twin pillars of Shaka's initative to break down kinship differences and create a wholly Zulu consciousness, subordinated the sexuality of men and young women to the state's needs.

We have seen that the north Nguni clans had a candid and uncomplicated appreciation of sexual pleasure and intoxication. The latter was available through beer, made from maize or millet, and cannabis, which was smoked through a horn, a process accompanied by much coughing, singing, storytelling and hilarity. Snuff was more a social lubricant than an intoxicant and, unlike cannabis, was shared among women as well as men. So far as sex was concerned, girls as well as boys were expected to enjoy the premarital form of intercourse known as *hlobonga*. Women expressed their sexuality frankly. Among some clans, young girls engaged in a bacchanalian celebration of adolescence known as *mtshopi*, involving dancing naked and singing sexually explicit songs. One such verse goes:

> The vagina starts whistling in the legs
> and calls the penis,
> Ha yi, ya yi, oh mothers,
> We are deprived.[28]

Much of this freewheeling sensuality was put out of bounds by Shaka. It had been standard practice since before Dingiswayo's time that, after a boyhood spent tending cattle, all young males were conscripted into age-group regiments. Shaka's innovation took matters a good deal further. Recruits were gathered at the annual first-fruit ceremony for induction, and then despatched to build their own military kraal, or *ikhanda* where they were isolated, both from their own clans and from women. During military service no man could marry, and even the occasions on which he could meet his sweetheart and engage in *hlobonga* were strictly controlled. Only when an *ibutho* was discharged did its members have the right to take a wife and don the *isicoco*, by which time they were forty or more. The sole feminine touch at the *ikhanda* was the presence of a matriarchal figure from the royal house. Shaka's aunts, like Mkabayi and Mmama, lived at *ikhanda* as symbols of the kingdom – and, no doubt, as its eyes and ears as well.

Enforced celibacy, and a rough barracks egalitarianism that cut across kinship ties, engendered a ferocious regimental spirit which sometimes spilled over into faction fighting. The *amabutho* did have some non-military functions, notably agricultural work, but it is clear that the defensive roots of the Zulu military system had changed course. This new creation required victories to refresh it, and an almost limitless supply of cattle to sustain it, cattle which would be awarded to those who had distinguished themselves on campaign. War, and the plunder of cattle, became both cause and effect.

From around 1821, young women were also recruited into guilds to perform national service. But the means by which Shaka exploited sexual politics among his female subjects is most clearly visible in the *isigodlo*, the so-called royal seraglio. Tributary chiefs sent daughters to kwaBulawayo to signal submission to the royal house. These girls, numbered in their hundreds, became part of a great pool of political patronage on which Shaka could draw – not, it would seem, for his own gratification, but to seal alliances with other clans, or reward favoured *izinduna*. The girls, known as Shaka's 'daughters', were supervised by his women relatives, including his mother, Nandi, and their marriages were arranged by him, as if they were indeed his relatives. Those for whom they were chosen were generally wealthy enough to part with the high *lobola*, or bride-price, of one hundred cattle which Shaka demanded for the honour.

Shaka's own sexuality has been, like so much else about the man, a matter of endless, sometimes wild, speculation. The few known facts are open to different interpretation, and no definitive finding is possible. Donald Morris asserts that Shaka was 'unquestionably a latent homosexual', in which Max Gluckman concurs. A.T. Cope finds a similarity with Napoleon that goes beyond their military careers: 'Napoleon also suffered from hypogenitalism, he also failed in his relations with women, and he is also supposed to have tended towards homosexuality.' Quite why the notion of homosexuality has won such acceptance is hard to say; there is no more than the slightest circumstantial evidence for it. What is reasonably clear is that Shaka had an aversion to sex. This had a rational side: he feared, to the point of obsession, fathering an heir who might challenge him. The suspicion remains, however, that his sexuality was troubled by other phobias. Women of the *isigodlo* who fell pregnant were forced to abort and quite often killed, and the fact that men other than Shaka were implicated in these pregnancies, and were put to death as well, suggests that he was seldom, if ever, responsible. A rare reference in the oral sources to his own sexual activity is a strange account of how, when he was once engaged in *hlobonga* with a girl of the *isigodlo*, he summoned his personal attendant, Nongalaza, to hold a lighted torch over them during the act.[29]

Shaka would often surround himself with these *umdlunkulu* girls, but this was probably no more than an attempt to demonstrate the virility expected of him. When, after the arrival of the whites, he became interested in the ways of English royalty, he asked whether George IV had as many girls as he. On being told that George had only one wife, it was reported, 'he laughed and said that King George was like him, who did not indulge in promiscuous intercourse with women, which accounted for his advanced age.'[30] In all probability, Shaka, like many other conquerors, was only really interested in sex as an instrument of statecraft.

On the subject of discipline we are on firmer ground. Shaka was arbitrary and capricious. Certainly there was a disciplinary code: the man who showed cowardice in battle and the adulterer were in no doubt about their fate. However, no offence was necessary for Shaka to have an individual killed, so the notions of innocence or guilt had little meaning. The bearer of bad tidings, or the man who sneezed in his presence, were just as likely to be put to death. It might simply be an individual's misfortune to have his eyes alight on him at the wrong moment. At a sign, a man or woman could be dragged away to death. Baleka, a Qwabe woman, testified to the whimsicality with which Shaka could order an execution:

That man used to play around with people. A man would be killed though he had done nothing, though he had neither practised witchcraft, committed adultery, nor stolen ... He [Shaka] would say, 'Hau! How ugly this fellow is! Take him away.'[31]

The method of execution varied. Usually, the victim's neck was broken with a single, practised wrench. There was also, it is clear, sometimes resort to impalement. Charles Rawden Maclean, an early white visitor whose testimony need not be doubted, wrote that the victim was first stunned by a blow with a club, which was sometimes itself fatal, and was then skewered by a sharpened stake inserted up the anus. Maclean marvelled at the courage demonstrated on these occasions.

It has often excited my pity, admiration and astonishment to witness the fortitude and dignified calmness with which a Zulu will go forth to execution. No fetters or cords are ever employed to bind the culprit; he is left at liberty to run for his life or to stand and meet his doom. Many do run, but few escape for, alas, every man they meet is an enemy. Many stand and meet their fate with a degree of firmness that could hardly be imagined.[32]

For the large part of his rule there was method to Shaka's use of this terrible power. More, he held it by general consent. We will return to this subject. For now, it necessary to note that, the Qwabe woman's revulsion notwithstanding, it was usually Europeans who recoiled in horror from Shaka's conduct, not his subjects. As another of those whites, Henry Fynn, remarked of Zulu justice in general: 'The chief is obliged to consider what effect his commands will have on the minds of his followers; even Shaka, one of the greatest despots that ever governed any nation, constantly kept this consideration in view, being perfectly aware that his reign would soon terminate if he opposed the general will of the people.'[33]

Shaka's standards have to be set, too, against the anarchy of the time. Out of the turmoil of inter-clan conflict, the time of Dingiswayo and Zwide, had come peace. Elsewhere there was conflict aplenty. But the Shakan state now offered its citizens an era of unprecedented stability and prosperity. Executions, however arbitrary, touched few lives compared with the scale of misery wrought by invasion and famine.

For generations afterwards, a legacy endured in which this golden age was associated with a startling concept of justice. One old *induna* named Nzobo told Stuart: 'The killing of people is a proper practice, for if no killing is done there will be no fear.' Another elder, Lunguza ka Mpukane of the Tembu clan, reflected on the confusion since the substitution of chiefly authority by European courts, and while noting approvingly that 'people are now permitted to die natural deaths,' simultaneously lamented the passing of the old ways: 'the misbehaviour of nowadays is due to it being impossible to kill off people as formerly.'[34]

If the Zulu kingdom was largely comfortable with itself, the same cannot be said of its neighbours. Flames of conflict had spread across the Drakensberg and down the coast and, although Shaka bore little responsibility for the troubles on the Highveld, in the latter-day provinces of the Transvaal and Orange Free State, the peoples south of the Tugela were paying a price for Zulu prosperity, in terms of the cattle necessary to maintain it.

In 1824, Shaka launched his most ambitious campaign yet. By now the Natal tribes had been reduced to the status of favoured tributary or abject supplicant and the region had been denuded of surplus stock. Beyond the Mzimkulu river, however, lay the lands of the Mpondo, a south Nguni people living under an able *nkosi* named Faku. Mpondoland, between the Mtamvuna and Mzimvubu rivers, was scarcely less bountiful than Zululand itself, its people rich in cattle. It was on this distant target, more than two hundred miles away, that Shaka had set his sights. For the first time he had decided not to lead the army personally. An *impi* of perhaps eight thousand men, roughly a third of the army, set out under the command of Mdhlaka ka Ncidi.

Faku had heard enough about his northern neighbour to know what to expect. Tens of thousands of refugees from Natal had streamed down the coast in recent years in search of sanctuary on or within his borders, among them the Tembu chief, Ngoza. The Mpondo were not a warlike people but gave a good account of themselves. The story goes that Mdhlaka tested his opponent, a Mpondo *induna* named Manci, with a light, skirmishing force and was astonished to find him ready and able to engage in a close-quarters stabbing fray. The skirmishers were slaughtered and Mdhlaka had quickly to deploy his main force to win the day. After the Mpondo withdrew, the Zulu rounded up what cattle they could find and started on a march home that rapidly became an ordeal. The cattle and grain brought as rations had run out, and as the plundered beasts belonged to Shaka and could not be touched, the *impi* was forced to live off the land. The Natal terrain through which it passed was a deserted waste, however, and the warriors were reduced to foraging for melons and plants to survive. To top it all, when they finally reached the royal kraal Shaka was unimpressed with his booty, grumbling, 'Zulu, you are deceiving me. The cattle of the chief who killed Ngoza are not here. That chief is a great one.'[35]

Although the *amabece* campaign, 'the war of the melons', had brought little glory, Shaka had made his point: the Zulu army could wage war successfully far beyond his borders. Campaigns against his oldest and now-distant foe, Zwide, and even the Xhosa chief Hintsa, were possible.

One other significant, and more disturbing, item of intelligence was brought by the returning *impi*. A week's march south of kwaBulawayo, on the bay known as Thekwini, the warriors had encountered an apparition of which many had heard, but none had seen before. Although the solitary figure had not spoken their language, the warriors were left in no doubt why he was there, or who he wanted to see. Repeatedly, the white man had said: 'Shaka. Shaka.'

4

THE MAKERS OF WONDERS

There used to be a folktale. The old women of former
times, those who bore our fathers and Shaka, would
say, 'There are white people who wear clothes. They
will one day come to this country.' Our forefathers
would ask, 'Where will they comes from?' The
answer was, 'They are on the other side of the sea.'
Our people would query this, saying, 'How could
they cross the sea?' But, indeed, there came white
people who wore clothes.[1]

Lugubu ka Mangaliso, Tembu *induna*,
May 1916

Chronicles of the South African past commonly portray the Zulu
as having been oblivious to the existence of Europeans right up to
the point that the two came face to face. The reverse is the case.
The existence of whites, and a host of associated images, were
established in the Zulu collective consciousness long before the
vast majority had actually seen any of those known as *izilwane*, or
wild beasts. A mythology was born out of tales from the fireside
and the rare sighting of an individual wanderer or castaway. Shaka
was aware of such stories, but by a quirk of fate he also became
privy to far more substantial information about the advancing

whites. Few African leaders can have been better prepared for the inevitable encounter when it came.

Trade with the Portuguese settlement at Delagoa Bay had shaped the political and military organization of coastal clans for more than fifty years. Now the resources of Shaka's empire were brought to the ivory trade and columns of men made the five-day journey to the bay, carrying tusks of elephant and hippopotamus. Neither the brass nor the beads with which they returned had any practical usefulness, but to a utilitarian society in which ornaments were made from materials readily to hand, such as shells, this made their allure all the greater. It also conferred a status on those who produced such treasures. In the beginning, whites were known to Zulu speakers not just as *izilwane*, but *abalumbi*: the makers of wonders.

The first European to venture into Delagoa Bay was Antonio de Campo, a companion of Vasco da Gama, who came upon it in 1502 during the great navigator's second epic voyage to India. Other Portuguese followed, along with Dutch, English and French mariners seeking a toehold on the tricky traverse of the Indian Ocean to the spice riches of the East. All these groups carried on a trade with the interior clans of the north Nguni, but European presence was sporadic until 1781 when the Portuguese built a fort on the estuary they called Espirito Santo, and established a trade monopoly.

For all the influence it radiated over the region, Delagoa Bay had been founded almost as an afterthought to the Portuguese settlements further up the east coast. It remained in Shaka's time a listless, unprepossessing place, far inferior to the ports of Sofala or Mocambique. A small mud fort accommodated the entire Portuguese population, which generally numbered less than twenty, including the governor and a priest. If the rusty cannons had ever been fired they would have done more harm to those within the fort than those without. Such defence as there was consisted of a shabby and ill-armed soldiery levied from the local chiefs and commanded by half a dozen or so Portuguese officers who, in attempting to maintain a suitable pomp, dressed in glittering uniforms that were as grotesque in the subtropics as they must have been uncomfortable. Rarely did this motley force venture out to the fetid swamps and marshes that extended south towards the Zulu country. By 1820, the Delagoa Bay community was dependent on the Zulu kingdom for the ivory trade which kept its feeble pulse going.

In the wake of the Portuguese came the Dutch. In 1652, three ships of the Dutch East India Company berthed in Table Bay, on the southern tip of the continent and roughly 1,300 miles south-west of Delagoa. An aristocratic surgeon named Jan van Riebeeck was in charge, with orders to establish a victualling station for the Company's ships. The Dutch authorities did nothing to encourage the settlement but over the next fifty years or so a steady trickle of Europeans, mainly Dutch but also refugee French Protestants and Germans, migrated to what became known as the Cape.

The small and isolated European communities at Delagoa Bay and the Cape were too much in awe of the vast *terra incognita* between them – some 1,400 miles – to venture far in exploration, but sea traffic increased and so the coastal Bantu were inadvertently introduced to Europeans. In the seventeenth and eighteenth centuries dozens of Portuguese, Dutch and English vessels were wrecked along the coast. These encounters were no doubt as alarming for the hosts as for the bedraggled survivors decanted on to a strange and seemingly hostile shore. Some tried to find their way back to the Cape or Delagoa, usually to die in the wilderness; some surrendered to their new circumstances. Oral traditions tell of a white woman of unknown nationality who was washed up on a beach in Natal, probably in the late seventeenth century. Nothing else is known of who she was, or what became of her.

Men came along to gather mussels, and found a girl and tended her. They reported this. 'We saw a white person with long hair.' They said she had come out of an *uqwembe* [a wooden meat tray] not knowing what a ship was. The chief then told them to go and catch her on the beach. The girl cried. They escorted her back to the chief. They saw she had breasts and was a woman. She lived on fowl's eggs chiefly. She then saw that no harm was intended and was happy. The chief looked out for an *umnumzana* [household head] with much property. She was then married off.[2]

During the eighteenth century the Dutch East India Company fell into decline. Immigration was discouraged at the Cape, as was exploration of the interior, and a lethargy similar to that at Delagoa Bay set in. By 1780, just seven years before Shaka's birth, the colony was near bankruptcy and the vast majority of its 13,000 white inhabitants lived within a day's ride of the small, white-washed settlement called Kaapstad or Cape Town.

The exceptions were a few hundred hardy and nomadic farmers, the *trekboers*, who wandered eastwards up the coast with their wagons, their cattle and their slaves. Through this attempt to escape taxes, fences and government interference, a thin stream of half-wild frontiersmen penetrated the *terra incognita* as far as the Great Fish river, disrupting the hunter–gatherer societies of the Khoikhoi and San.

Far to the north-east, roughly six days' journey away, Shaka remained for long unaware of these events, his strategic consider-ations dictated by matters within his domain. From the beginning of the 1820s he may have heard distant rumblings; he may have heard reports of increased sightings of *abalumbi*. It is fair to say that he would have had little inkling of the significance of these phenomena until the arrival at kwaBulawayo sometime in 1823 of a remarkable figure. Jakot, also known as Sembite, was a member of the Xhosa-speaking people who lived to the south-west. As such he spoke a similar tongue and shared many cultural characteristics with the Zulu, but the breadth of his travels, from Cape Town to Delagoa Bay, made him almost a creature from another world. Shaka was greatly taken with him, calling him Hlambamanzi – he who crossed the water – and inviting him into the *isigodlo* where he interrogated him for nights on end. The infor-mation gathered in these sessions would lay the basis for Shaka's policy in the years ahead.

Like the Zulu, the Xhosa dwelt on the coastal strip of south-east Africa and were of the Nguni family. The term Nguni is seen as no more than a flag of convenience by anthropologists nowadays, but it remains useful in distinguishing the coastal people from the Bantu highlanders, the Tswana and Sotho who lived north of the Drakensberg. Nguni tribes spoke dialects of a common language and shared distinctive customs and taboos.

Xhosa historical traditions date from an ancestor named Tshawe who was roughly contemporaneous with the Zulu forebear, Mal-andela, but their modern age begins with Phalo, who founded a royal line in the mid-eighteenth century. Succession disputes were no less common among the south Nguni than among their north-ern cousins, and after Phalo's death the Xhosa split into two houses: the paramount house under Rarabe, which lived west of the Kei river; the other under Gcaleka, to its east. Rarabe was succeeded by his son, Ndlambe, who was to bear the brunt of the struggle that developed as the first wave of white migrants eddied eastwards from the Cape. Jakot was among Ndlambe's subjects and a witness to events from both sides of this turbulent eastern frontier.

Conflict was inevitable. The wandering *trekboers* were tough free-booters with an eye for fertile land, a lust for cattle, and with no inhibitions about slaving. The Xhosa, no less thirsty for cattle, were more mettlesome folk than any so far encountered by the Boers. Their meeting on the fertile plains of the Zuurveld, between the Sundays and Great Fish rivers, was the sociological equivalent of mixing sulphur and saltpetre. In the century after 1779, a series of nine frontier wars were fought between the Xhosa and the Cape Colony. It was probably in the first or second of these so-called 'Kaffir Wars' that the child Jakot was seized by *trekboer* raiders as a slave.

Over the next twenty years or so, Jakot lived precariously on both sides of the frontier. He grew into an imposing-looking man – being described by one of the many whites he encountered as 'very handsome, strong and tall and possessed of a commanding figure' – and learnt the language of the Boers, and their ways. Conditions were relaxed enough for Jakot to escape at one point and return to his people, only to be recaptured when he came back to raid cattle again. Beaten almost to death, he escaped once more, and then was witness to one of the epochal developments in South African history – the coming of a new breed of white man.

Britain was sucked into acquiring the Cape, as so many of her foreign possessions, with initial reluctance. At this stage her stra-tegic priorities were France and India. Twice, British soldiers seized the Cape from the Dutch to secure the route east, in 1795 and again in 1806. The second time they stayed, and established a series of forts on the eastern frontier. Among the local levies was Jakot, who acted as translator to the military commander of the frontier district, Major George Fraser.

Having inherited a frontier problem, together with their new colony, the British determined to set their eastern border along the Great Fish river, which meant, in effect, expelling Ndlambe's Xhosa from the Zuurveld. On Christmas Day 1811, Lieutenant Colonel John Graham with a force of two thousand men advanced on the Xhosa. Driving all before them in a series of skirmishes in which kraals were fired, and both women and children became casualties, Graham's army accomplished the first great forced removal in a land which was to become painfully familiar with the practice more than a century later. Withdrawing across the Great Fish, Ndlambe's people were forced into competing for resources with the rival Xhosa house, now under the chieftaincy of Ngqika. When civil war broke out, the British intervened on Ngqika's side. Roused to counter-attack, Ndlambe's warriors were led in 1819 in a direct assault on the garrison at Grahamstown by a messianic mystic named Makanna, only to suffer inevitable and catastrophic defeat. Xhosa resistance was not dead, but it had been quelled.[3]

Jakot, meanwhile, left Fraser's service and again returned to his own people, but still could not resist the lure of untended cattle. Arrested again for rustling, he was transported to Cape Town and, along with Makanna, became among the earliest black prisoners to be ferried to a small, bleak landmass a few miles offshore called Robben Island. Jakot, however, had an extraordinary knack of bouncing back: after two years' imprisonment he was returned to Cape Town and summoned into the presence of Lord Charles Somerset, the Cape's patrician and autocratic governor, who ordered him to act as interpreter to a naval expedition. It was the first of an extraordinary sequence of events that brought Jakot to the Zulu court. In September 1822, he was aboard HMS *Leven* in a two-ship Royal Navy squadron commanded by Captain William Owen that set sail from Table Bay to make the first detailed survey of the south-east coast of Africa.

His experiences as slave and levy had given Jakot little enough reason to care for white men, but he seems to have established a good relationship with Owen, who found him 'excellent and trustworthy', and he had every hope that on their return to Cape Town he would gain his freedom. Fate, and the unconscious contempt with which many Europeans assumed the right to dispose of their black servants, now played him a cruel trick. Anchoring in Algoa Bay, Owen found another vessel from the Cape, a brig called the *Salisbury*, with two former Royal Navy men aboard,

Lieutenant Francis Farewell and James King, and on learning that they were in need of an interpreter, he obligingly handed over Jakot. A few weeks later an attempt by the *Salisbury* to land a boat off the coast of Zululand, at St Lucia Bay, ended in disaster: the craft capsized in the surf and three men drowned. Although Jakot rescued Farewell from raging surf, one white crewman decided that the Xhosa was to blame and attacked him. Jakot turned his back on the whites and set off inland.

This final twist brought Jakot to Shaka's court. Local people initially treated the stranger with suspicion, but his was a novel-enough presence for him to be taken to kwaBulawayo. Shaka immediately recognized the importance of what had come his way. In discussions late into the night in the *isigodlo*, Jakot poured out his observations and experiences: of the Boers who invaded the Xhosa lands as farmers and the British soldiers who drove the Xhosa beyond the Great Fish River; of Cape Town, the great place of the whites; and of the white king, a remote but powerful figure known as George, who lived across the sea. In the years ahead Jakot became a key figure in all Shaka's dealings with whites, his interpreter and adviser. Above all, he was the visionary whose prophecies conditioned the Zulu response to the coming of the *abalumbi*.

❋

In June 1824, three white men arrived at kwaBulawayo. They were Lieutenant Francis Farewell, the same man who had been rescued by Jakot the year before, an intrepid young fellow barely out his teens named Henry Fynn, and a Dutch merchant known to posterity only by his surname of Petersen. These were the first whites ever seen by Shaka and the vast majority of his people, and a demonstration of appropriate pomp had been laid on to impress them.

As the visitors entered the great kraal, Fynn estimated that there were 80,000 Zulus present, including about 12,000 warriors in full regalia.[4] The entire assembly was stationary and remained so as an *induna* named Mbikwana, who had accompanied the party from the outlying country, introduced them to an unseen figure. Gifts of elephant tusks for the whites were then brought forward and Shaka emerged from a cluster of *izinduna*. At a sign from him, the assembly formed into regiments, some of which rushed away to take up positions on the surrounding hills, while others made a circle and began to dance with the gleaming figure of Shaka at the centre. They were joined by perhaps 10,000 young women of the female guilds, naked but for bead girdles and small staffs carried in the right hand, who sang and danced in a series of precise and coordinated movements. The stamping of thousands of feet in unison on the baked earth produced a sound like thunder. This display of the nation's might was accompanied by another of its wealth, as innumerable cattle, herded according to colour, were driven past the kraal. The first visitors to lay eyes on Zulu ceremonial were duly impressed.

Fynn noted in his diary: 'It was a most exciting scene, surprising to us, who could not have imagined that a nation termed "savages" could be so disciplined and kept in order.'[5] He rapidly formed the opinion that 'the frontier Kaffir tribes, also the tribes of Delagoa, can in no way be compared to the superior standing of the Zulu nation.'

Three months earlier Fynn and a rugged Yorkshireman named Henry Ogle, the advance guard of an enterprise launched in Cape Town by Farewell, had landed at a lagoon some ten days' journey south-west of Shaka's capital. It was a lush spot, surrounded by a high ridge and teeming with wildlife. Hippopotamuses wallowed in the shallows, while monkeys and other small game infested the thick bush that grew right down to the bay's edge. Here the youthful representatives of the Farewell Trading Company established a rudimentary settlement at what became known as Port Natal.

When Fynn and Ogle waded ashore they had no idea of what awaited them. Shaka's existence had come to light at Cape Town only two years before and the little that was known of him was not encouraging. Indeed, Farewell seems to have been only too willing to leave this critical test of Zulu hospitality to his youngest employees; he only followed them two months later when the coast was clear.

It had been a Cape merchant named Robert Thompson who returned from a venture to Delagoa Bay in 1822 with intelligence of 'a formidable tribe, governed by a chief named Chaka'.

This man, originally the sovereign of an obscure but warlike people, called Zoolas, or Vatwahs, has within the last eight or nine years, conquered or extirpated the whole of the native tribes from Delagoa Bay to Hambona;

and has established a barbaric kingdom of large extent, which he governs on a system of military despotism, strikingly contrasted with the loose patriarchal polity generally prevalent among the other Caffer [Xhosa] tribes.[6]

Thompson had decided that Shaka was the kind of powerful leader with whom profitable business could be done. Commerce was booming at the Cape following the first organized British migration scheme in 1820. The 4000 or so settlers, a high proportion of them Scots, were industrious and literate folk, shopkeepers and tradesmen, ideal foils in commercial enterprise of another breed of men suddenly descending on the colony – military officers and youthful adventurers seeking fortune in the aftermath of the Napoleonic wars. Farewell, for example, had joined the Royal Navy as a teenage midshipman in 1807 and seen action in the Mediterranean. After Waterloo, he left the navy and tried his luck in India before deciding that the ivory trade in southern Africa offered more opportunities. His first venture to Port Natal was sponsored by Thompson.

Farewell's plan was simple: to draw the ivory trade away from Delagoa Bay and end the 300-year-old Portuguese domination of commerce on the east coast.[7] It was a risky and ambitious enterprise and those who joined it were tough and often ruthless men. Fynn and Ogle were exceptional in finding admirable qualities in the native people among whom they were to spend most of their lives; Ogle, indeed, was one of a breed of Yorkshiremen who took so enthusiastically to Africa that they abandoned European ways altogether and becames natives in all but the colour of their skin. More characteristic of the men drawn to Port Natal in the next few years were Farewell himself, Nathaniel Isaacs, a teenage bravo from Kent who had few scruples when it came to making money, and James King, Farewell's partner and later rival, a charismatic rogue with higher ambitions.

On only his second visit to Shaka, Farewell placed before him a draft document ceding the Farewell Trading Company title to a large, if vague, tract of land surrounding Port Natal. Shaka, to whom ownership of land was a ludicrous concept, had no objection to putting his mark to a paper granting the whites control over the natives within the territory, about one hundred miles by thirty-five. It was, in fact, a pointless charade, as land ownership in South

Africa was invariably *de facto* rather than *de jure*, but Farewell was none the less pleased with himself and believed the title would be useful to him with his backers.

Port Natal became the traders' base. Here, in a Crusoe-like world of beaches and trees, they hacked away clearings in the lush bush that ran down to the water's edge, built a few huts and shanties, and ran up the Union flag. The infant settlement remained for some years a rude and insignificant place. Shaka's capital lay a week to ten days' journey to the north-east and, when the great Tugela river was in spate after the summer rains, Zululand lay beyond reach for weeks on end. But right from its inception, Port Natal exerted a profound, and malign, influence on the kingdom.

Thompson had asserted confidently to his co-sponsors of the Farewell company that Shaka 'cannot, of course, foresee that the admission of a few mercantile adventurers may perhaps ultimately lead to the subjugation of his kingdom'.[8] The truth is, Shaka was acutely aware, from his discussions with Jakot, of the peril represented by this intrusion. But the evidence suggests that he believed his best strategy lay in trying to come to terms with the whites in a partnership in which each group retained its sovereignty. Shaka had made himself master of the Delagoa trade and saw the Cape as a source of yet greater power and wonders. By now, it should be added, he was sufficiently intoxicated by his own power to believe that he might ride the tiger. He had conceived a rather fantastic notion of power sharing, in which the white king, who he called umGeorge, reigned over the whites, while he ruled the blacks. Fundamental to both ideas, however, was the conviction that only he was capable of carrying them out. It is a consistent theme of the oral traditions that Shaka forecast whites would overrun the country after his death, indeed, that he made such a prophecy with his dying words.

From the very beginning, he set out to impress the outsiders with his power and hence his worthiness as an ally. Barely had Farewell and Fynn arrived at kwaBulawayo than they were obliged to witness a casual, summary execution of a man, for no crime that anyone could explain. Other visitors would be subjected to similar demonstrations, increasing in frequency and magnitude, of Shaka's omnipotence. Some accounts of such executions need to be treated with caution: Isaacs, who for more than a century was the only contemporary published source on the Shakan era, later characterized the Zulu king as a malevolently savage beast in a sensationalist account that attempted to establish Isaacs as a bestselling author. But allowing for exaggeration, there is still a wealth of reliable evidence from oral sources to prove the awful despotism of Shaka's final years.[9]

We are in an area abounding with contradictions and paradoxes. Arbitrary exercise of power over life and death had, as we have seen, always been part of the Shakan regime. Those picked out for despatch accepted their fate without demur and even, sometimes, with a certain pride. Some *izinduna*, for example, are singled out in the oral sources for welcoming death because it issued from Shaka. To understand something of this attitude we must remember that the *nkosi* was the incarnation of the nation, its achievements, its destiny. Anyone who died at his command could be seen in a sense as serving the wholeness of the nation, renewing a pact with the ancestors that assured its might and invulnerability. It may seem fanciful, but for much of his reign it is possible to see Shaka and his victims as partners in a sacrificial ritual which strengthened the bonds of a new-found Zulu identity.

Over the years, however, absolute power had wrought its inevitable corruption. Shaka was no longer just a great *nkosi*. He was already more myth than mortal. He had occupied the collective psyche of his people in a way that no one had before, nor has since. As Jung once said of Hitler and Germany, he obtained his power not because he ruled the Zulu, but because he *was* the Zulu. And the way in which he used that power now gave expression to the dark side of the African soul. The dread and awe which this human icon inspired had to be sustained with ever more extravagant displays of power. In the end, it could only be refreshed by the blood of its children.

Shaka had started to refer contemptuously to commoners as his 'dogs', and a chillingly dispassionate account by Mkotana, the son of one of his favourite *izinduna*, Komfiya, demonstrates how he sometimes disposed of them as such.

My father told me that Koto ka Msomi of the Langeni people had a daughter who was one of the *isigodlo*. She accidentally made water [urinated] while sleeping in the *isigodlo*. This was noticed and she was accused of causing the *isigodlo* to smell. Shaka now decided to test the girl's father. He sent the daughter to Koto and ordered him to kill her.

This he proceeded to do. As soon as he had done so he picked a beast, drove it to Shaka and gave praise, saying he had killed a dog and that his only child was Shaka.[10]

Shaka's perception of the bounds of his power was obviously spinning out of control anyway, but the whites' arrival had a further destabilizing effect on him. His policy now was to try to get on even terms with these formidable intruders while maintaining before his own people the dignity and authority of a king. For the four years after the coming of the whites, up to his assassination, Shaka showed them every friendship, while publicly disparaging everything about their appearance, artefacts and customs – from their pallid skins and their guns, to what struck him as their cruel and inhuman habit of locking up miscreants, rather than simply killing them. Perhaps in trying to demythologize the whites, he introduced a linguistic change. The term *abalumbi*, with its connotations of wonder-working, was abandoned for the more familiar *abakwetu*, meaning 'people of our house', although it was another word, *abelungu*, which stuck; it is still used.[11]

Fynn noted in his diary: 'Whilst in the presence of his people he placed the worst construction on everything, ridiculing our manners and customs, though in perfect good humour. When none of his subjects were present he would listen with the greatest attention and could not help acknowledging our superiority.'[12] A later white visitor, Charles Maclean, echoed Fynn. Maclean was scarcely into his teens when he arrived at Shaka's court. The king, fascinated by the young Scot's shock of red hair, took a shine to him, and once told him: 'I see and feel that you are a good and superior people; a strange and wonderful people.'[13]

While it is possible to read too much into these remarks, it seems that in his private interrogation of whites, Shaka was seeking blindly, and with increasing desperation, a key that would put him on equal terms with them. He asked them about the numbers of the English soldiers, the size of their cities and the greatness of their king, 'umGeorge' – and was delighted by the sentiments of their song 'God save the King'.

Firearms appeared not to impress him, even when an elephant was brought down with a single fluky shot from a muzzle-loader for his benefit. His view – that a gun's effectiveness would be diminished by the time it took to load in the face of a charging *impi* – was to be tested with interesting results a half-century later. Medicine was another matter. It is fairly certain that Shaka laboured all along under the illusion that the secret of the whites' power involved some kind of magic.

Just how strong Shaka's belief in sorcery was is unclear. Many of those he had executed as *abathakathi*, people possessed by evil spirits, were no doubt political opponents, but there is no reason to suppose that he did not share the common belief in the efficacy of potions and spells both to cure and to curse. When Fynn, on his way to meet Shaka, healed a feverish woman who had been pronounced all but dead by a *sangoma*, it caused a sensation. An even more potent demonstration of Fynn's powers followed soon after his arrival at kwaBulawayo.

While the king was taking part in a dance one night, the unthinkable happened. A group of would-be assassins, whose identities have never been fully resolved, set upon Shaka with assegais. Six men around him were wounded, while he suffered a stab wound that penetrated his arm and the left side of his chest. It was a severe wound, causing him to spit blood. Amid scenes of mass hysteria, crying of the *isigodlo* women and an uproar among the men, an apprehensive Fynn was taken to Shaka's side. While a *sangoma* treated the wound with roots, Fynn washed it with camomile tea and bandaged it.

Shaka cried nearly the whole night, expecting that only fatal consequences would ensue. The crowd had now increased so much that the noise of their shrieks became unbearable, and this noise continued throughout the night. Morning showed a horrid sight in a clear light. The immense crowds that arrived hour after hour from every direction began their shouting on coming in sight of the kraal, running and exerting their utmost powers of voice as they entered it and joined those who had got there before them. They then pulled one another about, men and women throwing themselves down in every direction. Great numbers fainted from over-exertion and excessive heat. The females of the seraglio were in very great distress, having overtaxed themselves during the night. They suffered from the heat and want of nourishment, which no one dared to touch. Several of them died.[14]

For four days, Shaka hovered near death himself. In all probability, his ox-like strength and the herbal skills of his own doctor would have saved him, but Fynn remained at his side, washing the wound and dressing it with ointment. On the fifth day the king's condition started to improve, and on the sixth he was well enough to appear before his people. As thanksgiving celebrations began, news came that three men had been apprehended and killed as the supposed would-be assassins.

Shaka's eventual recovery raised the white man's stock as a wonder-worker. But now, more than ever, the king sought control of the whites' medicine. Hearing that Fynn had cured the feverish woman, he remonstrated: 'Why did you give my dogs medicine? I am very angry with you. I shall send a messenger to umGeorge and request him to kill you.' His anger was only partly feigned. Such wizardry, clearly, could undermine the hierarchical order unless Shaka was able to dispense it as patronage in the same way as beads, brass or cattle. All the more important was it to have the *abelungu* on his side, and prevent them finding their way to his enemies. Following the attempt on his life, there could be no mistaking that he still had enemies, and that they were getting closer to him.

The sources of opposition to Shaka remain a mystery. Few solid facts are known about those who attacked him at the dance in August 1824; the three men put to death were variously identified as Ndwandwe agents or Qwabe dissidents, but their connection with the attack is not conclusive. And although the identity of Shaka's assassins three years later is well known, even their motives are not very clear. The oral sources are confused and contradictory, and the accounts of Isaacs and Fynn are surprisingly opaque, given their proximity to events.

Rising Qwabe resistance may indeed have been behind the first attack, for it provoked Shaka into a slaughter of Qwabe at the royal kraal. The greater danger, however, was posed by the Ndwandwe. Since being defeated at the Mhlatuze in 1819, Zwide had nursed his resources and plotted revenge. Although lacking the army to invade Zululand, he was still formidable enough to make Shaka anxious about his northern frontier. A Zulu attack was inevitable sooner or later, but the old fox Zwide cheated his arch-enemy. He suffered the unusual fate of dying peacefully in about 1824, leaving his son, Sikunyana, to preside over the final dissolution of the Ndwandwe empire.

In June 1826, messengers from kwaBulawayo arrived at Port

Natal to summon the traders to join Shaka's forces in battle against the Ndwandwe. Fynn and Isaacs later claimed to have been reluctant conscripts, pressed into service by threats from the king, and that they agreed only because he required them not as combatants but totems whose mere presence would help cause panic and confusion among the enemy. In any event, when the massed Zulu army set out northwards with Shaka at its head, it included the first English mercenaries to take up arms with the Zulu. Fynn left a vivid account of this final campaign against the Ndwandwe:

The whole body of men, boys and women amounted, as nearly as we could reckon, to fifty thousand. All proceeded in close formation, and when looked at from a distance nothing could be seen but a cloud of dust. Every man was ordered to roll up his shield and carry it on his back — a custom observed only when the enemy is known to be a a considerable distance. In the rear of the regiments were the baggage boys, few above the age of twelve, and some not more than six. These boys were attached to the principal men, carrying their mats, headrests, tobacco etc., and driving cattle required for the army's consumption. Some of the chiefs, moreover, were accompanied by girls carrying beer, corn and milk; and when their supply had been exhausted these carriers returned to their homes.[15]

Nine days after setting out, the Ndwandwe army was sighted, having taken up its position on a hillside, surrounded by cattle, with women and children in the rear:

Shaka's forces marched slowly and with much caution, in regiments, each regiment divided into companies, till within twenty yards of the enemy, when they made a halt. Although Shaka's troops had taken up a position so near, the enemy seemed disinclined to move, till Jacob [Jakot] had fired at them three times. The first and second shots seemed to make no impression on them, for they only hissed and cried in reply: 'That is a dog.' At the third shot both parties, with a tumultuous yell, clashed together, and continued stabbing each other for about three minutes, when both fell back.

Seeing their losses were about equal, both enemies raised a cry and this was followed by another rush, and they continued closely engaged about twice as long as the first onset, when both parties again drew off. But the enemy's loss had now been the more severe. This urged the Zulus to a final charge. The shrieks now became terrific. The remnants of the army sought shelter in an adjoining wood, out of which they were soon driven. Then began a slaughter of the women and children. They were all put to death. The battle from the commencement to the close, did not last more than an hour and a half. The numbers of the hostile tribe, including women and children, could not have been less than forty thousand. The number of cattle taken was estimated at sixty thousand. The sun having set while the cattle were being captured, the whole valley during the night was a scene of confusion.

Early next morning Shaka arrived, and each regiment, previous to its inspection by him, had picked out its cowards and put them to death. No man who had actually engaged in the fight was allowed to appear in the King's presence until a purification by the doctor had been undergone.[16]

Despite this final defeat of his oldest foe, Shaka remained restless, and his behaviour became increasingly erratic. Soon after his return, he announced that the royal kraal would be moved from kwaBulawayo to a site about seventy miles to the south called kwaDukuza. The move made little apparent sense. The site was near the coast and on inferior pasturage. It was even further away than kwaBulawayo from the valley of the Emakosini, the revered Zulu ancestral home, and, being across the Tugela river, was not even in Zululand proper. However, kwaDukuza was far closer to Port Natal and the traders with whom Shaka was spending more and more time. Unlike kwaBulawayo, the new kraal could not be cut off from the settlement by a flooded Tugela.

Still he could not make up his mind. He returned briefly to kwaBulawayo and, while he was dithering, there occurred one of the most macabre and ghastly episodes in Zulu history.

There are two versions of how Nandi met her death. Shaka's mother had for years maintained her own kraal, only a couple of miles or so from kwaBulawayo. She was now into her sixties and, as her life was nearing a natural end, it is unsurprising that the generally accepted account has not been more questioned. Fynn, the source for it, states that having been called to tend Nandi, he found her suffering from dysentery and in a hopeless condition; a few hours later she died. Zulu sources questioned by Stuart tell a different story.

Shaka's intolerance of heirs meant, as we have seen, that women of the *isigodlo* who fell pregnant were forced to abort; if a child was born it would immediately be put to death. It is a strong and consistent strand of oral history, however, that one such birth was

THE MAKERS OF WONDERS

successfully concealed and that the boy child was brought by the
mother to Nandi who, seeing this as the grandson Shaka had so long
denied her, took him in. The deception could not long be kept up.
According to one version, a woman went to Shaka out of spite or
jealousy, saying: 'Go to your mother. You will find something
beautiful.' On discovering the child Shaka became enraged, turned
on Nandi and, crying, 'so you are inciting the nation against me for
it to kill me,' plunged a small assegai into her side.[17] Mortified, he
then bound up the wound, but a few days later, after it had been put
about that the *inkosikazi* was sick, Nandi died.

One might be inclined to dismiss this story as just another of
the myths cloaking Shakan lore. But one of Stuart's informants, an
early Natal settler named William Bazley, related a similar version,
saying that he had heard it from Fynn himself, who had concealed
it 'for fear of what people would say in England'.[18] Quite why
Englishmen would care if Shaka had killed his mother was left
unstated. Certainly, Fynn pulled no punches in his description of
the dreadful events that followed.

Nandi was dead. Shaka appeared before his people surrounded
by *izinduna* in war dress. A long, profound silence was finally
broken by Shaka who burst into a series of great bellows of grief.
This immediately started a demonstration of mass lamentation by
the fifteen thousand chiefs and people assembled. By the next
morning the number had swollen to about sixty thousand, as those
living in outlying kraals descended on kwaBulawayo. All through
that day and night the weeping and shrieking continued. The next
day there commenced a massacre as, in the words of James Gibson,
a perceptive historian, 'each member of the assembled throng perceived the importance of establishing his own innocence [of
involvement in Nandi's death] and of manifesting a readiness to
destroy the guilty.' The slaughter was observed by Fynn.

Those who could not force more tears from their eyes, those who were
found near the river panting for water, were beaten to death by others
who were mad with excitement. Toward the afternoon I calculated that
not fewer than seven thousand people had fallen in this frightful indiscriminate massacre. The adjacent stream, to which many had fled exhausted, to wet their parched tongues, became impassable from the corpses
which lay on either side of it; while the kraal in which the scene took
place was flowing with blood.

93

Amidst this scene I stood unharmed, contemplating the horrors around me; and felt as if the whole universe was at that moment coming to an end. I stood there alone, a privileged being; and I felt truly thankful, not only that I was a British subject, but that I had so far gained the respect of this tyrant as to hope for escape even from this horrible place of blood. While standing thus, motionless, a regiment of young Zulus passed by me, when two of them with their uplifted knobkerries [a club-like stick] rushed towards me, the leader demanding fiercely why I stood there without a tear. I made no reply, but gazed upon them sternly and steadily. They moved on shouting vengeance. The sun again set, and Shaka now put a stop to this ungoverned general massacre.[19]

Two days later Nandi was buried, in a sitting position. Today those grim events seem also to have been interred. The grave site, hard to find but still known to local people, is a lovely spot, situated on a hilltop overlooking a few scattered huts, where a gentle breeze stirs the long veld grass.

For a one-year period of mourning after Nandi's death, it was ordered that no crops should be cultivated and no milk consumed. Furthermore, the entire nation was to desist from sexual intercourse; any woman falling pregnant would be put to death along with her husband. Over that period, three further lamentations were held.

It is difficult to know even now just what to make of this grim affair. Was Nandi's death natural, or murder? Was Shaka's grief genuine, or, as some Africanist historians believe, an excuse to rid himself of political opponents? We know that a conspiracy was indeed growing, and that Shaka could sense it; his actions sometimes seem those of a man losing his grip on reality, a Macbeth even, tortured by guilt, ghosts, and premonitions of his own death.

Fynn's view was trenchantly down to earth: 'I cannot help suspecting,' he wrote, 'that reasons of state policy had as much to do [with Shaka's actions] as any feelings of regret for his dead mother; and that he wished his people to infer, if such a sacrifice was necessary upon the occasion of her departure, how frightfully terrific would be that required at his own.'[20]

If a warning it was intended to be, however, it failed to have the desired effect.

5

THE DEATH OF SHAKA

In May of 1828 one of history's odder diplomatic missions set out from Port Natal for the Cape. It consisted of two senior Zulu *izinduna*, Sotobe and Mbozamboza, Shaka's interpreter Jakot, Nathaniel Isaacs and James King. They were aboard a rude schooner named the *Elizabeth and Susan*, which had been knocked up over the previous two years out of timber growing at Port Natal, replacing a wrecked brig, the *Mary*, as the traders' link with the outside world. On this none-too-buoyant platform rested Shaka's hopes of a friendship treaty with umGeorge and the British at the Cape.

James King now emerged as a key figure, reflecting the radical change that had occurred in Port Natal politics. At first, Shaka had been content to deal with Farewell. However, he was a stiff, remote figure who could summon little enthusiasm for the company of those he regarded as savages and Shaka made it clear he much preferred Fynn. Then, in October 1827, James Saunders King arrived on the scene. He had made a brief earlier visit to kwaBulawayo, but now had big things in mind. Garrulous, charming and thoroughly untrustworthy, he made a strong impression on Shaka. The Zulu king had little hesitation in signing over to King the same Natal land he had once granted to Farewell.

Nominally partners at the outset, Farewell and King had already fallen out and divided the traders' little community into two camps. Isaacs had always been King's protégé; Fynn, while generally independent, also leaned towards King; of the leading men at Port Natal, only John Cane stood by Farewell. Shaka was well apprised by his spies at the port, and drew the logical conclusion: King was the strong man among the whites.

The trouble was that King was playing a deep game in which Shaka was, for once, out of his depth. Shipping difficulties – due mainly to a sand bar at the entry to Port Natal on which the *Mary* had foundered – had inspired King and Fynn to consider opening up a land route to the Cape, through the countries of the Mpondo chief, Faku, and the Xhosa chief, Hintsa.[1] Other opportunities might be in the offing, too. Fynn had made ivory deals in the Mpondo country and could see the rich pickings to be had if these southern coastal lands could be brought under the order and discipline of Zulu administration. Now that Shaka had disposed of the Ndwandwe threat in the north, the *impis* were free for other campaigns. There seems little doubt that King, probably supported by Fynn, encouraged Shaka in a mad plan for regional domination, a power-sharing arrangement in which Shaka would rule the black peoples, and the British the whites. This would be set in motion by a Zulu invasion of the southern Nguni lands, at the same time as King was leading an embassy to the Cape proposing a treaty of friendship.

The idea clearly appealed strongly to Shaka. He told the young Scot, Charles Maclean, who had been wrecked with King on the *Mary*: 'I wish that there should be only two great kings in the world; that King George should be king of the whites, and I king of the blacks.'[2] In his increasingly uneasy state of mind, an alliance with umGeorge which recognized Shaka's dominance of all the coastal peoples had much to commend it. The idea of sending envoys to the Cape had occurred to him a year earlier, and now he agreed readily that King should accompany such a mission, acting as a broker between Shaka and umGeorge.

King did all he could to lay the ground carefully. In a letter published in Cape Town's first newspaper, the *South African Commercial Advertiser*, he announced that Shaka intended to launch a southern campaign, while emphasizing that this involved no threat to the colony and that Shaka was friendliness itself towards white people. This evaluation happened to coincide with the general view at the Cape at the time, where a Royal Navy officer had recently reported that the traders were 'living on the best terms of friendship with the natives and under the protection of King Chaka'.[3]

Shaka's preparations took a more symbolic form. The issue of who would go on the mission is said to have been resolved at a gathering of leading men on the coast just south of kwaDukuza, where the royal kraal had been permanently sited since Nandi's death. No Zulu had ever crossed the sea before and the elements needed to be consulted. Each man was given a stick and ordered to throw it into the sea: if the stick was carried away it would signify that the thrower would himself not return from the journey; if it came back, he would return in safety. Shaka is said to have cast a stick, but in common with most others it was carried away.[4] One stick which did come back belonged to Sotobe ka Mpangalala, an aristocrat of the Sibiya clan, and he was chosen to represent Shaka at umGeorge's kraal. Jakot would go as interpreter, although the business at hand was clearly set out in a document drafted by King. In it, Shaka conveyed wishes of friendship and esteem to His Britannic Majesty and authorized King and Sotobe to negotiate on his behalf, 'a treaty of friendly alliance between the two nations'.

So far as Shaka was concerned, the mission also had another purpose. He had once asked Fynn idly if whites had any medicine to change the colour of their hair and, on being told of a popular hairdressing called macassar oil, which could dye grey hairs, immediately announced that he must have some. Having entered his fortieth year, a few grey hairs had started to appear on his chin and Shaka seems to have been convinced that the oil would conceal his ageing. It may even have occurred to him that it was an elixir of life. According to Fynn, 'we endeavoured to assure him of our great doubts as to its powers, fearing should it not prove what we had led him to believe it was he would be displeased; but the more we attempted to deprecate it, the more he thought of its value. He said he could plainly see it was an oil used by umGeorge and that none of his people were allowed to touch it.'[5] When King left for the Cape, Shaka presented him with eighty-six ivory tusks, and announced to the kraal that the whites would return with much bounty. Privately, he told King that he was only really interested in macassar oil and medicine.

Soon after Sotobe's mission left Port Natal, Shaka launched a full-scale military expedition across the Mzimkulu, the southern boundary of his sphere of influence, telling his *izinduna* that this was so other nations would be made to share the Zulus' suffering over Nandi's death. The target was Faku, the Mpondo chief and the nearest of the southern Nguni leaders, who had been attacked four years earlier. Now Shaka himself led the expedition, accompanied by Fynn. The grandeur of the enterprise in which he was involved overwhelmed the king. Watching his army cross the river, he burst into tears and turned to Fynn asking if he had ever seen so great a man as he.

In Shaka's absence, the plot against him which had been festering for months came to a head.

The conspiracy against Shaka involved his half-brothers Mhlangana and Dingane, his powerful aunt Mkabayi, and his body-servant Mbhopa. As acknowledged sons of Senzangakona, the two brothers had seen their prior rights of succession usurped by a bastard. The usurper now having become a tyrant, the princes may have considered that self-preservation dictated pre-emptive action. Mkabayi is said to have encouraged the plotters in order to avenge Nandi's murder. All this fits with the common explanation that Shaka's assassination was a simple consequence of his tyranny. But other factors nourished the conspiracy as well, one of which has received scant consideration.

The traders' presence at Port Natal was by now a powerfully disruptive influence on the kingdom. Trade goods, once rare enough to give the Zulu aristocracy a coercive hold over the population, were becoming more readily available. Authority was also being undermined by the very existence of Port Natal, as refugees from the rough justice of the kingdom began to realize they could find asylum among the traders. By 1828 perhaps a thousand Zulus had opted for the white man's authority in preference to that of the king. Meanwhile, it was not lost on the *izinduna* that the whites, who were responsible for this creeping erosion, had gained the status of demigods, were free to move and act virtually without constraint and, moreover, held Shaka himself increasingly in thrall. It seems reasonable to speculate that some of the opposition to Shaka stemmed from his pursuit of alliance with the whites: among a people now persuaded of their superiority and military invincibility, prominent voices were raised that the few puny intruders should be cast out. Shaka once told Maclean that many would have rejoiced at the opportunity to murder the whites. 'I have often been told by my *indaba* (council) to kill you wild beasts of *abelungu*.'[6]

There is no direct evidence linking Dingane with this movement, but it is perhaps relevant that as Shaka's successor he demonstrated a far more muscular policy towards Europeans, and that the final act of his reign was to attempt to expel them from the kingdom.

Whatever resistance there was to white influence could only have been fomented by Sotobe's mission. The expedition was a disaster from the time that the *Elizabeth and Susan* arrived in the Cape Colony.[7] The envoys had been led to expect great things of umGeorge's place but, instead of Cape Town, they had been taken to Algoa Bay, where the infant town of Port Elizabeth was unlikely to have impressed anyone. There the party was left to kick its heels for almost three months before the arrival from Cape Town of Major A.J. Cloete, representing the governor, Sir Richard Bourke. Cloete viewed the mission with extreme suspicion. King suffered the humiliation of missing the interview that followed, at which Isaacs, rather than Jakot, was asked by Cloete to interpret. Worse, Cloete treated Sotobe and Mbozamboza more as criminal suspects than envoys. Although they were not to know it, the mission had come to grief precisely because of King's part in it. By now the Cape authorities knew enough about the erstwhile midshipman – he affected the rank of captain or lieutenant – to distrust anything in which he had a hand. Cloete's parting shot was to tell Sotobe that King enjoyed no status with umGeorge, or any other British authority. Shaka had sought a friendly alliance. Instead he was to receive a case containing a few copper sheets, a piece of broadcloth and some medicines.

Nothing daunted, King tried another tack. He approached the commissioner at Uitenhage, north of Port Elizabeth, issuing dire warnings about the approach of Shaka's hordes, and claiming to be the only man capable of averting an invasion. Again he was snubbed. News of the Zulu advance had already reached the Cape, where it was recognized that Shaka intended no harm to the colony. But refugees from previous Zulu campaigns had unsettled the frontier districts and in 1827 Bourke had resolved to protect the Xhosa and Mpondo chiefs, 'as long as by their friendly and peaceable conduct they prove themselves deserving'. Now he despatched a small force under a Major Dundas to enter the tribal lands and find out what was going on.

Dundas arrived at Faku's kraal on 18 July, in the wake of the Zulu *impi*. The devastation was a good deal less than might have been expected, as the Mpondo had also gained prior knowledge of the invasion and scattered. Rather sheepishly, Faku admitted to Dundas that he had pacified the Zulu by parting with some thirty thousand head of cattle and pledging allegiance to Shaka. More startling, to Dundas's way of thinking, was Faku's report that the marauding army had been accompanied by armed Englishmen, among them one he knew as Henry Fynn. Dundas reported:

Chaka's people had assured [Faku's] people that resistance was unavailable & flight to the Westward useless as the Englishmen were the friends of Chaka and that the Englishmen were sent by their countrymen to the Westward to assist them in fighting and overcoming all the people between him [Faku] & the country of the white man [the Cape].[8]

Following up directions from local people, Dundas came across what he took to be part of the withdrawing Zulu army. In fact, it was another band of raiders, not Zulus at all but Ngwanes led by the chief Matiwane, who, since his expulsion from northern Zululand by Zwide years earlier, had been causing havoc on the Highveld and in the northern Cape. Dundas attacked this *impi* and dispersed it. A month later, Colonel Henry Somerset, commanding a stronger British force, made the same mistake of identification, destroying the Ngwane at the Battle of Mbolompo and returning to the Cape proclaiming triumphantly that he had routed the Zulu army.

Bourke, one of the more capable men to occupy the governor's office (and subsequently to hold the governorship of New South Wales), reported to the Colonial Office that he had 'explicitly declared' to the envoys and King the government's view, 'with respect to the invasion of Caffreland by the Zoolas'. He added: 'I am in hopes that as King is now fully convinced of the determination of the Colonial Government to oppose Chaka's progress in Caffreland, he may persuade that Chief to remain within his own ample territory, or if not, to turn his arms to some other quarter where less resistance may be expected.'[9]

Soon afterwards a navy vessel, the *Helicon*, arrived at Port Elizabeth to transport the envoys back to Zululand. It was not a moment too soon for them. Thoroughly disillusioned with umGeorge and everything else about the *umlungu*, Sotobe arrived back at kwa-Dukuza at the end of August and made his report to Shaka. What the Zulus had seen of King's humiliation was bad enough, although one suspects it would have gone a good deal harder with the whites had Shaka known half of the full story. As it was, King had fallen seriously ill and it was left to Isaacs to make the crowning admission: the macassar oil had been forgotten.

Remarkably, even now Shaka did not lose his patience. He simply said that John Cane should return to the Cape for the oil, and make clear to Bourke that he desired only that the Zulu people 'might come come along with their sticks in their hands, without assegai or any other weapon, to see the white people.'[10] If there had been any misunderstanding before, there could be none now. In the Zulu tradition of pledging allegiance, Shaka had *konza*'d umGeorge.

Unfortunately, the damage had been done. The Zulu kingdom, so recently seen at the Cape as a power friendly to the white man, had been established in the common mind by King's alarmist report as a possible danger looming on the frontier.

The mission had been back for less than a month when James King died. His fellow traders regretted his passing in varying degrees – even Farewell attended his funeral – but accepted it as being in the nature of their risky existence. Fynn diagnosed the cause as a liver disease. For Shaka, however, King's death came as yet another evil omen. He was convinced that his go-between had been poisoned by the British.

By now Shaka was almost certainly aware that a conspiracy was closing in on him, and his utterances were full of foreboding. Barely had the *impi* returned from Mpondoland than he despatched it to march against Soshangana, Zwide's former general, who had established his own state far to the north of Delagoa Bay. It was unheard of for regiments fresh back from campaign to be allowed no leisure for dancing, storytelling and dalliance but, like Caesar, Shaka now wanted about him only sleek or fat men. While the army was away, he rounded up perhaps four or five hundred warriors' wives, accused them of witchcraft and put them to death. It was the bloody throne's last outrage.

Mhlangana and his inseparable brother Dingane had been ordered to accompany the exhausted regiments but soon after their departure returned to their own kraals near kwaDukuza, complaining of illness. With Mbhopa, the king's body-servant, they made their final plans.

On 23 September 1828, Shaka was at kwaDukuza where he was awaiting tributaries bringing him blue crane feathers. It was after nightfall and the kraal at which he was waiting, some distance off from his main *umuzi*, was lit by torches when the men arrived. In shadows at the edge of the kraal the assassins waited with assegais and heard Shaka berate the tributaries for their tardiness. At this, Mbhopa rushed out and joined his master in belabouring them. As they fled, Dingane and Mhlangana emerged. Most of the oral sources have it that Mbhopa turned on Shaka and made the first thrust. The brothers then joined in. Astonished, Shaka rose and, as the assegais rained down, burst out: 'Children of my father, what is the wrong [I have done you]?'[11]

Some hold that as he fell back he pleaded for mercy – 'Leave me alone, sons of my father, and I shall be your menial,' – to which Dingane replied: 'Leave you? The evil-doer who kills the wives of men who are away?'[12]

On one point the sources are unusually unanimous. As he lay dying, Shaka uttered a prophecy: 'The whole land will be white with the light of the stars, and it will be overrun by swallows.'[13] The words sound apocryphal but Stuart had them repeated to him many times as having forecast that the white man would take over the country. He wrote: 'Every elderly native of Natal and Zululand knows the king said this, and the words have, I am told, been sung as a dirge.'[14]

The assassins seem initially to have been overwhelmed by the enormity of what they had done. Shaka's body was left where he had fallen and, as the news spread, the kraal inhabitants fled into the bush. In the days following, however, Dingane and Mhlangana moved swiftly to deal with the two most pressing aspects of their inheritance.

First, they despatched Mbhopa with a three-hundred-man *impi* to the kraal of Ngwadi who, as Shaka's favourite half-brother, would have regarded himself as the natural successor. Fynn noted admiringly that Ngwadi's men fought 'only as warriors of Shaka could do' and accounted for far more than their own number before they were annihilated. Only twenty or so of Mbhopa's men returned.

Meanwhile, Dingane and Mhlangana consulted Sotobe as to how they might make their peace with Shaka's spirit, so that it would help rather than hinder them. On Sotobe's advice, a piece was cut from Shaka's *umutsha*, or loincloth, and placed in his mouth. Then a great pit was dug and his personal effects, years of accumulated tribute of beads, brass, cloth and trinkets, were placed in it with his body, his headrest and his blanket, and the earth was shovelled back in. Atop the grave a hut was erected, and a guard was set to stand over it day and night.

Shaka's last capital was abandoned. The royal kraal was relocated in Zululand, close to the Emakosini valley. As his prophecy was fulfilled and white men spread out over the hinterland of Port Natal, a town named Stanger was built where kwaDukuza had once stood. Stores and public buildings arose on the spot where the *amabutho* had once drilled. Shaka's grave fell into neglect, until eventually even its exact location became unclear. But his memory burned bright in the Zulu consciousness, and soon after the centenary of his death the nation erected a memorial near where he was murdered. It is a poignant spot, not for any art that went into its making, but for what it betrays of the fate that had overtaken the Zulu people. A mowed square of lawn beside Stanger's main street is surrounded by whitewashed colonial houses with spacious verandahs, and a row of rather shabby stores. An effort has been made to keep faith with the past – three beehive huts are set on the rear of the lawn – but they are contradicted by the memorial itself, which shows the effort made to strike an imposing effect in the manner then thought appropriate by a subjugated people. The high, vaulted plinth, set on a marble base and surmounted by a garlanded urn, would befit a colonial servant or, perhaps, a senior clergyman of the Edwardian era. The inscription reads:

> IN MEMORY OF
>
> TSHAKA KA SENZANGAKONA
>
> THE FOUNDER, KING AND RULER
> OF THE ZULU NATION
>
> ERECTED BY HIS DESCENDANT
> AND HEIR SOLOMON KA DINUZULU
> AND THE ZULU NATION,
> AD 1932

Shaka was no more than forty-one when he died, and had ruled for just twelve years. He had not alone been responsible for the north Nguni revolution that had reshaped southern Africa and societies as far away as the Great Rift Valley but he had, more than any other, seized and built on the opportunities offered by the era. Quite clearly, he was one of Africa's great men, yet his legacy continues to baffle us, and his accomplishments have been exaggerated in some quarters no less than his vices have in others.

Comparisons with the great men of western history fail because of the vast dissimilarity of political culture. It is time that analogies with such figures as Napoleon and Alexander were abandoned, although it is tempting to make a new one with Bismarck. He, at least, was a leader thrown up by a revolutionary age, who exercised a ruthless form of militarism and political authoritarianism to build a nation. Shaka would have thoroughly approved of the doctrine of Blood and Iron.

There are more apt historical parallels with Shaka and his Zulus, above all in central Asia, with its tradition of conquering empires and tribal culture. Mahmud of Ghazni gave birth to a great medieval dynasty in the country now known as Afghanistan, where today the conflict and feuding between the great Pathan clans, the Durani and Ghilzai, and once-subject groups of Hazaras, Tajiks, Uzbeks and Nuristanis, have an echo of the intra-black violence in South Africa. Timur of Samarkand and the Mongol emperor Genghis Khan are part of the same tradition.

The comparison between Shaka and Genghis needs to be carefully drawn. It has been a handy prop for sensationalists such as Isaacs, and a ready image for negrophobic historians who cited the Zulu past as evidence of irredeemable barbarity. We cannot escape the fact, however, that where life is by and large nasty, brutish and short, leadership will be harsh and arbitrary. Shaka rose in a time of anarchy and imposed not only order and prosperity but a strong degree of homogeneity with it. Whatever the cost, he was venerated for much of his reign – as he has been ever since.

Of the Zulu monarchs, Cetshwayo and Dinuzulu are remembered with the greatest affection and respect. But Shaka is something greater, an elemental force who gave those who call themselves Zulus their history and identity, and a social fabric of astonishing durability, despite the short period over which it had been woven. Fynn, who was as ambiguous as any in his regard for the Zulu founder, gave this as his final verdict:

The success that had always attended him in his numerous wars, and his own pretensions to superiority, led his followers to believe that he was more than human; and in this light he was ever adored by his subjects.[15]

Magema ka Magwaza, the first literate Zulu historian, echoed in 1921 this hint of supernatural intercession:

If a person thinks and looks at the activities of Shaka, he cannot conclude that he was merely the progeny of Senzangakona and Nandi; he can see clearly that he was a special product appearing from above, who arrived here expressly for the purpose of bringing unity to the country instead of disunity.[16]

Although the Zulus had lost their first king, the instruments of state control remained in place and the pillars of agriculture and trade were healthy. Militarily, the kingdom constituted the most formidable entity in southern Africa: the Mpondo were cowed, Moshesh's Sotho were respectful, and Mzilikazi and his Ndebele were far across the Drakensberg. At this stage, the Cape authorities had not even contemplated aggression against the kingdom. But although insidious, the European advance had already begun.

PART 2

INFILTRATION –
1828–1872

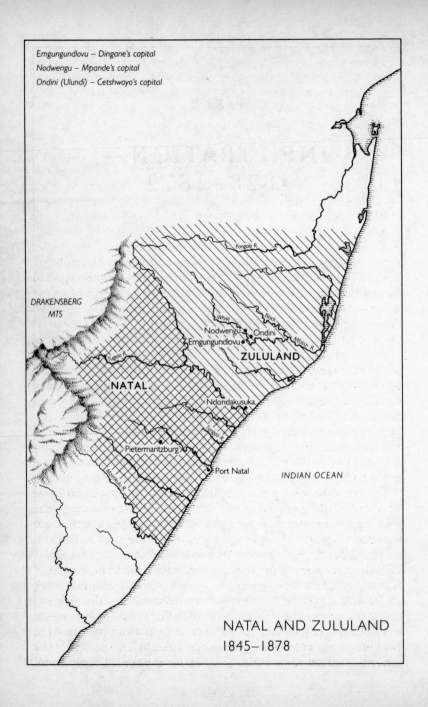

Emgungundlovu – Dingane's capital
Nodwengu – Mpande's capital
Ondini (Ulundi) – Cetshwayo's capital

DRAKENSBERG
MTS

Pongolo R.

White

Black

Nodwengu
Ondini
Emgungundlovu

ZULULAND

Tugela R.

Mfolozi R.

NATAL

×Ndondakusuka

Pietermaritzburg

Tugela R.

Port Natal

INDIAN OCEAN

Mkomazi R.

NATAL AND ZULULAND
1845–1878

6

THE QUIET ONE

Fifty years after Shaka's death, his predictions had been fulfilled. The Zulu were surrounded. Across the Tugela, the *abelungu* had indeed descended 'like swallows', to cultivate and multiply. Half of Shaka's empire had been a British colony called Natal for two decades. To the north, another breed of white colonist, the *amabuna* or the Boers, had also chipped away at the old kingdom.

Even now, in 1878, the nation remained confident and secure in its heartland. Many warriors, eager to test themselves, were adamant. The *abelungu* had gone far enough. When a demand came from Natal for the surrender of half a dozen men who had intruded across the Tugela, the young bloods were all for defiance. Older heads counselled submission. Mnyamana ka Ngqengelele of the Buthelezi, chief adviser to King Cetshwayo, urged in council: 'Let them be sent. We shall not remain in our good houses if we are ordered to fight these whites.'[1]

The question was, would the British accept peace? And if so, at what price? Everywhere across the Tugela was evidence of the transformation they had wrought. On the castaway settlement founded by Henry Fynn in 1824 had arisen the port of Durban, where buildings of steel and brick clustered at the sea's edge. A railway snaked along the coast to the Mgeni river, and a team of horses hauled an omnibus up the escarpment three times a week to the little capital of Pietermaritzburg. To the Zulus, the very soil of Natal seemed to be bringing forth alien life; the lands over which Shaka's *impis* ranged had been turned over to a crop unknown in his time, sugar, cultivated by labourers from India. The tide of the advance seemed inexorable. Even as he counselled submission,

Mnyamana reflected grimly: 'The country is being swept away by the water.'[2]

Now, on a sweltering December day, a Zulu delegation was coming down to the Tugela from the royal kraal of Ondini to hear Britain's demands.

It had been one of the worst growing years in memory, but the rains had at last broken; the hills sprouted green and the Tugela ran in rich, muddy-brown spate as the two parties drew up on a bluff overlooking the river and, away to the east, the sea. The Zulus, about forty *izinduna* and their attendants had left behind weapons and war finery. The British group, 150 imperial and colonial soldiers, had brought two field guns and Gatling guns. They stood beneath a sparse tree and a large tarpaulin which hung limply in the still, humid air. A British official started to read.

There were no surprises to start with: within twenty days Cetshwayo was to hand over the six men accused of raiding, along with 600 cattle as compensation for the border violation. The Zulus listened in silence. Then came the thunderbolt: Cetshwayo's army was to be disbanded. Furthermore, a British resident would be stationed in Zululand, with powers over the king. Missionaries must be readmitted. In future, war could be conducted only with the resident's approval. These conditions were to be accepted within thirty days, or Britain and the Zulu would be at war.

Whatever else might have been open to negotiation, the very basis of Zulu life was not. After half a century of uneasy and confusing coexistence, the blade was at last out in the open.

By striking when they did, Shaka's assassins embalmed the lustre of his name and reputation. His successor fared not half so well. The events of the next decade would have taxed the greatest of leaders – and Dingane was far from being that. But he deserves a better press than he has had. Whatever his shortcomings, Dingane resisted vigorously the European encroachment that started undermining the kingdom even as it emerged from the first period of its evolution.

As a monster, the second Zulu king has no peers in South Africa's history books. Shaka, although generally portrayed as a bloodthirsty demon, cannot be denied his greatness. No such plea can be raised in Dingane's defence and, when the time came for history to be written by white victors, he was duly excoriated. In truth, he is not remembered with any great love by his own people either, but his failings were more of leadership than anything else. He frittered away much of Shaka's legacy and it was left to the sibling they had both dismissed as a half-wit to restore stability to the kingdom. It cannot be said of Dingane, however, that he failed to read the signs correctly. Only the rash clumsiness of his response was wrong.

He was not the natural successor. It was Mhlangana who had jumped over the prone body of Shaka and who, it was assumed, would take his place. But the old intriguer, Mkabayi, matriarch of the kingdom and a leader in the conspiracy, had other ideas. First it was said that, having stabbed Shaka himself, Mhlangana could not succeed him under the old taboo that 'a man may not rule with a red assegai'. The same principle theoretically disqualified Dingane, but a way was found around this; it was put about that Dingane had not actually joined in the stabbing. A story told by Baleka the Qwabe woman gives one version of how the succession was then resolved:

Mbhopa went to Dingane and said, 'Hau! Mhlangana is going to kill you.' Then he went to Mhlangana and said 'Dingane is going to kill you. Cut short an assegai and hide it in your clothing.' Mhlangana did so. Mbhopa then rose up and went to Dingane and said, 'Mhlangana is carrying an assegai against you.' Mhlangana was caught and indeed an assegai was taken from his clothing. He was then killed, saying '[Mbhopa] have you done this to me?'[3]

Shaka's assassins had chosen their moment well. For all the madness of his final days, he had retained the army's loyalty and, had it been on hand, the conspirators would have been slaughtered. As it was, the army was in the midst of a disastrous expedition hundreds of miles to the north. Still fatigued from earlier campaigns, short of food and suffering from fever, the Zulus were sent reeling back by the Ndwandwes. The weary and emaciated survivors who straggled back to Dukuza over the first two weeks of November 1828 were fully expecting to feel the edge of Shaka's wrath. Any regrets at the news of his death were thus tempered with relief. Leading *izinduna* were then singled out by

Dingane for what Fynn described as 'excessive' gifts of cattle. Other palliatives followed thick and fast. At least one regiment was demobilized and the warriors were allowed to don the *isicoco* and marry. The entire army, supposedly in disgrace, was sent on an extended leave of rest and recreation. Exhausted men took gratefully to the cool of their huts and were allowed to mix freely with the women for *hlobonga*. Here was change indeed.

Dingane spoke of an end to killing. The assegai would be laid aside, he said, and the dancing stick taken up. Still the warriors were uneasy. Even beyond the grave Shaka seemed to hold his subjects in thrall; many suspected that this was merely one of his tricks, that he would shortly announce himself and make them answer for their lack of loyalty. As for Dingane, he was still an unknown quantity.

No high reputation had preceded him to the royal *isigodlo*. Until power was within grasp, he was content to live in Mhlangana's shadow, although self-effacement may have been only prudence in one so close to the throne. His mother was Mpikase, Senzangakona's sixth spouse but not the 'great' wife. The name Dingane means 'the needy one'; he was also known as 'the quiet one' and is said to have been a solitary, moody youth. As a young man, he is also supposed to have shared his father's sensuous disposition. Early in Shaka's rule he so disgraced himself in the sight of his prudish half-brother that he fled to the Qwabe in fear of his life, only being allowed to return after an abject apology.

Dingane was no warrior king, but nor was he the bloated and brutal coward of South African school textbooks. He had been on many campaigns and gained an honourable chest wound in a battle against Matiwane's Ngwane. Temperamentally, however, he was the antithesis of Shaka – artistic, fond of trinkets, perhaps even somewhat effeminate. He loved pageantry and was never happier than when designing some new item of apparel or a manoeuvre to be executed by the women who danced in his honour. Like all his people, he loved to dance himself, spontaneously and with furious energy, the sweat pouring off his gleaming body as onlookers chanted his *isibongo*, 'You are the Quiet One, O Heaven above! You are the Quiet One, O Lion! You are the Quiet One, O Great Elephant!'[4]

Tall and powerful in build, he turned rapidly to fat once authority relieved him of the need for exertion. A notable feature was the smallness of his teeth in a great moon of a face, which, it was said, accounted for the immobility of his features;[5] self-conscious about laughing or smiling, he expelled air when amused with a sound like 'phoo!', which some found unnerving. Although undoubtedly cunning, as noted by the lines of his praise poems which characterize him as 'the slippery rocks', he was neither astute nor strong.

One of his earliest acts was an attempt to free himself from his predecessor's shadow by moving the royal kraal from Dukuza to Nobamba. The site was well chosen. Nobamba was back in the Zulu homeland, the Emakosini valley, birthplace of his father, Senzangakona. With this move Dingane established his legitimacy and role as intermediary with the ancestors. His great kraal was built in 1829 and named Emgungundlovu, 'the place of the elephant'. It lay roughly midway between the Mhlatuze and White Mfolozi, about fifty miles north-west of kwaBulawayo, and for size and grandeur exceeded even Shaka's kraals. It was approached from the south by a hill, covered with flowering aloes and mimosas, which looked down on a series of ridges and over to a blue range of mountains. Water came from rocky streams on either side of the kraal, the Mkumbane and Nzololo, tributaries of the White Mfolozi.

The kraal was a vast oval more than a mile in circumference and from the opposite ridge looked 'like a distant racecourse', according to one visitor. It sprawled across a gently sloping hillside and contained a ring of more than 1700 beehive huts, six deep, and had a population of about 5000. At the top end was a fenced enclosure containing the royal quarters and the huts of the *isigodlo*, which were much larger than the average and overlooked the entire kraal. Just inside the fence was an earth mound, on which Dingane often stood to issue orders, or simply to survey his domain. At the centre was the arena where military parades, reviews and dances took place. At the bottom end, large cattle enclosures stood on either side of the entrance. Beyond, the hill sloped down to a gully. On the other side, the land rose again to the hill of execution.[6]

The grand design of Emgungundlovu reflected Dingane's talents for display and show. During his rule, ceremonies and rituals took on a new splendour. At the annual first-fruits festival, he would make a brilliant appearance, a girdle of buck and monkey skin around his waist, his body covered in decorations and his headband highlighted by the scarlet wing feathers of a bird called a lourie. During Dingane's reign, the *umkhosi* festival was a showpiece military review that never failed to impress visitors.

Women played an important part in Dingane's rituals. Although reduced since Shaka's time, the women of the *isigodlo* still numbered some three hundred. They were kept in a state of near-isolation in two enclosures, the *engome* and the *ebeje*, and lurid tales surrounded the doings there. Dingane remained childless, however, and once in power his main interest in women was as role-players in spectacular ceremonials. One warrior recalled: 'They were stark naked, with only a strip of beads round the waist. When they went out to the river to wash they were escorted by men with shields and assegais, and if you came in sight you must fall down in the grass face downwards in order not to look. They were very fat, they were like pigs. I never had a feeling of affection for them, for it was death to do so.'[7]

Dingane initially believed that it was possible to rule a state with all the might of Shaka's kingdom, but without its internal discipline. Once power was in his hands he was unsure of how to proceed. Although he ensured that the *amabutho* were kept sweet with generous rations of beef, matters soon began to drift. Fynn noted in his diary that although 'the people at large were released from the state of perpetual terror they had experienced there appears to be a want of that affection and respect which Shaka always engendered or commanded.' It even seemed to Fynn that the character of the dance had changed. In Shaka's time this most natural of Zulu expressional forms had an energetic, fiery character. Under Dingane, 'there is now a coolness, sedateness and formal regularity.'[8]

The mildness of the regime did not last. Dingane, whatever his natural inclination, found rapidly that, in a state founded on blood and steel, discipline could not readily be relaxed. Gradually, and then more rapidly, the hill opposite the royal kraal became littered with bleached bones.

His first important victim was Shaka's extremely able military commander, Mdlaka ka Ncidi. This caused no great stir; Mdlaka's days had probably been numbered since Shaka's death, and he was replaced with another respected *induna*, Ndlela ka Sompisi. The quiet elimination of Mbhopa also came as little surprise; it was to be expected that the new king would be leery of a regicide, albeit one who had been his fellow conspirator.

Few tears were shed for Matiwane either. The Ngwane chief, as we have seen, had spilled more than a little blood in his own time. His power broken by British troops at Mbolompo, Matiwane came to Emgungundlovu looking for sanctuary, blithely ignorant of the wound that Dingane had sustained at Ngwane hands a few years earlier. He was impaled on a stake at execution hill, which was ever after known as kwaMatiwane.

What did cause shock was Dingane's disposal of his own brothers.

It is said that he discovered they had been sporting in the *isigodlo* but it is just as likely that the fear of usurpation common to Zulu chiefs had begun to infect him. Jantshi ka Nongila recounted how the royal kraal was ordered to assemble early one morning:

Dingane left his hut and came out through the narrow gateway of the *isigodlo*. When he came to where the people were, he stood with a black blanket on. He said at once, 'Seize that fellow Mfihlo!' They caught him. Dingane said then, 'Catch that fellow Ngqojana! Catch Mqubana!' and so on to in regard to all his brothers. He caused them to be at once killed with thick sticks.

Ndlela rebuked him saying, 'You have removed the blanket that covers you. How will you cover yourself now?'[9]

One of Senzangakona's sons escaped this slaughter. Mpande had gone into hiding and, on being discovered, was about to suffer his brothers' fate when Ndlela interceded with Dingane. 'Surely you are not going to kill Mpande, one who is just a simpleton? You are not going to kill this idiot, *nkosi*?'[10] And so the Claudius of the house of Zulu was spared, and with him a dynasty.

Dingane's shortcomings as a king were exposed by the first major test of his reign. In around March 1829 he had a disagreement with Nqeto over the Qwabe chief's right to wed a woman of the *isigodlo*. Nqeto had ever been an awkward ally, a man who responded to strong leadership; it was said that only he could spit in Shaka's presence and get away with it. Now Nqeto sent messengers to all parts of the kingdom, summoning his clansmen to join him in revolt.[11] Many heeded the call, making the journey to the Qwabe ancestral lands in south-west Zululand and seizing cattle from kraals along the way.

Dingane dithered for days as the rebellion gathered force, before sending so small an *impi* that it was forced to retreat after no more than a skirmish. Nqeto decamped across the Tugela and imposed himself on another of Shaka's oldest allies, the Cele chief Magaye, whom he urged to join him. Magaye refused and had his maize and cattle plundered for his pains before Nqeto set off again down the coast. A large Zulu army finally caught up with the Qwabe about forty miles north-west of the trader settlement at Port Natal. Although each side prepared for action, neither, in Fynn's words, 'felt disposed to attack the other'. The Zulus contented themselves with rounding up some of their missing cattle, while Nqeto continued his southern migration, ending up in Mpondoland where he proceeded to plague the long-suffering Faku.

The loss of the prestigious Qwabe connection was bad enough, but Dingane now managed to turn his error into catastrophe. Having decided that Shaka's oldest southern allies were not to be trusted, he had the innocent and noble Magaye put to death, supposedly for having hesitated before rejecting an alliance with Nqeto. The Mbo were also attacked and their chief Zihlandlo, yet another of Shaka's favourites, and his brother Sambela killed. So was Matubane, the Tuli chief.

This ferocious round of blood-letting is illustrative of Dingane's kingship at its worst: he had allowed the Qwabe revolt to develop through weakness and hesitation, and then over-reacted. Or at least that is how it appears. In the suspicious, brooding way of Zulu blood feuding, others interpreted these events differently. Magaye's son, Melapi, said: 'Dingane resented the intimacy between Shaka and Magaye. By killing Magaye, who was called *mnawe* (my younger brother) by Shaka, Dingane was finishing off the house of Shaka.'[12]

Whatever the reason, Dingane had succeeded at a stroke in alienating the entire trans-Tugela region, almost half the land area controlled by Shaka. He had severed forever the blood-knot between Zulu and Qwabe. The ties that bound Zululand to the Natal clans through the large Cele chiefdom were also cut. Trusted friends had been shamefully dealt with and a way was left open for those hostile to the kingdom to exploit. A poisonous gap had been opened up between Zululand and Natal that would never be fully repaired.

The episode had also exposed a flabbiness creeping into the army. Dingane continued to recruit *amabutho* and, on the surface, Shaka's military system remained intact; militarism was still the dominant influence of Zulu culture. But Dingane's army was not Shaka's. The king never accompanied his warriors on campaign and morale declined. Moreover, the *isijula* or *iklwa*, Shaka's short-hafted stabbing spear, which had revolutionized warfare as had once the Roman *gladius* or thrusting sword, was abandoned by Dingane. Fighting men reverted to carrying a bunch of long assegais, *izinti*, which were hurled in a shower on the foe.[13]

All the time, however, Dingane had his eyes on more formidable weaponry. Unlike Shaka, he had no doubt about the superiority of firearms, and set his diplomatic sights on acquiring them from the only two possible sources: the Portuguese at Delagoa Bay and the English traders at Port Natal.

The traders' first reaction to Shaka's murder was one of alarm. Only his protection had guaranteed their safety, and there seemed a real prospect of Port Natal being caught up in an anarchic power-struggle. Reassuring messages from Dingane allayed these fears, and it was soon being said that he was actually an improvement on Shaka. Isaacs, still hoping for his big break, came away from an audience with the new king convinced that he was the man to throw open the door to unlimited trade and would show 'respect and friendship' to Englishmen.

Lieutenant Farewell, too, was confident of doing business with Dingane. In 1829 he set out from the eastern Cape on the overland journey back to Port Natal with a wagonload of trade goods. On passing through Faku's lands, Farewell was invited to visit Nqeto at his new kraal and, despite warnings from his servants that the Qwabe meant him no good, spent a night camped near by. Just before dawn, Nqeto's men surrounded the camp and Farewell and his two white companions were slain. In the absence of any obvious motive, it is generally assumed that Nqeto suspected Farewell of spying for Dingane. The Qwabe chief did not long survive Natal's founding father, having his kraal burned and cattle seized by a yet stronger marauder named Ncaphayi, and dying by an unknown hand soon after.

Farewell's murder shook his former comrades. No black hand had ever been raised against a white man in Shaka's time. Where life was cheap, theirs had been sacrosanct. That spell was now broken.

In the years ahead, strains accumulated in the relationship between the kingdom and the embryonic colony. Port Natal, as we have seen, had already become something of a haven for refugees from Zulu justice. Shaka tolerated this small exile community, saying the whites were his 'relatives'. Dingane's disastrous southern policy, however, had made enemies of three big southern clans, and as other people in the Tugela region incurred his displeasure, so the flow of refugees to Port Natal increased, to the point that it became a nest of opposition to the kingdom. Fynn noted: 'The natives living under the protection of the traders have the most inveterate hatred for [Dingane].'[14]

The trans-Tugela rift was deepened by the traders' continued efforts to stimulate Cape interest in Natal. In 1830 they helped organize a new Zulu diplomatic mission to the colony. Once again it backfired, this time with disastrous consequences for themselves.

The choice of John Cane to accompany Dingane's envoys was the first and biggest mistake. Cane had represented Shaka at the Cape after James King's débâcle two years earlier, but he was completely unsuited for diplomatic work. A deserter from the merchant navy, he had been Farewell's strong-arm man and was both rough and careless of responsibility. Moreover, he and Jakot, who was acting as interpreter as before, did not get on. Cane, with Henry Ogle, Jakot and seven Zulu envoys, arrived in Grahamstown, headquarters of the eastern frontier garrison, on 21 November. Cane's real interest was in convincing the authorities of Natal's suitability for colonization and in assuring them that Dingane would have no objection; this intelligence was duly communicated to Cape Town by the civil commissioner. But Dingane's gift to the governor of four ivory tusks was declined, so Cane bartered them for beads, cloth and blankets before starting back for Zululand.

Quite what happened over the next few weeks cannot be reliably established now, but certain points are clear. On arriving back in Natal, Cane sent the gifts ahead to the royal kraal but did not follow immediately to report on the mission. Instead, he went off hunting. Meanwhile, Jakot sent Dingane an extraordinary message, describing the changed conditions that he had found in his Xhosa homeland. The message was a time bomb. Fynn divulged its contents later as proof of Jakot's perfidy; in fact, it was as clear and devastating an exposition of the white man's advance in southern Africa as there is to be found.

First the white people came and took a part of the [Xhosa] land, then they encroached and drove them further back, and have repeatedly taken more land as well as cattle. They then built houses – missionary establishments – among them for the purpose of subduing them by witchcraft; that at the present time there was a *mlungu* in every tribe; that they had even got as far as the Mpondo; that lately no less than four kings had died, and their deaths were attributed to witchcraft by the *abelungu*; that during Jakot's stay in Grahamstown the soldiers frequently asked what sort of a country the Zulus had; if the roads were good for horses; if they had plenty of cattle; and had said 'we shall soon be after you'; that he had heard a few white people had intended to come first and get a grant of land as I, Farewell, King and Isaacs had done; they would then build a fort, when more would come and demand land, who would also build houses and subdue the Zulus; that Colonel Somerset, who is the terror of the frontier tribes, was about to advance with soldiers to see Dingane, because of having heard so much about the Zulus and that he [Jakot] thought Cane had remained at home to guide them.[15]

The accuracy of Jakot's observations unnerved the traders, just as they rang true with the Zulus. Cane's absence seemed to clinch matters. Dingane did the least he could in the circumstances, sending a small *impi* to raze Cane's kraal and seize his cattle. In a desperate attempt to retrieve the situation, Fynn hastened to reassure Dingane and denounce his interpreter as 'a consummate villain and an atrocious character'. But although the king seemed to accept his word that no British invasion was contemplated, Fynn saw the *izinduna* 'believed all Jakot had asserted'.

As he rode back to Port Natal, Fynn was, in fact, extremely anxious about the sudden change in the tenor of relations. The traders had never been in doubt where they stood with Shaka. Dingane, on the other hand, was capricious and gave outward show of a friendliness that he clearly did not feel. Individual Zulus whom Fynn had known for years, including his servant Lukilimba, were suddenly behaving aggressively towards him. It was widely rumoured that an *impi* was about to descend on Port Natal. Although humid summer had turned to temperate autumn, the air remained thick with menace.

Fynn summoned an emergency meeting of the traders at which it was decided to flee. Cane and Ogle took to the bush. Fynn himself started down the south coast towards Mpondoland with an entourage that included his five Zulu wives, numerous children and cattle. The mood of alarm and betrayal was infectious, and when Fynn learned that Lukilimba was advising others to desert the party, he shot his old retainer through the head in cold blood.[16]

The Zulus attacked at dawn as the party was camped by a beach in south Natal. A child raised the alarm just before the warriors fell on them, and in so doing saved many lives. Fynn took to the water and swam around a river mouth to reach the far bank, returning to the camp after the *impi* had withdrawn. Among the dead were four of Fynn's children. They had been laid out on the ground and covered with a blanket. A fifth child, a daughter named Nomanga, was found alive in a bush where she had been tossed by a woman in flight. Forty members of the party were dead, five men, twenty women and fifteen children, and all Fynn's possessions and cattle were lost. The seventy or so survivors, including seventeen wounded, pressed on, and just over three weeks later reached a mission station near Faku's kraal, which took them in.[17]

As suddenly as it had come, the storm passed. Within a month, Fynn was on his way back to Natal with a party of settlers from Grahamstown, having received Dingane's assurance that he would be welcome: it had all been a misunderstanding. Ogle and Cane also emerged from hiding.

The traders' leverage with Dingane, as a source not only of beads and cloth, but now also of firearms, ensured their survival. Scapegoats for the attacks were found, including Jakot. A demand for the interpreter's head was granted by Dingane, who suggested that Cane carry out the execution himself. Only Ogle had the stomach for the task. With a few of his black henchmen, he surrounded Jakot's homestead and shot him. So died a prophet who had the misfortune to be right in his own time.

A façade of normality returned to Port Natal. Beneath it, everything had changed. When a devout family among the new settlers held an open prayer service, Fynn fretted that it might be misconstrued by the Zulus, who ritually invoked their ancestors' spirits when preparing for war. The uncertainty and suspicion were all too much for Isaacs, whose dreams of wealth had so far come to nought. He moved to an island off Sierra Leone in west Africa where he established a lucrative trading operation in slaves. Fynn left two years later and served as a colonial official in the Cape for almost twenty years before returning to Natal where he died in 1861.

Others would soon take their place. Eight years after the founding of Port Natal, the Cape authorities were starting to take an interest in the region. In April 1832, Andrew Smith, a Scottish-born doctor, arrived at Emgungundlovu with secret orders from Sir Lowry Cole, the Cape governor, to study the Zulu kingdom and Natal's prospects as a colony. Although Smith was astonished by the size and grandeur of Dingane's court, and much taken with the lushness and fecundity of Natal, his report had no immediate impact. However, the message carried back to the Cape by one of his companions fell on more receptive ears. Hermanus Barry's connections were with the frontier Boers, whose instinctive wanderlust had been rekindled by their resentment of British rule. Barry had taken one look at the new terrain and invoked the Almighty. '*Allemagtig*! I have never in my life seen such a fine place.'[18]

When he got back to Uitenhage and said very much the same thing, the word spread like a veld fire.

Dingane made little effort to restore his tattered southern flank. Instead he looked north, and here he temporarily succeeded in regaining some of his lost prestige. The army, champing at the bit since Shaka's death, was sent on a series of northern campaigns after 1832 that replenished the royal herds and renewed the *amabutho*'s battle honours. Indeed, the sacking of the Portuguese fort at Delagoa Bay and execution of the governor must mark one of the very few occasions on which an African power had the daring and capability to invade a colonial neighbour.

In 1832, the Ndebele of Mzilikazi, who had fled from Shaka eleven years earlier, were attacked by a Zulu army under Ndlela near present-day Pretoria in Transvaal. The three-month expedition took the army 350 miles from the warmth of the coastal hills to the arid plains of the Highveld where, in mid-winter, night temperatures were freezing and warriors suffered acutely from cold and hunger. After a few skirmishes, Zulu and Ndebele met in strength on open veld near the Sand river. Casualties were high on both sides, although oral sources generally concede the Zulu the better of the day. Dingane, however, was far from satisfied with his cattle booty.

The Swazi kingdom, too, would suffer Zulu raids across the Lebombo mountains, but Sobhuza, the Swazi king, preferred for years to submit to paying tribute. When Zulu demands turned to incursion, Sobhuza was too wily to be lured into battle. Most ambitious of these northern ventures, however, was the coup against the Portuguese administration in Delagoa Bay.

Dingane had evidently decided to treat his European neighbours as no more and no less than tributary chiefs. His dealings with Port Natal reflect just such a pattern: the traders were not only expected to provide him with gifts but had to demonstrate loyalty by serving occasionally in his *impis* as well. At the same time, Dingane looked to individuals to assume the leadership of the trader community – to be white *nkosi* through whom he could control the others. In 1830, he adopted a similar policy towards Delagoa Bay, sending a message to Dionisio Antonio Ribeiro, the new governor, demanding that he pay tribute like other chiefs. Failing this, Dingane said, he would come with an *impi* and make a trader named Anselmo Nascimento governor.

Here was audacity. Admittedly, Delagoa Bay remained a pretty wretched colonial outpost; nevertheless, a garrison of half a dozen Portuguese officers and around a hundred native levies, all armed with muskets, seemed to offer some deterrent. Ribeiro responded by showing Dingane's envoys two cannon-balls, saying they were the best beads he had and the Zulu were welcome to come and get them. Dingane backed away, sending a few head of cattle to Ribeiro as a peace offering.

A form of cooperation between the two developed over the next couple of years. Dingane sent warriors to assist Ribeiro in raids on the Matola chiefdom, west of the bay. The governor, in turn, helped Dingane in 1831, sending 'five soldiers and five negroes, good marksmen, provided with powder and balls' to sort out some other difficulty. But slave raiding, in which the Portuguese were particularly active between 1825 and 1831, led to a rupture. At some point, it appears, Ribeiro made the mistake of seizing Zulus in a raid.

In July 1833, a Zulu army marched on Delagoa Bay and set fire to a number of villages near by. Ribeiro sent a gift for Dingane and the *impi* left, but a few weeks later it was back. This time Ribeiro withdrew to an island in the bay. On 17 September, the Zulus stormed into the settlement and sacked the fort. The remaining troops offered no resistance and were not harmed; nor were the traders or their homes interfered with. The *impi* had come for Ribeiro and settled down to wait on the coast opposite the island. Three weeks later Ribeiro tried to escape by boat, but he was blown ashore and captured. The Zulus took him back to Delagoa where he was paraded before the population. According to one Portuguese trader, the Zulu *induna* then made a speech.

This governor will die because of his treachery and tyranny, for having usurped the land of the king Dingane and of Makasana [a Zulu tributary], made war on him without motive and sent his people to Mocambique [headquarters of the Portuguese slave trade].[19]

Ribeiro was then put to death. The method is not recorded, but Zulu executioners usually broke their victims' necks with a wrench of the head. So torpid was Portuguese colonial administration that this cavalier treatment of an official was ignored. Ribeiro's successor was also approached by Zulu envoys for tribute but managed to excuse himself on the grounds of poverty.

By 1834, Dingane had recovered from his bad start. Shaka's shadow had receded and there was no sign of rivals. Moreover, the *abelungu* whom Shaka had treated with such deference had been exposed as mere mortals. Dingane seemed to have hit on the way to handle them.

7

THE WORD AND THE GUN

John Philip, superintendent of the London Missionary Society station in South Africa, sat at his desk drafting a reply to the letter from America. Mission House, Philip's headquarters, nestled among the whitewashed, flat-roofed buildings at the foot of Table Mountain. It was a spectacular backdrop which never ceased to make Capetonians and their visitors marvel, but Philip's mind was, as usual, on his work. His eyes went back to the letter from Princeton Theological Seminary, '. . . Thirteen have decided to become missionaries and the question with them is, "Where shall we go? What field shall we enter?"'[1]

Philip set out a heading, 'Condition and Character of the Zoolahs' and began to write, '. . . they are the most war-like and courageous people we have heard of in Africa in modern times . . . should the churches of America think of assisting us in South Africa, I would strongly recommend that they should send a mission to them.'[2]

Eighteen months later, on 22 November 1834, six missionaries and their wives gathered at Park Street Church in Boston to receive final instructions. George Champion, Aldin Grout and Newton Adams were to labour among Dingane's Zulu. Daniel Lindley, Alexander Wilson and Henry Venable were destined for Mzilikazi's Ndebele. They were an exemplary inter-denominational group, dedicated and well educated, and keenly aware of the daunting task ahead. Savage men and wild beasts, deserts and wildernesses, trial and peril, these would be their lot. But as they set sail for the Cape ten days later, they did so with the assurance that the renowned John Philip awaited them as mentor and guide.

Like David Livingstone, Philip was much more than a simple

missionary. The two men shared a humble Scottish background, an indomitable will and a philanthropic zeal in the cause of the oppressed that brooked neither opposition nor question. But while Livingstone crusaded in God's name beside the rivers, lakes and marshes of the African wilderness, Philip's struggle was waged in the urban jungle, along wooden corridors and among the influential and powerful in Cape Town and London. He was influential and powerful himself, especially in the turbulent debate over the colony's racial affairs. When Livingstone arrived in South Africa as a young missionary in 1841, his first reaction was that Philip was an authoritarian with a dangerous penchant for political dabbling. However, he shared many of the superintendent's opinions.[3]

Philip's creed was based on the principle of the equality of all citizens before the law. It followed that the humblest Cape inhabitants, the 'Hottentot' or Khoisan, should have the same rights of movement and property as any burgher. Beyond the colony was another matter. The most pressing need, Philip felt, was to restrain white colonists from expanding across the eastern frontier. Five 'Kaffir wars' – with further trouble with the Xhosa looming – had given notice of the combustibility of Bantu, Boer and Briton. The solution, in his view, was for Britain to annex the country up to Delagoa Bay while at the same time guaranteeing the inhabitants' territorial integrity. Missionaries would, meanwhile, be introduced to spread the gospel and civilization.

To humanitarians in Britain, these concepts were commonsense. To Sir Benjamin D'Urban, the new governor, they were worthy of consideration. To the great majority of white colonists and frontier Boers, they amounted to heresy and betrayal; not only had Philip given the black man ideas above his station, he now wanted to fence the white man in.

Philip was not one to be bothered by criticism and right now, in December 1834, he was ebullient. His prayers, so long seemingly in vain, had been answered. On the first day of the month, a blight had been removed from the world with the emancipation of almost a million slaves in Britain's colonies, including some 39,000 at the Cape. It had been a day which Philip regarded as among the most glorious in Britain's history, and his campaigning had played a part in it.

Missionary work was, meanwhile, proceeding with vigour. Under Philip's office, the number of LMS stations in South Africa had increased from five to eighteen. Even while the Americans were still on the sea, the gospel was being carried into Zululand. A month earlier, Allen Gardiner, a former Royal Navy officer of feverish piety, had passed through Cape Town, barely stopping for wagons and supplies before starting up the coast for Dingane's country. Gardiner was attached to no missionary group, but Philip was not concerned about rivalry in God's work.

None could recognize it, but that month of December was significant in South African history for more than the emancipation of slaves. The colony was on the brink of a series of upheavals that would cause frontiers to tumble and open up a fault to the north through which waves of white migrants would debouch. As some barriers fell, so others arose. The old Cape had been an easygoing place, generally tolerant of its ethnic diversity. When eventually the tremors subsided and the pieces came to rest, the outline and the psyche of the modern South African state was discernible.

The first vibration was felt in Cape Town on 28 December. An army galloper clattered up to Government House with news that the week before about twelve thousand Xhosas had invaded the colony, murdering male settlers. Farms and stores were burning and cattle being plundered. Seized by panic, the frontier settlement of Grahamstown had gone into laager.

The Xhosa had been provoked by white encroachment and the killing of one of their chiefs. When colonial reinforcements arrived they melted away into the Amatola mountains. After coming in to parley, Hintsa, the Xhosa paramount, was shot and his body mutilated. By this time Philip had arrived on the scene but so far as the settlers were concerned, his efforts to understand the Xhosa reaction, and to justify it, only added treachery to his list of misdeeds. More than any previous conflict in the eastern Cape, the Sixth Frontier War left a poisonous legacy of hatred and mistrust. For many in the Boer farming community, it was the final straw. Three decades of British rule had left an abiding sense of resentment. It seemed to the Cape's original white inhabitants that the British, through missionaries like Philip, were constantly meddling in their affairs, and the emancipation of slaves, for which they received little compensation, was only the last in a string of grievances over labour laws passed by the colonial administration. A great cry arose for an escape from both British yoke and Xhosa threat, to the old *laissez-faire* days and a land without frontiers.

But where to escape to? Again it was that fateful month of December 1834 that brought the answer. A party of twenty-two Boers, led by one Pieter Uys, an Uitenhage farmer, had been entrusted with investigating the bounteous land which, it was now known, lay beyond the Xhosa. The so-called *kommissie trek* returned with news of a paradise where rivers were plentiful and the grass grew taller than a man, where sheep might grow as fat as cattle, and which would produce two crops a year.

Between 1835 and 1841, some fifteen thousand Boer men, women and children, abandoned their farms and homes on the frontier and decamped in great heaving and creaking caravans, trailing servants, dogs and herds of livestock. They saw themselves as an oppressed people, and they hoped to live in peace with the black folk whom they would encounter. But land was their primary concern, and the great majority were bound for the Zulu country.

The royal kraal was a showpiece. The kingdom had not attained such a richness of display under Shaka, nor would it again. Emgungundlovu was glutted with brass and beads, the latter obtained by barter from whalers calling at Delagoa Bay. Trade with Port Natal had also contributed to the capital's prosperity. Printed cottons, calico and blankets were in circulation, and the *isigodlo* was like a treasure trove.[4]

Dingane had an inordinate fondness for objects. One end of his great hut was bursting with presents from the traders, snuff boxes, brass bugles, iron pots, and sundry pieces of cloth. The supporting wooden pillars were covered by matted beadwork in which the Zulu had become expert and innovative, and which Dingane himself wore about his upper body. Bead mats also hung from the sides of the huts, which were blackened by smoke from the fire. The clay floor, smoothed over regularly with cow dung and polished with a stone, was as smooth as glass and deliciously cool. Here the king dallied with his many concubines, although without ever producing an heir. Now aged about forty, he insisted, 'I am but a boy – I am too young to marry.'[5] Like Shaka, he never did.

All the show and finery could not conceal the fact that there was something rotten in the kingdom. It started with Dingane himself. The adventurousness which had brought him success in the north did not last. He is sometimes represented as a sybarite, but his real vice was sloth. In his slow-moving bulk, he came increasingly to resemble one of his praise-names, 'the elephant'. He spent a great deal of time just lying on a reed mat, his head supported by an *isigiki*, a wooden rest. Since assuming the throne, he had never gone on campaign with the army and confined his military duty to the occasional visit to the *amakhanda*, regimental kraals in the outlying country. One of his chief interests was devising new costumes and manoeuvres for the women who were required to perform dances and chants before him.

When Dingane did exercise his authority, it was usually ill-judged. Beneath the superficial splendour of Emgungundlovu, the mood was uncertain and anxious. The place acquired an evil reputation and its inhabitants were known for their sulky hostility to outsiders. 'It was a place of death,' said Lunguza ka Mpukane, a Tembu whose kraal lay in the northern districts. 'One always lived in a state of dread and trembling at Emgungundlovu, and was only relieved when one went home.'[6]

Killings probably never reached the levels of Shaka's final years, but then the purpose of discipline was not as clear as it had been. Dingane appeared to make up reasons for having someone killed. 'The birds are hungry,' he might say – or, if a man was ill, 'He is afflicted; go and finish him off.'[7] There is almost nothing in the oral sources to suggest that Dingane was remembered with any warmth – except, perhaps, one story told by Lunguza, about a man who was to be executed:

Dingane said, 'Fellow, what thing that you prize do you leave on earth?' He replied, 'I leave my king who, like a child beginning to talk, can only grow in greatness.' What else do you leave?' He said, *'Nkosi*, I leave my child.' The king said what is it? He answered, 'It is a boy.' Then the king said, 'O Zulu! Let him be, for he says that he leaves two things of value, his child and his king.'[8]

Day to day running of affairs had passed into the hands of two men whose power grew throughout Dingane's reign. One was Ndlela, the army commander-in-chief. The other was Nzobo ka Sobadhli, usually known as Dambusa, a high-ranking member of the Ntombela clan. As Dingane's interest in matters of state waned, so did that of Ndlela and Dambusa grow. In the second half of

Left: Shaka. This illustration, from a drawing by James King, is the only contemporary portrait of the founder of the Zulu state

Below: Dingane, Shaka's half-brother, assassin and successor – from a drawing by the missionary, Allen Gardiner

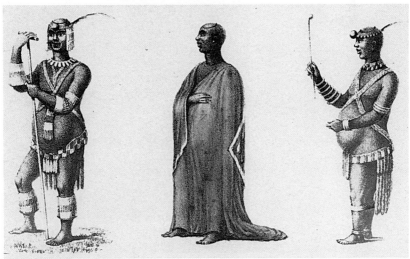

Above: An early painting depicting the massacre of the Boer leader, Piet Retief, and his followers at Emgungundlovu in 1838

Right: Henry Fynn, the first white man to visit Shaka's court – a photograph taken in 1858 towards the end of his life

INTERIOR OF A ZULU HUT.

Above: The interior of a Zulu hut, as seen by a nineteenth-century traveller

Left: A man tending the *isicoco* of one of his fellows – a photograph taken in the 1860s. The fibrous headring was a badge of the mature, married man

Above: A group of
warriors, photographed
shortly before the
Anglo-Zulu war
in 1879

Right: A Zulu warrior
in full ceremonial
regalia at the time of
the war

Theophilus Shepstone

Bishop Colenso and his
daughter, Harriette

Far left, above: Ngoza, a Natal chief, with his *izinduna*. Ngoza was to send his children to Colenso's mission, Ekukanyeni, to be educated

Far left, below: Ekukanyeni before the fire which destroyed it. The figure on the right is William Ngidi, Colenso's first convert

Above: The British ultimatum to the Zulu kingdom being read out on the bank of the Tugela on 11 December 1878

Left: King Cetshwayo – a photograph taken in London

Dabulamanzi, Cetshwayo's fiery half-brother and leader of the failed attack on Rorke's Drift

Isandlwana – a photograph taken some months after the British catastrophe, when the field was still littered with the debris of battle

Dingane's reign there were clearly occasions on which they exercised power without reference to him. In Shaka's time, only the king himself had the authority to order executions. Now these *izinduna* had the power over life and death and Dambusa, for one, was reputed to abuse it in the pursuit of his own aggrandisement. One source later said that Dambusa 'caused people to be killed off in every direction, especially those with property, cattle or girls'.⁹

Ndlela, who had been appointed army commander by Dingane in succession to Mdlaka, was not up to so important a task. Respected, kindly and clear-headed, he was politically ambitious, but had not the ruthlessness required to lead men in war. His record was undistinguished. Apart from the raid on Mzilikazi's weakened forces in 1832, and the Delagoa Bay overthrow of Ribeiro the following year, the *amabutho* had failed conspicuously to win credit, let alone glory, under him. Expeditions against the Bhaca, a people living in the Mpondoland region to the south had returned virtually empty-handed. No campaigns of any sort were undertaken in 1834 and 1835.

Loyalty in the army declined along with efficiency. In 1834, a large section of one regiment deserted its *ikhanda* and crossed the Tugela. Three others set off in pursuit, but with orders from Dingane not to cross into Natal, as the bloodshed that would inevitably follow might alarm the traders. The deserters duly reached Port Natal, where they swelled the growing ranks of Zulu exiles. This incident was especially serious as the *ibutho* had been posted on the Tugela not as a line of defence but specifically to prevent desertions.

Other methods of controlling the southward flow of refugees had been no more successful. It is clear that more than just a fear of punishment was causing this haemorrhage. A loss of direction within the kingdom and reports of the free and easy life that awaited those who could attach themselves to the trader community at Port Natal were additional lures. Dingane had tried to erase the impression that once in Natal refugees were beyond his control by getting traders to carry out executions at his behest. Such was the case involving the Cele *izinduna*.

We have seen that early in his reign Dingane murdered the Cele chief, Magaye. His son, Mkhonto, was installed in his place by Dingane and, for a year, all was well. Then, without warning and for no known reason, a Zulu *impi* descended on the Cele kraals and massacred the inhabitants; the once-powerful Cele clan scattered. Some of the survivors went to Zululand. Others took shelter with the traders Henry Ogle and James Collis, while six of Magaye's brothers sought the protection of Henry Fynn. On his next visit to Dingane, Fynn was horrified to be told that he must have the brothers killed. For eight months he prevaricated and wheedled; if Dingane wanted them dead let his own men do the killing. The king was obdurate. Fynn's diary leaves the brothers' fate unstated, but it is reasonable to infer that he had them done away with.

By midway through the 1830s, the thousands of exiles living at Port Natal had become the most pressing foreign policy issue confronting the kingdom, and Dingane's relations with the traders were at an all-time low. There were *izinduna*, among them Dambusa, who were all for sweeping down on Port Natal and blotting out the settlement, the whites as well as the king's foes. The only obstacle was Dingane's fondness for the increasingly lustrous objects with which the whites plied him.

At this critical juncture, the Zulu were introduced to the first of a new kind of *abelungu*, those who called themselves 'teachers'.

What made Allen Gardiner choose the Zulu for his mission has never been explained, but then the man's whole life seems to have consisted of a series of profoundly felt but unresolved impulses. He defied his parents' wishes to join the Royal Navy and, while still a teenager, fought in the 1812 war with the United States. He rose in rank to commander and had visited the four corners of the world – including South Africa, where the Zulu first came to his attention. Then, in May 1834 his wife died and, within three months, he was on his way to the Cape. He had no commission from any missionary organization but with some private funds, immense energy and a willing spirit, he set out for Zululand to preach the gospel. En route, he was lucky to run into Fynn, now working for the colonial administration in Grahamstown.

Fynn had seen trouble coming. He had always thought that Port Natal could only sustain three or four white traders. More than that and 'the Zulus will and must look on us with suspicion'. Meanwhile, the population had grown to about thirty male residents, swollen by itinerant hunters and traders. However, Fynn approved of Gardiner's mission, offering advice on dealing with

Dingane, and suggesting a splendid red baize cloak as the kind of gift that would sweeten the king.

Dingane, too, was prepared. It had been as the prophetic Jakot had said: first, the white men came and took part of the land; now a 'teacher' was following to build houses among the people. No doubt it was his intention to subdue them by witchcraft.

Gardiner fulfilled his expectations. The missionary, a dark, thin and intense figure, plunged in headlong, explaining that he had come to teach the Zulu 'the Book' and requesting that he be allowed to build a house at Emgungundlovu. Gravely, Dingane asked to see the Book and turned the pages with much curiosity for a few minutes before handing it back. He then asked a few questions which convinced Gardiner that he was no fool – about the whereabouts of God, the Last Judgment and eternal life – before concluding the interview affably, saying that he would have to consult Ndlela and Dambusa.[10]

Gardiner found the following four weeks a trial. He was left waiting in anticipation of a reply that seemed never to come. The mood of the kraal was ugly and Dambusa's behaviour towards him so hostile that several times he feared for his life. Finally, he was summoned to where Dingane was sitting on a chair under a tree with the two *izinduna*. Once again he explained his purpose. Now Dambusa interjected: the Zulu did not want the teaching of the Book; what they wanted was teaching in how to use the muskets brought by the traders. Ndlela supported him. When Gardiner turned imploringly to Dingane, the king replied that he could not overrule his chiefs.

Gardiner's mission might have ended there and then but for the exile crisis. He returned to Port Natal where the traders induced him to act as an intermediary with Dingane. In April 1835 he was on his way back to the royal kraal with the draft of a treaty pro-posal: in return for the king's guarantee of safety for all Port Natal's white and black residents, the traders would guarantee to send back all future fugitives. Gardiner had no need of the gewgaws he had brought for the king, including a pair of naval epaulettes, three gilt bracelets, some sporting prints and a portrait of William IV, Britain's new. ruler; Dingane was delighted with the treaty. Dambusa, hitherto so surly, declared that his heart was glad and that Gardiner was a good man, to be trusted.

Gardiner was, in fact, a decent man far out of his depth. He had accepted a poisoned chalice from the traders and it was not long before he found himself obliged by his own agreement to carry back to Dingane, and certain death, seven fugitives, including a woman and three children. They were starved before being executed. Dingane's glee only added to Gardiner's distress, and not all his hand-wringing and prayers could relieve him of his terrible responsibility. The king was delighted to have found a European who carried out orders in a way that accorded with his own notions of loyalty. 'Now we see that you belong to the Zulus,' he said. Gardiner would be his *nkosi* among the white people. 'You must have power. I give you all the country [of Natal] – you must be the chief over all the people there.'[11]

The final twist of this bitter morality play was perhaps the most poignant. Sacrificing the fugitives gained Gardiner the permission he had been seeking, to preach the Word north of the Tugela. The first mission station in Zululand was a series of grass huts about twenty miles south of Shaka's old capital, kwaBulawayo, which Gardiner called Culoola, a transliterated version of the Zulu word *kalula*, or freedom.

At the end of 1835 Gardiner set off for the Cape, to take advice from D'Urban, the governor, and seek support in Britain for his missionary work. Passing through Port Elizabeth he encountered Grout, Champion and Adams, the American missionaries, on the final leg of their journey to Dingane. Gardiner was cool, saying they had no chance of success and going so far as to suggest that they abandon their mission entirely, 'lest we destroy all the good he had done'.[12]

By now the Americans must have been wondering why they had come to South Africa at all. Since their arrival at Cape Town little had gone right. The first group, of Lindley, Wilson and Venable, had duly set out north for Mzilikazi's Ndebele, but the trio bound for the Zulu had their departure delayed for weeks by the frontier war, which had cut the coastal road. Philip, whose encouragement had inspired the mission in the first place, appeared to have lost interest, declaring that it had little chance of success among so barbarous a people as the Zulu. Then, on arriving in Grahamstown, the missionaries had been assailed in an article by Robert Godlonton, the negrophobic editor of the *Graham's Town Journal*, as associates of the detested Philip, and agents of American imperialism. Doggedly, they pressed on. The American mission would be at centre-stage in the cataclysm about to break across South Africa.

Mutual incomprehension characterized early dealings between Zulu and missionary. The Americans were immediately impressed by 'two remarkable traits for a heathen community, honesty and chastity'. Yet they were entirely ignorant of the spiritual system they were intent on replacing, and blind to the king's centrality in the religious life of his people. Although pleased by the friendliness of his welcome on their first visit to Emgungundlovu, they were puzzled by the impression created by Gardiner, and the expectations Dingane had of them as 'teachers'. The king, they noted, 'has erroneous views in regard to our work'.[13]

Dingane had found in his dealings with Gardiner that missionaries were not only able to supply many of the goods he desired, but were more pliant and eager to please than the traders with whom he had previously dealt. By now his paramount concern was firearms. Early in his rule, Port Natal had been the source of a steady trickle of muzzle-loaders, although the traders had deliberately rendered some useless by removing vital parts. Now he was receiving a few guns from Delagoa Bay, but not enough. Equally vital was instruction in how to use them. Dingane, Ndlela and Dambusa were all convinced that the 'teachers' could explain the mysteries of firearms.

Guns conclusively proved their worth in the 1836 expedition against the Swazi. Dingane had been intending to strike against his northern neighbours for some time, to replenish his herds and exercise the *amabutho*, who had not seen active service for about three years. At the same time, concern about the army's decline gave him reason to seek the traders' support.

The growing community at Port Natal had decided a year earlier to name their town in honour of the Cape's governor, D'Urban, in the evident hope that he would grant their wish for annexation to the colony. In the meantime, they remained vulnerable, and the summons for assistance from Emgungundlovu offered an opportunity to heal a two-year rift with the kingdom. About thirty settlers, led by John Cane, took up their guns and joined the Zulu *impi* that set forth against Sobhuza's Swazis. So significantly had Zulu military morale declined that, it is said, Ndlela deferred to

Cane in the matter of command. After a skirmish in which the whites blazed noisily away for a while, the Swazis took refuge in the mountains. The raiders returned with thousands of head of cattle, being greeted as conquerors, and Cane and the other whites were liberally rewarded for their help.

The missionaries had their own reasons for thanksgiving. Their first station, Umlazi, just south of the port, had been opened and was teaching the children of Zulu exiles. Furthermore, Dingane had granted them permission to found a station in Zululand itself, although still keeping it at arm's length. Ginani (I am with you) was built near Gardiner's abandoned Culoola, in the Tugela border district of Hlomendlini, and two days' journey from Emgungund-lovu. Here the local *induna*, a brother of Dambusa, was politeness itself, but requests that children be sent for teaching were ignored. While matters were still at this relatively promising stage, news arrived of the disaster that had befallen the mission to the Ndebele.

The second American trio had arrived on the high grassy plains of the Highveld trailing the migrant Boers from the Cape. Scarcely had the missionaries established themselves with Mzilikazi than trouble broke out. In raids on trekker camps near the Vaal river, the Ndebele killed more than twenty Boers and plundered sheep and cattle. But in casting themselves against the defensive laager of Boer wagons, the Ndebele lost more than four hundred men. The trekkers withdrew to await reinforcements and brood on revenge.

On a warm early morning in January 1837, a mounted Boer commando swept down on the Ndebele, firing from the saddle with their long-barrelled *roers*. The stunned missionaries watched helplessly as the people they had come to save were slaughtered around them. Fifteen kraals were destroyed and between four and five hundred Ndebele killed. Lindley reported to his superiors in Boston: 'Few of the men belonging to them escaped, and many of the women were shot down.'[14] The survivors scattered, eventually mustering under Mzilikazi's leadership to start a northward migration of their own. To the missionaries, however, it seemed that there was nothing more to be done for the Ndebele. They set off south for the Zulu country with deep foreboding. Lindley feared he was witnessing a repeat of the fate of the American

Indians who had been driven from their lands. Wilson was more specific:

This emigration of the farmers is going to form a new era in the history of the native tribes beyond the colony. We are now on our way to join our brethren in the country of Dingaan. We have our fears that the farmers and Dingaan will come into conflict in a few years.[15]

The assegai had been tested against gun, horse and wagon, and been found wanting. For the time being, however, Dingane was less interested in learning the lessons of Mzilikazi's calamity than profiting from it. The Ndebele had long been the Zulus' only rival for military supremacy in the interior and their previous encounter had been indecisive. On hearing of the Boer victory, Dingane sent out an *impi* under Ndlela to take advantage of his old foe's weakness.

As in 1832, the Zulu crossed the Drakensberg in mid-winter and suffered fearfully in the march to the freezing Highveld. Allowing for privation, however, it is a sign of how enfeebled the Zulu army had become that it was unable to gain a decisive advantage over Mzilikazi's debilitated men. In their only set-piece battle, near the Pilanesberg mountains in west Transvaal, neither side could gain the upper hand and both endured heavy losses, although this time the Zulu were able to round up an immense number of Ndebele livestock. The ragged army that arrived home in September 1837 presented Dingane with the greatest cattle booty to be seized during his rule. But the missionaries were shocked to see at what price it had been bought. More than a thousand men failed to return, many having died on the march.

A few weeks later another band of armed men filed over the Drakensberg passes and looked down on the tall swaying grass of the Zulu country. Wilson's forecast had been out only in its timing. The Boers had come.

For many months the trekkers had been encamped north of the Cape Colony, around a mission station named Thaba Nchu. They had done little but quarrel: about the direction in which they should proceed; under whose leadership; and, because they were independent, pugnacious folk, about anything else that occurred to them. Then, in March 1837, Piet Retief arrived. He was already known by reputation to many, as a respected eastern frontier farmer. A tall, bearded man of great presence and unusually good education, he was an obvious choice to resolve the leadership crisis. It was forgotten that in his business enterprises Retief had sometimes demonstrated injudiciousness amounting to rashness.

The Great Trek, as the movement of migrant Boers was known, was at a crossroads. Many were in favour of continuing north, across the Vaal river and settling on the plains from which Mzilikazi's Ndebele had so recently been swept. The further away from British rule, the better, went the reasoning of men like the prickly, redoubtable Hendrik Potgieter. A majority, however, were drawn by the tales they had heard of Natal, recalling the words of Hermanus Barry on his pioneering visit five years earlier: '*Allemagtig*! (Almighty). I have never seen such a fine place.' The Zulu country had become in the minds of many the Promised Land.

In October, Retief, accompanied by fifteen men and four oxwagons, descended from the Drakensberg and rode on to Durban. The Boers were surprised but nevertheless relieved by the warmth of the British community's greeting. For the time being, they shared interests and concerns. The settlers' efforts to get Natal annexed as a colony to the Cape had come to nothing and, meanwhile, relations with Dingane had soured again. Alexander Biggar, Durban's new civic leader, was delighted to learn that the Boers had come to stay.

Retief was no pirate. His manifesto as trek leader, published in a Cape newspaper, averred: 'We will not molest any people, nor deprive them of the smallest property, but if attacked we shall consider ourselves fully justified in defending our persons and effects.'[16] He had secured friendship treaties with the Rolong and Tlokwa on the Highveld, and he intended to deal openly with Dingane in seeking land on which Boers could settle. From Durban he wrote a letter to the king which allayed the forebodings of the missionary Lindley, who performed the translation and was 'much pleased with the entire spirit' of it.

Neither trekker nor missionary was prepared to admit the heart of the matter. Wherever white men had so far gone in the subcontinent the native inhabitants had been forced either to submit or to retreat. It was being disingenuous not to acknowledge that, for all their protestations of peace, the trekkers were invaders. And it was naive to suppose that the most martial black nation in southern Africa would not recognize them as such. Either that, or it was to underestimate the blacks' intelligence.

In November, Retief rode out from Durban with six men, bound for Emgungundlovu. Thomas Halstead, one of the last of Farewell's original trading party, was among them to act as interpreter.

❀

To Dingane it had become a race against time to obtain guns. Mzilikazi's rout and all the information he now received only emphasized the point made by John Cane's raid on the Swazi – the superiority of firearms to assegais. But mere knowledge of the fact was not enough, and his sources had dried up.

All through the first half of 1837, frustration mounted. The whites' refusal to give him guns could only mean that they were not friends but foes. Old grievances resurfaced as the new white chief, Biggar, renounced the pact to hand back exiles. So far as Dingane was concerned, Durban had become a nest of opposition and defiance. Then, in mid-year, Allan Gardiner returned from England, bringing another missionary, Francis Owen. Dingane rejoiced. Here, at last, was the one white who had always done his bidding. As a sign of good faith, he allowed finally that a teacher might live at Emgungundlovu. Owen's home was built on a hillside opposite the royal kraal and about a mile distant from it.

Owen was an unworldly, rather prissy man, more suited to an English country parish than the fraught situation in which he found himself. Dingane quickly tired of his earnest proselytizing, ridiculing the idea that man has a soul and, Owen complained, 'even made light of the name of God, which he went so far as to laugh at'.

The real trouble was that the pastor could not, or would not, unlock the magic of firearms. Within a few weeks Owen recorded Dingane's protest in his journal:

He was much displeased. He had expected the teachers would instruct him in all things; however, they chose certain things which they would teach him, but they would not instruct him in that which he most wanted to know – alluding to firearms. First one teacher asked to instruct his people, then another, and he granted all. He said that I was like the rest; for when he asked me only to lend him a bullet-mould, I refused.[17]

137

Thus were matters poised when Retief and his small party arrived at the royal kraal on 5 November.

Elaborate preparations had been made. Warriors were gathered from all the military kraals and cattle herds mustered from around the country for a display of the king's might. For three days the Boers were fêted at feasts, parades and dances. The climax was a massed demonstration of Zulu warfare by the *amabutho* at which Dingane appeared resplendent in his kilt of monkey skins and a striped robe of black, red and white. The rituals over, Retief presented his petition.

Dingane's response was a characteristic combination of opportunism and prevarication. He was willing, he said, to 'give' Natal to the Boers, but first they must prove their friendship. Kraals in northern Zululand had been losing cattle to rustling by the Tlokwa under their chief Sikonyela. Let the Boers bring back these beasts and he would see that they were indeed friends. Retief, who had been impressed both by the 'terrific exhibition' of martial prowess and Dingane's friendliness, had no hesitation in agreeing.

Just what Dingane intended by this pact has been the subject of much speculation. From the Zulu perspective it can only be understood in the context of previous dealings with whites. The land in question had been assigned to Farewell, King and Gardiner before Retief – not in the form of a title to ownership, which was alien to Zulu thinking, but as a fiefdom to be administered by a loyal surrogate. At this stage, Retief appeared to Dingane as just another of the many white *amakosi* who had come to Natal, stayed for a while and then gone. The test of friendship he had set Retief was the same, in form if not detail, as those required previously of Fynn, Cane and Gardiner.

Retief duly started back for the Highveld on his errand. He had not been long gone, however, when the size of the Boer party suddenly became clear to Dingane. Without waiting for the king's permission, hundreds of trekker wagons came over the Drakensberg passes into the Zulu country and camped along streams less than a hundred miles from the royal kraal. As the Boers clustered around their fires, smoking pipes while the womenfolk boiled great pots of maize meal and children splashed in the cool *spruits*, they were oblivious to the provocation this offered. Retief's manner only aggravated matters. In a letter carried back to Dingane, he boasted of Mzilikazi's defeat, of the hundreds of Ndebele killed without any Boer losses. Another letter preached that 'wicked kings' like Mzilikazi were punished by God 'and not suffered long to live and reign'.[18] Owen, who was by now thoroughly disillusioned with his host, read the letter and thought it 'excellent advice'.

Sikonyela was bearded in his den by the Boers. The Tlokwa chief was clamped in irons until he agreed to hand over about seven hundred cattle. He also parted with a dozen muskets and fifty horses used by his banditti. Word of the capture was sent back to Dingane, with the assurance that the proceeds would shortly be brought to him.

Back at the Boer camp in northern Natal, Retief consulted his staff on the next step. He had decided that the way to deal with Dingane was to overawe him, and proposed returning to Emgungundlovu with a large *kommando* to claim the reward. Gerrit Maritz, his deputy, dissented, not because he felt a larger force might challenge the Zulu, but because a small force would be less of a loss if Dingane turned treacherous. On such reefs of misunderstanding have relations between Boer and Bantu often foundered: one man had reached the wrong conclusion, the other the right conclusion for the wrong reason. Sending a small force was the only way that tragedy might now have been averted. As it was, Retief's counsel prevailed.

The Boers returned to Emgungundlovu with the subtlety of an elephant herd. Retief led a *kommando* of seventy-one men that thundered across the Tugela and into Zululand on 1 February; there were sixty-five Boers, five mixed-race servants, and Thomas Halstead, still acting as interpreter. Two days later, having announced themselves from a distance with a volley from their *roers*, they rode into the royal kraal, still brandishing guns and herding the captured cattle.

The Zulus, drawn up in assembly, were astounded by this unprecedented demonstration. In the dusty arena at the centre of the kraal, the Boers then put on a cavalry display in which, as Owen put it, 'they danced on horseback, by making a sham charge at one another'. The air resounded with the crash of muskets. Dingane seemed enthralled.

Retief handed over the cattle. Then he was asked for the guns and horses taken from Sikonyela. Laughingly, he tugged at the grey hairs of his beard.[19] The gesture said it all; only a child would be fool enough to give guns to the Zulus.

It has been suggested that Retief's refusal was critical to what followed, that Dingane was driven by his desperation for firearms. But it was already too late to avert disaster. According to Mmemi ka Nguluzane, an informant of Stuart's:

The Zulus, finding [the Boers] coming in large numbers became suspicious. They thought they came in a hostile manner and these suspicions were increased by the Boers proposing to put on a display for the king. There was nothing wrong in that, but when the display consisted in firing guns so that the smoke of the guns smelt about the kraal, as well as riding round the main kraal as if to try and encircle it, the intentions of fighting were translated into the possibility of success unless the affair were nipped in the bud.[20]

It was probably that night that Dambusa proposed a plan for nipping 'the affair' in the bud.[21]

Over the next three days the Boers were fêted as before, with feasting, dancing and singing. None appeared to notice the steady arrival of men in war-dress from outlying kraals. Nor could they comprehend the warriors' chants. One who did was a lad of thirteen named William Wood, the son of a Durban trader, who was acting as Owen's interpreter. On the evening of 5 February, Wood muttered to the Owen household: 'You will see. They will kill the Boers tomorrow.'[22]

The following morning Owen was at his devotions in the shade of a wagon when a sweating and anxious warrior hurried up from the kraal and poured out his message from Dingane: the missionary and his family were not to worry, but they should know that the Boers were about to die. Thunderstruck, Owen turned and looked across the valley to the hill of execution, kwaMatiwane. He recalled:

'There!' said someone, 'they are killing the Boers now!' About nine or ten Zulus to each Boer were dragging their helpless unarmed victims to the fatal spot.[23]

Retief's party had prepared to depart that morning. They had what they had come for, a piece of paper to which Dingane had put his mark, making over the land between the Tugela and Mzimvubu rivers. Leaving their camp under a pair of euphorbia trees, the Boers strolled up to the kraal in twos and threes to take their leave.

Young Wood was already there. As some of the Boers strolled past, he warned them that he feared treachery. They smiled and replied: 'We are sure the king's heart is right with us.'[24]

Shortly, Dingane emerged from the *isigodlo* and seated himself in a large armchair which had been the gift of a trader some years earlier. In one of those inconsequential matters of detail that can stick in the mind *in extremis*, Wood was later to recall that it had become rather threadbare. Dambusa and Ndlela were on either side of the king. About two thousand warriors were drawn up in a vast circle but they were not armed. Weapons were not allowed within the great enclosure, and the Boers had left their guns at camp. Word was sent for them to approach.

Dingane made a brief speech wishing the party a good journey, then proposed some refreshment before they set off. Retief squatted on the ground near the king, with his men a short way off. Pots of sweet maize beer started to circulate and the by-now familiar chanting and dancing began. After perhaps a quarter of an hour, Dingane suddenly shouted in Zulu: 'Seize them!'

The Boers were initially uncomprehending. Not having understood the words, most were still seated when they were engulfed in a rush by warriors. Halstead, however, recognized what was happening and shouted: 'We are done for!' He struck out with a knife, eviscerating one assailant.

Amid the mêlée, Dingane remained seated in his armchair, crying: '*Bulala abathakathi*!' – Kill the wizards.

Kicking and flailing, the Boers had their hands bound with thongs and were dragged from the kraal. Seething clusters of bodies moved down the hill, across the gurgling Mkumbane stream and up the opposite ridge to kwaMatiwane. The bones from previous executions already lay scattered among rocks and aloes.

There is some disagreement over how the Boers were put to death. According to oral sources, their necks were broken.[25] Wood said that they were clubbed, Retief being saved for the last. One of the Boers who later found the bodies claimed that some had been impaled. What is certain is that all seventy-one perished.

According to one story, Retief's heart and liver were cut out and taken in a cloth to Dingane to be used for magic which was then sprinkled on the road by which the Boers had come. It is possible, but unlikely in view of the fact that Retief's remains were found months later fully clothed, in the leather waistcoat he had donned that morning and with Dingane's concession in a shoulder bag.[26]

All this Owen watched in horror through a telescope from the hill opposite. In less than half an hour, the slaughter was over and the Zulus streamed back to the kraal where Dingane remained in his tattered armchair. As shields and assegais were issued, the warriors set up a clamorous *giya*, declaiming the king's praises and stamping and gyrating through a war dance. At midday, the *impi* set off northwards at a run.

The rivers of north Natal rise in the Drakensberg and flow down in gathering volume to the Tugela. It was among these rivers, amid the sounds of cicadas, chuckling waters and the call of the red-chested cuckoo, or *Piet-my-vrou*, that the trekkers were camped in family groups on the night of 17 February. No word had reached them in the eleven days since the Retief massacre and they suspected nothing.

A moonless night and the thick bush beside the smaller rivers hid the *impi* until the last moment. Many of the trekkers failed to stir until the Zulus were in their wagons. Then, amid screams and cries, the assegais rose and fell. Beside the Bloukranz, Malanspruit and Moordspruit, the trekkers died almost to the last servant and child. The few shots which they managed to get off warned more distant groups, in time for hasty defences to be prepared. Along the Bushmans river, the Bothman family set up a withering fire until the Zulu mingled with their cattle and, driving them in on the wagons, breached the laager. Riders galloped from camp to camp, shouting warnings.

When dawn came the Zulu were gone and the survivors gathered at a spot called Doornkop. The toll was counted; among the Jouberts and Engelbrechts, the Loggenbergs, De Beers and others, forty-one men, fifty-six women and 186 children were dead. The high number of children reflected the proportions of Boer families, although sixty-five men had been away on Retief's *kommando*. Less attention was given to counting the number of 'Hottentot' servants who died; it is roughly estimated at 250. In all, more than five hundred members of the trek party had been slain in ten days. No comparable disaster had ever been experienced by whites in southern Africa, and the flame of a terrible hatred was kindled.

Even as the *impi* loped back to Emgungundlovu, driving ahead thousands of sheep and cattle, news of the disaster reached Durban, where a new wave of Boers was just arriving from beyond the Drakensberg. Hunger for revenge burned in every heart. In Durban, John Cane was organizing a punitive expedition, composed mainly of Zulu exiles, to avenge Halstead. At Doornkop, Maritz was joined by Hendrik Potgieter, Piet Uys and their followers. In messages between Boer and Briton, an alliance for a twin-pronged invasion of Zululand was agreed.

It went hopelessly awry. Cane set off in fine fettle, an ostrich plume waving from his old straw hat, an elephant gun across his shoulder, and at the head of about four hundred Zulu exiles breathing fire and brimstone and vowing death to Dingane. The expedition quickly became nothing more than a glorified slave-raid. At the first large Zulu kraal, they found that the menfolk were still away with the *impi*, and stopped only long enough to round up five hundred women and children and a few thousand cattle before returning to Durban.

The Boers, meanwhile, were beset by their old fractiousness. Potgieter and Uys were not even on speaking terms, which caused problems as they were supposed to be in joint command of a punitive *kommando*. A powerful force of 347 men crossed the upper Tugela into northern Zululand and on 11 April ran straight into an *impi* under Ndlela. Zulu casualties in a running battle were high, but it was the Boers who broke off and fled, leaving the bodies of Uys and ten others on the field.

Zulu rejoicing over this victory had barely subsided when Dingane's men won further laurels. On 17 April, another punitive force set out from Durban, this time consisting of seventeen whites and about eight hundred Zulu exiles, perhaps half with firearms. Despite the earlier reverse, morale was high and as they marched the exiles sang how they would 'kill the elephant and eat his cattle'. But no sooner had they crossed the Tugela, near its mouth, than they were ambushed by a section of the Zulu army led by Dingane's brother, Mpande, and Komfiya the Qwabe, who, almost twenty years earlier, had fought in Shaka's great defeat of Zwide. On this occasion the battle was scarcely less ferocious. Finding themselves surrounded, the exiles fought desperately. Most were killed. So were thirteen of the Englishmen. John Cane, one of the last survivors of Farewell's original party, was among them. When his body was found later, it was surrounded by the bodies of dozens of his followers, who remained loyal to the last to their white chief.[27]

The survivors fell back on Durban, which dissolved into a state of mourning and panic. Among those clamouring to leave were the American missionaries who had fled Zululand, despite Dingane's assurances of their safety. The entire white population transferred to a brig, the *Comet*, moored in the bay, while the black exiles, who had trusted for years to the traders' protection, were abandoned, in the words of young William Wood, 'to make for themselves the best shift they could'.

Next morning, after years of rumours and false alarms of invasion, a Zulu *impi* finally swept down on Durban. It stayed nine days, looting traders' homes and butchering those of the exiles not fleet enough to escape. As the Zulus pulled back to the Tugela, half a dozen or so of the bolder whites, including Biggar and Ogle, returned to their sacked town. But most of Natal's former inhabitants gratefully accepted passage on the *Comet* to the Cape.

By the end of April, the Zulu king's praises were being sung with a fervour not known since Shaka's time. A ghostly wind blew through the mission stations that had been opened in such high faith, and Boer encampments were mute with despair. Across the Zulu country, gun and gospel were in retreat.

8

THE BREAKING OF THE ROPE

Dingane's hour of triumph was brief and he paid dearly for it. So did his subjects. Boer revenge was to be bitter and implacable, and the Zulus' noses were still being rubbed in the Retief and Bloukranz massacres more than 150 years later. Within two years, the kingdom had been divided by civil war, carved up and forced to pay ruinous reparations; thousands of Zulus had been killed. Yet, paradoxically, these same traumas enabled the kingdom to survive and ushered in an era of tranquillity and reform.

Through the winter of 1838, Dingane pursued the Boers while persisting in the hope that he could restore relations with the English. Almost the last thing that he asked Francis Owen to do before quitting his mission was write a letter to the Cape authorities, saying that 'he would not allow white people to build houses in his country,'[1] and that he had killed the Boers because they were planning to murder him. At Dingane's request the American missionary, Wilson, took down another letter 'to the king across the waters' (presumably, William IV, although he had died and been succeeded by Victoria in June 1837) with a similar explanation, and a request that friendly relations should continue.[2] These diplomatic initiatives were conducted simultaneously with raids on the Boer laagers still in northern Natal.

Dingane had no intrinsic preference for Briton over Boer. The English had simply been associated in the Zulu mind with a limited presence and the Afrikaner with a larger, more intrusive one. However irritating the handful of scallywag traders might be, they had their uses and could be controlled. But, although it seemed initially that Britain was prepared to enforce a return to the *status quo ante*, Natal's days as a rough trading post were already over.

In May, Lord Glenelg, the Colonial Secretary, wrote to Sir George Napier, his new governor at the Cape. Britain, he said, would 'punish by all lawful means the acts of aggression and plunder which, there is too much reason to believe, it is the practice of [the Boers] to perpetrate'.[3] Glenelg was, in fact, referring to the trekkers' treatment of Mzilikazi, but the same concerns would soon apply to the Zulu. Napier's reply put sympathetically the Boers' case for leaving the Cape, but proposed that in the final resort, the only way to protect the Zulu 'from extermination or slavery' by people still regarded as British subjects, was by military occupation of Port Natal. On 10 September, Napier cut off supplies of guns and powder to the Boers in Natal and, three months later, about a hundred 72nd Highlanders under Major Samuel Charters landed in the bay with orders to keep the peace.

That winter the trekkers had suffered further losses in their camps on the upper Tugela. In August, an *impi* seized many of their remaining cattle. The following month, Maritz, the last of the original trek leaders, died of fever. Potgieter had already turned his back on Natal and headed back to the Highveld with his followers. Through all these trials the trekkers clung to their vision of the Promised Land and now, at last, their Moses was at hand. As spring gave way to summer, there arrived from the Cape one Andries Pretorius, an ill-educated but self-assured farmer, forceful and clear-thinking. In a few weeks he had organized and inspired his fellows to raise a new *kommando* of which he was made leader.

Charters, hearing of these preparations, fired off a message advising Pretorius that Britain was determined to protect 'the native tribes of Africa', and warning him to desist from 'offensive measures against the Zulu chief', and to withdraw from the Zulu country.[4] It was too late. When Pretorius received the message he had already crossed into Zululand at the head of 470 mounted men, sixty-four ox-wagons and two cannons, bound for Emgungundlovu.

Dingane was not oblivious to the possibility of defeat. He had spoken about it, remarking that he knew places where, in the event, he could go and not be found, and where the Zulu would be able to regroup. At the same time, the military establishment had been consumed by a dangerous hubris after its early victories.

As the Boer wagons creaked onward, they were shadowed by Zulu spies. Bands of warriors were in their vicinity and, as Pretorius dispatched mounted patrols of up to a hundred men to locate and attack them, dozens of Zulus were ridden down and killed. Dingane had marvelled years before at his first sight of a horse and wondered aloud how any man could stand against such a terrible creature. Now the *amabutho* were discovering to their cost the vulnerability of lightly armed infantry against cavalry.

On 15 December, the *kommando* was about fifty miles north-west of the royal kraal when Pretorius called a halt on the west bank of the Ncome river. Word came in that evening that the Zulu army was advancing in force. A laager was formed, all sixty-four wagons being drawn up in a circle and lashed together to prevent the attackers forcing an opening between them. It was Pretorius's intention to remain within his fortification the following day, the sabbath, and launch his cavalry on the Monday morning. But he was ready for a Zulu onslaught; cattle and horses were brought into the laager, and the cannons set in firing position. The position was well chosen. To the east, the Ncome river ran too deep to allow any advance from that direction, while a deep *donga*, or ditch, cut off the approach from the south. The open terrain between the river and the ditch funnelled down to a neck where the *laager* stood. It was from there that any Zulu attack would have to come.

Dingane had not committed his entire army. *Amabutho* known to have been at the Ncome battle were the Dhlambedlu, the first regiment formed during his reign and his favourite, the Imkulutsh-ane, the Ukokoti and the Izinyosi, the last of Shaka's regiments. There were others as well, but estimates that put Zulu numbers at up to twenty thousand are exaggerations; between eight and ten thousand would be closer to the mark. However, for the first time an *impi* came to battle carrying guns, the muskets belonging to Retief's men having been distributed among about sixty men. Their failure to hit anything, because of an apparent misapprehension that bullets would curve in flight like assegais, was to be a conspicuous feature of Zulu marksmanship for many years.

Other deficiencies were even more glaring. Tactics and caution were thrown to the wind as the warriors advanced, extolling their ascendancy over 'Piti', as Retief was known, and their defeat of the first *kommando*. Ndlela's failings as a general were to be pitilessly exposed. It is inconceivable that Shaka's old commander, Mdlaka, with his record of stealth and night attacks, would have committed his force to a full frontal assault over open ground against a better armed foe in an almost impregnable position.

As dawn broke clear and bright on 16 December, Boer lookouts saw the *impi* advancing at a distance through knee-high grass. Thousands of baritone voices were raised in war-song, and the drumming of assegais on shields, the *ingomane*, set up a thunderous rattle. One of the Boers, watching in awed silence, noted: 'Their approach, although frightful on account of the great number, yet presented a beautiful appearance.'[5]

There is just one Zulu eyewitness report of what South Africans call the Battle of Blood River. Lunguza ka Mpukane was in the Ukokoti regiment, which was held back from the massed charge because of its youth, and was only to be sent in for blooding if the Boers were overcome. What his account lacks in detail it makes up for in starkness.

The Boer fort was made of wagons closely drawn together with branches put in between. The rushes of the Zulu on the fort were repulsed. There was a flight in various directions. The Boers charged; four came in our direction riding red horses, five in another direction, six in another. They fired on the Zulu with their guns. Our men hid in antbear holes, under antheaps while others hid themselves under heaps of corpses. Men were shot who were already dead. I found that as many as thirty elders from our tribe alone had been killed.[6]

The Zulu had, in fact, charged four times in great waves. The Boer cannons and muskets carved swathes through the glistening bodies, and on each occasion the line had wavered and broken before the wagons were reached. What Ndlela lacked in guile he made up for in courage. Each time, he rallied his men with challenges and exhortations for another dash to the wagons. By the blazing mid-morning, bodies lay in heaps amid the long, still grass, and the Boers' guns were almost too hot to handle. Then, with his ammunition running low, Pretorius unleashed the cavalry. As the wagons parted and the horses thundered out, the slaughter commenced. Warriors leapt into the Ncome or scrambled down the sides of the *donga* in an attempt to flee, only to find themselves in deeper peril. From the banks, the Boers picked off their targets methodically and mercilessly. Some Zulu tried to hide themselves among the reeds, others submerged holding their breath.

A year later, Adulphe Delegorgue, a French naturalist who travelled with sympathy among both Zulu and Boer, came upon the spot and found piles of whitened bones and skulls:

It was these same fiery black warriors, tainted with the blood of white women, whose bones we had found. They who had been without mercy asked for none. Once discovered, they knew that death was inevitable but, obeying the instinct of self-preservation, they dived underwater until forced to the surface, where their heads were immediately shattered by the avenging bullets of the Boers.[7]

Carcasses of another sort litter the site today. Sixty-four wagons, drawn up in a circle in imitation of Pretorius's laager, were painstakingly cast in steel, blown over with bronze and set in concrete on the banks of the Ncome in 1988. It is a typically bizarre and barren example of white South African triumphalism – made to endure but already doomed. Few visitors venture off the main Vryheid–Dundee road, twelve miles down a rutted track in northern Natal, and the place still celebrated annually by Afrikaner nationalists as the site of their delivery from heathendom has a desolate, abandoned air. However, scientific experts have given an assurance that the bronze-steel wagons will last for at least two hundred years.

At first it seemed a disaster rather than a catastrophe. Dingane had lost many of his best fighting men – up to three thousand had died, for not a single foe – and the capital was lost, but he had his fall-back position prepared. When the Boers reached Emgungundlovu four days later, the once-grand Place of the Elephant had been burned to the ground and no living thing remained. Among the aloes on kwaMatiwane, they found the remains of Retief and his companions.

While Dingane retreated northwards with the main body of the kraal's population and cattle, the *amabutho* were ordered to decoy and harass the *kommando*. On one occasion, a group of Boers was drawn into an ambush in which they lost five men, their first deaths in the campaign. However, the Zulu continued to take high casualties, and the Boers rounded up about five thousand cattle. At this stage, evidently believing that he had broken Zulu power, Pretorius started to withdraw to the Tugela.

Dingane set up a new kraal near present-day Nongoma, across the Black Mfolozi and about fifty miles north-east of his ruined capital. Here his hopes were revived by news of the British warning to the Boers to quit Natal. 'Now I shall be able to make all right,' he rejoiced. 'Tell the English government to assist me and send the Boers out of the country.'[8] But the English government was in no position to send anyone out of the country. On hearing of the Ncome battle, the British had sent a formal protest, regretting 'the slaughter of the Zulus and the unwarranted invasion of their country,' and warning that any similar aggression in future would be 'followed by the strongest marked displeasure'.[9] It sounded an empty threat and it was. When Captain Henry Jervis, the new garrison commander at Port Natal, strove to convince the Boers that they remained Crown subjects, they replied that this was clearly nonsense, as they were outside the colony. Then they selected a spot in fine, high country about fifty miles north-west of the port and started to build their new capital, which they called Pietermaritzburg.

Jervis did succeed, however, in bringing about an *indaba* between Boer leaders and a group of Dingane's *izinduna* at which a basis for peace was agreed in principle. The trekkers were to be given the land south of the Tongati river – which lay roughly half-way between the Tugela and Port Natal – while the Zulus would return Retief's arms, horses and all stolen cattle and sheep. Until this issue was resolved, the Zulus were to remain north of the Tugela.

Dingane was not one to worry overmuch about promises and had no intention of observing this pact. But the deal struck at Port Natal in March 1839 introduced him to the European version of realpolitik which, he discovered, was every bit as ruthless as his own. For the first time the Zulu had, in European terms, formally renounced rights over a large area of Natal. From there, control over events slipped rapidly from Dingane's hands. It had been his intention to shift the nucleus of the kingdom away from the threat to the south and towards the north. The key to this strategy was the Swazi kingdom, and there he had sent three *amabutho*, the

Mbelebele, the Imkulutshane and the Nomdayana, to occupy and settle the country. They, however, managed to establish just one kraal before the Swazi attacked and drove them out.

Loyalty to the king started, at last, to waver. Through these disasters, Dingane's surviving brother, Mpande, had remained at his homestead in south Zululand. In the ten years since Dingane had put their other siblings to death, Mpande had served him unstintingly. Now, however, word came from the king that Mpande must abandon his southern comforts and join the north-ward migration. Loath to obey, Mpande also suspected that his life would no longer be secure if he was at Dingane's side in these troubled times. To what extent disaffected elders had starting rally-ing to Mpande we cannot be sure. Evidently, however, his sus-picions were well founded. It is said that his guardian angel, Ndlela, who had saved him before, discovered that Dingane meant to kill Mpande and warned him through a messenger named Matunjana:

Ndlela said: 'Matunjana, the Zulu nation will not survive if Mpande dies, for he has fathered children, while Dingane, like Shaka, has none. Mpande will save the Zulu nation from crumbling.' Matunjana then went off to carry the message. He said to Mpande: 'On no account come to Dingane. You will be killed. Ndlela says, "Cross the river, and go to the Boers." So that when Ndlela has died because of what he has done for you, you will care for his orphaned children.'[10]

While Dingane was still preoccupied with his misadventures, Mpande decamped across the Tugela with elders, warriors, women and children. As the news spread, others flocked to join him. What had started as an individual act of self-preservation became an exodus: demoralized and fearful in the wake of Dingane's failure, the Zulu people were doing what they had always done, *konza*'ing, or submitting to a new leader who appeared to offer better pros-pects of protection. From that point Dingane's cause was lost.

An estimated seventeen thousand people crossed into Natal that October of 1839, in a movement known as *ukudabuka kwegoda* – 'the breaking of the rope' (that bound the nation)[11]. It signalled the onset of the first Zulu civil war.

Mpande was an improbable revolutionary. Dismissed by his more ambitious brothers as too feeble-minded to be dangerous, he was enormously fat, had been almost totally idle since Dingane's accession, and was seen as a weak, rather contemptible figure. It is not an impression that bears scrutiny. As the historian, Shula Marks, has pointed out, it must have taken a shrewdness akin to genius for a brother to have survived the regimes of both Shaka and Dingane.

Further virtues would emerge during the long reign of the Zulu Claudius. Energy was never one of them, however, and it was with some reluctance that Mpande was mobilized against Dingane. Brought before the Volksraad, the Boers' ruling council in Pieter-maritzburg, on 15 October, all he requested was land south of Tugela, between the Umvoti and Umhlali, where he might live with his people, free from the half-brother who, he readily agreed, was a bloodthirsty tyrant.

Pretorius, however, was not going to miss the opportunity that had fallen into his lap. So long as the British maintained diplomatic contact with Dingane, the threat of an Anglo-Zulu axis could not be discounted. Dingane's destruction and replacement with a pro-Boer puppet had become a priority. Mpande, it was clear to Pretorius, was the ideal candidate.

A Boer embassy attended Mpande at his new kraal on 26 October, proclaiming him the 'Reigning Prince of the Emigrant Zulus' pending his accession as Dingane's successor. The rest of the envoys' message was less sweet-sounding. Mpande was advised that the land he was presently occupying would soon be required for the many Afrikaner colonists now on their way to Natal. In order to secure a place for himself on the other side of the Tugela, he should raise an *impi* 'for action against our general foe'. More-over, the envoys added, on Mpande's death, his successor would be chosen 'subject to our approval'. In the meantime, 'war, cruelty or faithlessness towards our government' would be avenged.[12]

Any lingering constraint on the Boers was removed by the with-drawal of the British from Natal in December. Napier had been forced to admit the failure of his efforts to cut off supplies of arms and ammunition, and his small garrison had been 'of no avail in protecting the native tribes'.[13] As the British sailed, the Boers celebrated and, in the words of the French traveller Delegorgue, 'decided to take immediate advantage of the favourable circum-stances'.[14]

Even from the far north of Zululand, Dingane could see the dangerous drift of events. He had returned Retief's arms, horses and a small number of cattle, but demands from the Volksraad that he pay penal reparations of some 14,000 head were becoming insistent. Dambusa and another *induna* were dispatched as envoys to the Boers with two hundred beasts. Identified on his arrival as Dingane's chancellor and accused of instigating Retief's murder, Dambusa was promptly clapped in irons. A new *kommando* was raised to invade the Zulu country, accompanied by an *impi* of Mpande's men. Delegorgue thought it looked like 'a hunting expedition'. A new advance across the Tugela started on 18 January in two columns. Pretorius's force consisted of more than 400 armed men. Mpande had some 5000 warriors, commanded by Nongalaza ka Nondela. Few records exist of this expedition, but it is fairly clear that Pretorius had no intention of involving his men in combat unless absolutely necessary. Let the opposing Zulu armies slog it out; Pretorius's real interest was in vengeance – and plunder.

It is Pretorius who must bear responsibility for the shameful disposal of the Zulu envoys. Eleven days after crossing the Tugela, the Boers reached the site where the Ncome battle had been fought a year earlier and it dawned on Dambusa and his fellow envoy why they had been brought along in fetters. They were arraigned before a military court at which Mpande, pressed into service for the prosecution, testified to their many crimes. Dambusa held himself erect, admitted all that was alleged against him, and professed his readiness to die. But he asked that his companion be spared as he was blameless. Pretorius was unmoved. He sentenced both to die by firing squad, then urged them to save their souls by turning to God. Dambusa replied that Dingane was his only master and, if the white man's God existed, then He would surely recognize one who had done his duty.

Delegorgue, who likened this episode to a revolutionary tribunal during the Terror, watched appalled as the two envoys were lined up before a firing squad. Dambusa's companion died at the first volley, but Dambusa was only wounded.

Then, as calmly as ever, and in spite of his suffering, he arose and stood steadfastly facing the guns, until the second round of shots rang out and he fell to the ground. These men know how to die, I thought, and I went away full of admiration, but a prey to a thousand regrets, for this act of Boer justice seemed to me despicable.[15]

The *impis* of Dingane and Mpande clashed among the Maqongqo hills near Magudu in the far north of Zululand. Dingane was evidently in retreat and had already abandoned his second capital, but his men still gave a good account of themselves as Zulu fought Zulu. The tide was turned when Dingane's warriors started to cross over to Mpande. A thousand men are estimated to have died on either side, and a Boer who later visited Nongalaza's camp estimated that he had 1200 wounded. Once again, however, Ndlela had failed, and this time the outcome was to be fatal for his master.

Although Pretorius made a show of trying to capture Dingane as he fled north across the Pongolo into Swazi country, the purpose that underlay the expedition now became clear. The *kommando* started a round-up. In part the booty was legitimate spoils of war: around 30,000 Zulu cattle returned with the Boers to Natal. So also, however, did up to a thousand Zulu children. They were supposedly 'apprentices', orphans of war who would be assigned to a family until the age of around twenty in order to learn a trade. In reality, they were slaves. Delegorgue noted the shamefaced way in which one Boer man confessed: 'If it was up to me, I would not have them at all, but what will my wife say if I do not take some home? It is difficult to find servants in Natal.'[16]

His Zulu foes disposed of, Pretorius turned to his Zulu friends. Mpande's delight at being told that he could now assume the title, King of the Zulus, was tempered a few days later by the news that his kingdom, already reduced by half, was to be halved again. Pretorius, as commandant of the South African Society of Port Natal, had announced the 'seizure' of all the land south of the Black Mfolozi.

Dingane did not last long across the Pongolo. The despot whose court had been synonymous with style and luxury was now a fugitive in enemy territory, abandoned by all but a few of his most faithful followers. One of these was his oldest servant, Ndlela, who had served as Dingane's military commander since his accession. Whatever his failings as a general, Ndlela had not been found wanting in loyalty.

It was in the order of things, however, that loyalty was taken for granted and, although adrift in the wilderness with this old retainer, Dingane had him killed without compunction. The reason had nothing to do with military incompetence. Recalling that Ndlela had persuaded him to spare Mpande all those years before, the king said, 'You were harbouring a snake for me.'[17] Then Ndlela was put to death. He had expected no less, and no doubt met his end stoically. His place in Zulu history was secure; singlehandedly, he had ensured the survival of Senzangakona's house. Mpande honoured his trust and took care of Ndlela's children, providing them with homesteads of their own.

There are a number of accounts of Dingane's death, some fanciful. For years the Boers took comfort in a report that he was captured by hostile people who humiliated him before slowly torturing him to death. The simplest version is probably the closest to the truth: in a land where his name was feared and loathed, he threw himself on the mercy of the Nyawo people, a sub-clan of the Swazi, who decided that he was too dangerous a client to tolerate; he was murdered by three members of the ruling house, but his body was buried with the deference due a king.

Dingane had ruled for eleven years. During the early part of his reign, the kingdom acquired a superficial splendour while losing much of the vigour and direction that Shaka had given it. By the end, it was in ruins. The Zulu domain had shrunk, and an overweening neighbour was at the door. The nation's will and capacity for self-defence had been sapped. By any criteria, Dingane had been a disastrous ruler. His memory is reviled not only by whites but his own people too, among whom his treachery towards the Cele and Qadi is seen as no less heinous than the murder of Retief. Magema ka Magwaza, the Zulu historian, wrote: 'Although a person in form, he had the heart of a dog and the nature of a witch. Dingane was truly like a poisonous snake.'[18]

This is harsh and simplistic. The second Zulu king was a complex and, in the end, rather pathetic character. His instinct was to turn power to the pursuit of pleasure, rather than conquest; war was an unwelcome companion to the beauty and ceremony in which he delighted. In a less testing time, he might have been fondly remembered as a jovial and pleasure-seeking ruler who indulged his people; but his weakness and indecision were fatal in the face of outside challenge. Now the Zulu needed neither a sun king, nor a warrior king, but a healing father able to bind up their wounds. Fortunately, they had found one.

Mpande's reign lasted thirty-two years, the longest of the Zulu kings and, perhaps, the happiest. Apart from a brief, bloody struggle, midway through his rule, over who would succeed him, Zululand remained at peace. By now the kingdom's independence was limited by the white presence that continued to burgeon in Natal, but Mpande was naturally placid. After two decades of almost constant turmoil, Zulu society was able to rediscover its soul. For this, Mpande is still remembered with gratitude and affection.

His name meant 'the Root' and, enhanced by his enormous bulk, it came to represent solidness and dependability. Unlike his predecessors, Mpande was a traditional and fecund Bantu patriarch. In all, he had at least twenty-nine sons and more than thirty daughters by his twenty or so wives. His bearing had none of the innate arrogance of great men among the Zulu; indeed, he could seem quite humble. The French traveller, Delegorgue, thought he had great natural dignity and quoted a missionary as calling him, 'a Caffir gentleman'.

His first duty, in the aftermath of what had amounted to civil war, was reunion and reconciliation. Given the nature of the Zulu – quick to dispute, equally quick to forgive – this was not in itself a great task, but it required magnanimity. When the remnants of Dingane's forces straggled back to their homesteads and kraals, they were at first ostracized and insulted by the term 'Ndlela's arse'. Mpande quickly put a stop to this and ordered that former foes should meet to *uxoxa impi*, to talk and boast of their deeds as comrades of old.

The new king was aged about forty-four when he assumed power, having been some eleven years Shaka's junior. In recent years, he had lived in the south near present-day Eshowe. However, his new kraal, Nodwengu, was sited in central Zululand, between the White and Black Mfolozi rivers, reflecting the steady retreat towards the north. While Shaka had moved his capital to be closer to the whites, Dingane and Mpande had each moved theirs to be farther away. Mpande's highly successful foreign policy was founded on maintaining a cordial but distant friendship with the whites, while keeping open a sphere of interest to the north, among the Ronga chiefdoms around Delagoa Bay.

It helped that Pretorius's self-proclaimed annexation of the land between the Tugela and the Black Mfolozi was never ratified by treaty. The Tugela was now officially acknowledged as the border between Natal and Zululand, and would remain so. But what had once been a wholly Zulu domain, in which a handful of traders lived in one sector under sufferance, had now been partitioned. One half remained wholly under the king's authority. In the other, Zulu-speaking exiles were to be increasingly torn between the demands of European rulers and the emotional ties of kinship and culture; at the same time, other African migrants were gradually drawn into the region by stability and the prospect of wage-earning employment.

We need not concern ourselves here with the protracted bout of arm-wrestling that saw the Boer republic of Natalia become the crown colony of Natal in 1845. Both Boer and Briton had, however, made distinct and contrasting impressions and, up until the Anglo-Zulu war at least, there was little question which of the two most Zulus preferred. For all that Natal's first whites, the old English traders, were by and large ruthless opportunists, their code of rough egalitarianism held an implicit acceptance of native ways. Men like Fynn, Cane, Ogle and, later, the 'white chief' John Dunn, lived like Zulus themselves and were regarded as such. 'They all had a number of wives and ordinary native kraals,' recalled Dinya ka Zokozwayo, a Cele. 'The sexual intercourse with these wives took place on the Zulu plan; that is, any woman required would be sent for. The man would not go to each woman's hut, carrying his blanket with him, as less important men are in the habit of doing.'[19]

The Boers, in contrast, held themselves aloof. They had transported their entire way of life as well as their families from the Cape; and the rigid Calvinism they observed brooked no social, let alone sexual, intercourse with heathen. However, it was not for their separateness that they were disliked and feared, but for their cruelty and contempt for native people. In a society in which summary executions were commonplace, such objections sound perverse but it was less death that the Zulu objected to than the indignity of a whipping with a *sjambok*, the insults, forced labour and lack of respect for chiefs. Stuart records one old man who was indignant at being called a 'crow', and another who complained that 'Zulus governed people with a rod of iron, but as soon as they conquered people they treated them with dignity.'[20] According to Dinya ka Zokozwayo:

Boers would take hold of a man by his headring and pull it off for nothing, and beat him. They liked having young boys and girls to work for them. Natives used to build in out-of-the-way places to get out of the way of the Boers. They would think nothing of halting beside maize gardens and half-filling their their wagons with maize in spite of the women's remonstrances. Any man interfering would be skinned with the whip.[21]

For their part, Boers were alarmed to see their 'Promised Land' being resettled by blacks who had scattered during the reigns of Shaka and Dingane. Mainly they came from the south, to where some Zulu-speaking clans had fled from Natal between 1820 and 1824 and where they had intermarried with other groups. Now these people were back, reclaiming ancestral lands and intending to stay. To the north, Mpande made no effort to restrict migrant movements. Between 1840 and 1845 many thousands of people crossed from Zululand to Natal. Boer farmers complained of 'squatters' and, occasionally, resorted to vigilante action against them. As early as 1841, because of 'complaints that the Kafirs begin to multiply amongst us', the Boer parliament, the Volksraad in Pietermaritzburg, attempted to establish the first black 'homeland' for the 'surplus' black population, between the Mzimvubu and Mtamvuna rivers. On this occasion, the plan came to nothing.

Over the next few years, the Boer influence waned as many trekkers decamped once more. Some stayed in the fertile districts of northern Natal, around towns with names like Vryheid (freedom), Utrecht and Paulpietersburg. Others crossed into the nascent republics of Transvaal and Orange Free State. Until emigration schemes started being organized from Britain to Natal, from 1849, Afrikaners composed the majority of the white population. Thereafter, Natal became and would remain the most English of South Africa's provinces.

9

A WHILE IN ELYSIUM

Mpande endeavoured to respect God, knowing that
the people he ruled did not belong to him, but to his
father, Senzangakona. He knew that his father was
responsible for them to God. Mpande ruled until he
was given milk to drink, ruling well.[1]

Magema ka Magwaza, Zulu historian,
1922

Weakness was the strength of Mpande's regime. Despite Shaka's
best efforts, the kingdom had never been entirely monolithic. Now
an era of mild rule led to a revival of chiefly authority. For, remarkably, Mpande first allowed his powers to be constrained and then
fostered the growth of a grass-roots tribal democracy. The day of
the Zulu tyrants was over.

Superficially, the kingdom remained much as before. Mpande
recruited *amabutho* as his predecessors had done, and the military
system continued to be the central organizing institution of the
nation; by 1850 the army numbered 35,000–40,000 men – larger
than it had been under Shaka. Mpande looked far more a king
than Dingane, and was a figure of ponderous dignity and calm.
He still symbolized to the Zulu their identity and the annual gathering for the first-fruits ceremony was as dazzling a show of national
unity as ever. Although placid by nature, Mpande made occasional

use of his authority to order executions and, indeed, when once taxed about this by a white official, retorted: 'You cannot rule a Zulu without killing him.'[2]

A number of factors abetted the limitation of royal power. One was the new constraints on the king's capacity to wage war. Those two old theatres of operation, Natal and the Highveld, had been put off limits by white settlement. Although the Ronga chiefdoms and the Swazi remained possible targets for raiding, the latter at least were not easy prey. Warriors did not exactly beat their assegais into ploughshares but the emphasis on the regiments' activities turned from warfare to labour, usually chores for the king, such as building new *amakhanda* or collecting tribute. Devolution was assisted by Mpande's own personality and his reputation as a simpleton; it is unlikely that he would have been accepted by the increasingly powerful regional chiefs as an autocrat, even if he had aspired to the role. A few chiefdoms, notably the powerful Qwabe, no longer recognized the paramountcy of the Zulu king; since Dingane's alienation of Nqeto, the Qwabe had reverted to the conviction that theirs was the senior line – 'the reedbed of the Mhlatuze' – a view which some continued to hold well into the twentieth century.[3]

Above all, however, devolution was a symptom of the flexibility which the Zulu ruling establishment has generally demonstrated at times of stress. The forces of fission and integration which characterized early political organization had been merely dormant and were at work again. Amid the instability that follows any civil war, it now behoved all rulers, from the lowliest homestead chief to the king himself, to heed the wishes of their people. As one saying had it: 'The people respect their chief, but the chief ought to respect his people.'

The tight-knit clan organization of old was becoming blurred. Members of one clan might be scattered across the country, having attached themselves and their relatives to the kinship groups of different chiefs while retaining their own clan names. Under Mpande and his successor, Cetshwayo, the ties that bound these chiefdoms into a federation were loosened. As always, freedom had its price: jealousies, intrigues and rivalries burgeoned, throwing up factions and divisions so that at times it seemed the only thing binding the Zulus together was their language. Beneath these tensions, however, a system of consensual leadership was being forged, and there remained a capacity to unite in the face of a common enemy.

Mpande made no new laws without the approval of the leading chiefs. A great council was held every year, usually after the first-fruits ceremony in December. The anthropologist, Max Gluckman, has well described the conduct and tone of such an *indaba*: the king would put the issue before the council, but speak last himself so that no one would be afraid to express his own opinion; he would not put himself in a position where he might be contradicted, although he might have told his closest councillors his own views; no councillor would express a strong opinion, but would rather introduce his points with some oblique phrase deferring to the king. The king ended the discussion and generally adopted the views of the majority.

Under the legal code, most offences against individuals other than the king could be settled by restitution or a fine. Adultery and rape were usually punished by a fine. Murder was punishable by death, but might be redeemed by the culprit paying cattle to the victim's family and undergoing ritual purification. Mpande's successor, Cetshwayo, explained it thus:

A murderer is punished by death; but if a man kills another, and runs away for a time, he may be forgiven. The people interested have their hearts softened if he has been wandering about the hills for some time.[4]

As ever, witchcraft was the most perilous charge, for it could be made against an individual purely out of malice and there was no sure defence. Fynn had estimated in Shaka's time that about a third of those so accused had actually tried to use magic, either in the hope of gaining advantage or to harm a foe. Under Mpande and Cetshwayo, fewer alleged *abathakathi* were executed; Cetshwayo was sceptical about the ability of diviners to 'smell out' witches and to prevent executions he started sending accused people to other kraals where they might start a new life. Only if the charges of witchcraft followed them to two or three kraals might they be put to death.

Virtually all offences against the king were still liable to be fatal. Most serious was the act of disrespect, which amounted to treason. The 'almost holy awe' for authority noted by Bryant remained paramount. One individual who was normally exempt from this stricture was the *imbongi* or royal praise-singer. He functioned additionally as a kind of court jester and had a degree of licence to remind listeners of the king's shortcomings as well as his greatness. Mpande's *imbongi*, Magolwane ka Mkatini, the most renowned of all praise-singers, took candour a step too far in the end. When the executioners came for him, he ordered them to stand off, arranged a feast and beer-drink and, when he had had his fill, declaimed Mpande's praises for hours until his voice gave out and then said: 'Now you can kill me.'[5]

The nature of the Zulu had always been blithe. Consciousness was of the moment and, to a lesser extent, the past, but never the future. Thus death always came, blessedly, as a surprise and daily life was largely free of fear. In the peaceful era of Mpande's reign his people experienced something new, however, which was stability. The Frenchman, Delegorgue, recorded a Zulu idyll that contrasts starkly with the accounts of earlier travellers like Nathaniel Isaacs. Delegorgue's depiction of the Zulu, their dignity, their manners, their intelligence and physical fineness, came close to incarnating the nineteenth-century European conception of the noble savage. The Zulu were 'the French of south-eastern Africa', he reported. In one lyrical passage he celebrated tribal pageantry:

Our clothes are constantly buttoned up; theirs reveal and conceal their bodies as they move; in rapid action, their floating tails, their widowbird plumes, stream out behind them, suggesting that the individual who wears them is imbued with the spirit of long-maned horses and the courage of lions.

In battle, their songs and their movements combine with their appearance to produce an effect so terrifying that even the bravest are momentarily filled with fear. I will confess that I likened these black men to the fearful devils with which the good Fathers endeavoured to terrify my adolescence. There is, however, nothing repulsive about these warriors. On the contrary, they are the finest soldiers imaginable.[6]

We do not need to share Delegorgue's youthful romanticism to identify Mpande's reign as an all-too-brief golden age. The pageantry and élan remained, but now in tranquillity. The atmosphere of the period was captured by another young visitor from Europe, the English artist, George Angas, who travelled in Zululand in 1847 and recorded the kingdom in its idyll. Like Delegorgue, Angas was deeply impressed by the beauty of his surroundings, and the harmony as well as the pageantry of the society which he observed. His studies remain among the most vivid and moving pictures of African tribal life before the European conquest.

The peacetime duties of men were, to say the least, untaxing. Agriculture was the province of women, and herding that of boys, although the paterfamilias took great pleasure in surveying the fruits of others' labours, gazing out at the evening hour over his fields and cattle. After ablutions, the day might start, as it would probably end, with a smoke from a cannabis pipe, although at this early hour it was intended to clear the head rather than intoxicate. Thereafter, unless there was hunting to be done, or perhaps a fence to be made, the day might be spent in other male company, drinking *tshwala* and passing snuff while discussing an issue of the moment.

Men did take a keen interest in matters of trade and regularly made expeditions to the Ronga country around Delagoa Bay where the most prized pelts were to be obtained. Bikwayo ka Noziwawa, a Tuli, described making such trips during the 1860s to buy genet skins for warriors' dancing girdles; leopard and otter skins for headbands whose velvety thickness provided something of the protection of a helmet; blue skins of the samango monkey for the flaps worn over the ears; cloth for the *isigodlo*; beads, calabashes, gourds, ornamental sticks and ostrich feathers. These would be paid for in cattle, and borne back to Zululand, not by Zulus, but by the local people.

Like portering, cultivation was regarded by a Zulu man as beneath him. Hoeing, sowing, reaping and carrying water and wood were women's work. Habit died hard. Much later, Zulu men worked willingly enough in apartheid's mines but declined what was termed 'coolie work', like cane-cutting. To this day, it is common to see Zulu women swaying up a hillside path like slow-moving gazelles, long and heavy bundles of wood seeming to be precariously balanced on their heads.

Each married woman had her own hut and a field in which she cultivated maize and vegetables for her household. The greatest misfortune that could befall her was that she should be childless. Then a *sangoma* would be consulted to diagnose whether she was the victim of witchcraft; if her barrenness continued, she might be returned to her parents, or have her child-bearing duties taken on by a sister, in which case she remained with her husband. Few men had more than two wives, mainly for economic reasons, but also because, according to one source, 'many wives would have the effect of a love charm – to have intercourse with so many, a man's back would break and he would find an early grave.'[7] Visits to the husband's hut were rotated among wives – quite strictly if he wanted to keep a happy homestead and prevent jealousy. A ditty which was sung by wives complaining of neglect went:

> O! We love our husband,
> Why does he sleep only in one house?
> Look at the husband who sleeps in one house![8]

Mpande was less successful in maintaining peace in his household than in his kingdom according to one contemporary, who recalled his being occasionally scolded by one or other of his two-score wives:

She would have some cause for grievance, and she would lash out at him in the wildest manner, the reason being that she wanted him to consort with her. This was due to jealousy – others were 'called', she not. She might in her fury even say, 'Let the king take me and put me to death.'[9]

To this day traditional Zulu society remains strongly patriarchal and, in rural areas, a woman may still be subject to male guardianship. A big step forward was made, however, in the semi-independent KwaZulu 'homeland' in 1981 with an Act which places Zulu women in almost the same legal position as white women.

Another durable relic of the past is the custom known as *hlonipha*, a system of respectfulness shown by a woman to her male in-laws. She would not address directly her husband's father, nor would she eat in his presence. Both before and after giving birth, she would be isolated and subject to various taboos: as she was unclean she could not, for example, drink curds lest she bring down some pestilence on the cattle of the kraal.

As so often in male-dominated societies, a special reverence was accorded the woman who had attained the status and seniority of a matriarch; we have seen how maternal figures wielded power and influence in the Shakan age. On a cultural level, matriarchs were the trustees of folklore and the oral traditions; the wisdom and mythology of ages past was learned by children at the knees of their grandmothers.

In a land blessed by sunshine and relatively free of disease, children stayed naked until the age of about eight and grew strong and robust. From the outset they mixed mainly with others of the same sex and similar age. Spending days out herding, boys challenged one another to vigorous bouts of stick-fighting or games of spear-throwing in which, for example, a gourd was set rolling down a hill with the aim of impaling it with an assegai. Life out in the open was a carefree affair. At home, though, children were required to submit totally to their parents. Etiquette – of which there was a great deal – honesty, and respect for elders were learnt the hard way. The ideals of conduct cultivated by this discipline were manliness and civility among boys, and submissiveness and cleanliness among girls. Physical punishment helped to instil these traits, but we do well to bear in mind that the authority of the father was also based on spiritual grounds, for he was destined to be the most immediate and powerful of the ancestors to be invoked in due course by his children.

Sexual awareness existed from an early age, and licence to indulge in *hlobonga*, or external intercourse, was generally given in the teenage years when a girl was advised by a mature woman, '*Phumuzani abafokazi*' – to, literally, give the men a rest. Despite this injunction, a youth was expected to obtain the permission of a girl's parents to *hlobonga* with her. Prostitution was unknown, but a traveller offered hospitality at a kraal for a night might find a sexual partner among the comforts of the road.

Rarely would his host's hospitality have extended to meat. The mainstay of most meals was *amasi*, or curds of milk, eaten with vegetables and maize. A beast was slaughtered only on special occasions. These naturally included welcomes for honoured guests and ceremonies such as weddings and funerals, but also sacrifices and acts of reconciliation between feuding kraals. Then an animal would be cut up, the prized cuts of the sirloin and the head going to the senior men. Women were given the ribs and children the offal and offcuts. No part was unworthy to be eaten. The choicest parts were roasted over a fire, the tougher ones stewed. Then, while children slept, the men would gather round the fire, the cannabis pipe would circulate again and stories of great deeds would begin.

Fastidious care was given to washing. Water coursed abundantly off the highlands to the sea and the nearby river or stream was a forum for ablution and fellowship in much the same way that communal baths were for the Romans. In the sweltering midsummer, streams became a refuge where all society gathered, lovers to dally on the banks, herdboys to play.

There is dispute over whether the Zulu ever actually believed in a Supreme Being, or whether, as is more likely, the concept was introduced by Christianity. Appeals to the spirit world were directed to one's ancestors and the shades of revered kinsmen as a process of communion rather than worship. Beyond that, the image of creation was rooted in a reed-bed from which *Unkulunkulu*, or the First One, was held to have sprung (reeds were a symbol of primacy). The notion of God, Lord-of-the-Sky, or *Umvelinqangi*, followed on the heels of the missionaries. It then acquired a potent force, seeming to confirm a divine origin of the Zulu clan, as the name of its founding father, Zulu, meant 'of the sky' or heavens. In time, Christianity did take a hold on the Zulu, especially on those living in Natal. But among rural folk, God always remained a remote presence; it was the shades, or ancestors, who were seen as all-present and all-loving.

Dreams were the messages of the ancestors. In many instances, they still are. One modern researcher was told by an informant: 'The dreams show the truth, because the shades never deceive their children.' Another said: 'We see them very closely and hear them saying things to us.'[10] A failure to dream gave rise to anxiety. Diviners were the ancestors' servants, able to interpret dreams as well as cure ailments and smell out *abathakathi*, or evil-doers. Paradoxically, given their subservient role in daily life, the majority of diviners were women. Diviners were held in awe and, although some modern day practitioners undoubtedly exploit the credulous, they continue to have a large following. Many Zulu Christians and professional people still set store by the herbal remedies and dream counselling of the *sangoma*.

All wrongs were attributed to *abathakathi* – and no evil was beyond their capacity to perform. Premature death, infertility, drought, disease, injury – none had a natural cause. One authority on spiritual life, Axel-Ivar Berglund, has noted that the concepts of chance and luck, whether for good or ill, had no validity among the Zulus. Good came from the ancestors, evil from witches who were as likely as not to be dwelling in one's own kraal. As no misfortune might arise without cause, it was therefore necessary to locate a source to blame. Perhaps in this understanding of the sources of good and evil may be found an explanation for extremes of behaviour that sometimes baffle outsiders.[11]

A peace treaty between Mpande and Britain had formally demarcated the boundary between Zululand and Natal in October 1843. Zulu sovereignty and independence were recognized north of the Tugela and Buffalo rivers, while Mpande agreed to withdraw his remaining chiefs and kraals from Natal. Two years later, Natal was annexed to the Cape as an autonomous district of the colony. Finally, in 1856, Natal became a separate colony with a lieutenant-governor.

Stability in Natal caused a population explosion in what had once been a wasteland. A small established population of Zulu exiles was swelled by many thousands who flocked to the colony either as a land of opportunity or to reoccupy the lands they had abandoned during Shaka's conquests. In the main, they came from the south, from Faku's lands beyond the Mzimvubu river, with families and enlarged horizons: as refugees they had struggled, survived and, in some cases prospered; they had learned to live outside the kinship network. From a population of around eighty thousand in 1844, the number of so-called 'Natal natives' almost doubled in a decade. The tongue spoken by most of them was Zulu, but many were of Pondo or Bhaca origin. The cultural gulf between those on either side of the Tugela widened steadily from the 1840s onwards.

The question of how to enforce Her Majesty's writ over these new subjects in the 20,000 square miles of territory that had suddenly fallen to her was to throw up an intriguing experiment in colonial rule. However, as a first step towards establishing 'some salutary influence' over blacks, the authorities turned to two surviving members of the American mission.

Aldin Grout had abandoned Zululand in despair in 1842, driven out by Mpande who saw no benefit to be had from missionary influence. Thereafter, Grout prayed fervently for the destruction of the kingdom. It was an emotion shared by most missionaries, who came to identify closely with the advance of imperialism and white settlement. Newton Adams, on the other hand, was dubious about the value of making Zulu converts and preferred the idea of schooling their minds. From 1844, a sum of £300 a year was set aside from imperial funds for these two men to pursue their labours in Natal. Grout lived to see his prayers answered with the fall of the kingdom but Adams' pragmatic vision accomplished a good deal more in the nature of Christian love. Adams College, at Amanzimtoti, south of Durban, and high schools for boys and girls founded by the American mission, were for long the finest educational institutions to which blacks had access in Natal.

A high moral tone had been struck for dealing with blacks in the colony. Lord Stanley, the Colonial Secretary, insisted that there 'shall not be in the eye of the law any distinction of colour, origin, race or creed'.[12] But the new migrants who were starting to flow in to the new colony from the British Isles – at least 5000 arrived between 1849 and 1852 – were looking for cheap labour, not fellow citizens. Sir John Scott, an early governor of Natal, once reflected ruefully: 'It seems impossible for a body of white men to live in proximity to the coloured races without adopting the conviction that as the dominant people they have the right to command the services of the less civilized.'[13] Natal's policies towards blacks might at times have been characterized by a form of benevolent paternalism unusual in South Africa. Individual whites showed respect for, and an appreciation of, Zulu life and customs. But there was never any question of equality.

One man loomed over the affairs of Natal's black population to the end of the century and beyond it, almost as much as the shadow of Shaka. In some respects, Theophilus Shepstone might have served as a model for the benign paternalist among colonial servants. He extolled African virtues where negrophobes saw only savagery, defended tribal society when others sought to destroy it, and created a model for ruling aboriginal peoples that was widely admired and copied elsewhere in the empire. But Shepstone was no dewy-eyed idealist, and his motives were almost invariably self-serving. He would have survived among the Borgias and prospered with the Bourbons. Simple, broad features gave him the appearance of a butcher, but his real métier was for intrigue.[14]

His was an unlikely career for the son of a West Country pastor. Shepstone was born near Bristol in 1817 but was taken to South Africa in early childhood and grew up on the eastern frontier where, with a linguistic gift, he learned to speak excellent Xhosa and, later, Zulu. After serving in a number of posts in the Cape administration, he was given the influential job of diplomatic agent to the Natal tribes in 1845 when still aged only twenty-eight, and became the new colony's first secretary for native affairs.

Shepstone's task was a monumental one. He was expected to administer, and to prepare for the requirements of an industrial society, tens of thousands of 'Natal natives' still living in traditional society. He had to do so at no cost to the colonial exchequer and in the face of a new settler community outraged by the idea of leaving the black man to his own indolent devices when their crying need was for labour.

He made one invaluable early discovery. This was that the Africans of Natal still expected to be ruled by a *nkosi*. Accordingly, he installed himself as one. For many years it worked remarkably well. He proceeded to carve out an empire of his own in which he ruled as a great white chief, revelling in the pomp and mystique of his position, and encouraging his charges to think of him as 'Father of the People'. However, his sympathy with Africans and preservation of their culture extended only insofar as it sustained his own position and reputation. Once his imperialist convictions placed him on a collision course with the Zulu monarchy, he plotted the kingdom's downfall as pitilessly as any conqueror.

He was intensely secretive and the enigmatic aura which he cultivated, of the man versed in native lore, worked almost as effectively with whites as with blacks. Even when his reputation was highest, many members of the British establishment thought him distinctly rum – a sort of 'Afrikaner Talleyrand' as one put it. Like Cecil Rhodes, another extraordinary Englishman who had 'gone native' in South Africa, Shepstone never seemed quite to add up.

One of his first duties in Natal was to sit on a commission that laid the basis for African administration. The key provision was for the creation of a series of 'locations' in which Africans would live by traditional law, purged of its more draconian features, and under a chief answerable to Shepstone himself. There was no attempt to establish an education system beyond that run by the missionaries, and those Africans who aspired to emulate the white man's ways received short shrift from Shepstone. He actively discouraged those who were starting to take an interest in Christianity. Stuart noted in one of his notebooks: 'Shepstone favoured the raw native . . . he did not wish the native to rise to the higher civilization . . . He advocated a separation between Europeans and natives instead of promoting unity.'[15]

This then was the basis of what became known as 'the Shepstone system' of native policy. In fact, as Shepstone himself acknowledged, it was hardly a policy at all. He simply 'took advantage of circumstances' to save the young colony expenditure. His success was based on his adoption of Shaka's tactics of divide and rule. To keep Natal's 'natives' in the requisite state of political weakness, Shepstone manipulated their differences, breaking down hereditary chiefdoms wherever possible and replacing troublesome incumbents with men amenable to his instructions. His assumption of kingly prerogative was breathtaking in its audacity. One of his decrees prohibited the celebration of the first-fruits rituals without his express permission.[16] Shaka had done no less himself.

The American writer, Donald Morris, has given us an irresistible portrait of Shepstone at his work:

A chieftain, summoned to an *indaba*, could expect no casual encounter. Shepstone would be seated on a throne-like chair, and from his shaded eminence would parley with the man squatting in the dusty sunlight before him. Shepstone would listen gravely, take snuff in native fashion, nod sagely. When he spoke his rhetoric was that of a tribal elder and his allusions those of a Bantu savant. His edicts were delivered with the awesome finality of the Judgment Seat, and no matter how petty the agenda had been, a native who had consulted with Shepstone knew that he had been in a Conference.[17]

Whitehall's insistence that the new colony was to be self-supporting was applied to blacks as well as whites and gave rise to complaints by Shepstone that he had been set 'the Egyptian task of making bricks without straw'. In 1849, chiefs in the Natal locations were told that every man would have to pay a tax of seven shillings a year for each hut in his household 'towards the government of the country under which they enjoy all the privileges and amenities of security to life and property, and peace'.

The concept of tax was foreign but not entirely alien. Chiefs had been required to demonstrate loyalty to Shaka or Dingane in a concrete form and the hut tax at least took the size of a man's family, the number of his wives, as a yardstick of wealth. Shepstone noted with relief that the tax was paid 'cheerfully and readily'.

The blacks, it had to be grudgingly admitted by most colonists, were not bad citizens – upright but respectful, law-abiding and quite astonishingly honest. Nevertheless, they succeeded in constantly reducing the settlers to purple rage. Quite simply, they would only work until the needs of the moment were met. Time and time again, a farmer would employ a man who worked willingly for a month or two, but then collected his wages and disappeared. Back on the location, he would husband his resources until new needs arose. His sins were thus doubled; he was an unreliable worker *and* he was a poor consumer.

Through the 1850s, the pressures grew on Shepstone from the rapidly growing settler population to break up the traditional system which enabled blacks, in the words of a colonial commission, 'to follow idle, wandering and pastoral lives or habits, instead of settling down to fixed industrial pursuits'. The kaffirs, it added, should be 'ordered to go decently clothed'. This would have the dual benefit of forcing them to seek work, and raising customs revenues through clothing sales. It had become necessary to 'destroy the power and independence of the kaffir chiefs'.[18] In 1854, there was further criticism of the Shepstonian system from a Whitehall visitor who complained that the 'savages' were being 'dangerously indulged', adding 'they have made little or no progress in civilization or Christianity since they were taken under the wing of the British government.'[19]

To such attacks Shepstone responded with two incontrovertible arguments that won the day. Whatever the faults of his policy, peace prevailed in Natal and the black inhabitants were contributing substantially to the Treasury – if not in labour, then through the hut tax. In the six years to 1855, it had raised £10,000.

These benefits, Shepstone could have added, had been achieved against a background of turmoil elsewhere. Britain was digging itself into a hole in South Africa. It had pursued the Boers across the Drakensberg, annexed their new territory, the Orange Free State, and then fought them in what was to be only the first of many Anglo-Boer battles, at Boomplaats in 1848. British troops had also been involved in two small-scale conflicts against the Sotho and, between 1846 and 1853, two very much uglier wars against the Xhosa on the eastern frontier. What had been regarded as the most savage part of the country had meanwhile become a sea of tranquillity.

10

TWO BULLS, ONE PEN

Mpande had ruled for sixteen untroubled years when there occurred the event that blighted his later life and his legacy. Like most of the saddest stories, it was about parental love and loss. But the effects went beyond mere personal tragedy. The succession struggle of 1856 handed to the kingdom's enemies the instruments with which to bring about its downfall. Chief among those foes was to be Theophilus Shepstone.

Devolution of authority had checked despotism but done nothing to remove the real flaw of the Zulu political system: the principle of succession had not evolved beyond the bare-knuckle stage. 'Our house did not gain the kingship by being appointed to sit on a mat,' Mpande once said. 'Our house gained the kingship by stabbing with the assegai.'[1] The first three kings had seized power by force; the fourth would be no exception. But now the situation was further complicated: whereas Shaka and Dingane had no children, Mpande had more than sixty.

The brew of dynastic chaos was laced with confusion over the status of Mpande's numerous wives. It was rare that a chief's first spouse produced his heir. That usually fell to the so-called 'great wife', a high-born woman who was wed relatively late in the chief's life, possibly to reduce the risk of usurpation by a vigorous princeling. In Mpande's house, however, no such demarcation had been made. Among his wives were at least two by whom, as was customary, he had sired children for his less fecund siblings. He had also taken more than twenty wives of his own choice, who fell in and out of his affections, but no official 'great wife'. His first wife, Ngqumbazi, had genealogical advantages, being a chief's daughter of the well-connected Zungu clan. The eldest of their four children, Cetshwayo or 'the Slandered One', had many of the virtues of kingship. He was intelligent and capable, and he dreamed of restoring the Zulu to the greatness of the Shakan age. He looked the part too, a handsome man with a natural *gravitas* and proud bearing that commanded attention. Just over six feet tall, he was powerfully built with the heavy hams characteristic of the Zulu aristocracy.

Cetshwayo had been proclaimed by Mpande as his successor during their sojourn among the Boers in Natal. However, after the return to Zululand and the establishment of the new royal kraal at Nodwengu, Mpande's rather fickle favours started to fall on another of his sons.

According to the oral sources, Mbuyazi was an even more imposing figure than Cetshwayo. One of his partisans, who might have been embellishing the picture, told Stuart that Mbuyazi was a giant of a man, some six feet four inches tall. His fearsome appearance was accentuated by a shock of hair, which made him stand out. In one line of his praise poem he was called 'the elephant with a tuft of hair'.[2] He was one of Mpande's seven children by Monase, a woman of the Nxumalo clan, who had been sent by her father to join Shaka's *isigodlo* and so bind their houses. She was handed on by Shaka to Mpande and became for some years his favourite wife. Their first son was born not long after Cetshwayo and named in honour of Henry Fynn, who had been called Mbuyazi by Shaka.

Two more of Mpande's formidable list of progeny were born at about the same time: Shonkweni was the son of an aristocratic beauty named Masala, and was either fathered by Mpande to 'raise seed', as it was said, for his brother, Dingane, or may have been Dingane's own son; Hamu, who was destined for a notorious role in Zulu history, was sired by Mpande for his brother Nzibe.

Normal sibling tensions were aggravated by the fact that seven of Mpande's sons were of a similar age. Through their adolescence and youth, rivalry grew between these 'young bulls', as Mpande called them, and it is hard to escape the conclusion that it was fomented by their father to test them.[3] When they reached military age, Cetshwayo, Mbuyazi and their five peers were inducted into a new regiment. The illustrious membership of the Tulwana ensured that it would be an elite unit; one of the kingdom's great men, Mnyamana ka Ngqengelele, was made *induna*, being the only man of whom the boisterous princes would stand in awe. Competition for honours was fiercest between the two eldest. However, when the Tulwana was given the chance to wash its spears in 1852, on a rare foray against the Swazi, Cetshwayo returned bloodied, while Mbuyazi did not.[4]

It made no difference. By now nothing that Cetshwayo could do would win his father's praise. What followed was a case study in twisted paternal love.

Mpande demonstrated his preference for Mbuyazi in many small ways. Once summoning both sons to a great hunt, the king ordered that an ox be slaughtered for shields, then ensured that Mbuyazi's was cut from the favoured side of the beast. When challenged by an *induna* that he seemed to be renouncing his first-born, Mpande explained feebly that when he was a 'commoner' he had intended Cetshwayo to be his heir, but now that he was king, Mbuyazi was to succeed him. When that failed to convince his councillors, he claimed that he had actually fathered Mbuyazi on Shaka's behalf, as a secret successor.[5] This invocation of 'the king of the earth' was received with scepticism.

A reckoning was only delayed by the fact that the rivals lived in different parts of the kingdom. Mbuyazi's *umuzi* was north of the Black Mfolozi, Cetshwayo's was south of the Mhlatuze. But on ceremonial occasions at the royal kraal, they would confront one another, strutting and flaring like fighting cocks. At one great dance, Cetshwayo declaimed a verse before the assembly lamenting his rejection. Mbuyazi responded with a furious war dance, provoking his opponent. As factions formed around the princes, it became clear that Cetshwayo was still regarded as the legitimate heir. His partisans, known as the Usuthu, included many of the kingdom's most senior men; it is a mark of how far authority had devolved that Mpande's chief adviser, Masipula ka Mamba, could publicly oppose his king over the issue. Another important Cetshwayo ally was Mapitha ka Sojiyisa who, as head of the Mandlakazi lineage of the royal house, was perhaps the most influential man in the kingdom. Among the rank and file of the army, too, Cetshwayo's standing was high.

Mbuyazi's faction was called the Isigqoza. His most ardent supporters were his brothers, including Shonkweni, who could call on their own regional reservoirs of manpower. Otherwise, his only significant advantage was his father's foolish love.

It was Mpande himself who brought on the inevitable. Recognizing that his favourite needed a wider power base, the king advised Mbuyazi to move south of the Mhlatuze, near Shaka's old kraal of kwaBulawayo. Here, it was reasoned, he would be able to build up his following. Cetshwayo, seeing that the moment of truth was upon him, sent out messengers to raise an army. Men from all the king's regiments responded and by the time the Usuthu advance began he already had a formidable force. As it swept through southern Zululand, the strong leader for whom the kingdom had yearned since Shaka's death emerged from youth and entered his maturity. Warriors flocked to Cetshwayo's standard, drawn by a proud and commanding figure who marched at the head of his army as Shaka had done. A few kraals hesitated, conscious that in abandoning Mbuyazi they would be defying the king's wishes, but soon fell in too.

Mbuyazi fell back to the Tugela with his remaining Isigqoza followers: seven thousand or so warriors and twice that number of dependants. They halted on high ground above a tributary that fed into the great river near its mouth. Once again the Tugela was to be the setting of an epochal event.

In the last resort, Mpande had advised Mbuyazi, 'go to the country of the whites. I too was brought to power by them.'[6] This time, however, flight to Natal was impossible as the summer rains had broken and the Tugela was in flood. Reduced to desperation, Mbuyazi and some of his *izinduna* managed to cross and made their way to a frontier outpost manned by Joshua Walmsley, the Natal agent, who was asked for military support. They returned with a handful of Natal native border police under the command of a colourful buccaneer named John Dunn. Thus was launched a political career of glorious improbability, in which Dunn became for a while one of the most powerful rulers in Zululand.

Reinforcements of a few well-armed and mounted men made little difference to Mbuyazi's plight. By now his advancing foe numbered between 15,000 and 20,000 men. But he refused to lose heart, encouraging the men with memories of his father's victory over Dingane: 'Do not be dismayed. Mpande's army was also small.'[7] Dunn, seeing the peril of their position, urged him to withdraw to the north. Mbuyazi retorted that he would hold his ground. All the gulf that separated their cultures was captured in that exchange: on the one hand, the pragmatic man who calculates on purely rational grounds; on the other, one who lives by pride, trusts in instinct and, ultimately, is careless of death.

On 2 December, a terrific storm broke over the Tugela, turning the swollen river into a torrent. Early the next morning, a dark mass arose on the horizon.

Cetshwayo's army advanced in the old manner, with the thunder of beating shields, the *ingomane*, intended to strike fear into the waiting foe. But now was heard for the first time the drawn-out rhythmic chant, '*Usuuuthu . . . Usuuuthu,*' the rallying cry of Cetshwayo's followers. According to one of his warriors:

Cetshwayo had on his black loin-cover of the skin of a silver jackal, and his buttock-cover of genet skin. He had a black shield with a white patch at the side. He had on his head a band of otter skin, with tassels of blue monkey skin, and a crane feather. He also had a gun. He walked in the midst of the companies of men.[8]

The battle of Ndondakusuka was as brief as it was bloody. It is said that beforehand Mbuyazi ordered a section of grass to be burnt, marking a line beyond which the Isigqoza would not retreat. His 7000-strong force lined up with backs to the Tugela as Cetshwayo deployed men of five regiments in the traditional horn formation. Their initial foray was repulsed and, for a moment, the Isigqoza were exultant, hurling insults after the retreating foe. But Cetshwayo had held back the cream of his men, the Mandlakazi and an inner circle of the Usuthu. In the next great onslaught the Isigqoza were engulfed. Mbuyazi died hurling himself into a pack of his enemies. Five other sons of Mpande also fell. Those men who escaped the assegai were driven back into the Tugela, to be swept out to sea.[9]

John Dunn, who, until the line broke, had been picking off the warriors of the next Zulu king with a precision that would have alarmed his colonial employers had they been aware of it, was saved by his own foresight. He had asked a friend named Jack Hill on the Natal side to have a boat in readiness and, in the midst of the massacre, Hill paddled across. On the way back, they passed through clots of drowning Zulus who grasped for the side of the boat. 'They had to knock the natives on the head,' one of Dunn's contemporaries remembered laconically.[10]

Now the Usuthu turned on Mbuyazi's dependants. Among the thousands who died that day, the majority were not fighting men at all but the elderly, women and children. As they fled, ghastly-eyed and shrieking, they too were pursued down the high-sided ravine to the Tugela and to the sands at the edge of the Indian Ocean. There, they were butchered. Dunn, whose testimony is not entirely to be trusted, claimed to have seen babies skewered to their mothers by a single assegai. Each body was disembowelled, enabling the victim's spirit to escape so that it would not haunt the perpetrator. More than fifty years later, one of Cetshwayo's warriors, Mvayisa ka Tshingili, recalled stabbing three men as they fled, but he could put no figure on the number of women and children he had killed. 'I don't count women and children,' he said, adding in explanation: 'Women were not allowed to escape in war because they bore fighting men.'[11]

For days afterwards, bodies were washed up on the coast down to Durban. Others remained where they had fallen and, for many years, the area round Tugela mouth was known as Mathambo, or 'the place of bones'. When Cetshwayo was brought to where his half-brother lay on the battlefield, he leapt over the body in the ritual gesture of ascendancy, then ordered Mbuyazi to be buried in a manner befitting a king's son. A new star had arisen in the kingdom.

The annihilation of the Isigqoza did not quite end there. Yet another of Mpande's sons was unaccounted for. Mkhungo, full brother to Mbuyazi, had reached sanctuary in Natal, where he was taken under the wing of Theophilus Shepstone.

The blood lust that can overtake fighting men with a civilian population at their mercy is as old as the species. Biblical history is replete with massacres. The Mongol armies that swept through Asia and eastern Europe as far as Austria in the thirteenth century, are but one element in the saga of Asia's conquering hordes, from the Avars and Huns through to the Turkic-speaking marauders such as the Comans and Petchenegs. Asian cavalry was mobile and highly organized, and the nomads overran their foes, who included the flower of European chivalry, with almost contemptuous ease.

Where they met resistance, they put civilian populations to the sword and razed their cities. Setting his troops loose on the gem that once was Bukhara, Genghis Khan is said to have roared: 'The hay is cut; give your horses fodder.'

One explanation advanced for the destructive ferocity of Asian nomads is that they found the organization of urban settlements and those who inhabited them disturbing, repulsive and threatening. In the seventeenth century, Wallenstein's nominally Catholic army in Protestant Bohemia in the Thirty Years' War and Cromwell's supposedly Protestant forces in Catholic Ireland, manifested similar intolerance, for supposedly religious reasons. Like the nomads, they left a trail littered with infamous deeds.

American and Turkish cavalrymen also found their quarries disturbing and repulsive, although in the late nineteenth century the distinction tended to be ethnicity. The killing by the US Seventh Cavalry of 153 Sioux men, women and children in 1890 at Wounded Knee creek, a reservation to which they had just been forcibly moved, is notorious. On the atrocity scale, however, it barely compares with the Ottomans' suppression in 1876 of a Bulgarian revolt. Among Turkish irregulars, the Circassians – a tribal people from the Caucasus noted as much for the warmth of their hospitality as their baleful vindictiveness – stood out for their part in the massacres that followed. No distinction was made between old and young, women and children. In the little town of Batak alone, 5000 were butchered and the final toll was some 15,000. Gladstone was inspired to one of his crusades and penned a pamphlet that aroused the indignation of Europe.

The focus of these comparisons is on hot-blooded slaughter, rather than the icy scientific genocide of industrial man. Still, if we go back to Mvayisa's explanation of events at the Tugela – 'women were not allowed to escape in war as they bore fighting men' – it sounds shockingly lame. Can there be an explanation for what makes a man impale a child on an assegai, a sword, a lance? If there is, it surely belongs to the realms of the subconscious rather than the rational world.

In a study of group or crowd psychology at the beginning of the twentieth century, Gustave Le Bon outlined a series of differences between the psyche of the individual – conscious, reasoned and more or less peaceful – and that of the crowd – spontaneous, passionate and, above all, subconscious. Le Bon's theory, born out of Europe's era of revolutionary turmoil, was that a collective sub-conscious takes over large groups, fusing individuals into an entity which has a great capability for both positive and negative action, for nobility and heroism on the one hand, but also, and more commonly, for baseness and barbarity. Other studies have linked Le Bon's work to the military sphere and concluded that armies provide 'powerful incentives for releasing forbidden impulses, inducing the soldier to try out formerly inhibited acts which he originally regarded as morally repugnant.'[12]

The collective subconscious, of which Carl Jung spoke, is innate to Bantu society. Through dreams and rituals, it helped forge the profound emotional and psychological stability that were the black man's best defences against institutionalized humiliation, the cleavage of families and all the other harmful influences that came with the modern South African state. The military milieu unique to the Zulu kingdom had provided a platform on which the collective subconscious could function at an even more potent level. Bonding age groups of both men and women to the service of the king had added a further dimension to the collective identity natural in traditional societies. It made the Zulu among the most resilient of communities in the face of threat or change. It would be perverse not to recognize that the military milieu also nourished a capacity for blind and unreasoned bloodshed.

Acceptance of the value of human life is implicit in Zulu war ceremonials. Before a battle, warriors would be doctored with sprinkled medicines and would then purge themselves by ritual vomiting; thus internally and externally cleansed, they washed in a stream and set forth. A man who had killed an enemy was not allowed to mix in the community or drink curds until he had been cleansed anew; otherwise, he was thought liable to go mad. Those who had washed their spears were isolated for days in order to be doctored with herbs and potions which were painted on their bodies.

Whether individuals felt either guilt or responsibility for the killing of innocents is another matter. What little evidence is available would suggest not. The collective subconscious conferred a collective responsibility which was assuaged by collective cleansing. Then life went on as it had before, free of guilt and care. Lest this be taken as suggesting that the Zulu or other Bantu societies were either callous or cruel by nature, it must be emphasized that there was an almost total absence of domestic violence. Mistreatment of children was virtually unknown and no man would raise his hand against his wife. Elderly people were revered. For all its martial and disciplinary aspects, those most malevolent forces, hatred and, especially, sadism had no accepted place in this world.

That still leaves the question of the motivation for mass killings: Mongols supposedly razed cities out of hatred and fear; Christians slaughtered Muslims, and vice versa, just as they slaughtered other Christians, out of blind fanaticism; Europeans killed Indians because they regarded them as subhuman and wanted to be rid of them. Zulus killed because if they did not establish their ascendancy and that of their *nkosi*, they would surely perish themselves. Whatever the motivation, one suspects that the same primeval force is at work in each case, and that those who take part in such massacres make a terrible discovery of some kind of pleasure in the process. Those who have experience of these things maintain that this capacity exists in all of us.[13]

Cetshwayo returned in triumph to the royal *umuzi* of Nodwengu. He was confident of having earned the position of heir but, at the same time, was intent on showing his continued loyalty to Mpande. All the cattle seized from the Isigqoza were driven ahead to be presented to the king. But on hearing of Mbuyazi's death, Mpande was stricken with grief and would have no part of this tribute. 'I don't even want to see them,'[14] he said. So, rebuffed again, Cetshwayo departed for his own homestead. As a symbol of the supremacy he had established in southern Zululand, he built a new kraal about fifteen miles north of the Tugela which he called Gingindlovu, meaning the Swallower of the Elephant.

Mpande never fully recovered from the death of his favourite son. Blind to his own fault in the tragedy, he blamed Cetshwayo for his loss and for years could not bear to have his first-born near him. When Magolwane, his praise-singer, reflected Cetshwayo's growing popularity in an *isibongo* which began, 'The wild beast which looks up at its father's sons and they bow down,' he was silenced.

Mpande said, 'Hau, Magolwana! What emotions you awaken in me! I want to weep on account of my sons. Do you mean to rouse me by giving Cetshwayo the praises of my sons who died?'

Magolwana replied, 'And you? Did you not kill the sons of your father? Have I not composed praises for you? Who was it that gave you the praise, "You who crossed all the rivers on the way to restoring yourself"?'

The king said, 'Enough, Magolwana. Give praise now. Let no other men praise Cetshwayo, for I shall weep.'[15]

Cetshwayo's apprenticeship for the throne presented further evidence of an unusual personality. He suffered his rejection without complaint, earning another line of his *isibongo* as 'the one who remains silent and provokes quarrels with no one'. Although many *izinduna* were starting to look to him for leadership, he remained loyal to his father. In the normal course of events, the heir apparent might have been tempted to nudge the natural process along but Mpande was to remain king for a further sixteen years.

Perhaps it was respect for the office, rather than the holder, that made Cetshwayo act as he did. For one thing, he felt Mpande was far too beholden to the white interests pressing in on the kingdom. Cetshwayo himself was innately suspicious of the *abelungu* and regarded as shameful the way that Mpande had allowed himself to be manipulated and used by the Boers to overthrow Dingane. Once, allowing his personal bitterness to show, he called his father *kafula*, a term dripping with contempt, used of the Natal exiles and returnees living among the white man and dependent on him. Whatever his feelings, Cetshwayo was under no illusions that either Boer or Briton could now be driven away. During the silent but deadly feud with Mpande that followed, each had a white confidant who advised him on how to deal with the Europeans and acted as a scribe. Cetshwayo's choice was entirely typical. It was not his way to harbour grudges, and when a down-and-out John Dunn returned across the Tugela on a trading expedition, he was invited into the *isigodlo*. Cetshwayo never mentioned Dunn's earlier support for Mbuyazi, but studied him keenly and decided that he fitted the bill.

Dunn was then in his early twenties, a lean, rangy man with dark eyes and a full beard. At the age of twelve, he had seen his father killed by an elephant and had spent most of his life in the wilderness since then, earning a living by his rifle. He was a fine marksman, had shot more elephants than anyone else in Natal's history, spoke Zulu and Xhosa like a native and was as tough as biltong. Offered land by Cetshwayo in return for his services as a diplomat, Dunn set up a kraal near Gingindlovu with his first wife, Catherine, and proceeded to accumulate new Zulu wives and political influence with equal energy. With wealth came an appreciation of the good things in life. Dunn recognized good wine, was well spoken and could hold his own in company with any European grandee willing to overlook his domestic arrangements. Although an outrageous snob, Sir Garnet Wolseley, an early administrator of Natal, was fascinated by him. Mostly, colonial society treated him like a pariah.

Mpande's white adviser was another piquant figure. Hans Schreuder was a Norwegian missionary of filthy appearance, indomitable will and enormous strength; he once strangled a leopard with his hands. Mpande had repeatedly refused him permission to set up a Lutheran station in Zululand, but Schreuder persisted for more than eight years until the king accepted him as a physician. Once more, however, the 'teachers' were to be frustrated. The three Norwegian missions built in the 1850s had no more success in winning converts than the Americans before them.

If Cetshwayo was right to fear European mischief-making, the Zulu had only themselves to blame for the opportunities that they presented their foes. The next internal crisis was entirely of their own making.

Mpande was infatuated again. Nomantshali was among the youngest of his wives and voluptuous with it. Big buttocks were the normal yardstick of feminine allure, but Mpande's eyes were for another part of Nomantshali's anatomy. He called her Somapa, 'the thighs that become the centre of attraction'.[16] Others noted the way she fed the king with wild vegetables and herbs; it was whispered that she had bewitched him with love potions. Nomantshali had borne Mpande at least three children, including a son named Mthonga. When the old king started showing favour towards the lad, unease stirred at court. When he announced one day, 'Ha! Zulu people, the heir will come from among the calves,' the Usuthu decided it was time to intervene.[17]

Cetshwayo later claimed that the men who arrived at Nodwengu late in 1860 exceeded his orders. Initially they were frustrated, as Nomantshali and her sons had received warning and fled. Over Mpande's ineffectual protests, the men searched the kraal and moved on. Nomantshali was traced to another *umuzi* and murdered.[18] Mthonga, however, had eluded the assassins. A few days later he fled across the northern border – into the welcoming arms of the Boers.

❋

Theophilus Shepstone had taken the other refugee princeling, Mkhungo, into his care gratefully. It was clear that the succession was far from resolved and the Boers had shown with Mpande how a prominent refugee could be put to good use. So when Mkhungo was brought to Shepstone after the battle of Ndondakusuka, he had a quiet word with his friend, John Colenso, Bishop of Natal, who enrolled the youth in the new Anglican mission school, Ekukanyeni, or 'place of light', near Pietermaritzburg.

Shepstone's small measure of renown had already been enhanced by a greater part of mystique. He was regarded by Natal's whites as the man who 'knew the native mind', one who was as at home sitting under a tree with a bunch of savages as other men were once the ladies had departed and the port was circulating. It was the best card Shepstone had – and he played it for all it was worth. From the small office in Pietermaritzburg which he ran with a single clerk and two black messengers, he gave the impression of running a vast intelligence network with tentacles reaching out among African peoples as far north as the Zambesi.

A good deal of this was humbug. Shepstone was indeed well versed in Nguni lore and had acted ably in defence of 'native' interests in Natal. He played the role of sage to perfection, being mainly taciturn and enigmatic, although loquacious on esoteric matters of which most whites were ignorant. However, much of his information was derived at secondhand; any messenger from a distant chief would be interrogated on issues mundane and arcane, but Shepstone rarely visited Zululand itself and the two men closest to affairs of state in the kingdom, Schreuder and Dunn, regarded his posturing with derision.

All this time, Shepstone was grooming the young prince Mkhungo for the role of puppet king. It was an audacious idea, but feasible, and it appealed strongly to Shepstone's love of intrigue. (The plot involving Mkhungo foreshadows Shepstone's even more ambitious attempt a decade later to install an impostor on the Ndebele throne after Mzilikazi's death, in order to gain

access to the supposed mineral wealth within the kingdom.[19])
Shepstone had even managed to involve Bishop Colenso in his
designs, after convincing him that Mkhungo was actually the true
heir. The bishop, who was tutoring the young prince, wrote:

If ever the British Government interferes, as, I imagine, some day it must,
in the affairs of Zululand, a youth like this, civilized and (may God in His
mercy grant it) Christianized, would surely be the person whose claims
would be most likely to receive our support, more especially as he is even
now regarded, both by friends and foes, as the rightful successor to
Panda's authority.[20]

Just as the British had their pretender, the Boers were championing the cause of Mthonga, who had taken refuge among them.
A covert, cynical game of land-grabbing and king-making was now
played out.

Cetshwayo was aware of the machinations of both sides and,
already, anxious about the threats to his position when Boer
envoys arrived at his homestead early in 1861. The import of their
message was that the British were preparing an invasion of Zululand to install Mkhungo. The Boers, Cetshwayo was assured, had
no such treachery in mind. Under the right conditions, they would
surrender their princeling, Mthonga, to the Zulus and 'put Cetshwayo in the Royal Hut'. The conditions were that he should cede
a stretch of land in north Zululand, around present-day Utrecht,
and guarantee Mthonga's safety. Reluctantly, Cetshwayo agreed.

When reports of the Boer deal reached Shepstone, he realized
he had been trumped. It was a serious blow and the only way he
could see of retrieving the situation was to go to Cetshwayo and
attempt to regain his trust. Hastily, he made preparations to make
one of his rare visits to Zululand, while putting it about that he
had been invited to recognize Cetshwayo officially as Mpande's
successor. This explanation, and Shepstone's account of his deft
handling of a perilous situation at Nodwengu and eventual trium-
phal acclaim, was allowed to stand for many years. The truth was
that Cetshwayo saw through Shepstone's bluster and sent him
packing, as Schreuder's account of what happened makes clear:

On Thursday Ketshwayo asked Mr S what had he come for? He said to
acknowledge him as successor. Ketshwayo replied, we do not thank you
for that, the Zulus can settle that for ourselves and we have settled it.

'What have you come for, you had some great thing to say, what is it?'
Mr S said 'I think that is a great thing that Panda has acknowledged you
in my presence as his successor.' 'No Mr S, that is not a great thing, he
has done so three times before and it is just as uncertain as ever as far
as he is concerned. What have you come for Mr S?'

He [Cetshwayo] then became very angry and said many things he
ought not to have said, his captains [*indunas*] interfered to quiet him and
the meeting broke up in great excitement.[21]

Shepstone returned to Pietermaritzburg claiming that he had
been hailed by the Zulu as a king with a great cry of '*Bayete*' and
another anecdote was added to the Shepstone legend. Privately,
the humiliation rankled and he conceived a hatred of Cetshwayo.
For the time being, though, there was little he could do about it.
Cetshwayo had now been recognized by both Boer and Briton as
Mpande's successor.

The Boers, meanwhile, took full advantage of the land that had
fallen to them. At first, they confined themselves to the area of
Cetshwayo's grant but northern Zululand was a pastoralist's
dream. Gradually the old pattern established itself, and encroachment began.

In his final years, Mpande was hardly ever seen to walk. Hauling
his immense bulk up from a rush mat and, wheezing with exertion,
he would waddle towards a little wooden cart. A man waited
attentively and reached out to help the king as, gingerly, he
climbed aboard. Another stood by holding a shield with which to
ward off the sun. Creaking and bumping, the cart was then
wheeled around the royal homestead to cries of '*Bayete*!' His
rounds done, Mpande returned to the shelter of the *isigodlo*. And
so another day would go by at Nodwengu.

The king in his cart, made by a white trader as a gift for the old
king, could be a metaphor for the torpor and isolation that overtook Zululand in the final years of his rule. For so long on their
guard against the visible threats of land-hungry Boers, the Zulu
were cut off from the new and more subtle forces that had come
into play and were reshaping the subcontinent around them.

For a start, the map had been redrawn. Since their withdrawal
from Natal, the Boers had formed two embryonic and, as ever,

fractious states north of the Drakensberg. The independence of the Orange Free State, between the Orange and Vaal rivers, was re-established in 1854 after a brief British occupation. North of the Vaal lay the South African Republic, generally known as the Transvaal. It was to the Transvaal that Cetshwayo had made the Utrecht land grant.

For more than two centuries, white men had clung to the Cape. Now, within three decades, the Boer migration had split open the subcontinent like a ripe melon. Suddenly the fruit within started coming spectacularly to light.

In March 1869, a Griqua herdsman found a hard, opaque stone in the drab and dusty wilderness where the Vaal and Orange met to the north of the Cape Colony. He showed it to a Boer and came away with a horse, ten oxen and five hundred sheep in exchange for the lump of rock. The farmer was equally pleased when it was sold soon afterwards for £25,000 to the Earl of Dudley. 'The Star of South Africa', as the 83-carat diamond was known, started a rush of prospectors to the Griqualand diggings. The first of South Africa's two mineral revolutions continued the transformation of the political landscape. When it happened, Britain had just about given up hope that its South African possessions might become paying concerns. Discovery of the Diamond Fields changed all that. The Cape's boundaries were hastily redefined to incorporate the diggings. Sleight of hand would not be so easy when the yet greater riches beneath the Reef of the White Waters, the Witwatersrand, were discovered in the Transvaal fifteen years later.

It was not just the Boers who were opening up Africa. Between 1853 and 1856, David Livingstone had captured the imperial imagination as no man would ever do to quite the same degree again with his epic journey up the Zambesi river, 'God's highway to the interior' as he called it, traversing the continent and drawing back the curtain on all the raw promise and energy of Central Africa. Livingstone's address to Cambridge students a year later rallied a generation to the causes of commerce and Christianity in Africa. In the main, though, it was commerce that prevailed. Within twenty years, the great powers of Europe were gorging themselves on the continent like hungry tribesmen at the carcass of an elephant.

Shepstone was among the first to feel the stirrings of the Scramble for Africa. His efforts to intervene in the Ndebele succession stemmed from the claims of a German geologist, Carl Mauch, to have discovered the legendary gold workings of Mono-motapa north of the Limpopo river. Few had ever even heard of Monomotapa (which did not stop Shepstone pronouncing that it meant 'the place of the mines') but Natal was seized by gold fever. When Thomas Baines, the artist—explorer, set out from Pieter-maritzburg in 1869 with an expedition to assess Mauch's findings, he carried with him a letter signed by Shepstone to 'all chiefs of native tribes and their people residing northward and eastward of the Colony of Natal'. It warned:

If gold exists where it is said to exist, no power can stop the stream of those who seek for it, however much it may be wished to do so; and it is the way of a wise man to guide what he cannot prevent.[22]

Monomotapa turned out to be a disappointment so far as gold was concerned, but an idea had been lodged in Shepstone's head. This was that in the opening up of Central Africa, which was now inevitable, Natal would be the slipway from which British enterprise would be launched into the interior.

Twilight came gently on the last of Senzangakona's sons. Towards the end, he had little to do with the exercise of power and even his little cart was rarely used. Traders who called at Nodwengu noted that, while he still asked to hear gossip from the world beyond, the old king would often doze off while they were in mid-recitation.

Resolution of the succession had greatly eased the internal strains of the state. There were troubles during the remainder of the 1860s, but they were of a kind that any rural community might have experienced: an outbreak of lung sickness in the cattle herds, an epidemic of smallpox, a severe drought. By 1872, as Mpande's life drew to a close, the kingdom had been at peace with itself for more than sixteen years. He even became reconciled with his first-born. In 1867, at the age of forty, Cetshwayo was allowed to don the *isicoco*, or headring, signifying his full maturity and readiness, both to take a wife and rule his people. His first wife was Msweli and a year after their marriage she gave birth to a boy, Dinuzulu.

Right to the end, Mpande officiated at the one great ritual celebration of national pride, the first-fruits festival. Then, as they had
since Shaka's time, the clans would set out from their kraals at the
full moon and stream down from the hills to the royal *umuzi* to
sing the praises of Shaka, Dingane and Mpande, to dance with joy
and abandon, to see their king make his communion with the
ancestors, and to revel in their own greatness as a people. They
came in columns from every corner of the country, and when they
departed three days later they carried a sense of national renewal
back to the most distant homesteads.

It was shortly before the festival of 1872 that Mpande summoned
his *izinduna* for the last time. One of his grandsons, Mkebeni ka
Dabulamanzi, related the legend:

Mpande spoke. 'I am going. Send for Mapitha, and tell him to pick out
an old white ox. Let him select four men, and let them drive this ox,
which is old like me, to fetch a cloak for me.' By this he meant the skin
of a lion, an old one, one which was now chief among the lions, one
which no longer hunted game but had its prey caught for it by others.

They did this at a place where lions were very numerous, like the
grass. But the lions paid no attention to the beast. As it was getting dark,
an old male, old like Mpande, could be heard roaring. As the sun rose it
approached them. The ox then lay down. The lion came up to the ox
and made a wound on its neck. The ox died, upon which the lion lapped
up the blood. It then lay down. One of the men cried '*Bayete!*' to the lion.
'Do not take fright; now I am taking you.' Saying this, he flung an assegai.
The lion died. It did not fight.

The king had said that the lion should be tied in the skin of the white
ox. This was duly done, and it was brought to Nodwengu. Then Mpande
said, 'Wrap me in the skin of the lion and bury me in it. Now I am going.
Stay well. Cetshwayo will rule my people well, but he will reign for only
five years.' Upon this, Mpande died.[23]

That night, many inhabitants slipped away from Nodwengu,
fearing a slaughter such as had accompanied Nandi's death. But
Cetshwayo quickly ordered that there would be no killing. A Zulu
king had died naturally and a succession was taking place in peace.
The bloody eras of Shaka and Dingane were well and truly buried.
Surely, this was an omen of yet better times to come.

Strangely though, in Cape Town and Pietermaritzburg they were
talking of Cetshwayo as 'another Shaka'.

PART 3

RESISTANCE AND
RUIN – 1882–7

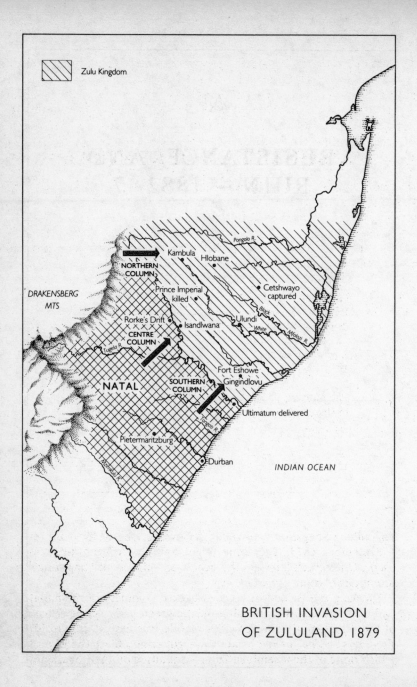

Zulu Kingdom

NORTHERN
COLUMN

Kambula

Hlobane

DRAKENSBERG
MTS

Prince Imperial
killed

Cetshwayo
captured

Pongolo R.

Rorke's Drift

CENTRE
COLUMN

Isandlwana

Ulundi

Black

White

Mfolozi R.

NATAL

SOUTHERN
COLUMN

Fort Eshowe
Gingindlovu

Tugela R.

Ultimatum delivered

Pietermaritzburg

Tugela R.

Mkuzi R.

Durban

INDIAN OCEAN

BRITISH INVASION
OF ZULULAND 1879

11

'A SOURCE OF PERPETUAL DANGER'

> I love the English. I am the child of Queen Victoria.
> But I am also king in my own country. I shall not hear
> dictation. I shall perish first.[1]

King Cetshwayo,
1877

> The monster Shaka is his model. To emulate Shaka
> in shedding blood is as far as I have heard his highest
> aspiration.[2]

Sir Bartle Frere, governor of the Cape, on Cetshwayo,
1879

Theophilus Shepstone 'crowned' Cetshwayo king of the Zulu on
1 September 1873. The scene might have come from an *opéra
bouffe*. Only much later did the deadly seriousness of Shepstone's
intentions become apparent.

The king was seated in a broad-backed colonial armchair that
had been set out that morning on the green early spring shoots
of the Mhlabatini Plain. A scarlet mantle was draped around his
shoulders, while on his head was a glittering object the like of
which none of the assembled Zulus – squatting on their haunches

in front of him, wrapped in blankets and clasping assegais – had ever seen before. A brass band played and the Durban Volunteer Artillery thundered out a 17-gun salute. With a pop and a cloud of smoke, a photographer recorded the scene for posterity.

Shepstone sat beside the king, in the shade of an umbrella held by a soldier. His expression was calm, impenetrable, but inwardly he seethed. He had intended that by officially installing Cetshwayo he should finally establish an ascendancy over the king, sealing a relationship as overlord and client; instead, like his previous expedition to 'recognize' Cetshwayo as Mpande's successor, the whole affair had become a huge embarrassment.

Shepstone's entourage, which included the explorer–artist Thomas Baines, prominent colonists and over a hundred Natal troopers, had arrived the previous month, only to find that Cetshwayo had already been installed by his own people. Furious, Shepstone demanded to know who had authorized the royal salute. So angered was he that he considered turning back, before deciding that this would deal an even bigger blow to his dignity. However, his embarrassment was then compounded as the party was left to kick its heels for more than two weeks while Cetshwayo carried out burial rituals for an old adviser.[3] The boredom of the colonists at this time, lying listlessly about in tents while the Zulus completed their ceremonials was captured in a sketch by Baines.

Now, with the official 'coronation' finally under way, it was evident to Shepstone that even the crown perched ludicrously on Cetshwayo's head had been a bad idea. A garrison tailor had knocked it up, using ostrich feathers and some scraps of tinsel left by a travelling opera company; the connection had proved to be unfortunate, for the crown resembled nothing so much as a prop from an amateur production of *Aida*.

Shepstone rose, and started speaking. 'Here is your king. You have recognized him, and I now do so also in the name of the Queen of England. Your kings have often met violent deaths by the hands of your own people, and if you kill this one we shall require his blood at your hands.'[4]

To his superiors Shepstone later reported with ill-conceived satisfaction: 'Thus, he, who a few minutes before, had been a minor and a prince, had now become a man and a king.'[5]

Next to him, Cetshwayo could afford a smile. Shepstone's visit had turned out just as he had hoped. For years rumours had circulated that Mbuyazi had survived and was living in Natal. Of course, Mkhungo, another of Mpande's sons, was known to be there. To the Zulus the implication was clear: Shepstone, or Somseu as he was known to them, was offering Cetshwayo's rivals not only help but support. Hence the king's invitation that Somseu come and publicly acknowledge him, as he had just done.[6] At long last, the ghosts of Ndondakusuka had been laid to rest.

But Somseu was not quite done yet. He had other reasons for participating in this diplomatic *pas de deux*. There, on the Mahlabatini Plain, he proclaimed that, as Cetshwayo was recognized by an English monarch, he should in future behave more like one. In future, no Zulu should be killed without a trial, or before he had been able to appeal to the king. People accused of witchcraft should not be killed at all, but sent away.

Later, in a marquee erected nearby, Shepstone warmed to his subject. Cetshwayo listened but was noncommittal. He was more interested in hearing how Somseu proposed to stop the Transvaal Boers encroaching on Zulu land. Now it was Shepstone's turn to counter: when would Cetshwayo allow more missionaries into the country?

So it went on, without give or take. Shepstone was obliged to admit that the new king was an impressive figure who had conducted his side of the discussions 'with great ability and frankness'. Cetshwayo, he wrote, 'ranks in every respect far above any native chief I have had to do with'.[7] When the colonists started back to Natal, with a parting gift of cattle to feed them on the road, only one thing had changed. Britain had officially recognized Cetshwayo's sovereignty. Nothing had been done to suggest that the Zulu king had surrendered his right of independent action. The admonition against killing, so far as everyone was concerned, was just another of Somseu's little homilies.

Shepstone himself acknowledged as much. It had, he said, been a sort of 'ordination sermon or bishop's charge' which was 'but sowing the seed which will still take many years to grow and mature'.[8]

This little 'sermon', however, was shortly to be invested with all the weight and imperative of the Commandments, handed down from on high in tablets of stone.

✸

Mpande had been dead a year when Cetshwayo was installed. The new king's own 'great place' was built not very far from Nodwengu, between the Black and White Mfolozi rivers, and was called Ondini. With around 1500 huts, it was much like previous circular capitals, although Cetshwayo made one concession to the changing times and had a brick house of European design built for himself within the *isigodlo*.

Cetshwayo was now forty. He reigned over some 300,000 subjects and could summon an army of up to 30,000 men. His prowess as a war leader was proved and he was young enough to command respect among the young bloods, while also mature enough to impress the *izinduna*. Reserved and softly spoken, he was none the less forthright and assured, and was quite capable of taking up an opposing position to his entire 'cabinet', the chiefs of the *umkhandlu* who were now so influential in matters of state.

More than any previous king, Cetshwayo was steeped in tradition, and it is in the light of tradition that his resistance to Britain must be seen. He has been described as 'the noblest manifestation of the old order', his domain as 'a magnificent anachronism'. In fact, a transformation had taken place since the days of Shaka and Dingane. But Cetshwayo revered the Zulu past and was utterly determined to uphold the principles by which his people governed themselves. This would be demonstrated when, years later, under a long and intensive interrogation in Cape Town, he refused with calm dignity laced with touches of humour to compromise any of the values that his British captors found strange or abhorrent. He had none of Dingane's artfulness or Mpande's pliancy.

The historian Magema ka Magwaza, his contemporary, said he was 'a good man who loved all his people and disliked favouritism'. The king had a Solomon-like reputation for resolving disputes, listening patiently to the claims of both sides and then generally ordering each to produce a goat to be shared in a joint feast. No less important for a people living under authoritarian rule, he was neither whimsical nor capricious. Discipline conformed to well-understood principles. Because Natal colonists were so sensitive to the supposed ferocity of Zulu justice and as by now few incidents went unreported, we have a fairly good idea of the occasions when killing occurred during Cetshwayo's reign. Executions were comparatively rare. Probably the most notorious was a consequence of a 'rebellion' by one of the female *amabutho* in around 1876.

The women of the Ingcugce regiment were of marriageable age and it had been decided that they would take husbands from the Indhlondhlo, which was due to put on the headring. However, some of the women had already found lovers among other regiments and rejected the Indhlondhlo, demanding instead that the uDloko and uDududu be disbanded for them to marry. Such defiance was unknown, and when the women cut off their top-knots in protest and fled, Cetshwayo sent warriors after them. By one account, thirty-one women were killed.[9]

It was probably this incident that brought a messenger from Natal to the king, with a reminder about his 'coronation vows'. Cetshwayo shot back:

Did I ever tell Mr Shepstone I would not kill? Did he tell the white people I made such an agreement because if he did, he has deceived them. I do kill . . . it is the custom of our nation and I shall not depart from it. Why does the governor of Natal speak to me about my laws? Do I go to Natal and dictate to him about his laws?[10]

Although popular, Cetshwayo's leadership was not without contending pressures. Like Shaka, he was unhappy about the power of *izangoma*, or diviners. The 'smelling out' and execution of supposed witches had become subject to much corruption and abuse. In his father's time Cetshwayo had supported a policy to move accused witches to new kraals. He would later complain of having encountered opposition to this. As he was not specific, we can but surmise that certain chiefs, as well as the *izangoma* themselves, wished to retain this power over their people.

Most formidable of a number of potential rivals was the king's cousin Zibhebhu, a fiery and intelligent young general who had succeeded his father, Mapitha, as head of the Mandlakazi lineage which held sway in the north of the country. Mandlakazi support had been crucial to Cetshwayo's victory over Mbuyazi and Zibhebhu seemed loyal enough, but the strongest men in Zululand were rarely without ambition.

Hamu was another who showed signs of awkwardness. He, too, was one of the *abantwana* – royal princes of Mpande's line – and had a following in the north-west. Although popular, he was already showing signs of the weakness for the Natal gin, called by the Zulus 'the Queen's tears', that was to be his eventual undoing.

His Ngetsheni lineage was less prestigious than the Mandlakazi.

Question marks over the loyalty of these two men were dispelled for the time being at Cetshwayo's installation, just before Shepstone's visit. Hamu, in particular, made a great show of pledging allegiance to the new king. The omens were good. Mnyamana, respected head of the Buthelezi clan, who had known Cetshwayo since his youth and had been his commanding *induna* in the Thulwana regiment, was appointed prime minister. His father Ngqengelele had served Shaka in the same capacity. Mnyamana automatically became a member of Cetshwayo's inner circle of advisers, the *umkhandlu*, consisting of the chiefs of such important clans as the Biyela, the Mdlalose, the Tuli and the Hlabisa.

Foreign policy was founded on friendship with Britain. Zulu leaders had initially kept an open mind about the Transvaal but, when encroachment by Boer farmers to the north persisted, they turned to Natal for help. Incidents flared regularly in the border Hlobane region. Between 1861 and 1876, the Zulu made eighteen requests for Shepstone to intercede with the Transvaal over territorial violations. Somseu was sympathetic in principle, being anxious that the Boers should not manage to open up a corridor to the sea via Zululand; but he was able to give little practical help and encroachment continued.

In 1876, after a series of particularly serious flare-ups, Cetshwayo made military deployments to counter the threat to the north. Once again the Boers seemed poised to invade. In fact, like the British at Singapore, the Zulus were facing the wrong way.

In Natal, the egalitarian principles of the 1856 charter tumbled as the settler population grew. Where only a few decades earlier whites had petitioned African leaders for favour, now they assumed it as a right. And, like Kurtz in Joseph Conrad's *Heart of Darkness*, they gazed into the black interior with horror and dread.

The colony's white population was about 23,000 by the 1870s. Gone were the old 'white chiefs' with their black wives and rough familiarity with native people. Dunn was living in Zululand, and Fynn, the last of the breed, had died in 1861 at his home on the Bluff, looking down on the bay where he had landed almost forty years earlier, now transformed into the busy town of Durban. Their places had been taken by English settlers, recruited by commercial companies to populate the dominions like Australia, New Zealand and Canada. In the depressed economic conditions of the 1850s in Britain, there had been no shortage of farmers, traders and artisans willing to make a new start in the sun. They were clearly industrious and enterprising: Natal thrived modestly as an agricultural producer, one crop in particular being found suitable to local conditions, sugar. On the back of their prosperity, the newcomers, like settlers everywhere, tried to recreate the society they had left behind. Newspapers were started, clubs and societies founded, schools opened.

Surrounding the white centres of Durban, Pietermaritzburg and the new Midlands settlements of Richmond and Greytown were about 250,000 Natal natives, still mainly living in the 'location' system devised by Shepstone. A day's journey away by horse lay the Tugela, and the start of the Zulu country. Neither intended any harm to settler society and, indeed, when whites encountered 'natives' they were treated with deference, if not reverence. It is perhaps not surprising, however, that a people transported across the world, isolated from other whites (even Cape Town was more than a thousand miles away), and nourished on the beliefs of social Darwinism, should have started off on the wrong foot with their black neighbours. Partly it was because of the natives' refusal to work for wages: an editorial writer for the *Natal Witness* fulminated: 'Unimpelled by want, they have worn away their lives up to the present time in slothful indolence, to the full depravity of human nature.' But in the main, the problem of race relations was founded in a pathological white fear of being overwhelmed: the Langalibalele affair brought this hostility and fear to a head.

Langalibalele was one of Shepstone's charges, the chief of the Hlubi people who dwelt beneath the Drakensberg in the north of the colony. At their first meeting, Shepstone had been impressed. Langalibalele had 'that dignity and grace in his actions which so commonly, among the most savage nations, proclaim the king'. Now, twenty years on, the old 'savage' posed a problem.

Members of the Hlubi, the scattered remnants of an ancient and war-like folk, had recently returned from working on the now-flourishing Diamond Fields with guns bought with their earnings. Firearms were supposed to be registered with magistrates, but in the African experience registration usually led to confiscation. On being summonsed to register the firearms owned by his people, Langalibalele first prevaricated. Finally, issued an ultimatum by

Shepstone, the Hlubi abandoned their location and started up the Drakensberg to the Highveld.

They simply wanted to escape, but what African people had always done when facing an intractable situation was no longer tolerated. Shepstone sent a few hundred colonial troops and volunteers with about 8000 native levies to head off the Hlubi at the top of the mountains and drive them back. Among these troops was Major Anthony Durnford, the Chief of Staff, a forty-three-year-old Irish officer. An inglorious mêlée ensued at the top of Bushman's Pass with a small party of Hlubi who were not even among Langalibelele's group. When the smoke cleared most of the volunteers had panicked and fled, three others were dead and Durnford was wounded. Langalibalele, who had witnessed none of this, was meanwhile long gone with the great majority of his people.

Vengefully, the troops set upon Hlubi stragglers and elderly men and women. About two hundred were flushed from hiding in caves and shot. Some five hundred younger Hlubi were rounded up and forced into labouring work. Then the troops turned to the Putini, neighbours of the Hlubi. They were held accountable by Shepstone for sympathizing with their brethren and had their kraals burned and 8000 cattle seized. The Putini, too, were then dispersed and drawn into the colonial labour market.

A few weeks later the wandering Langalibalele was betrayed by the Sotho. A travesty of a trial, over which Shepstone presided and at which Langalibalele was undefended, saw him convicted of murder, treason and rebellion. He was sentenced to life imprisonment on Robben Island. Colonial society, which had been roused to a frenzy by his 'rebellion', thought he should have been strung up from a tree.

There matters would have rested, but for John Colenso, the Bishop of Natal. Colenso was a slight, irascible leprechaun of a man, with an untidy white mane and a gift for mathematics. Raised in Cornwall, he was already an outrageous figure in colonial society. His Low Church views had set him off on a study of the first five books of the Old Testament, the Pentateuch, which caused him to be branded a heretic. Although excommunicated in 1866, Colenso continued to preach at St Peter's Cathedral, Pietermaritzburg, and opened up a schism in the Church of England in South Africa that still endures. Most of his heresies are the orthodoxies of today's churchmen but it was the manner by which he came to them that, as much as anything, had caused so much of a stir. According to the bishop, it was one of his Zulu converts, William Ngidi, who started his spiritual quest. On being told the story of Noah's ark, Ngidi asked:

'Is all that true? Do you really believe that all this happened thus – that all the beasts and birds and creeping things, large and small, from hot countries and cold, came thus by pairs, and entered into the ark with Noah? And did Noah gather food for them *all*, for the beasts and birds of prey as well as the rest?'

My heart answered with the words of the Prophet, 'Shall a man speak lies in the name of the Lord?' Zech.xiii.3. I dared not do so ... I was thus driven – against my will at first, I may truly say – to search more deeply into these questions.[11]

A less well-known story of this quixotic, gallant man's spiritual pilgrimage in Africa, was told to Stuart by another convert, John Kumalo.

One day Colenso's *induna* William said:
'Sir, you say God destroys the wicked. Would you, if your son did wrong, destroy him?'
'No', replied Colenso.
'Then how can you say that an all-mercifull and loving father, whose own children we all are, will destroy us if we do wrong?'
Colenso found this a hard question. He submitted it. The Archbishop replied, 'You should turn your mind to prayer. You have gone astray.' Colenso got furious.[12]

As a result of exchanges like these, Colenso gave up preaching about hell, while his admissions of doubt duly inspired a limerick by a contemporary wag.

> A bishop there was of Natal,
> Who took a Zulu for a pal,
>   Said the Kaffir, 'Look 'ere,
>   Ain't the Pentateuch queer?'
> And converted my Lord of Natal.[13]

From his beloved mission of Ekukanyeni, or 'place of light', high over Pietermaritzburg, Colenso further flabbergasted his colleagues. He baptized polygamous converts without insisting that they cast aside all but one of their wives and, even more outrageously, implied that all men had within them the gift of the Holy Spirit. He brought the same uncompromising integrity to his political views as he did to his spiritual beliefs. His daughter, Fanny, was in love with Anthony Durnford, and when the major confided his misgivings about the atrocities that had been committed against the Hlubi, the bishop was moved to investigate further.

As we have seen, Colenso had been in perfect agreement with his old friend, Shepstone, that native powers such as the Zulu kingdom would, and should, submit to the influences of Christian civilization. But he also had an abiding faith in English justice and humanity. The more he found out about the Langalibalele affair, the more shocking he found it. Most painful of all was the discovery that during the chief's trial Shepstone, his most intimate friend for twenty years, was prepared – indeed, insistent – that the injustices done to an innocent man and his people should stand. The rift between the two was complete and permanent. As Colenso's wife, Sarah, wrote: 'As soon as John found the line [Shepstone] had been taking, he said in this case "it must be war to the knife between us", and [Shepstone] has not been to the house since, though of course they salute in public . . . Like Luther, he could not do otherwise.'[14]

The Langalibelele affair marked a turning point. Henceforth, no tribal power in southern Africa could doubt that the days of its independence were numbered. However, it made a difference that one white man had taken up the Hlubi cause. Cetshwayo, hearing that Colenso was sailing for Britain to plead the case with Lord Carnarvon, the colonial secretary, sent him a messenger:

Cetshwayo rejoices exceedingly to hear that you have gone to the great *izinduna* of the Queen to tell them about the treatment of the black people of Natal. Cetshwayo says that he is in good hope, and, even if you are worsted that is of no consequence, you will have done what becomes a faithful *induna* of the Queen.[15]

Colenso's lobbying in London did secure an amelioration of the Hlubi punishments: Langalibalele was eventually allowed to return to Natal, after thirteen years in imprisonment and exile. However, another visitor from Natal was in London at the same time as the

202

bishop, and was listened to at the Colonial Office with even more attentiveness.

Shepstone had arrived trailing a reputation for Machiavellian skill in dealings with South African natives, white as well as black. Extraordinarily, his role in the Langalibalele fiasco was overlooked and it was Sir Benjamin Pine, Natal's governor, who came home under a cloud. Carnarvon, meanwhile, called Shepstone in and was completely taken in. Here was a man, he told Disraeli, the prime minister, 'heaven-born for the object in view'.[16]

The object was to be the extension of British dominion over the whole of southern Africa. Somseu was about to step from the backwater of 'native affairs' to the mainstream of imperial policy-making, from where he would help chart the downfall of the Zulu kingdom.

Perhaps the most charitable interpretation of Britain's reasons for starting the war of 1879 was given by a Zulu. 'It had been decided to destroy this savage government,' wrote Magema ka Magwaza, 'because the Natal government feared that one day it would suddenly and unexpectedly be attacked. It seems that the white people had in mind the events and bad deeds of Dingane. But Cetshwayo on his part was a man of good character who would never have committed acts like those of Dingane.'[17]

The words of Magema, a protégé of Colenso and author of the first Zulu-language history, *The Black People, and Whence They Came*, cut with a direct simplicity through a forest of debate and dissertations that have polarized the 'liberal' and 'radical' schools of South African historiography over the causes of the Anglo–Zulu War. This is not the place for an analysis of British policy in the 1870s – of the supposed capitalist imperative to conquer the Zulus to acquire their land and suck their labour on to the Natal sugar plantations and the Cape Diamond Fields.[18] Magema's words still have a hard edge of truth. War was by no means historically inevitable, but in the late nineteenth century an assertive European power was bound to make an independent African one bend the knee sooner or later. Had he been on the other side, Shaka would have done no less himself.

Carnarvon, at the Colonial Office, was the architect of the policy that led to war; Shepstone provided the raw materials; and Sir

Bartle Frere, the governor of the Cape, was the messy draughtsman whose fingerprints were found all over the plan when a scapegoat had to be found.

Since 1874, Carnarvon had pondered how the jumble of ethnic and political blocs that made up the subcontinent – British colonies, Boer republics, and Bantu kingdoms – could be neatly composed into a South African confederation. He had previously fashioned a similar dominion out of the territories of Canada, and the process of streamlining and economizing was self-recommending. Gradually, the obstacles were whittled away so that, two years later, the main ones left were the Boers and the Zulu. The Transvaal, Carnarvon was sure, would be easily dealt with. The Boers were chronically divided, the republic was vastly indebted and the treasury contained 12/6d. Shepstone was again called to London, knighted, and sent home with secret orders and a free hand to effect the annexation of the Transvaal – peacefully. So secret was this mission that even Frere – who was about to be appointed governor of the Cape, with the task of securing confederation – was given the barest details.

The new era announced itself dramatically. Frere, who came to South Africa as a proconsul of Indian renown, stepped off the Balmoral Castle at Cape Town on 31 March 1877. Shepstone was already in Pretoria, putting the wind up President Burgers with, among other things, a story that the territorial dispute had provoked Cetshwayo beyond endurance; a great Zulu *impi* was mustering across the border, Shepstone said, and only British protection could save the Boers from invasion. The fact that there was not a shred of truth in all this made little difference; the bankrupt and demoralized Burgers government was ready to submit. On 12 April, Shepstone's clerk, a weedy-looking youth named Henry Rider Haggard, read the proclamation in Church Square.

Britain's annexation of the Transvaal changed the face of South Africa and opened a vein of Boer resistance that would lead to two wars. The initial Zulu reaction, however, was enthusiastic. The Boer foe in Pretoria had been replaced by a British ally. Somseu had supported the kingdom in its land dispute with the Transvaal. Now Somseu would see to justice.

The fact was, however, that annexation had changed Shepstone's perspective. The Transvaal's land dispute with the kingdom had now become Britain's. From a Zulu gamekeeper, Shepstone had just been turned into a Boer poacher.

❋

On being told by Shepstone that he was going to 'settle affairs' with the Boers, Cetshwayo sent back an offer of help. Clearly this alluded to armed support. Shepstone, naturally, declined.

More than two decades of peace had started to tell on the Zulu army. Since the 1852 raid on the Swazi, fifteen *amabutho* had been recruited, none of which had seen action. A despatch by Frere to London about 'celibate man-destroying gladiators' baying for the chance to 'wash their spears', was a gross distortion, but it was not without a grain of truth. Cetshwayo's warriors were confident and virile young men who had been nourished on a folklore of military glory and then denied a chance to test themselves. Other stimuli existed for a military adventure. Between 1872 and 1875, Zulu cattle were again ravaged by an epidemic of lung sickness which by some accounts took off half the national herd. As usual in such circumstances, Zulu leaders looked to the Swazi country to replenish their stocks, only to find that even that old stamping ground was now cut off from them. John Dunn, the king's leading counsellor in matters relating to the whites, was insistent that a raid on the Swazi would cause an outcry in Natal. Cetshwayo swallowed his pride and stayed his hand.

Provocation, meanwhile, increased in the north. Cetshwayo was later to say that had the Transvaal not been annexed by Britain, war would probably have broken out between Boer and Zulu. From 1873 it became a priority to ensure that the army was prepared for conflict with the Transvaal. In this Dunn played a crucial part. From his homestead near the coast, Dunn set up a gun-running network through Delagoa Bay which brought thousands of firearms to Zululand. Instruction in their use was harder to arrange and Zulu marksmanship remained appalling. Dunn, however, prospered, raking off profits from both the gun trade and an agency recruiting Tsonga labourers from the Delagoa Bay region for Natal farmers. This bounty enabled him to live in a manner that combined the best of both his worlds: he paid *lobola* for all forty-eight of his Zulu wives, while the quality of his hospitality became renowned among fascinated European visitors who sought him as a hunting companion.

The kingdom was not without internal tensions. Competitiveness between Zulu regiments often produced rivalry that resulted in massed stick fights. Although vigorous enough to produce plenty of broken limbs and the occasional fatality, such affrays were regarded as a natural consequence of manliness and pride. The conflict between the Tulwana and the Ngobamakosi at the royal kraal, Ondini, in around 1877 was far more serious than that, however, and gave a hint of the enmity stirring between Cetshwayo and his half-brother, Hamu. The Tulwana was Hamu's regiment, while the Ngobamakosi was Cetshwayo's favourite. During a clash between the two, the Tulwana, at Hamu's urging, dropped their sticks and took up assegais. Many Ngobamakosi were killed.

It was at around this time that Shepstone sent a message to Ondini, requesting a meeting to discuss the territorial dispute between the kingdom and the Transvaal.

The delegation that came to the Ncome river on 18 October was composed of the most senior men of the kingdom, headed by Mnyamana, the king's chief minister. The man they had come to see was not native secretary any more and it did not take them long to realize that, as administrator of the Transvaal, Somseu had new loyalties. Hitherto, it should be recalled, he had professed support for the Zulu position. Now he went directly on to the offensive, saying they should give up the Utrecht district and accept the Boer boundary claim. The *izinduna* spent a few moments digesting this. Then one stood up and accused him of betraying the son of his old friend Mpande. At first Shepstone resorted to playing the white chief. 'Go and tell my child (Cetshwayo) these words. He will understand me.' Another *induna* stood up. 'Somseu, *we* do not understand you.' At this, Shepstone started to bluster. How dare they call him Somseu and not *nkosi*? Well, responded one, as they were all chiefs themselves, they called other chiefs by their names too.[19]

Enraged, Shepstone turned away. To one of his accompanying troops, he muttered that he would march a force across the Tugela just to show who was in charge. Like his rift with Colenso, Shepstone's break with Cetshwayo was acrimonious and final. It marked a point from which the Zulu would later date the slide to war.

When Cetshwayo was told of Shepstone's *volte face*, he appealed to Colenso and Sir Henry Bulwer, the new governor of Natal. Bulwer had experience of native peoples in a host of exotic places, from the Caribbean to Borneo, and his advice to the Zulu throughout the ordeal ahead was unprejudiced and well meant. Alone among British officials, he would stand out against the war. Now he suggested that Cetshwayo submit his boundary case to arbitration by an independent commission. Colenso agreed. He had only met Cetshwayo once long ago – finding him 'a fine, handsome young fellow with a very pleasant smile and a good humoured face' – but was instinctively sympathetic to his plight and anxious about the direction matters were suddenly taking.

Messages from Bulwer and Colenso satisfied the king that there were still those in Natal who desired that he should 'drink water and live'. He would have been less reassured if he had seen the letters that had started to pass from Shepstone to his superiors in Cape Town and London. Writing to Carnarvon in December, he portrayed the king as:

... the secret hope of every independent chief, hundreds of miles from him, who feels a desire that his colour should prevail, and it will not be until this power is destroyed that they will make up their minds to submit to the rule of civilisation. The sooner the root of the evil which I consider to be the Zulu power and military organisation is dealt with, the easier our task will be.[20]

Frere was even more receptive than the colonial secretary to this kind of warmongering. Without any evidence of aggressive intent from the Zulu, he had bought, lock, stock and barrel, Shepstone's description of the kingdom as 'a source of perpetual danger to itself, and to its neighbours'.[21] Soon Frere was adding Shepstonian touches to his own despatches. It was known that Cetshwayo had been in diplomatic touch with Sekukuni, the Pedi chief, who had recently humiliated a Boer *kommando* sent to drive him out of the northern Transvaal. Taking his cue from Shepstone, Frere built this contact into a conspiracy, the makings of a Bantu resistance movement. Blacks were uniting to oppose 'the flood of new ideas and ways which threaten to sweep away the idle, sensuous elysium of Kaffirdom'.[22]

The boundary commission gathered on 7 March 1878 to start hearing evidence at a farm called Rorke's Drift, just on the Natal side of the Buffalo river. The members included John Shepstone, acting in his elder brother's stead as native secretary, and Anthony Durnford, now promoted to lieutenant-colonel. Most significantly, the chairman was Michael Gallwey, Natal's first attorney-general and an Irishman of forthright independence. Hearings continued for five weeks, but before the end Gallwey had signalled his belief that no proper concession of the Utrecht district had been granted by the Zulus. The Boers had always been reluctant to have a commission and, as their evidence was subjected to scrutiny, it became apparent why. Zulu *izinduna* who had testified returned home rejoicing and reported that they had been told: 'You have beaten the Boers and we are convinced that the land claimed is rightly yours, and we are going home to tell the English nation of this.'[23]

Frere, too, must have been informed of the likely outcome. He had been depending on a report favourable to the Transvaal, both to reconcile the Boers to annexation and to challenge the Zulus. Now, it seemed to Colenso, he would surely take stock and reflect calmly. Sir Michael Hicks Beach, who had succeeded Carnarvon at the Colonial Office, made it plain he wanted to avoid the 'very serious evil of a war with Cetshwayo'. But Frere still had his *carte blanche* for confederation and, for reasons that have never been fully explained, he was now beyond recall. When the boundary report, duly upholding the Zulu case, was presented to him in June, he concealed it. Meanwhile, quite deliberately and wilfully keeping the Colonial Office in the dark, he made his preparations for war. General Frederic Thesiger, commander of imperial forces in South Africa, was sent to Natal to draw up an invasion plan.

The incident that served as a *casus belli* occurred while Cetshwayo was still awaiting the commission's findings. On 26 July, two adulterous wives of Sihayo ka Xongo, a border chief, crossed into Natal with their lovers and took sanctuary among a kraal of border police. Hot on their heels came a son of Sihayo's, a young firebrand named Mehlokazulu, who seized the women, returned with them to Zululand and put them to death. Bulwer protested directly to Cetshwayo, requesting that Mehlokazulu and four other male relatives who were also implicated be handed over for trial in Natal. Cetshwayo replied that he could not comply without consulting his leading men. While recognizing that the matter was serious, he was clearly reluctant to lose face in the sight of his chiefs. Adultery was a capital offence and the women had been killed on

Zulu soil. Moreover, Sihayo was one of his oldest comrades and had given staunch support at the battle of Ndondakusuka. Pending a meeting of his councillors, he sent back £50, which Bulwer rejected.

Soon afterwards, Frere arrived in Pietermaritzburg to take charge of the situation. Scenting blood, newspaper editorials started a clamour for war in which they were abetted by the missionaries.

Schreuder and his Norwegian brethren had been followed to Zululand by German Lutherans of the Hermannsburg Missionary Society and the Church of England. By 1872 there were twenty-one stations north of the Tugela, but the 'teachers' failed to unlock any of the doors to white technology expected of them and what they did have to offer was inimical to traditional culture. Mpande had once complained: 'The people soon began to call themselves the people of the missionary, and refused to obey me.'[24] As for Cetshwayo, he declared that a Christian Zulu was 'a Zulu spoiled'.[25]

Denied converts, in effect by royal decree, the missionaries soured and brooded. Robert Robertson, a shrewd observer of Zulu affairs, disgraced himself in the eyes of his Anglican colleagues by drunkenness and fornicating with Zulu girls. Robertson and others who had set out with such high hopes to take the Word to the heathen, began to pray for a Zulu 'deliverance' by invasion. Amid the rise in tension along the Tugela, most missionaries left their stations and crossed into Natal. There Robertson pursued his campaign, writing articles in the press claiming that the Zulu 'would hail English rule tomorrow'. An Anglican monthly periodical, *The Net Cast in Many Waters*, circulated missionary hostilities in Britain.[26]

While Bulwer deplored 'absurd rumours' and a 'tendency to panic' among colonists, Frere was baffled and irritated to find in Natal 'a mass of half-informed and prejudiced people who, to much contempt and ill-will towards the Transvaal Boers, add a curious sort of sympathy for Cetshwayo, such as one might feel for a wolf or hyena one had petted'.[27]

Cetshwayo, meanwhile, was puzzling over what had turned his old friends into enemies. He found it hard to believe that they would now 'kill the country because of two foolish children'. One message in particular, for all its occasionally disingenuous tone, captures his genuine bewilderment:

What have I done or said to the great house of England, which placed my father Mpande over the Zulu nation, and after his death put me in power? What have I done to the great white chief? I hear from all parts that the soldiers are around me, and the Zulu nation asks me this day what I have said to the white people.

I hear that there is war intended, and the reason for it is that I said I was as great as the Queen of England – that Somseu was only as great as my chief Mnyamana.

I feel the English chiefs have stopped the rain and the land is being destroyed. They have told me that a kraal of blood cannot stand, and I wish to sit quietly according to their orders, and cultivate the land. I do not know anything about war, and want the great chiefs to send me the rain.[28]

In mid-November, a message arrived at Ondini from Frere that the findings of the boundary commission would be delivered to a Zulu delegation at the Tugela on 11 December, along with 'other communications'. It was clear to all that the British would raise the Sihayo incident, and the royal council met to consider its response. At the same time, Cetshwayo prepared himself against the possibility of a sudden invasion. Three *amabutho* were summoned to the capital as a praetorian guard. Another, the Ngobamakosi, was sent to build an *ikhanda* near St Lucia Bay as the king had heard the British might attack from the sea.

The consensus of the great men was that Sihayo's son should be handed to the British. According to Mkando ka Dhlova, one of Stuart's sources:

Mnyamana, Hamu and Zibhebhu said 'The country should not be destroyed on account of minor people. Let them be caught and handed over. It should be destroyed only your account, *nkosi*.' Hamu said: 'Even I, who am of the royal house, should be surrendered rather than let the whole country perish on my account.'[29]

Mnyamana, Cetshwayo's chief adviser, said:

Let Sihayo be taken and given to the whites. Let us not fight. We shall not remain in our good houses if we are ordered to fight these whites.[30]

Cetshwayo temporized. How much this was due to his friendship for Sihayo, and how much he might have been influenced by the young warriors who were now bursting for a fight, it is not possible to say. The king himself still shrank from war, but he was bound to take account of all shades of opinion, even when important individuals like Hamu protested that Sihayo's sons should be killed, and the bodies sent to Natal.

On the morning of 11 December, a large Zulu delegation came down to the edge of Tugela Drift and were ferried across to the Natal side in flat-bottomed punts. There were half a dozen *izinduna*, about forty leading men, and a similar number of mat-bearers, but no member of the king's inner circle. It was a swelter-ing mid-summer day, and John Shepstone stood under a tarpaulin hanging limply from a large fig tree as he read from a sheaf of papers. He started with the boundary award, which duly went in favour of the Zulus, and was greeted with a murmur of approval. Shepstone then suggested a break for lunch, and presented the delegates with an ox.

Soon after 1 p.m., Shepstone again appeared under the tarpaulin and started to read. This time it took him almost three hours to get through the document in his hand, and with each page his listeners became more apprehensive. Reduced to essentials, he announced that Cetshwayo had thirty days to disband the army and abandon the military system; to accept his 'coronation vows' as outlined in 1873 by Somseu; to allow all men to marry at the age of maturity; to admit a British diplomatic resident; and to re-admit all missionaries who had left the kingdom and allow them to teach the people without hindrance. Twenty days were to be allowed for Sihayo's sons to be handed over, and for payment of a fine of six hundred cattle.

It was called an ultimatum but it was more a declaration of war.

12

END OF THE BEGINNING

'It is like a ball of sand, with no larger base than a
ball would have, and with only shape enough to keep
its shape while undisturbed.'[1]

Theophilus Shepstone, of the Zulu kingdom,
1878

Frere went to war bolstered by Shepstone's assurance of Zulu fra-
gility. One touch and the whole thing would disintegrate. That
was what he was banking on, to get it all settled in the two months
that Thesiger had told him would be necessary for victory, before
London had a chance to intervene. It seems astonishing now that
a lone colonial official could go so far out on a limb without Whitehall's approval, but Frere had the authority and he was staking all
on one big gamble. Once he had been able, as he put it, 'to draw
the Monster's teeth and claws', a demilitarized Zululand would fit
tamely into his confederation, like an Indian 'subject ally'.[2]

Signals from Hamu had given further grounds for optimism.
Unknown to Cetshwayo, his half-brother had been hinting in messages to border agents that he might defect even before the ultimatum. Hamu was thought by Natal's spy network to command
a large following and the signals that went back assured him of a
welcome, protection, and an important role in a new Zululand. In
the event, Hamu sat tight for another three months and, when he

did finally cross over, assessments of the value of his support turned out to have been as faulty as most of Frere's intelligence.

John Dunn did not hold out as long, crossing into Natal two weeks before the expiry of the ultimatum with all his wives and around 2000 followers. He had put his best efforts into preserving the peace, as Cetshwayo's scribe and go-between with Bulwer, but now that the inevitable was approaching he felt keenly the ambiguity of his position. His rediscovery of his true loyalties, after so long enjoying royal patronage and the benefits of being an *induna*, earned him general contempt on the Zulu side. Dunn protested loudly that he would remain neutral but, gradually, became drawn in to helping the British. Cetshwayo never forgave him.

Over those final weeks, the king played for time. Eventually, he had accepted that Sihayo's sons would have to be surrendered, but was still asking Bulwer for more time to collect the fine, pointing out that written terms had only reached him ten days after the Tugela meeting. At the same time, he had to proceed cautiously as dangerous divisions were starting to show; elders who were in favour of accepting at least some of Frere's terms were being openly insulted by young firebrands. However much time was bought, talk of peace always foundered on an immovable rock: nothing would induce Cetshwayo or any other chief to agree to disband the *amabutho*.[3] As Frere must have known, they were much more than an army; they were the kingdom's organized labour force. Disbanding them would have dislocated the entire society.

The last great first-fruits ceremony to be held in the kingdom was a grave affair, lacking in any of the usual pageantry or celebration. The appointed day, when the moon would be full, was 8 January, only three days before the deadline expired, and Cetshwayo ordered that the *amabutho* should assemble, not in their ceremonial finery, but armed for war. As warriors set out for Ondini from every corner of the kingdom, reports came in that British forces were massing along the Tugela. The three-day rituals switched rapidly from harvest renewal to doctoring for war. As part of the preparations, each regiment was put in an enclosure with a wild young bull, which had then to be wrestled to the ground and killed by breaking its neck. War doctors cut the meat into long strips, *umbengo*, which were treated with medicine and roasted on mimosa wood. Every part of the animal had to be accounted for, lest the enemy obtain a portion and, with his own medicine, use it to gain the ascendancy. The carcass of the bull was incinerated. Cooked *umbengo* were meanwhile flung to the warriors and each man took a single bite before passing it to his neighbour.

Warriors with guns brought them forward to a vessel containing a smoking mixture and pointed them down over the container so the vapour passed up the barrel; this doctoring was to ensure that the bullets would find their targets. Another secret concoction was smeared on each warrior's forehead; for the first time, but not the last, warriors were assured by their *izangoma* that they would be invulnerable to the white man's bullets, which would turn to water. Finally, the *amabutho* gathered at a stream that fed into the White Mfolozi where a series of deep pits had been dug. Each man took a gulp of a potion mixed by the doctors, then ritually vomited into one of the pits. Some of the vomit was smeared on the *inkatha yezwe*, a sacred grass coil symbolizing national unity which had been passed down since Shaka's time. The pits were then sealed while the warriors washed in the stream. Thereafter, until the onset of war, they were to stay in seclusion and abstain from sexual intercourse.[4]

No record exists of Cetshwayo's spiritual preparation for the war but kings, no less than their warriors, had rituals to perform. He was supposed to consult the spirits of the Emakosini, his ancestors. According to Mtshapi ka Noradu, a warrior of the Mcijo regiment:

He would dream that the past kings had agreed. 'Let the army go forth. The kings have given their agreement.' He would then order the great chant of Senzangakona which he had received from Jama, to be sung. The whole army becomes fired with courage, their hearts become enraged, and they thirst for battle.[5]

On this occasion, Cetshwayo was reluctant to the last. His final request for an extension of the deadline was received in Natal on 11 January. Bulwer replied the next day. Only unconditional surrender was acceptable. Britain was at war with the Zulu.

In the regimental museum of the South Wales Borderers in Brecon, hangs a martial canvas on the grand scale. A meticulous and detailed work, compiled by Alphonse de Neuville from a soldier's sketches, it captures a critical point in the defence of Rorke's Drift, depicting a defiant little circle of bewhiskered redcoats in white sun helmets, their bayonets flashing. The air is thick with cordite and in the background smoke rises from a burning building and mingles with a mist coming off the Oskarberg mountains. Lieutenant John Chard VC reaches for a cartridge to slide into his Martini-Henry rifle. Private Henry Hook VC is carrying the wounded Corley to safety. It is all there – all the pride and gallantry of the Anglo-Zulu war.

And there is not a Zulu in sight.

It has been well said by the historian Norman Etherington that the 1879 campaign appeals to military enthusiasts because it seems to lack the most abhorrent features of war – flagrant abuses of civilians, rape, pillage or concentration camps – and has a great deal to gladden martial hearts. The courage and comradeship on both sides was the stuff of legend and it was, indeed, a most theatrical war. To that might be added a rarer quality. Both sides fought without quarter or pity but, by and large, without rancour either. By the end, the Zulu had earned a respect that transcended the ubiquitous references to them as 'savages'. The British army is itself innately tribal and no soldier could fail to admire the full-frontal assaults of the Zulus in the face of withering fire. 'My, how they do come on,' was a refrain heard in British ranks from Kambula to Ulundi.

But like the missing figures in the canvas, the Zulu side of the war has been largely overlooked. *Zulu*, a well-known film about the war, based largely around events at Rorke's Drift (in fact, a relatively minor engagement) was not about Zulus at all. Its stars were Michael Caine and Stanley Baker, playing Chard and Lieutenant Gonville Bromhead, another hero of that battle. The centenary of the war produced a spate of publications which, with one splendid exception, also focused on imperial heroics. It took an academic work, Jeff Guy's *The Destruction of the Zulu Kingdom*, to look beyond the mustachioed redcoats and that other Zulu War cliché, the self-immolating *impi*, to demonstrate that the kingdom was destroyed not by the war, but by the peace. (Another academic, John Laband, has since followed this with a fine and detailed study of the war from the Zulu side, *Kingdom in Crisis*.) The final battle, Ulundi, was just a curtain-raiser to the ruin of Zululand and the death throes were to last another thirty years. Romantic, heroic – it may have seemed so. Yet the British invasion of Zululand was one of the most terrible of wars, for it was not about territory or resources, but about a way of life.

The British force that assembled on the Natal frontier in January numbered 18,000 men, including 5500 imperial regulars, 1200 mounted colonial volunteers and roughly 2000 transport and supply staff. However, by far the largest contingent consisted of more than 9000 Zulu-speaking levies. Bulwer had resisted the raising of this force to the last. Some whites were alarmed by the idea of showing natives how to use guns and the governor worried, with good reason as it turned out, that it would cause lasting enmity between Zulu-speakers on either side of the Tugela. However, Thesiger – who had just inherited the title of Lord Chelmsford – insisted that he had insufficient men, and his demands prevailed. The black recruits ranged from 100 Edendale *amakholwa*, or Christian converts, who had adopted European dress and came with their own horses, to about 300 deserters from the Thulwana *ibutho* who retained all their own regimental attire. Otherwise, the levies were mainly to be distinguished from Cetshwayo's men by the red bandanas around their heads. It is a little remarked fact that in the first stage of the campaign, Chelmsford was as dependent on Zulu mercenaries as Pretorius had been on Mpande's rebels in 1840.

The strategy was simplicity itself: a three-pronged advance across the seventy-odd miles to Ondini (or Illundi, as the British called it) to depose the king and enforce the terms of the ultimatum. Chelmsford's experience of war against the Xhosa had convinced him that black warriors 'had only to be hunted', but he hoped fervently that the Zulu would come out and fight, for they would then have to throw themselves on highly disciplined infantry squares. He would accompany the centre column of 4700 men under Colonel Richard Glyn, which was to cross the upper Tugela at Rorke's Drift. To the south, the right column of 4700 men under Colonel Charles Pearson would cross at Tugela Drift near the coast. The left column, the 2250 men of Colonel Evelyn Wood, would come in from the north and drive down into the heart of the kingdom. Two other forces were kept in reserve.[6]

The crossing started at dawn on 11 January, and Chelmsford suffered his first losses even before enemy territory was reached. Several Natal Zulus were swept away while fording the Tugela. The next day brought amends. In the opening skirmish of the war, about twenty of Sihayo's men were killed, and his brother gave himself up with a few dependants. There was to be precious little else for the British to cheer about for some time.

The Zulu army assembled at Ondini 'seemed to stretch from there right to the sea',[7] according to one warrior present. Every man capable of bearing arms was at the royal *umuzi*, from the greybeards of the Mbelebele and Dlambedlu, now nearing their sixtieth year, to the newest *ibutho*, the Uve, in their early twenties. It was the largest force to be mustered in the history of Zulu arms: not fewer than 29,000 warriors awaited the king's command.[8]

Cetshwayo's army was built on essentially the same principle as Shaka's had been fifty years earlier, a fast-moving, marauding infantry. One vital, new, but untested element had been introduced – firearms. Just how many guns had been imported by means of Dunn's clandestine operations is uncertain. A figure of twenty thousand is often cited but, even if this figure is accurate, the vast majority were antiquated muskets, and there was a severe shortage of ammunition; many Zulu had to resort to firing pebbles and metal fragments during the war. Fewer than a thousand Zulu had modern breech-loading rifles. None the less, the availability of firearms gave a formidable defensive potential.

Further uncertainty surrounds Cetshwayo's intentions. We know that the lessons of the Ncome river battle against the Boers forty years earlier had been absorbed. The *izinduna* were under instructions that under no circumstances should they attack fortified positions, wagon laagers or otherwise. It is also clear that there was never an intention to threaten Natal itself, even after the initial British disaster. Judging from his actions, Cetshwayo hoped to hurl back the invaders and then play for time. Despite all previous evidence to the contrary, he still believed that if he gained a chance to put his case across, it would prevail because of its justice.

The news that 'the country was red with soldiers'[9] decided Cetshwayo to gamble most of his force in one concentration. Chelmsford's central column was the most immediately threatening; a great *impi* would confront it. Holding operations would meanwhile be launched by smaller forces against the columns in the north and south. A reserve of the older *amabutho* would be held back as a final resort at Ondini.

The day before the *impi* set out, Cetshwayo summoned the *amabutho*, 'so that I may hear what you will do on the day you see the enemy'.[10] Then, men of each regiment started to dance and *giya*, provoking and challenging one another with the deeds they would perform. Typically, one of the Ngobamakosi taunted a Mcijo: 'I shall surpass you, son of Ndhlovu. If you stab a white man before mine has fallen, you may take the kraal of our people, you may take my sister, you may take my father's cattle.'[11] The king watched, occasionally wagging a finger in approval. Amid the singing and stamping of feet, the dust rose on a red setting sun.

The largest Zulu *impi* in history, between 20,000 and 25,000 men, started to move down the Mahlabatini Plain towards the White Mfolozi on the afternoon of 17 January. Over the next four days, two great columns traversed the rolling country through the sweet, green waist-high grass, cutting a swath across the landscape that was still visible weeks later. It was high summer, and they travelled in the morning and evening, conserving their strength as Cetshwayo had urged, and feeding as best they could from kraals along the way.

More than twenty years had passed since the Zulu had last gone to war and inexperience was apparent as much in the leadership as in the ranks. It was also a weakness that, like the British army of the Crimea, commanders tended to be appointed for their social standing, rather than any proved ability. The commander was Ntshingwayo ka Marole. Aged sixty-eight and head of the Koza clan, he was revered as a link with the age of Shaka; his father had been a herdboy with Senzangakona. He, certainly, was more aristocrat than general. The chief of staff was Mavumengwana, who was aged around forty-five. A son of Dingane's old commander Ndlela, he had been an *induna* in the Tulwana and might have been expected to offer tactical guidance. Dabulamanzi, a full brother of the king's, was a fire-eater who smouldered with barely restrained aggression. Wrongly identified by the British as the Zulu commander, perhaps because of his overweening manner, his influence was to be disastrous. Perhaps the most able military man was Zibhebhu, whose loyalty was under some question.

218

Vumandaba, who had received the British ultimatum, marched with the *impi*, as did the king's old friend, Sihayo. That chief's volatile son, Mehlokazulu, who had been held responsible for much of the trouble, was a junior *induna* in the Ngobamakosi.

Ceremonial regalia had been set aside and the warriors were stripped to kilts and cowtail leggings. Some regiments were distinguishable by their shields, those of the Tulwana veterans being white with a black patch. But the main identifying feature of a particular *ibutho* was its war chant. As the Mcijo marched, they sang of themselves as 'we who smash the rocks'. Their great rivals, the Ngobamakosi – whose name meant 'bend the chiefs' – praised themselves as 'the lightning of the sky'.[12] These two regiments, the youngest in the army, with a knowledge of combat limited to the lore of the fireside, were to be in the forefront of the cataclysm that followed.

By 21 January, four days after setting out, the *impi* had covered about fifty miles and was within ten miles of the Natal border. That evening it was strung out along the floor of the Ngwebeni valley. Scouts had come in with intelligence that the British were camped between five and six miles away.

Chelmsford's progress over rocky broken country had been methodical and slow. He had arrived the previous day on a comparatively open plain, with clear views extending more than four miles to the east and perhaps two to the north, whence any Zulu war party would be expected to come. He set up his camp in the lee of a striking conical hill, about seven hundred yards across at the base, which would guard his rear. The hill was called Isandlwana, meaning 'little house'. For once, the Zulu gift for linguistic imagery was found wanting. The British soldiers thought it looked like a sphinx, or a crouching lion.

The foe lay at hand, but the Zulu were not yet ready. A moon was dying and activity of any kind at such a time invited a dreaded condition known as *umnyama*. In war, this would bring evil upon the *impi* and fortune to the enemy. On the evening of 21 January, *izinduna* told their men there would be no fighting the next day but to be ready for the new moon on 23 January. That night fires flickered briefly along the valley before being extinguished for fear of alerting the British.

At dawn on 22 January, about half of the British force rode out of camp. A message received in the night from a patrol indicated that the Zulu army had been located and Chelmsford hoped to catch it unawares. In fact, the patrol had spotted only a small force, well to the east of the main *impi*. Oblivious of the real danger, Chelmsford had committed the cardinal error of dividing his force in enemy country. He had also ignored the advice of men experienced in 'kaffir' campaigns, including the Transvaal leader, Paul Kruger who, at a brief meeting in Durban, admonished him about the necessity to laager his wagons as the Boers had done at the Ncome river.

Despite the camp's vulnerability, there is no reason to suppose that the Zulu would have attacked that day, but for coincidence.

Midway through the morning, the *impi* was still strung out for a mile or so on the valley floor, lying up, resting and talking, when a crackling of gunfire was heard well to the east. Chelmsford's force had caught up with the stragglers. At around the same time, and also to the east, Zulu foragers were returning with cattle rounded up for the hungry army, when a mounted volunteer patrol under Captain George Shepstone, one of Somseu's sons, spotted them at a distance and set off in pursuit. The cattle were being driven down into the valley as the patrol reached the top of the ridge.

The response of the scouts to seeing what must have seemed the entire Zulu nation spread out below is not recorded. For a long moment they could only look down on the host below. Then they reached for their rifles and a volley rang out.

Spontaneously, the nearest *ibutho*, the Mcijo, rose and started up towards them. With a roar, the Nokhenke were up and following on the right, the Ngobamakosi and Mbonambi on the left. The commanders, further up to the valley to the left, managed to restrain about a third of the *impi*, but there was no way of stopping the 13,000 or so youngest warriors who were now streaming up the side of the ridge. Ntshingwayo and Mavumengwana mustered their veterans, including the Thulwana and the Dloko, then set off down the valley on a flanking movement to the right. They were to be remote from the main theatre of action.

As the fleetest warriors reached the top of the ridge they could see Isandlwana about five miles away to the south-west, protruding from open but gently undulating veld. Shepstone's party was falling back towards the camp in orderly fashion, stopping occasionally to fire as they went.

Automatically, the *amabutho* started to take up the traditional horn formation for attack. Massing on the escarpment, they started to pour down on to the plain, fanning out to left and right as they came. It was shortly after midday.

Chelmsford had left 1770 men in camp, including six companies of the 24th Regiment, four of the Natal Native Contingent, and two seven-pounder guns. By coincidence, the senior officer was Colonel Anthony Durnford, who had been summoned from Rorke's Drift that morning to make up the strength. However, he was out on a sortie to the south-east and it was left to Colonel Henry Pulleine to deploy his men in a large semicircle almost a mile across and 800 yards beyond the wagons. A small group went up to support the retreating scouts. Between them, they kept up a sharp fire at the centre of the horns, or 'the chest', consisting of the Mcijo and the Nokhenkhe. Durnford had meanwhile returned in time to set up a fighting outpost of about 200 men, including the Edendale *amakholwa*, on the southern flank of the camp. They watched the oncoming left horn: the Uve, Ngobamakosi and Mbonambi.

The Zulu ate up the ground with loping strides. All the pent-up energy and aggression of years went into that charge. It had a single objective – to get to close quarters. One warrior fighting for the first time that day recalled being told: 'Don't bother about those of your own who are hit, but press on ahead.'[13] They made little use of their own guns. Those with firearms blazed away randomly, apparently without aiming and certainly without effect. It later emerged that many believed that their guns, like their assegais, would only prove effective once they were within the enemy enclosure. Instead of a steady volley of fire, the oncoming warriors set up a sound that the defenders found even more unnerving, a low murmuring hum like a vast swarm of bees.

As they came to within two miles of the camp, both left horn and right horn started to falter under the fire from the Martini-Henrys of the two outlying groups who were still falling back, and the two seven-pounders, which were 'cutting roads through them'. For perhaps fifteen minutes the attack was stalled. Men, pouring with sweat after the dash across the plain in sweltering heat, lay flat in the dust and gratefully drew breath.

It was at this critical stage, according to the Zulu chronicler Magema, that an *induna* of the Mcijo roused his men with a reminder of their bravado in the *giya* at Ondini. 'You did not say you were going to lie down!' he roared.[14] Again the Mcijo rose and hurled themselves forward. As they did, another *induna* named Sikizane shouted a taunt across to the Ngobamakosi: 'Why are you lying down? What was it you said to the Mcijo? There are the Mcijo going into the tents.'[15]

Stung, the left horn also rose and raced on again, sweeping out even further on the left. Durnford's men resumed an intense fire but, still more than a mile from camp, were gradually being out-flanked. They were also running short of ammunition. Without haste or panic, they started to fall back.

The defenders had so far suffered few casualties but the sheer stamina and determination of the attack was starting to work on them. One volunteer later uttered a common refrain: 'We shot hundreds but it seemed to make no impression, they still came on.'[16] The redcoats, the *amasoja*, had been firing for an hour, and they too had started to run low on cartridges. A tremor went through the ranks; here and there gaps started to appear as indi-viduals broke and fell back on the camp. Suddenly, the right flank was open and exposed. Sensing their advantage, the *impi* surged into the gap yelling Cetshwayo's war-cry, '*Usuthu! Usuthu!*'

At the top end of the camp, the redcoats had been pouring fire into the Nokhenkhe but they too were now infiltrated and were starting to fragment. Pulleine ordered firing to cease and a retreat to camp.

It was the consensus afterwards that the Mbonambi were the first among the tents. On their heels were the Ngobamakosi and the Mcijo.[17] Suddenly there was no line. The solid blocks of red-coated men started to dissolve and mingle with the flailing tawny tide that was engulfing the camp. Isolated bands of soldiers held together, fighting back to back. One group of men from C Com-pany, 24th Regiment, under Captain Reginald Younghusband, fought a retreat up the side of Isandlwana itself and on a flat grassy outcrop took up a position for a last stand. Others, at the bottom end of the camp, seeing all lost, had started to flee to the south-west.

The British fired until their bullets ran out, then fought on with fixed bayonets. It was the pitiless, face-to-face combat of Zulu tra-dition and yet, even now, in their hour of triumph, the warriors were learning an awful lesson. The fact was, a long bayonet at the end of a heavy rifle thrust made a far more effective stabbing spear than any assegai. Mehlokazulu later recalled: 'Any man who went to stab a soldier was fixed through the throat or stomach, and at once fell.'[18] But Zulu numbers were overwhelming. While one warrior hung impaled on a bayonet, others leapt forward. Some soldiers fell under an avalanche of bodies; sometimes, 'when a soldier was engaged with a Zulu in front, another Zulu killed him from behind.'[19]

Mpatshana ka Sadondo, who, as a member of the Ngobamakosi, was in the thick of things, agreed that it frequently took more than one warrior to subdue a foe. Men 'stabbed opponents who had already been stabbed by others'. This won respect because similar tactics had to be employed in killing lion. 'It was recognized that fighting against such a foe and killing some of them was of the same high grade as lion hunting,' Mpatshana said.[20] Another source was more down to earth:

Some [British] covered their faces with their hands, not wishing to see death. Some ran away. Some entered into the tents. Others were indignant; although badly wounded they died where they stood.[21]

At 2.29 p.m., while the slaughter was at its height, there occurred a partial eclipse of the sun. It was roughly two and a half hours since the Zulu had come surging out of the Ngwebeni valley, and the British army had suffered its most humiliating defeat since the turn of the century.

Those defenders who were still able, joined what had become a general flight towards Natal and the Buffalo river, which lay about four miles to the south-west over broken country. However, the Zulu commanders, Ntshingwayo and Mavumengwana, had ordered the right horn of about 6000 men to execute a flanking movement around the back of Isandlwana hill. As the fugitives made their way down towards the river, they saw to their horror warriors racing around to their right to cut them off. Here the killing continued, although in all the chaos, shouting and shooting it was now possible to take evasive action. The British survivors of Isandlwana were those who, like Lieutenant (later general) Horace Smith-Dorrien, managed, on horseback or foot, to scramble madly down the gullies, among rocks and red flowering aloes, to the river and plunge headlong into the rescuing waters of the Buffalo.

They were pitifully few. Of the 800 white soldiers who had been left in camp that morning, 779 were dead, including Durnford, Pulleine and George Shepstone. Every man-jack of the six imperial infantry companies had perished, although five officers had escaped. Of the 907 blacks, 471 had been killed. Many escaped only because they were less conspicuous than the redcoats.

In the camp, the aftermath was as grisly as the battle itself. Mopping up operations went on through the afternoon. Nothing was spared, neither the drummer boy of the 24th, nor the horses which were 'the feet for the white men'. One warrior acknowledged, 'our eyes were dark, so we stabbed everything we came across. But when we got light into our eyes again we spared what oxen and mules were left.'[22] The victors were too dazed and exhausted for rejoicing, but there were still rites to perform. Men wandered among the bodies, stripping off the red tunics and other garments to be used later in purification ceremonies. They disembowelled the bodies to dispose of troublesome spirits.[23] Zulu dead were too numerous for burial, so bodies were simply covered with their shields. The wounded were helped or carried from the scene. So many died afterwards that it was believed British bullets were poisoned. No reliable estimate of Zulu dead can be made: it is generally put at around 1000 but could as easily have been 1500.

The loot was considerable. Oxen were hitched to wagons to carry away spades, blankets and a mass of other useful objects. Overnight, the firepower of the Zulu arsenal was virtually doubled. No less important than 800 Martini-Henry rifles were some 40,000 bullets, although the two seven-pounder field guns that trundled eastwards towards Ondini that evening were never to be turned on the invaders.

Some days after, a few Zulu boys who had heard of the battle went to Isandlwana. One later recalled the scene:

We arrived early in the morning. We saw the soil was red, the sun shining very brightly. We saw a single warrior dead, staring in our direction, with his war shield in his hand. We ran away. We came back again. We saw countless things dead. Dead was the horse, dead too the mule, dead was the dog, dead were the boxes, dead was everything, even to the very metals.[24]

In the hour of its greatest victory, the Zulu military exposed to the enemy its Achilles' heel. The action at Rorke's Drift later that same day flew in the face of the tenets that had been laid down by Cetshwayo for waging the war, and enabled the British to salvage a morsel of comfort from defeat.

The honours of Isandlwana had been won by youth, by the raw warriors of the left horn and the 'chest'. The *amabutho* on the right horn, including the veterans of the Thulwana and Dloko, all men well into their forties, had missed most of the fighting. They felt cheated of glory and were liable to have their prowess and courage derided. The situation was now inflamed by the king's intemperate brother, Dabulamanzi, who roused between three and four thousand of the men on the right horn to launch an attack on the British depot at Rorke's Drift, inside Natal. Cetshwayo had ordered that the *impi* should not enter Natal, nor should it attack fortified positions. That a man of status but no rank could have acted as Dabulamanzi now did – despite the presence of the commanders Ntshingwayo and Mavumengwana – demonstrated one of the most fundamental flaws in the military system.

The story of Rorke's Drift is well known and, as one of the less significant engagements of the war, needs no lengthy retelling here. Under the command of two young lieutenants, Chard and Bromhead, 130 British troops, some of them sick and wounded, staged a doughty twelve-hour defence of the depot. Dabulamanzi handled his force atrociously and, by the time the Zulu withdrew, he had sacrificed another five hundred or so men for a mere seventeen of the defenders. Chard, Bromhead and nine others were awarded Victoria Crosses.[25]

Good though all this might have been for soldiers' morale in the field, no number of VCs could paper over a disaster as great as Isandlwana. The shock waves were felt from Pietermaritzburg to Durban, from Cape Town to London.

There is no indication that the victory was accompanied by any rejoicing at Ondini. Paradoxically, Cetshwayo saw his victory not as an opportunity to drive home military advantage with an invasion of Natal, but a chance to renew negotiations. His *impi* had 'eaten up' the British; it seemed only logical to him that the British would now be willing to hear his peaceful intentions. A message from Ondini to the Norwegian missionary, Schreuder, stated that the king still did not understand British demands, but was willing to listen to any proposals. In all, peace envoys were sent to Natal eighteen times in the five months of war.

Possibly, the price of victory had brought home just how fearful would be the cost of defeat. Cetshwayo evidently did not believe he could continue to hold the British back indefinitely. True, Chelmsford had withdrawn immediately to Natal for reinforcements, but one victory had required the efforts of almost the entire Zulu army. In the meantime, the British left and right columns had got the better of some heavy skirmishing against small *impis* and remained deep inside Zulu territory, in fortified positions.

Colenso pointed to another critical factor. The Zulu, he wrote, were 'an armed people, not a standing army'. In the aftermath of victory, many of the fighters did not return to Ondini in triumph, but made directly for their own kraals, desperate for food, and so that they could carry out their purification rituals. The military leadership had failed to think through the conduct of this new kind of war. For all the enduring quality of the Battle of Isandlwana as a feat of arms, it gave ample notice of the problems ahead.

If the response to Isandlwana was muted at Ondini, it was not at Pietermaritzburg. Unaware of Cetshwayo's hopes for peace, Natal saw only Chelmsford's hasty retreat and, assuming that an invasion of black supermen was now imminent, went into an understandable panic. Barricades went up in the centre of every town, local militia were drafted, and all ships leaving Durban were crammed with women and children.

At Ekukanyeni, the Colenso household was caught between mourning for Durnford, friend of the bishop and beloved of his daughter Fanny, and anxiety over the public clamour for revenge. Colenso, who was just embarking on a crusade for Cetshwayo that was to be every bit as courageous as his defence of Langalibalele, noted gloomily: '"Extermination" is the cry.'

The news of Isandlwana did not reach London for another three weeks. Disraeli's cabinet was still absorbing the fact that they were at war with an unknown but reputedly savage people when Hicks Beach, the colonial secretary, presented them on 12 February with the news. 'Stricken', the prime minister took to his bed.

Disraeli was to be much troubled by the Zulu War. It was a significant factor in his election defeat the following year, when a Liberal landslide threw the Tories 'forward' policy of expansion in southern Africa into reverse. In South Africa itself, Frere and Shepstone, and all their schemes, were irretrievably discredited. There would be no confederation, or union – not, at least, for another thirty years.

13

BEGINNING OF THE END

We are the boys from Isandlwana!

Zulu *impi* en route to defeat, Battle of Kambula,
29 March 1879

In some respects, defeat at Isandlwana would have served the Zulu cause better than victory. For the British, humiliation required nothing less than the redemption of overwhelming victory. As for the Zulus, defeat might have stung the military into a re-examination of its ossified tactical concepts. Instead, a diehard conservatism that has at times seemed a feature of the Zulu character prevailed and a headlong rush to disaster began.

It has been customary to assume that, after Isandlwana, Britain was always going to have its face-saving victory. That may be so, but other wars of resistance against the British were fought and lost in South Africa, with consequences a good deal less catastrophic to the vanquished than that of 1879 proved for the Zulu. For decades, the Xhosa had demonstrated on the eastern frontier an almost infinite capacity for ducking and weaving away from the decisive confrontations which British generals sought to engineer. Twenty years later, the Boers of the Transvaal were to show just how effective a guerrilla campaign could be against a mighty imperial army. Both of these options were open to the Zulus. So was a third, of defensive hit-and-run tactics. The logistics of operating in

Zululand had given Chelmsford nightmares from the start, as the country was completely unsuited to supplying by ox wagon. Slow-moving transport in hostile territory would be susceptible to breakdowns on the rough tracks and overworked pasturage, and vulnerable to disruption by mobile marauders. So it proved on the one occasion that a supply convoy was attacked.

Often it was patience and discipline that were lacking on the Zulu side, as for example at Rorke's Drift. There was also perhaps an even more critical flaw. Pride had always been close to hubris in their way of war and, in 1879, it riddled the *amabutho* and undermined the opportunities created by their unquenchable courage. The condition can be seen in the attitude of a warrior like Mpatshana ka Sodondo of the Ngobamakosi, whose understandable pride in the feat of Isandlwana blinded him to alternative tactics. When, almost thirty years later, an uprising against white rule took place and Zulus finally resorted to concealment and ambush, elder warriors shook their heads and Mpatshana commented: 'They waylaid Europeans wherever they could. We laughed at them for this. Zulus would have taken up a position in the open and come face to face with the foe.'[1] Zulu conduct in 1879 brings to mind nothing so much as General Bosquet's observation on the Light Brigade at Balaclava: '*C'est magnifique, mais ce n'est pas la guerre.*'

There followed a lull after Isandlwana, as Chelmsford withdrew with the survivors of the centre column to Pietermaritzburg to await reinforcements, leaving Wood and Pearson to hold their positions in north and south Zululand. Pearson's right column had advanced to find the countryside abandoned, but was harried by an *impi* of 5000 men under Godide ka Ndlela. After a heavy skirmish at Inyezane, where British troops used the Gatling gun in anger for the first time, Pearson fortified the old mission at Eshowe and went into laager.

Cetshwayo had none of his regular *amabutho* left over for the northern sector. Defences against Wood's left column were left to, on the one hand, fervent royalists of the northern Qulusi section, who would have fought to the last man to defend the king and, on the other, chiefs of uncertain loyalty, such as Sekethwayo ka Nhlaka, and semi-independent mavericks like Mbilini ka Mswati, a renegade Swazi prince. They nevertheless provided stout resistance in a series of skirmishes in January. After the news of

Isandlwana, Wood set up a strongly fortified camp atop Kambula hill, about sixty miles north-west of Ondini.

With a disaster to be avenged, Whitehall lurched from parsimony to open-handedness. Its response to Chelmsford's request for reinforcements was to issue orders by the end of February for six infantry battalions, two cavalry regiments, two artillery batteries and various support staff to take ship for Durban. Chelmsford could do little while waiting impatiently for them to arrive. Pearson's right column was bottled up at Eshowe, although safe enough from attack. Wood's position was also a secure one, and he at least could launch occasional forays under the energetic command of his deputy, Major Redvers Buller. Simultaneously, Wood was pursuing political advantage; after months of hesitation, the king's half-brother, Hamu, was at last ready to defect. He arrived at Wood's camp on 10 March, but with an entourage of only 600 instead of the great following that had been expected. It was the consensus, none the less, that Hamu would yet prove useful, and he was packed off to Natal with a generous gin ration against that day.

Two days after Hamu's defection, disaster befell the invaders again. A wagon convoy bringing supplies up to a garrison in the far north was surprised by about 1000 of Mbilini's marauders along the Ntombe river. Men of the 20th Regiment under Captain David Moriarty were still in their blankets when the raiders descended on the camp out of a misty dawn. Moriarty fell after shooting three of his assailants, but few of his men managed to reach their weapons. Only a handful, rallied by a sergeant who staged a fighting retreat across the river, escaped. The action at Ntombe Drift was one of only two occasions in the war on which imperial casualties clearly outnumbered those of the Zulu. Sixty-one British soldiers were killed, along with eighteen black and white transport staff. Only thirty Zulu dead were found.[2]

Although Chelmsford had to grit his teeth at this fresh setback, by late March enough reinforcements had arrived for him to proceed with his first objective – to relieve the besieged Pearson at Eshowe. Once that was accomplished, he would reassemble his army for a thrust at Ondini. On 28 March, a force of 3400 Europeans and 2300 Natal Zulus crossed the Tugela without incident and started the thirty-mile march towards Eshowe. This time there was to be no carelessness about laagering the wagons and the fact that John Dunn had been co-opted as head of intelligence ensured that English officers were well informed.

At Ondini, the leadership had been buoyed by the action at Ntombe and, at an assembly of all the great men, Cetshwayo issued orders which, had they been carried out, would have significantly undermined Chelmsford's plans. The king also sent out a new series of peace feelers to the British – who responded by clapping his envoys in irons.

So far as the Zulu were concerned, Pearson was harmless while shut up in his fort. The southern *impi* was to be reinforced with some of the men from Isandlwana to ensure that he stayed there, and to prevent any efforts to supply him. This force, of roughly 10,000 warriors, was under Somopho ka Zikhale, although Dabula-manzi was again to make his presence felt. Wood's left column was the more threatening, so it was northwards that the king now despatched the rest of his army. His orders were explicit, and sensible: 'to bring the whites into the open field' by driving off their cattle, or to surround their entrenched position on Kambula 'and make them die of hunger'[3] – in other words, to besiege them. This operation was to involve an *impi* of some 20,000 men, includ-ing most of the Isandlwana veterans. Their commanders were Ntshingwayo and Mnyamana, the king's venerable prime minister, who was now aged about seventy. The theatre for this decisive stage of the war differed vastly from the open terrain on which Chelmsford had come to grief. It was rocky and mountainous, ideally suited for defence or guerrilla warfare.

Wood had some warning of the advancing force, but had no idea of its whereabouts when he assigned a force of 670 men in late March to flush out about 2000 Zulus of the Qulusi section who had occupied the mountain fastness of Hlobane, about twenty miles to the east. In the early hours of 28 March, Buller led his mounted troops up the eastern slopes of Hlobane through a thunderstorm that lit up the rocky plateau to which they were ascending. Dawn was breaking as a few Zulus opened fire from the cover of caves and crags, but Buller reached the summit without significant casualties. He was skirmishing across the top, driving off what Zulu cattle were found when, in mid-morning, the horrified British looked down from Hlobane to see, about three miles off to the south, an *impi* almost as large as that at Isandlwana loping towards them.

The Zulu advancing on Kambula had heard the gunfire from Hlobane and changed direction to the north. It now became a race by Buller and his men to get off the plateau and withdraw down a precipitous pass westwards to Kambula before being cut off. They were chased and harried as they went by the Qulusi, who proved better marksmen than most Zulus, and the retreat became a rout. One section, which had become detached from Buller's main force and was caught between the Qulusi and an *ibutho* fleeter than the rest, was all but wiped out.

This third successive disaster for the British was exceeded only by Isandlwana. Fifteen officers and seventy-nine men lay dead on Hlobane, along with more than a hundred Natal Zulu levies. In the two months since the start of Frere's crudely provoked war, Britain had nothing to show but defeat and humiliation.

At this stage, with the foe on the run, and the war in the balance, the Zulu military proceeded to commit collective suicide.

Elation swept the encampment along the White Mfolozi that night. The ground was sodden from the earlier thunderstorm and a cold fog came off the hills, but the warriors were still flushed with triumph. Around the fires glittering beside the river, new praises were composed and voices were raised in *uxoxa impi* as pipes of cannabis circulated and fuelled the heady air. The next day, the *impi* ate a leisurely breakfast and, at mid-morning, started for Kambula, twelve miles to the north-west.

Wood's forces had recovered sufficiently from the trauma of the previous day to be fully prepared and their position was vastly superior to Pulleine's at Isandlwana. The Kambula fortification sat atop a narrow ridge with a commanding view of all approaches. A laager of wagons was drawn up on the west end of the ridge, while about 200 yards away, at the highest point on the east side, stood the redoubt. Four field guns covered the northern plain and another four the south. In the weeks that they had spent here, Wood and Buller had laid the ground meticulously: a series of white painted stones acted as range markers for the artillery. There were more than 1200 infantry and about 700 horse. Kambula was a formidable and forbidding objective: any attempt to storm it was bound to involve dreadful casualties.

Cetshwayo's orders, as he later related them, had been clear:

'Encamp close by, harass the camp, attack the horses and cattle out at pasture, force Wood to come out and fight in the open.'[4] Had these instructions been followed, no assault would have been made. The evidence as to why they were ignored is scanty. It is reasonably sure that the critical point occurred at around midday, as the garrison saw the *impi* mass on a hill about four miles south-east of Kambula where it was addressed by Mnyamana. The commander had been equivocal about fighting the British from the start and was still fearful of where it would all end. His irresolution angered his men. By now normal rivalry between the *amabutho* had been raised to fever pitch, particularly between the units that had carried the day at Isandlwana – the Ngobamakosi, the Mcijo and the Mbonambi. So long denied opportunities for honour, youth had seized destiny with both hands; traditional respect for elders had worn thin. Under pressure to abandon Cetshwayo's strategy and launch a direct attack, Mnyamana failed to stand firm.[5]

Later, perhaps trying to justify the rashness of the Ngobamakosi, Mpatshana said that Mnyamana's talk had made the men uneasy. 'He was unduly apprehensive and fearful of the results. When the battle occurred, the *impi* was not directed by Mnyamana but took up position by itself.'[6] Or, as another warrior, the headstrong Mehlokazulu, put it: 'Our hearts were full, and we intended to do the same as at Isandlwana.'[7]

For more than an hour the *impi* had been mustered in full view of the British when suddenly it started to fan out slowly in an encircling movement. One onlooker wrote home: 'The whole country round was black with the enemy and it seemed as if these legions would swamp us completely.'[8] First to start for the laager at a run were the Ngobamakosi, from the north.

Buller galloped out with a small band to bait this headlong charge. At perhaps 700 yards' distance they dismounted and fired a volley, then pulled back. Onward dashed the Ngobamakosi – on to the white stone range markers, set for the seven-pounders. At 1.45 p.m., the artillery opened up.

Across the plain from the south, six *amabutho*, including the Mcijo and the Nokhenkhe, also charged straight into the seven-pounders. From the east, into a wall of fire poured down on them from the redoubt, came the Dududu, the Thulwana, the Sangqu and others. A German soldier in the fort found himself marvelling at their 'dash, élan and fearlessness'.[9] But the carnage was frightful. As the flimsiness of cowhide shields was repeatedly exposed by shrapnel and bullets, some warriors were seen carrying rocks in front of them to shelter behind.[10]

The Ngobamakosi managed to get within about 200 yards of the laager before the hand of unseen death forced them to fall back and seek cover among some rocky ground to the north-east. Meanwhile, the charge from the south was maintained up the slope and to the British line. A few members of the Nokhenkhe got to the wagons before being shot down. Wood noticed a wounded *induna* being helped away by two comrades, but they did not get far before all three were felled. As the Zulus wavered, two companies of redcoats streamed out in a bayonet charge and drove them back. Other warriors, presented for once with an exposed target, used their firearms to an effect telling enough to drive the redcoats back. Most of the British casualties were suffered in this foray.

There was, however, little attempt by the Zulus to concentrate fire at the defenders within and, once again, it is as if they believed their guns could not kill unless they were face-to-face with the enemy, whether inside his enclosure or on open ground. Their marksmanship had undoubtedly improved, especially with the captured Martini-Henry rifles, but the concept of killing at a distance – the very basis of modern warfare – remained alien. Every instinct instead clamoured for the one objective: to get to close quarters.

Fury and frustration mounted at the redcoats' unwillingess to fight in the same way. Cornelius Vijn, a trader who was the only white to remain in Zululand during the war (and who was impeccably treated by Cetshwayo throughout) said:

The general remark of the Zulus was, 'Why could not the whites fight with us in the open? We have never fought with men who were so much afraid of death as these. They are continually making holes in the ground and mounds left open with little holes to shoot through. The English burrow in the ground like wild pigs. The Boers are of more worth, who dare to come into the open field.'[11]

Further assaults were launched up Kambula hill through the afternoon, but with less and less conviction as the pile of semi-naked brown bodies before the ridge rose. At 5.30, the spirit that had carried the *amabutho* into the tents at Isandlwana was dying with the sun.

As the Zulu fell back for the last time, Wood unleashed his cavalry. Buller's men charged among the exhausted *impi* with memories of their own defeat the previous day, wielding pistols and using captured assegais like cavalry sabres. The Zulus would have expected no mercy and received none. Only the cover of nightfall delivered them from what was becoming a massacre.

The War Office put Zulu dead at the Battle of Kambula at almost 2000, and it is fair to assume that Mnyamana's force was decimated. The *impi*'s painful passage back to the south was slowed by walking and supporting wounded and became littered with the bodies of those who died on the way. In contrast, this most decisive battle of the war had cost the British just twenty-eight dead and sixty-five wounded.

Disaster in the north was repeated four days later in the south.

Chelmsford had crossed the Tugela on 28 March to relieve Eshowe. On the way, Dunn, acting as intelligence officer, reported heavy Zulu activity in their vicinity and, on 1 April, he picked out a suitable knoll to defend in open country, fifteen miles south of Eshowe and near the burnt-out *ikhanda* of Gingindlovu. A square laager of wagons was drawn up with assorted artillery at each corner. Although Somopho had been told to prevent any help getting through to Pearson, he might have done better to have waited until Chelmsford was fording the Nyezane river, less than a mile away. Against this, the high grass in the area gave at least some cover for his men – or so it seemed as they swarmed across the river at 6 a.m. in the familiar crescent formation.

At the Battle of Gingindlovu, however, a new horror lay in store. While the warriors were still well over half a mile away from the laager, and partially concealed by the grass, a strange hammering rattle started from the wagons and bodies started falling like maize stalks under the hoe. The hand-cranked Gatling guns, capable of dealing death dozens of times a minute, had opened up.

Once again the ghastly tableau was enacted. Bounding across the open ground, the Zulus were scythed down by a barrage from a combination of more than 5000 Martini-Henrys, Gatlings and seven-pounders. Shrieking and spluttering volleys of Hale rockets, which were counted a useful psychological weapon against an unsophisticated foe, added to the clamour.

No doubt there were men in the laager who relished the slaughter, but there were also those to whom the war had become a pitiful waste. Few had been left unmoved by their enemies' bravery, a subject that had become a feature of campfire discussion. Of this occasion, Smith-Dorrien, one of the five imperial officers who had escaped from Isandlwana, noted: 'The poor Zulus hadn't a ghost of a chance.'[12] After forty minutes, Chelmsford released his first mounted charge to the north, but the Zulus had not yet lost their spirit for tackling a visible foe; one *ibutho* rapidly took up horn formation and started to encircle the cavalry, which retreated. The warriors to the south were being urged on by Dabulamanzi, who was himself mounted. Cetshwayo's warlike brother had been taught to ride by John Dunn and was one of the few Zulus comfortable on horseback. Now, while leading an attack against his former friend, he was hit, although not seriously.

It is said that one Zulu reached the laager, an unarmed mat-bearer aged about twelve who was plucked from the side of a wagon by a member of the Naval Brigade. The lad was reportedly adopted as a mascot by the men of HMS *Boadicea* and subsequently joined the Royal Navy.[13] Others got no closer than twenty yards. After just over a hour, Chelmsford ordered a second cavalry charge. This time the demoralized Zulus fell back, and as the riders thundered among them, they fled or fell. Coming up in the rear of the cavalry were more than 1000 Natal Zulus of the native contingent who put to the assegai those merely wounded by shot, shell and sabre.

Zulu casualties at Gingindlovu were proportionately probably the highest of the war, the War Office estimate of 1200 dead out of Somopho's 10,000 men being worse than the decimation at Kambula. Chelmsford's casualties, on the other hand, were the lowest on the British side for a major engagement, thirteen dead and forty-eight wounded. Pearson was relieved at Eshowe the next day and by 12 April the entire southern contingent was safely back in Natal, where preparations began for the final reckoning.

Two battles in four days had sealed the outcome of the war, and Cetshwayo knew it. It was more than a matter of casualties, grievous though they were: about 5000 men were already dead and every homestead in the country was in mourning; most chiefs had lost sons, some more than one. Still, the army remained full of spirit and would willingly carry on the fight. For all their losses, there remained some 25,000 warriors to answer the call.

However, Cetshwayo could not fail to recognize that his army had been unable to adjust to this new kind of war. In close-quarters combat it had proved itself the equal of any force in the world. But, tactically as well as technically, it belonged to the past. His own orders, based on an instinctive grasp of guerrilla methods, had been defied or ignored. Even further victories could only worsen the position, for, as he told Vijn, the Dutch trader, 'they will say, if white men lose their lives, "It is all Cetshwayo's doing!" whereas it is they who are doing it.'[14] Youth had invoked Shaka's legacy and this was now threatening to carry the nation to extinction. The time had come to call enough, to restrain the *amabutho* and redouble peace initiatives.

Cetshwayo now turned to Vijn as a scribe to communicate with the British. 'Say that Hulumente [Bulwer], Somseu [Theophilus Shepstone] and Mr John [John Shepstone] who have brought on this war, should come to speak with me to bring the war to an end.'[15]

From the time of Gingindlovu to the final battle of the war, three months later at Ulundi (as the British called the royal homestead of Ondini), no resistance was offered by Cetshwayo. Throughout that time, a series of new and increasingly desperate peace envoys were sent to Chelmsford and Frere. In a sample message, on 15 May, the king's bewilderment and anxiety are only too plain: 'What have I done? I want peace, I ask for peace.'[16]

These overtures were dismissed by officers on the ground as 'peaceful lies', and the envoys described as 'villainous-looking scoundrels'. Chelmsford was not interested in a ceasefire, as he showed by sending back the original ultimatum terms, topped up with a series of new and ever more confusing conditions. On 15 May, it was the surrender of all captured weapons and prisoners (of which there were none), plus 10,000 stands of firearms and 10,000 head of cattle. When the envoys came back again on 5 June, there were new terms – the surrender of an *ibutho* yet to be named by Chelmsford and a requirement that the king somehow prove that he retained the loyalty of all chiefs and could answer for them.[17]

Back in Pietermaritzburg, Colenso might well rail at these 'preposterous' demands, but no other voice was raised against the deadly vengeance of Frere and Chelmsford. The governor who had ruined his career by insisting on war, and the general who had blighted his with the blunder of Isandlwana, pressed on towards the destruction of Cetshwayo. Frere's standing order was that 'no overtures of any kind must be allowed to delay military operations.'[18]

Chelmsford's second invasion started on 31 May. He had bided his time to ensure that he had all the men, supplies and transport required. Nothing had been left to chance. His progress would be equally meticulous. It was to take him twenty-eight days to cover the sixty-five miles to Ondini. No resistance was offered to this army, but hardly had he crossed into Zululand than Chelmsford suffered one final, insupportable blow.

On 1 June, a band of Zulu scouts was monitoring the advance when they spotted a British patrol making towards a nearby kraal. The chief, a man named Sabhuza, anticipating a visit from the invaders, had withdrawn to a hilltop that morning, from which he and the scouts now observed eight white soldiers and their black guide dismount at the kraal. The Zulus decided on an attack and, advancing stealthily down the hill, reached the edge of the huts before one of the whites raised the alarm. All but two managed to mount their horses and gallop away. One was shot in the saddle and fell. That left a lone redcoat.

His horse reared and bolted, stranding the wild-eyed young soldier with a pistol and sword to face the oncoming warriors. Xamanga, a member of the Mbonambi, dealt him the first assegai blow, and though the young soldier fought furiously it was all over in a few moments.

The Zulu were not to know it – least of all Xamanga, who fell at Ondini a month later – but the death of Louis Napoleon, the Prince Imperial of France, created an even greater furore in Britain and Europe than the defeat at Isandlwana. Louis had received his military training as an exile in England where, despite his antecedents, he was a popular public figure, and on the start of hostilities had lobbied vigorously and successfully to go out to Zululand as a uniformed observer. His presence at the kraal that day was a monumental misfortune all round.

When Cetshwayo heard that a great *induna* had died, he did what he could; Louis' sword, which had been worn by his illustrious forebear at Austerlitz, was found at Sabhuza's kraal and sent to Chelmsford. That doomed general could only set his face to the east once more and proceed with what he now knew with certainty would be his last duty on active service. Still, he must have winced when the Prime Minister's reaction was reported back to him. The long-suffering Disraeli, realizing that the war had done for him too, remarked with masterly self-control: 'A wonderful people, the Zulu. They beat our generals, they convert our bishops, and they write *finis* to a French dynasty.'[19]

Chelmsford's column was covering barely two miles a day southeast towards Ondini. Simultaneously, a second column under General Henry Crealock was working its way up the coastal route. Despite their slowness, there was a new menace about the British advance. Previously, most ordinary homesteads had been ignored and ordinary life left relatively untroubled. Now, although encountering virtually no military resistance, the army was putting kraals to the torch and driving off livestock. Women, children and the elderly took themselves off into the bush with what food and possessions they could carry. This mailed fist carried a velvet invitation to local chiefs to make their own peace. Britain's quarrel was not with the Zulu people, but the Zulu king, Chelmsford's messengers were saying. Kraals which renounced allegiance to Cetshwayo and surrendered their arms and any royal cattle would be left in peace; those that did not would be destroyed. Most leading men now saw defeat as inevitable but disloyalty to the king would be unendurable, a denial of every spiritual and social tenet. Put in this impossible position, many chiefs did the only thing they could, and played for time.

Cetshwayo, too, was without illusions that the Zulus could stop those they called the *amasoja* but there remained genuine confusion over exactly what the British wanted. Watching Chelmsford's inexorable advance and the disintegration that was taking place around him, the king could only continue to send out messengers with peace offerings ranging from ivory tusks to cattle. On 25 June, a pair of his envoys pleaded that the British should halt their advance, or Cetshwayo would have to fight, 'as there will be nothing left but to try and push aside a tree that is falling on him.'[20]

A few days later, the king told the *amabutho* at Ondini that he was sending to Chelmsford one last peace offering, a hundred of the pure white royal oxen that were his personal pride. This poignant moment was related later by Mtshapi ka Noradu, a member of the Mcijo *ibutho*:

He came into the semi-circle of men and said, 'O, Zulu, I see that the white people have indeed come. I see that though you blunted them at Isandlwana, the next day they came on again. Though you blunted them at Hlobane, the next day they came on again. I say now that these oxen must go as a peace offering to the white people.'

Then Matatshila ka Masipula of the Emgazini said, 'No, *nkosi*. Is the king beginning to speak thus even though we Kandempemvu are far from finished?'

The king replied, 'Matatshila, what do you mean by "far from finished"? Where is Zikode ka Masipula? Where is Mtshoda ka Ntshingwayo? Where is Mahu? So you are far from finished? How is it that you can say that? Where is Gininda ka Masipula?' [This list of the dead included two of Matatshila's own brothers.]

When the king had finished speaking, Matatshila answered, 'Is the king afraid? Does he think he will be defeated because those who sit around the eating-mat have been killed?'

Again the king spoke: 'Yeh! Matatshila, if you look up the sky will be far off; if you prod the ground with your stick, the earth will be hard. If the white men advance when so many of them have been killed, and when so many of us have been killed, what is there to stop them?'

That was all. The cattle were taken off.[21]

Zulu destiny was being shaped by events far away of which they knew nothing and over which they had no control. At the end of May, a Cabinet exasperated with both Frere and Chelmsford had appointed Sir Garnet Wolseley as supreme civil and military authority in Natal and Zululand. To Chelmsford's earlier compulsion to erase his humiliation with a great military victory was added a new imperative: speed. Wolseley was even now on the sea off Zululand. Once he arrived on the scene any credit from a victorious campaign would be his. The final blow would have to be delivered swiftly.

❈

From the dry mid-winter plain, a cloud of dust shimmered around the advancing column. On 26 June, it reached the edge of the Emakosini valley, the hallowed ground where past kings were buried. Of the spiritual significance of this place the British were largely ignorant, but the valley contained half a dozen military *amakhanda* and a strong cavalry force rode down to the abandoned kraals and set them ablaze. Earlier that day, the Nokhenke *ibutho* had slipped away from their *ikhanda*, Esiklebeni, but had failed to take with them the *inkatha yezwe*, the symbolic grass coil of national unity dating from Shaka's time. The *inkatha* was consumed in the flames.[22]

Chelmsford came to the banks of the White Mfolozi, two miles south of Ondini, on 2 July. There, for the next two nights, the sound of singing and roars of '*Bayete*!' carried across the water as the Zulus readied themselves for the final onslaught. At daybreak on 4 July, the British advanced over the plain in a great hollow infantry square consisting of more than 4000 imperial troops, including three companies of lancers, almost 1000 Natal Zulus, nine fieldguns and two Gatlings. At 8.30 a.m. they halted and set up their stand on a gently sloping hilltop. The *amasoja* were at last going to fight the Zulu in the open. As Chelmsford put it grimly: 'We've been called ant-bears long enough.'[23]

Exactly sixty years earlier, Shaka had led his *amabutho* in defence of an embryonic kingdom against Zwide's invading Ndwandwe. Since then the Zulu had been invincible. Now they were going forth again to defend the land against an invader. It would be for last time.

They had followed the advance that morning and were concealed behind hills and stream beds to the west, north and east, but as the early mists lifted their movements gradually became visible to the British. From the west, *amabutho* worked their way round to the south to complete the encirclement. Once again, imperial officers found themselves admiring the order and synchronization of these deployments.

Eclipse was accomplished in less than two hours: the first shots were fired at around 8.35 by the lure of Buller's outriders who drew the warriors' charge into an inferno; the lancers galloped out of the circle at 9.25 and, by 10.07, shells from the nine-pounders were exploding among the huts of the royal homestead. In between, the warriors demonstrated their customary valour, although they clearly now recognized that neither the potions of the *izangoma* nor a disdain for death made them invulnerable. Officers like Wood, who had seen them at Kambula, thought them now hurried and less methodical. Mehlokazulu admitted that the warriors did not fight at Ulundi with 'the same spirit because they were then frightened'.[24] But Britons watching for the first time how Zulus hurled themselves into the shadow of death were still awed. Melton Prior, the war artist of the *Illustrated London News*, swore he had never seen anything like it.

If they were grand, they were also indisputably beaten. The remnants of the last great Zulu *impi* dispersed to the north mid-way through the morning to start making their way back to their own homesteads. It required no orders from the *izinduna*. The king's house was destroyed and it was now time to look to their own. For some, there were burned *umuzi* to rebuild. For all there were herds to be tended and lands to be prepared for a new growing season. Life would go on.

Shortly before midday, Buller arrived at Ondini to find it abandoned. Orders were issued for the huts to be torched, and from hills and valleys over the Mahlabatini plain, clouds of smoke could be seen rising from Cetshwayo's great kraal.

It seemed a great symbolic moment: the British had finally come out into the open; they had fought the Zulu army on its own terms and won; the place of the ancestors and the king's capital were reduced to ashes. More than 1000 warriors had died at Ulundi compared with thirteen on the British side, and the superiority of the white man's arms was inescapable. Altogether in the war, some 6000 Zulus had died, for 1080 white soldiers and 570 Natal Zulu but, since Isandlwana, the weight of casualties had been overwhelmingly on the Zulu side.

Chelmsford seized the moment. Isandlwana had been expunged and the Zulu military dealt a blow from which it would never recover – or so he maintained. Knowing that Wolseley was to arrive on the scene in a matter of days, he wrote his resignation on the spot, delighted to be able to hand the whole wretched business over to someone else.

All that had so far been achieved, however, was superiority in the field. And while it was true to say that the *amabutho* had been subdued for the time being, it was equally the case that the British officer who wrote home, 'We all felt the power of the Zulus had been destroyed,' was speaking prematurely. The burning of home-steads had no significance for the Zulus, or strategic advantage for the British. Most chiefs, whatever they might say to a redcoated officer, remained loyal to the king.

The king. As Wolseley raced up from the coast to assume his new command, it was clear to him that the king was the key to everything.

14

'A SATURNALIA OF WRONG-DOING'

Sir Garnet Wolseley seemed the obvious candidate to extricate Britain from the mess Frere and Chelmsford had got it into. Still only in his forties, Sir Garnet had combined a dazzling military career with a good deal of diplomatic experience. A colonel at twenty-six – the youngest in the British army – he had campaigned from Afghanistan to Ashanti, from the Crimea to China, and was no less zealous in military reforms. The star of his generation, he was the model for Gilbert and Sullivan's 'Modern Major-General'. Moreover, on the strength of six months as administrator of Natal in 1875, he counted at the Colonial Office as a South Africa expert.

Realization was starting to dawn in Britain that the war had been an awful mistake: Frere had been censured by the government for causing it but there was still no acceptance in Whitehall that his actions now obliged the government to bring about a durable settlement. The vast majority of Britons had never so much as heard of the Zulus until that year, and the government's view was that, with any luck, the voters would quickly forget them. Disraeli's Tories, facing an election within months, needed the speediest and cheapest peace Wolseley could impose. Annexation, or any other kind of responsibility, were simply not on.

Wolseley had not risen to dizzying heights by bucking orders and his solution was nothing if not cheap and speedy. Dealing with Cetshwayo was his first priority. The king had disappeared into the northern wilderness, fearful that he would be killed. Privately, Wolseley offered up a prayer that 'some amiable assassin' might do just that. He reflected in his journal on the prospects for setting the Zulus against the Swazi kingdom.

Up to the present beyond shooting & wounding some 10,000 men, we have not really punished the people as a nation. Our leniency may be mistaken for fear. I should therefore like to loose the Swazies upon these northern tribes, but I have to think of the howling Societies at home who have sympathy with all black men.[1]

Thus constrained, Wolseley moved instead to divide the fugitive king from his subjects. In meetings with the chiefs, he declared that Cetshwayo was finished, but said that if the chiefs gave up the king he would be well treated and that they in turn would retain their freedom and independence. For almost two months the king remained at liberty, being passed from kraal to kraal in the north, until his former leading men decided that, as further resistance was impossible, they might as well submit. It was Mnyamana, his former premier, who betrayed Cetshwayo in the end.

On 28 August, a squadron of dragoons ran to ground the exhausted and bewildered king, accompanied by a handful of attendants and relatives, at a kraal in the Ngome forest. Cetshwayo was identified to the troops by Martin Oftebro, who had been acting as an interpreter for the British and was the son of an old Zululand missionary. The king looked at the younger man reproachfully.

He said: 'Was your father a friend of mine for so long that you should do this to me?' I must admit that I felt somewhat embarrassed and attempted to explain to him that I was merely doing my duty.[2]

From there things moved swiftly. Brought to Wolseley's camp at Ondini, Cetshwayo surveyed the ruins of his great kraal while being told that he was being deposed for breaking his 'coronation vows'. That same day, he was driven down to the coast and put on a steamer, *Natal*, which would take him to exile in the Cape. For the first time, a Zulu king was to experience the white man's world at first hand.

Wolseley had established to his own satisfaction that self-interest could be as potent a tool in dealing with what he called 'these interesting niggers' as it had been with the troublesome Afghans; he now proceeded with a settlement similar in concept to that drawn up for controlling the North-West Frontier of India. The day after the king's departure, Wolseley addressed a gathering of all the great chiefs. Cetshwayo was gone and would never return, he said. The *amabutho* would be disbanded and the Zulu nation divided. Thirteen chiefs would rule in place of a king. They would be independent, with defined territorial boundaries but, in the event of any dispute, would have to submit to arbitration by a British resident.

Superficially, the plan might have seemed attractive to chiefs and commoners, for it left untouched the kraal economy that was the basis of community life; it did not penalize those who had fought in the war; and it appeared not to tamper with Zulu independence. The only obvious casualty was the royal house. Whitehall found the plan pleasing as well. Wolseley had informed the Colonial Office that, on Shepstone's advice, he was freeing the Zulu people from the tyranny they had always resented and resisted under the house of Shaka and restoring the region to its pre-Shakan state. John Dunn was another expert on tribal affairs who was offering his insights.

It was in Wolseley's choice of the thirteen chiefs that cracks started to show. He had found John Dunn's advice so valuable – indeed, Wolseley had been fascinated by the way the man effortlessly straddled the African and European worlds – that he wished he could actually make him king of the whole of Zululand.[3] As that was not possible, he did the next best thing. Dunn was made chief of the largest territory in the subdivided kingdom. Other chiefs appointed to rule supposedly 'pre-Shakan' tribes, were just as hastily and, in most cases, crassly chosen. A second non-Zulu was installed north of Dunn's territory: Hlubi, chief of a Sotho people, the Tlokoa, had no claim on this land at all and was simply being rewarded for his services in the war. So was Hamu, whose credibility as a ruler was compromised in Zulu eyes by his defection and, even among the British, because of his drunkenness, but who nevertheless received a large tract in the north-west.

Another of the new 'kinglets', Zibhebhu, had the virtue, at least, of having been a man of standing in Cetshwayo's kingdom. His appointment, however, was to prove the most disastrous of all.

Zibhebhu is one of the most complex and controversial figures of the time. Probably Cetshwayo's ablest military commander, he had distinguished himself during the war and came from a lineage of proven loyalty to the royal house, his father, Mapitha, having been a key adviser of Mpande's. He had considerable business acumen, too, and had already profited handsomely in trade with the colonists. Indeed, some whites found him 'a grasping, ambitious man'.[4] Now Zibhebhu sensed that his best advantage lay in transferring allegiance to Wolseley.

According to a story told by Mpatshana ka Sodondo, Cetshwayo had once saved Zibhebhu from execution by his own father.

Zibhebhu was showing cunning by taking cattle belonging to Mapitha and selling them to buy things for which Mapitha never saw any return. Hence, concluded his father, 'he is buying medicines with which to kill me.' Mapitha received Mpande's approval about killing Zibhebhu, but Cetshwayo sided with Zibhebhu and the action was never carried out.[5]

This was the man who was to become the scourge of the royal house. For, under Wolseley's dispensation, Zibhebhu was given supreme authority over members of Cetshwayo's family, a recipe guaranteed to produce enmity between the Mandlakazi and Usuthu. Hamu's area, it turned out, also included a high number of ardent royalists, notably the Qulusi section.

On close examination, it was found that similar powder kegs were littered everywhere. The *abantwana*, the forty or so sons of Mpande, had overnight been reduced to commoners. Each chiefdom contained men of established status and authority who had suddenly been set under men who were their inferiors.

Of all the plan's flaws, however, most glaring was that it abandoned without a supreme authority a land founded upon the principle of absolute power invested in one man. The king had been the administrative and spiritual head of his people, the head of the army and the supreme court, and the source of a mystical power which alone kept in check the jostlings and ambitions of chiefly rivals. To stretch a point somewhat, it was as if Tudor Britain had at one stroke lost its monarch, the See of Canterbury and its means of defence, and been handed back to the barons.

Although himself a leading beneficiary, Dunn thought the plan 'the maddest piece of policy ever heard of'.[6] His view was that the Zulu, having been defeated, could have been readily moulded into model British subjects had Cetshwayo been sworn to loyalty and left as head of state. Even Shepstone, who had favoured invasion in the expectation that Zululand would be annexed and the Zulus subjected to his administrative system, criticized 'the simple device of practically leaving them to themselves, after we have taken away their head, and advising them not to hurt each other.' Britain was bound, 'for the safety of the people whom we have conquered, to replace the government we have destroyed by one less barbarous, but equally strong.'[7]

Partisans of the Zulu were even more critical. To Colenso it was the worst of all possible outcomes. Into the open wounds of Frere's war had been poured the poison of Wolseley's peace.

Wolseley detested the bishop — 'a busybody at the bottom of every native trouble here'[8] — and was soon too busy with other matters to worry about such criticisms anyway. A boundary commission, whose job it was to divide the kingdom, pointed out that some of his 'kinglets' lacked the proper credentials. Wolseley ignored that too. For a man whose brilliance marked him out as one of the few intellectuals produced by the British military, Sir Garnet showed a singular lack of commonsense, as well as basic humanity, in his South African duties.

Like a whirlwind, he now passed on to deal with another of Frere's awkward constituents, the Transvaal Boers, leaving in his wake turmoil and the makings of civil war.

If it had been Wolseley's hope that Cetshwayo would be forgotten in exile, he was quickly disabused. The king's voice was soon being heard beyond the walls of Cape Town's dank seventeenth-century Dutch fortress, the Castle. With the assistance of two faithful white allies — Robert Samuelson, who was appointed his official interpreter, and Colenso in Natal — he mounted a campaign for his restoration that carried to Whitehall and Balmoral.

The conditions of the king's custody were not especially rigorous. In deference to his status, he had been allowed to take with him an *inceku*, an attendant who saw to his personal needs, and four of his wives. Samuelson, who also acted as his secretary, was allowed to write letters freely on his behalf and did so with considerable eloquence. Cetshwayo joked wryly that letters had become his 'only assegais', and although the content and idiom were his, it is clear that Samuelson helped to sharpen the points.[9]

A further asset was the king's own mien. Visitors who came in a steady trickle to his rooms at the Castle expecting to find a barbarian left having been impressed by a simple, naturally dignified figure who, despite his vulnerable circumstances, took respect as his due. Even hardened foes like Wolseley and Frere remarked on his regal bearing, although the latter added that he lacked other kingly attributes, apart from cunning. Certainly, the king was not above guile, but he was quite blind to the dissembling of European diplomacy. On meeting Frere, he was puzzled, describing the agent of his downfall as 'a kind, friendly man'.[10]

Above all, however, he had a compelling case, and it was attracting a growing band of sympathizers abroad. William Howard Russell, the great war correspondent whose crusading reports from the Crimea for *The Times* had inspired Florence Nightingale, wrote to Colenso confiding his shame in a war

. . . discreditable to our arms, disgraceful to our civilisation and injurious to our good name. It makes one despair of ultimate good to see such a Saturnalia of wrong-doing.[11]

William Gladstone, the opposition leader, took up the refrain with thunderous speeches in his election campaign. 'Remember the rights of the savage,' he implored. 'Remember that the happiness of his humble home is as inviolable in the eye of Almighty God as can be your own.'[12] Other Liberals were pointing out that if the Zulu had been Britons 'they would have had magnificent orations written in their praise and a tablet in Westminster Abbey.'[13] These sentiments seemed to have won the day when, in April 1880, the Liberals gained a landslide victory. A jubilant Colenso had high hopes that it would lead to Cetshwayo's early restoration. In fact, although the 'rights of the savage' made a fine-sounding election issue, the Liberals were to be as reluctant as the Tories to take responsibility for the Zulus' peace and welfare, and even less willing to spend money on them.

Although pleased by the reassurances he received from Colenso, that justice would now prevail, the king's longing to see his homeland was reinforced by anxiety over the news of events there. A month after Gladstone's election, a large delegation of leading Zulu arrived in Pietermaritzburg. Led by Ndabuko, a full brother of Cetshwayo's, they were representative of lineages loyal to the royal house and had walked about 150 miles to protest over the yoke of Zibhebhu and Hamu and to petition for the return of the king. It was, as the historian, Jeff Guy, has pointed out, the first major political reaction to the peace settlement and an attempt to show the colonial authorities the anomalies in it. More were to follow.

Zibhebhu and Hamu were ruling areas where loyalty to Cetshwayo was strongest. Both had reasons for antipathy towards the royal house and neither missed an opportunity to humiliate the reduced aristocrats under them. Of the two, Zibhebhu was the more aggressive and zealous, and he was in the powerful position of having many of Cetshwayo's household in his charge, including the king's son and heir apparent, Dinuzulu. The loyalists maintained that Zibhebhu had set out to seize cattle and property of the royal house and 'set himself up as king in place of Cetshwayo'. The king's brothers Ndabuko and Ziwedu were subjected to repeated indignities. Just as outrageous to the king receiving this news a thousand miles away were reports that Zibhebhu had taken some of Cetshwayo's wives to his own *isigodlo*. In Hamu's territory, the leading plaintiff was Mnyamana, the king's old chief minister, who remained head of the Buthelezi clan and had declined an offer of his own chieftaincy. He found himself persecuted and robbed by a man he regarded with contempt.

The self-interest that Wolseley had banked on in introducing his settlement was starting to become a threat to stability. But when these complaints were laid before the colonial authorities, they were either dismissed or ignored. Mnyamana was told that if he was being victimized, it was his own fault as he had been given the chance to be a chief himself and refused it. Natal's whites chuckled to themselves over the squabblings of the 'Kilkenny cats' as the thirteen chiefs were known. A more severe view was taken by Melmoth Osborn, the British resident in Zululand, who shared his mentor Shepstone's hostility to the royal house and was convinced that it had no support among most Zulus. It followed that those who petitioned on Cetshwayo's behalf were agitators, their real objective to obtain an independent territory from which the phoenix of a Zulu kingdom might arise.

For their part, the new chiefs were assured of the authorities' support and encouraged to deal with any opposition within their territory, violently if necessary. When, for example, a pretender appeared in the land of the Mthethwa, Osborn authorized four chiefs in neighbouring territories to send *impis* to suppress him.

Through 1881, the strains grew as Wolseley's settlement started a slide towards anarchy. A ruling by Osborn that Dinuzulu, Nda-buko and Ziwedu should move to Dunn's country – which would probably have been in the interests of their security – caused an outcry among the loyalists for, as one said, Dunn 'is not even a Zulu. He is a kaffir [meaning that he was from Natal] who the king made one of his *izinduna*.'[14] Fighting broke out when Zibhebhu and Hamu tried to drive out the loyalists. In October, more Zulus died in one encounter between Hamu's adherents and members of the Qulusi section than had at Rorke's Drift.

These grim tidings were brought to the king in letters. The con-ditions of his incarceration had been further relaxed since being moved to a farm called Oude Moulen, which he shared with another of Britain's native prisoners, Langalibalele. Cetshwayo was taken for drives through Cape Town's leafy suburbs, and once went to the theatre and to a dinner party. These occasional pleasures did not diminish efforts to regain his freedom, and the loyal Samuelson continued to plead his cause in letters to anyone of note who might take an interest, from Gladstone to the Prince of Wales, even to Victoria herself:

Cetshwayo begs permission to send his humble respects to the Queen; he is staying here awaiting the Queen's pleasure and will willingly and cheerfully go wherever the Queen directs. At the same time he is living in the hopes that at some future time he may be pardoned.[15]

The correspondence of Cetshwayo's campaign for freedom has been painstakingly researched by Jeff Guy, and the story, as he has pointed out, is an absorbing and moving one for which there is not adequate space here. Respectful though the king was towards Victoria, he did not shrink from upbraiding lesser captors. To Glad-stone he wrote: 'Why do you keep quiet and do not talk for poor sufferers like me?'[16]; to Lord Kimberley, the colonial secretary: 'Do you kill me like this because I am a black man? Who could have been a greater friend of the English than I, who remained quiet in my country until I was attacked?'[17]

He had won a new and influential convert. Lady Florence Dixie, the eccentric daughter of the Marquis of Queensberry, who mixed her time between travel and journalism, visited him and on her return to London trumpeted his plight in the *Morning Post*. But it took a tragedy to cause the breakthrough. In July, the king's *inceku*, his personal servant, hanged himself, and Cetshwayo was cast into despair. An official visitor reported to the Colonial Office:

He told me he would rather die than remain as he was at present. That he was like a bird in a cage and that he would follow the example of his follower and commit suicide. It was a painful interview, for Cetshwayo was in great mental distress, and his dignified and gentlemanlike deportment always inspires sympathy.[18]

It was the fear of a scandal if the king did kill himself that started the wheels rolling. In September, the new governor of the Cape, Sir Hercules Robinson, told him that he was to be allowed to put his case personally to the Queen. Some officials had started to talk of Cetshwayo's restoration as the only way to deal with the chaos wrought by Wolseley's settlement. However, it was to be another nine months before Cetshwayo sailed for England.

The ox-like pace with which Cetshwayo's case proceeded was partly due to the fact that Britain had its hands full in South Africa. Having accepted Shepstone's annexation of the Transvaal with barely a murmur in 1877, the Boers had a messianic new leader, Paul Kruger, and were vociferously demanding their independence back. When that failed, they went to war. Gladstone was much to blame. His castigation of Disraeli while in opposition had encouraged the Boers to expect that self-government would follow almost automatically when he took office. In the event, Wolseley had rebuffed them with calculated contempt when he visited the Transvaal.

The first Anglo-Boer war evened the score. At the Battle of Majuba in February 1881, British arms suffered a defeat almost as humiliating as Isandlwana. Because it was not promptly avenged, the shame went even deeper; Majuba was recalled almost twenty years later when the Jingoes were in need of a *casus belli* to plunder the Transvaal's gold. For now, Gladstone had no alternative but to hand back Boer sovereignty.

The Liberals proved as much of a disappointment to Cetshwayo's partisans as they had to the Boers. The Zulus had become impatient and in April 1882 by far the largest delegation yet – some 2000 loyalists, more than a quarter of whom were chiefs and headmen

– marched on Pietermaritzburg. Further complaints were made about the oppressions of Zibhebhu and Hamu and, again, the king's return was urged. Repeatedly, Zulu spokesmen reflected their bewilderment at the failure of their British conquerors to now accept them as subjects. Osborn was told by one leader: 'When a man beats his child he afterwards wipes his child's tears.'[19]

Finally, in July, Cetshwayo was taken to the harbour below Table Mountain where he embarked on the *Arab*, accompanied by three chiefs.

The British public was blasé about the crowned heads of Europe but the savage potentate of a race of black Spartans was another matter. Londoners flocked to get a glimpse of the king. Conditioned by the dramatic Zulu War images created by artists for the *Illustrated London News* and *The Graphic*, they might have been somewhat disappointed by the dapper figure in frock coat, kid gloves and bowler but the visit was still an enormous public success. A wave of sympathy followed the king and he and his attendants evidently attracted feminine admiration. On one occasion, some women in a crowd embraced the startled Zulus and a music hall ditty suddenly appeared that went:

> White young dandies, get away, O!
> You are now 'neath beauty's ban;
> Clear the way for Cetshwayo,
> He alone's the ladies' man.[20]

He was, perhaps, less comfortable with feminine company when the time came for his meeting with the Queen at Osborne. The audience was a rather stiff one. According to Guy:

The Queen, influenced by the military men who had led the 1879 invasion, had been opposed to Cetshwayo's visit to England. Nevertheless she told the king she had respected him as a brave enemy and trusted that he would now be a firm friend and the short audience closed with the Zulu visitors giving their royal salute.[21]

More to the point were the meetings at the Colonial Office. Although Kimberley, the colonial secretary, had decided that the king was to be restored, an undetermined area of Zululand was to be set aside for chiefs who refused to submit to his authority.

Cetshwayo was told of this formally on 15 August, but when he asked what part of the country would be his, Kimberley had to hedge. The king felt 'as if he had been raised up from the dead', according to the record of the meeting, although his kingdom was now very small, and the prospect of losing more of it 'buried him up to his knees again'.[22] Still, there was nothing for it but to accept the terms for now and do what he could to improve them when the opportunity arose.

On the afternoon of 10 January 1883, Cetshwayo stepped ashore on the land of his fathers after an absence of more than three years. There to meet him, like a dark shadow from the past, was Sir Theophilus Shepstone, out from retirement to oversee the restoration. Whether the king saw this as an omen or not, the triumph of his return was to turn rapidly to tragedy.

The new Zululand was divided into three sections. On the map it looked quite straightforward: Cetshwayo's reduced kingdom lay at the centre, 'a native independent territory under British protection and authority'; to the north, Zibhebhu retained his country, having convinced the authorities that he would fight before submitting to the Usuthu; to the south of the Mhlatuze river a reserve had been created out of the lands of John Dunn and Hlubi, where other chiefs unwilling to accept Cetshwayo could find sanctuary. The reserve, moreover, while it would initially act as a buffer with Natal, would also provide an overspill for the colony's own Zulu population and a reservoir of new labour. In attempting to dispose of previous sources of instability, however, the partition created new and even more potent ones. A large number of the king's Usuthu adherents remained in Zibhebhu's country, while Hamu, who was scarcely less hated by the loyalists, fell under the king. Five of the thirteen 'kinglets' renewed allegiance to Cetshwayo. Those who opted for sanctuary in the south, did so partly for fear of retribution over their disloyalty. As a model of Balkanization, dividing a single region into separate and mutually hostile elements, the partition could hardly have been bettered.

The warning signs were only too obvious. At Cetshwayo's installation on 29 January, all the loyalists' bitterness over the disaster that had befallen them since the invasion came boiling over. Almost all the great men of the old kingdom were there, the *izikulu* and the *abantwana* and, one by one, they rose to address Shepstone. After starting off with thanks for returning 'the bone of

Senzangakona', they proceeded to harangue him over the injustices done to the Zulu and their king. One Buthelezi *induna* was especially scathing, and prophetic:

Even today in bringing him back you are killing him, killing him, I say, as you have done all along! Did you not set him up at first and then destroy him for nothing? Did you not take him to his Mother [Victoria] and now do you cut off the land saying 'it is for those dissatisfied'?

You are his enemy from the beginning! You are the author of all our troubles! Why don't you enquire about those kinglets of yours, those murderers? You have sent them away and allowed them to keep all the king's property! How will you deal with us? We shall arm and seize the cattle, and stab those who try to keep them. For we have learned that with the government one who spills blood is not blamed; on the contrary he is praised, and is given the women, and the cattle, and the land of the peaceable ones![23]

Shepstone reeled away from this onslaught and retreated into retirement. He never saw Cetshwayo again. Although the system he had devised continued to be cited as a model for benevolent native administration, Shepstone's handling of the Transvaal annexation overshadowed his later years. He died an embittered man in 1893, defended only by his devotee, Rider Haggard.

Within weeks of the king's return, Zululand started dissolving into anarchy. The flame was lit by a spark in the north, where Usuthu loyalists clashed again with followers of Zibhebhu and Hamu. When news reached Ondini, which was being rebuilt, the Usuthu leaders from the north – notably Ndabuko and Mnyamana – left for their homesteads to raise an *impi*. The Usuthu were confident and rash. Late in March, they advanced deep into Zibhebhu's country, about 5000 strong. The Mandlakazi *impi* was a third of that, but Zibhebhu was a formidable fighter, a veteran of Isandlwana who had mastered the essentials of the new military culture, cavalry and firearms, in a way that his opponents still had not. On 30 March, in the valley of the Msebe stream, the Usuthu were ambushed. Retreating in disorder under rifle fire, they were then routed by cavalry, Zibhebhu himself charging about like a possessed horseman of the apocalypse. Mnyamana is said to have lost ten sons and Ndabuko five. No casualty figures were recorded but, according to the historian James Gibson, they were probably the highest ever suffered in a Zulu battle.

Loyalists in the north fled to forests and caves, leaving their crops and homesteads to be burned. At Ondini, Cetshwayo summoned support from loyal chiefdoms. On the sidelines, colonial officials whose actions had brought matters to this pass, washed their hands and looked away. Colenso, who had opposed partition throughout and appealed for the king to be given support, was denounced in the press as a socialist agitator. Colonial society, in favour of anything that was against the Usuthu, Cetshwayo's faction, had decided that Zibhebhu was 'fighting the battle of South Africa, and championing the cause of civilization and order.'[24]

Zulus not directly involved could only look on and lament. William Ngidi, Colenso's first convert, wrote:

The Zulus are set at loggerheads by the cunning of white men, who want to eat up their land. My heart is very full of grief, I cannot find words to express it, for this splendid old Zulu people.[25]

In the midst of this harrowing civil war, Colenso died exhausted at home. His struggle for blacks to be decently and justly treated had never wavered, and Natal's whites, most of whom had disagreed violently with everything he stood for in life, could not but acknowledge the greatness of the spirit that had passed from them. For the Zulu the loss was more painful. John Kumalo, one of his converts, lamented: 'Nothing which espouses our cause ever seems to prosper; Colenso himself did not prosper.'[26]

Though the loss was great, the legacy was too. Some years later, James Stuart held a series of discussions with Kumalo and another Colenso protégé, Lazarus Mxaba, on what they agreed were the great issues of humanity and race. As Stuart's notes make clear, he was profoundly moved by these discussions, finding in men like Mxaba, 'not merely my match, but my identity'. Though Colenso's Ekukanyeni was gone, destroyed by fire, Kumalo and Mxaba told Stuart that it had actually been the bishop himself who was 'the place of light'.

[They said] his deeds on behalf of the natives, his questionings, discussions, the briefs he held, were themselves the nature of light; they tended to produce light; they tended to glow. The circumstances in which he laboured may pass and vanish from view, but his example is a beacon of light. Thus, Mxaba remarks on behalf of me: If, should we at a later time tell our children of these discussions with you, these questionings of yours, answers and what-not, there will be no necessity to decry such as fruitless and without light because no tangible results arose, for out of the very effort of discussion and questioning some light is derived.[27]

Cetshwayo's message on hearing of Colenso's death was a request that:

. . . a stone may be bought in my name, which shall be set up over the grave of my father, to show that we loved him in return for his great love for us, and his efforts to deliver us out of our distress.[28]

Colenso lies today in the small and lovely stone cathedral of St Peter's in Pietermaritzburg, beneath a stone at the altar inscribed simply 'Sobantu' – his Zulu name, which means Father of the People.

Mercifully, he was spared the holocaust that followed a few weeks later and the final eclipse of the Zulu kingdom. Cetshwayo had been trying to organize his defences against an anticipated attack by a joint *impi* of Zibhebhu and Hamu, but the Usuthu had no general of Zibhebhu's ability and personality. On 21 July, the Mandlakazi forces, including a group of tough white traders, approached Ondini at dawn after an overnight march. The Usuthu were caught completely unawares. Warriors of the Tulwana, the Ngobamakosi, the Mcijo, roused from sleep, came out to confront the foe. But, like Shaka's kingdom itself, the great *amabutho* were a shadow of their former strength. Zibhebhu's men drove them back into the kraal, where there commenced a massacre.

It was witnessed at a distance by Henry Fynn, son of the first white man to meet Shaka, who was the British resident with Cetshwayo. In his report, he put the toll at around five hundred. The significance on this occasion, however, was not the number of men killed, but their status. The king had been attended at the time by chiefs from all parts of the realm and, while most of the warriors were able to escape, the great men were vulnerable. One white trader reported in the *Natal Advertiser*: 'Being all fat and big-bellied they had no chance of escape; one of them was actually run to earth and stabbed by my little mat-bearers.'

The list of the dead read like a *Who's Who* of the old order:

Godide ka Ndlela was chief of the Tuli and an *isikulu*, a member of the inner circle of great men; so was Mbopa ka Wolizibi, head of the Hlabisa; so too Ntshingwayo, commander of the army at Isandlwana; and also Seketwayo ka Nhlaka, chief of the Mpungose. Sihayo, the border chief and Cetshwayo's great friend, was dead; and Vumandaba, who had received the British war ultimatum.[29]

Here, finally, was the Zulu kingdom's *Götterdämmerung*. In all, Fynn reported, fifty-nine men of rank had been killed, many of them with links to Mpande's time. Cetshwayo narrowly escaped death himself. For the second time, he had been forced to flee Ondini, but was later found hiding in the bush near the White Mfolozi. It is said he was stabbed twice in the leg by youths before, remembering himself, he shouted 'Hau, boy! Am I stabbed by you then?' and the youths, recognizing him, fled mortified.

For a while, Cetshwayo hid with a band of followers among the gorges of the Nkandla forest before putting himself under the protection of Osborn, the British resident at Eshowe, where he established a small homestead. This was the final and most galling humiliation, for he and Osborn detested one another. Four months later, on 8 February 1884, King Cetshwayo died without warning after an evening meal. He was fifty-seven.

The Zulu were convinced that their king had been poisoned, possibly by Osborn who, it was said, had forbidden Cetshwayo's own people to prepare his food.[30] Colonial officials pointed out that a medical check conducted while he had been in Cape Town found evidence of heart disease. There is no certainty either way, as members of the king's household forbade a post-mortem examination. But although there is no forensic evidence for British culpability, it is not surprising that the imperial power should have been blamed. In the Zulu way of thinking, premature death and misfortune were invariably the work of a powerful enemy's magic. While the agents of this most tragic king's downfall were plain to see – the sombre-browed Shepstone, redcoated soldiers – the reasons for their actions remained to most a complete mystery.

The war, at least, had been comprehensible – an act of conquest. From that point, the Zulu had expected a new paramount authority to be installed. Instead, it turned out, the conqueror was prepared to admonish and to threaten, but not to rule. The Zulu were thus subjected to all the loss and indignity of subjugation, without any of the benefits of firm government. They were not to know that

British electioneering had made annexation politically inexpedient. When Cetshwayo was restored, it was not to put right a manifest wrong, but in the hope that his presence would restore order. It was far too late for that. By sending him back to a territory with enemies clustered on his borders and slender means of defence, Gladstone's government abandoned its own man to the whim of a fate that, in his case, had ever been unkind.

There is a tendency, natural enough, for accounts of Cetshwayo's end to become somewhat mawkish. So it may be appropriate to conclude with a robust Zulu oral tradition. According to Mangati ka Godide, son of the *isikulu* killed in the Ondini massacre, the king's downfall dated from the time he fell out with his powerful *sangoma*, Manembe. It is said that Cetshwayo angered the medicine-man by failing to inform him of his son's death and then, fearing the evil that might flow from this wrath, ordered that he be killed.

The *impi* surrounded Manembe's homestead. He called to it from the calf pen – he was seated there, not hiding – 'Do you come to kill me? Because my child is dead?' That was all. He said, 'Kill me, that I may follow my child.' Then they killed him. When the sun set he rose up, even though they had stabbed him, saying 'Things will not go well with you because of my death.' That was the end. Nor did Cetshwayo's affairs prosper, as history clearly sets forth.[31]

❋

But this was more than the tragedy of one man. Central Zululand had ceased to have any government and when the Natal authorities sought advice, Lord Derby, the new colonial secretary, telegraphed back: 'We prefer if possible to leave the Zulus to settle their own affairs.'[32]

If the British shrank from involvement, the land-loving Boers of the Transvaal did not. Three months after Cetshwayo's death, they reached a pact with Usuthu leaders acting for the king's heir, Dinuzulu, who was aged fifteen. In return for Boer recognition of Dinuzulu as king and protection against his foes, the Zulu leadership agreed to hand over an unspecified amount of farmland in the north to Boers who helped them.

Zibhebhu appealed in vain for British help. On 5 June 1884 an Usuthu army of around 6000 men, including 200 or so Boers, attacked a Mandlakazi *impi* about half that size and defeated them. Zibhebhu's power was broken and later that year he guided his people to sanctuary in the southern reserve.

The Usuthu were left standing in Pyrrhic triumph amid the ashes of everything that had been the Zulu kingdom. Gone was the social and political stability and the military security. The economic prosperity that flowed from these was disrupted, and whatever remained of territorial integrity disappeared when the Boers demanded the payment for their support – about 4000 square miles of the richest northern farming land, roughly a third of the former kingdom. This territory, which contained the homesteads of the staunchest Usuthu supporters, the Buthelezi, the Qulusi and Mdlalose, was to be called the New Republic.

By now, other European powers, notably Germany, were sniffing over the scraps overlooked by Britain as the Scramble for Africa gathered pace and this finally provided an impetus that had been lacking. The Tories defeated Gladstone in 1886 and, on 19 May the following year, Zululand was formally annexed as a British colony.

It had taken eight years for the most powerful and independent African society south of the Limpopo to be reduced to divided fragments. The process was being repeated all over the continent and however much one might mourn the passing of the old order, it had probably been inevitable. Now that the insulation of the Zulu people had ended and the advance of alien culture and industry begun, the question was what place they would find in an intimidating and still incomprehensible wider world.

'The house of Shaka,' said Sir Arthur Havelock, the white *nkosi* to his new people, 'is a thing of the past, like water that has been spilt.'[33]

PART 4

ENDURING – 1887–1990

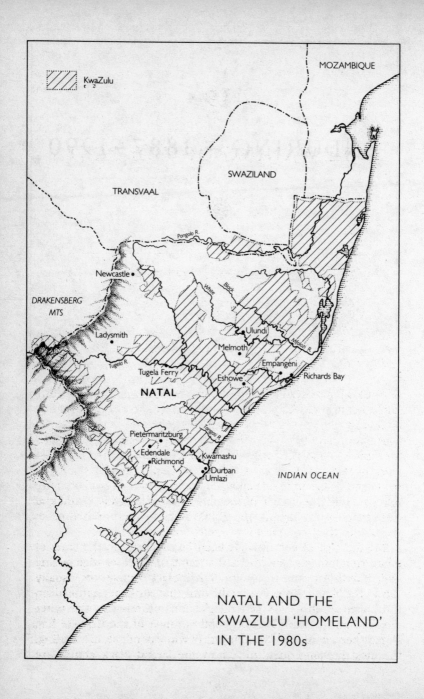

KwaZulu

MOZAMBIQUE

SWAZILAND

TRANSVAAL

Pongolo R.

Newcastle

DRAKENSBERG
MTS

Black

White

Ulundi

Ladysmith

Melmoth

Mfolozi R.

Tugela R.

Tugela Ferry

Empangeni

Eshowe

Richards Bay

NATAL

Pietermaritzburg

Tugela R.

Edendale

Kwamashu

Richmond

Durban

Umlazi

INDIAN OCEAN

Mkomazi R.

NATAL AND THE
KWAZULU 'HOMELAND'
IN THE 1980s

15

THE WANING OF THE PAST

This is Shaka's place. He made us a great people.

Lazarus, a boy aged ten, approaching
the author at the site of kwaBulawayo,
1991

The Zulus have survived. Indeed, in some respects they have done
rather better than that. A Zulu-speaking population of around one
million at the turn of the century has grown to between seven
and eight million. Along with South Africa's other black people,
they can look to the future, if not with optimism, then at least
with a sense that they are regaining control of their destiny; the
next century lies in their hands. The same cannot be said of many
other subjugated aboriginals, notably those of the New World and
Australia. To that extent, the Zulus' story in the hundred or so
years since their conquest is a positive one.

But the cost of survival has been enormous, and the scars of
oppression hideous. Apartheid, that catch-all label for stigmatizing
white South Africans' treatment of their black compatriots, usually
carries the blame. However, by the time that Afrikaner nationalism
triumphed at the 1948 general election, ushering in the bitter
modern era of South African politics, much of the damage had
already been done. Now that the era of white domination is ending,
the most pressing question is how the largest black groups are

going to come to terms with each other, and with power in a modern state. In particular, it is being asked what part eight million Zulu-speakers, the largest single population group, will play in South Africa's future.

The rise of the modern South African state brought blacks from all over the subcontinent together for the first time. Zulu rubbed shoulders with Pondo, Venda, Xhosa, Sotho and Tswana. Drawn to the cities as cheap labour, they discovered – amid the shanties and shebeens of the townships, the beerhalls and gambling dens – a shared humanity, and identified a common foe. Just as whites had established a common front to achieve domination, it was recognized that blacks would have to bury their own ethnic differences to escape it.

However, South Africa is an incorrigibly tribal nation. Through all the political and social upheavals which it has undergone this century, Zulu nationalism has remained a force in the land. The very term Zulu has always had a certain *éclat* among other blacks, who have often looked to Zulus for political leadership. It is sometimes forgotten today that the leading lights in the foundation of the African National Congress were Zulus, Pixley ka Isaka Seme and John Dube.

The reverse side of this instinctive deference to Zulu leadership has been a deep-rooted fear of Zulu dominance. The pride that comes naturally to many Zulus contains within it the seeds of arrogance, even chauvinism. At the same time, a traditionalism which is essentially conservative has remained stronger among Zulus than other ethnic groups. Zulus have thus often found themselves swimming against the tide – the target of resentment for assuming leadership as if by right, and the focus of denunciations by more militant blacks for embarking on what they termed *hamba gahle* (go carefully) leadership.

This is not to say that the Zulus themselves have spoken with a single voice. Indeed, it has sometimes seemed that the old quarrels have merely found new shape, as social pressures, land shortage and demands for pasturage have been felt by a rapidly growing population.

Narrow concepts of ethnic identity were watered down by urbanization and the black nationalist struggle. Ties of kinship and clan were in many cases eroded, to be replaced by a kind of class division between people who continued to live close to the old ways, and those who adopted European customs. Zulu-speakers are as diverse today as any other group, from the traditionalist of the north, who still owes allegiance to his chief, to the urban sophisticate of the south, whose only interest in animals skins, as the journalist Khaba Mkhize puts it, concerns the latest pair of Italian shoes.

However, the clearest feature of the divisions between Zulu-speakers is still the fault line of the Tugela. Traditionalism remained strong in the old Zulu country, where little development took place and cattle and land remained the first and last arbiter of status. South of the Tugela, meanwhile, industry and development flourished around the centres of Durban and Pietermaritzburg. Here the seeds planted by the first missionary among the Zulu, Allen Gardiner, were finally to bear fruit. From mission stations such as Inanda now came a new man: one who spoke the language of Shaka but who had been raised and nurtured on the gospel of forgiveness; one who had been educated in European ways and encouraged to believe that he was no less a man than the white. With the gift of literacy, he reached out for the rights and privileges which the law, in theory, offered him. He was the *kholwa*, the Christian convert, and from his ranks were to come the leaders of the African nationalist struggle.

The *amakholwa* were the new elite, an intelligentsia who looked on the masses from whom they had sprung with embarrassment, seeing them as uncouth and adopting the missionaries' term for them, 'heathen'. For their part, traditionalists saw the *amakholwa* as upstarts who had betrayed their past.

The distinction was to be critical. Although the two groups have sometimes buried their differences in a joint struggle against oppression – such as the 1906 rebellion, and the revival of Zulu nationalism in the 1920s – this cleavage always re-emerged. The most vivid, and tragic, evidence of that is to be seen in the intra-Zulu conflict of the past decade. Paradoxically, it is the traditionalists who resisted British imperialism in 1879 who are now identified with the forces of conservatism, while from the ranks of those who collaborated with colonialism, the Natal 'natives' who took up arms against the kingdom, have sprung the ANC militants of today.

❁

265

In 1897, Zululand was incorporated into the self-governing colony of Natal. At that point, Zulu-speakers north and south of the Tugela became subjects of a single ruler for the first time since Shaka. Natal's 500,000 or so Africans lived under some 200 chiefs, while authority over about 400,000 people in Zululand lay in the hands of 100 or so clan and lineage chiefs. Virtually all these people were governed by the Code of Native Law, which covered such matters as the succession of chiefs, laid down punishments for offences like adultery and prescribed the number of *lobola* cattle payable by chiefs and commoners. Most of this 'tribal' population continued to live in homesteads in the old way, giving allegiance to their chiefs, consulting *sangomas* for their physical and spiritual ailments, and practising polygamy when they could afford it.

The collapse of the military system left the rising generations of young men in Zululand without employment or purpose. Gradually, those who previously would have joined the king's age-regiments, started setting off for the towns and mines in search of jobs. The need for wage-paying work was stimulated by the imposition in Zululand of an annual hut tax of fourteen shillings, already in existence in Natal. At the same time, the cash economy brought independence for young men, who became able to buy cattle, marry and set up their own homesteads.

Natal was in constant need of African workers and a forced labour system, known as the *isibalo*, was in operation. Under this the Natal chiefs were required to supply a number of workers each year to work on the road system at wages lower than those obtainable in the private sector. This system was not applied to chiefs in Zululand, although in time many came to informal arrangements with industrial concerns, including the mines, to provide labourers.

Durban and Pietermaritzburg were the main towns to which migrant workers were drawn. Keenly though their services were sought, blacks were allowed into what had become white enclaves only under sufferance. They became subject to a baffling array of by-laws and regulations segregating them: they could not use public transport, were forbidden to drink alcohol and had to observe a night-time curfew or risk arrest.[2] Neither services nor amenities were provided for them, and even well-disposed whites made it clear that they were aliens without rights. The native, so the prevailing wisdom went, might ultimately progress towards civilization but, in the meantime, education or training would only give him ideas beyond his station. He was 'a minor who has to be safeguarded against things which he might otherwise think right,' as one old colonial hand put it.[3]

Defeated, dislocated and confused, Zulus came to the white man's door in the fast-growing towns of Natal – wary, respectful – seeking work as 'house boys'. In a curious way it was as if men felt they were thus keeping a part of their pride intact. Field labour such as cane-cutting was regarded as women's work and, as no traditional Zulu would do it, Natal's sugar farmers had to recruit their labourers elsewhere, among the Mpondo and from as far afield as India. Meanwhile, the descendants of those who had once marched with Shaka, donned the khaki shorts and tunic of the 'house boy' and meekly submitted to the haranguing of an over-bearing white madam.

If the white man's towns in Natal had become strange, the other places to which migrant workers travelled must have seemed fantastic. The hub of the Diamond Fields of Kimberley was the so-called 'Big Hole', a vast open-cast pit resembling a subterranean city, where thousands of miners swarmed like ants beneath a spiders' web of metal cables running down to each claim. It was a wild, brutal but nevertheless seductive place, where brandy and gin were readily available and men experienced for the first time the seductive power of having money in their pockets.

One of the first Zulus to visit the Diamond Fields was Ndhlovu ka Timuni, a scion of the royal house, who was recruited by a magistrate to take a group of about 180 men to Kimberley in the 1880s. Blacks were confined to compounds by ethnic group and, in an early example of the divide-and-rule principle which was to be used by administrators, the Zulu were employed as an irregular militia to keep order among other groups. This inevitably gave rise to conflict, especially with the Sotho, another proud and independent people. Ndhlovu recalled:

The Basutos one night caught one of the police, cut off his lips, showing all his teeth, slit both ears and let him go. In other ways too did the Basutos injure the police, smashing their teeth in with a grindstone. At the end of all these experiences those who returned came back with little or no money.[4]

Fast and furious though life on the Diamond Fields was, the full impact of South Africa's industrial revolution was only felt by those who went to the gold mines of the Transvaal.

It must have been a terrifying experience. They had said their farewells at the little homestead of huts and taken one last look over the green hills and the cattle pen, before taking up their few possessions in a cloth bundle or, perhaps, a small brown suitcase. They had walked up to a hundred miles to Durban and ridden up the metal line to Johannesburg. There, they were disgorged into a world of hissing steam, metal wagons and concrete buildings – of grey barracks and black mineshafts, gas headlamps and dynamite. In this hard, dangerous world, they worked all day in the bowels of the earth and at night they came up and went to their bleak, all-male hostels.

At first, even the most basic of home comforts, like sex, were unavailable. At least the man working in Durban was able to go back to his kraal and family occasionally. Migrant workers far from home had no such opportunity and homosexuality, rare in African society, started to occur. But as the mine communities of the Reef grew, throwing up Johannesburg, Africa's most seething, modern city, a leisure industry for black miners appeared. Shebeens were rip-roaring, illegal drinking dens where a man might find a woman, at a price. The oldest profession was late in coming to the Bantu world – all contemporary observers agree it was unknown before – but with the breakdown of tribal life, it flourished.

So did crime. Among the bandits who preyed on this society was Mzuzephi Mathebula, a man of obscure Zulu origins who arrived on the Rand and, finding it easier to steal than work for money, formed a gang. Mathebula was a fearsome figure who, at the turn of the century, ran his team of thieves and bandits from the hills south of Johannesburg like the *induna* of an *impi*. He has been represented as a kind of Zulu Robin Hood, keeping alive a spirit of freedom and resistance to the new order, but from his record he seems to have been little more than a colourful gangster.[5] Later, other ethnic-based gangs would also thrive in the township ghettoes of the Rand, such as the Sotho 'Ma-Rashea', the Russians, who concealed sticks and assegais beneath their Basotho blanket cloaks. These gangs acted much like the crime fraternities of Italy, being not only commercial concerns, but security 'families' for members of the same ethnic group in a tough environment.

On the surface, life in the homesteads of Natal and Zululand was largely insulated from these strains. As they had for centuries, the women worked the fields and boys tended the herds. Working men, now in the garb and ornaments of the townsman, returned with stories and gifts to a wide-eyed welcome from their kraals.

One white official took a keen interest in this society. James Stuart, born in Pietermaritzburg but educated in England, was among the greatest Zulu linguists produced by colonial society. Because most Zulus would not learn any language other than their own, many white farmers and civil servants spoke it, and Stuart was regarded as the finest practical orthographer and linguist of his generation. He was interpreter to the commissioner at Eshowe and chief magistrate, and made a point while travelling round the country on official business, of seeking out men and women learned in local folklore. Most of Stuart's research was historical but he also recorded the opinions of his subjects on contemporary issues. They evidently felt able to unburden themselves as they did to few white men: Stuart's notes reflect the ferment that lay beneath the placid surface.

I had an interesting talk with Dhlozi and Ndukwana last night. Dhlozi remarked that to Europeans' faces they pretend to be satisfied, whereas among themselves they speak discontentedly. At first Europeans were regarded as saviours, but now they are looked on as more tyrannical and oppressive than Shaka's wildest schemes.[6]

There was much confusion as Africans grappled with capitalism. One man complained: 'Natives should not be given money because they do not know its use. After we have worked, the money we earn is taken from us in every way. Our needs are increased. We then go out to work and wages are reduced.'[7] The seeming pettiness of the law also caused resentment. Another demanded to know: 'Why am I arrested for being drunk? Was not the money I got drunk on mine?'[8]

More than anything, though, it was the whites' aloofness, their refusal to accept blacks as fellow men, that baffled Africans. One man wondered why Europeans would not 'associate and become one with the natives, who are not only [willing] but actually place implicit confidence in them?'[9]

The case of Ndhlovu ka Timuni is illustrative: he had taken a band of men to the Diamond Fields to be the white man's police; he had no complaints about being attacked by Sothos, but he was baffled and pained that whatever service he rendered to whites, he was still treated as an outsider. In 1906, Ndhlovu would join the rural rebellion against white rule. Three years earlier, Stuart recorded a conversation in which the chief made a heartfelt complaint:

Ndhlovu says, 'We cannot find your gate; the gateway in our own times consisted in going and tendering our allegiance.' The chief laid stress on this. His meaning is that the native people, so far from being taken into our fold and becoming one with us, are standing outside and drifting further away as time goes on.[10]

In another remarkable conversation, Stuart noted the testimony of two Natal Zulu-speakers who had joined the English side in 1879 in the belief, as Ndhlovu had put it, that this might be the 'gate' to acceptance, only to be betrayed. The men were Mkando ka Dhlova and Dhlozi ka Langa.

Mkando says: 'When Shaka died he said the white man would overrun the land; the whole land would be white with the light of the stars. We are your dogs. We do not feel as if we were at home. You make a law; we obey it. Again you make a law and we accept and obey it. Over and over again you promulgate fresh laws and we abide by them cheerfully, until we have become old and grey-headed and not even now do we know the meaning of your policy.

'We cut away the the wild forests for sugar plantations and towns; we dig your roads. When will this digging of roads cease? We are made to live on farms and pay rent, and are imprisoned if we cannot pay. You chase our wives out of our homes by facilitating divorce. How is it you treat us thus, seeing we are your people?

'Our children go off and become converts. We have no control over them. Our children lose contact with their homes and we lose that wealth which according to ancient custom is vested in them.

'The natives belong to one ruler; they may not be owned by just everyone and anyone.'

Dhlozi follows and says: 'We came into sharp contact with the Boers. They were our enemies. War began and continued until the English arrived. Peace smiled on the land, and we rejoiced on getting what we thought were sweet people. From Zululand came refugees. As each arrived, he exclaimed, "How glad I am!"

'[Then] the English directed us to pay taxes. We did not demur because they were people we respected, even though the tax weighed heavily. Then many governors arose; the land was divided and cut up into islands. On this a great grievance arose. For when you built on a white man's land you would have something claimed from you in respect to what you had built. Thus we remained on top of a coal of fire, having no place to go to. The white man, as often as he found his wish uncomplied with, orders us to quit his farm. Seeing we are unprovided with wings, we are unable to fly off into the sky and build in regions perchance to be found there. The ground is hard or we would have dug ourselves away out of sight. You have come upon the bucks all cornered in one spot.'[11]

In 1904, Stuart warned the colonial authorities to be on the alert for unrest, even rebellion. He was ignored. That year, Frederick Moor, secretary of native affairs, declared blithely: 'We rather congratulate ourselves that our natives are the best-mannered, and the best-behaved, and the most law-abiding people that we have got in South Africa.'[12]

The kingdom had gone, but the king lived on. Dinuzulu was Cetshwayo's heir, an intelligent and muscular boy who had entered adolescence when the *amabutho* were broken at Ulundi, and was aged about seventeen when his father died. He inherited all the pride of his forebears and, in the words of Colenso's son, Francis, 'trod the earth as if he owned it'. Nothing that he endured altered his view of his destiny. Unable to adjust as others had before him, he was to spend his adult life in a state of embittered resistance, interspersed with long periods in exile and prison.[13]

We have seen how Dinuzulu had grown up in the clutches of Zibhebhu, the man seen by the Usuthu as a British puppet, who had never missed an opportunity to humiliate the members of the royal house left at his mercy by the partition of 1879. The young king was also unfortunate in falling under the influence of his uncle, Ndabuko, whose hatred for Zibhebhu knew no bounds and who encouraged him to think of revenge. Cetshwayo's old chief minister, Mnyamana, counselled caution:

My child, I advise you against fighting because if a man approached us here leading a dog on a chain and you hit that dog, you would really be attacking its owner. Zibhebhu is the dog but the British are the owners and they will attack you with their soldiers against whom you cannot fight.[14]

It was good advice, but Dinuzulu failed to heed it. Early in 1888 incidents involving his Usuthu followers and Zibhebhu's Mandlakazi faction preyed on the young man's mind; he brooded furiously on the loss of his position and on the partisanship shown towards Zibhebhu by British officials like R.H. Addison, the magistrate of Ndwandwe district. In June, Usuthu followers attacked a force of Zibhebhu's men, who had been summoned to help protect Addison's headquarters, and put them to flight. No violence had been offered against the Crown, and the fault for the attack lay with a policy which now exploited the enmity between Usuthu and Mandlakazi. But the following year Dinuzulu was tried at Eshowe, found guilty of high treason, and sentenced to ten years' imprisonment, to be served in exile on St Helena. Ndabuko was sentenced to fifteen years, and another of Mpande's sons, Tshingana, to twelve years.

These years were not entirely wasted. Dinuzulu had a private tutor appointed to him, Magema ka Magwaza, the historian and convert of Colenso, who taught him to read and write. The heir to Shaka's kingdom also learned to play the piano, well enough for one white visitor to remark later on his ability to 'rattle off a few tunes'. He took to European ways in other respects, having a special fondness for British military-style uniforms, and kept a pet parrot, a canary and a monkey. Having been allowed to take two wives into exile, he fathered a number of children. His successor as king, Solomon Nkayishana, was born on St Helena in January 1893.

While Dinuzulu and his uncles shared the island of Napoleon's exile, Britain was coming under intense pressure from Natal, after the granting of self-government in 1893, to give up control of Zululand. Farmers had their eyes on the fertile coastal plain, and gold and coal had been found in the interior. It was only a matter of time before the inexorable alienation of the Zulu from their land resumed.

Dinuzulu was eventually allowed home in January 1898, having served just under nine years in exile. The position to which he returned was extremely curious. Zululand no longer existed independently, having been incorporated into Natal the previous year.

Left: Cetshwayo in captivity, on his way by sea to Cape Town

Below: Zibhebhu, leader of the Mandlakazi, and scourge of Cetshwayo in the civil war

Above: Zulu maidens – as posed for the camera by an early photographer

Right: Zulu madonna

Above: Cannabis smokers

Left: Women *izangoma,* or diviners

A renowned Zulu chief (Tshingwayo) and his adjutants

Above: The traditional Zulu hut is clearly seen in this nineteenth-century portrait of Tshingwayo, a chief, and his headmen

Right: A woman dressing the hair of her daughter

King Dinuzulu at the time of his trial for treason

King Solomon and attendant

Above: John Dube, first president of the African National Congress

Right: A.W.G. Champion, Dube's great rival

Above: Bishop Alpheus Zulu reading a Shaka Day address. To his right are King Cyprian and the young Mangosuthu Buthelezi

Left: Albert Lutuli – ANC president and winner of the Nobel Peace Prize

King Goodwill Zwelithini, left, and Chief Buthelezi
at a Shaka Day rally

Dinuzulu himself was not recognized as king of the Zulus, but the authorities realized that he could be useful and he was employed by the colonial administration as 'government *induna* and adviser'. In return, he was to be well paid, receiving an annual stipend of £500.

All this was irrelevant to the hundreds of thousands of Zulus who still regarded Dinuzulu as their king. But he was a much changed man. The proud, handsome youth had become an over-weight and prematurely aged man. He quickly retired to Nongoma, about thirty miles north of Ulundi, where he proceeded to hold court in the manner of Zulu monarchs of old. This was all very well for appearances but it was of little benefit for his people, who now desperately needed effective leadership. For, dependent as they were on agriculture and the blessings of their ancestors, it was clear to many that they had incurred the spirits' anger.

Three years earlier, maize seed had been planted and watered by the spring rains. Plants grew strong and tall. Then, one day in the steamy midsummer, clouds started appearing in the sky, of swarms that whispered menacingly and fell upon the crops like black rain. Within days, the harvest in large areas had been wiped out by locusts. The fields beside Zulu homesteads were reduced to flayed stalks. Overall, two-thirds of the maize and half the sorghum crops were lost.

For the next two years, the plague returned. By then, the devastation of crops was being completed by another pestilence. Day after day, men emerged from their huts and scanned the skies for clouds of a different kind. None came. The rains had failed. But the worst was still to come.

In the second of these terrible years, youths tending cattle started reporting to their fathers that the animals were displaying little appetite for grazing. Anxiously, the men clustered round the herds that were their pride and wealth. Animals' muzzles were heavy with foaming saliva, a watery discharge seeped from their anuses, and they smelt foul. Nothing like it had ever been seen before and none of the usual remedies of the best stockmen, or the *izangoma*, made any difference. Within days of displaying these symptoms, an animal was dead.

Among white farmers the disease was called bovine typhus, or rinderpest, and it was known to have spread to Natal and Zululand via the Cape. By fencing and inoculation, the whites managed to bring it under control. To the Zulu, it came as the wrath of God. With their tradition of communal grazing, the disease spread like a veld fire and with as devastating an effect. In two years, the black people of Natal and Zululand had lost between 80 and 85 per cent of their herds. The social impact was cataclysmic. Some of the wealthiest homesteads were, in effect, bankrupted, without so much as the means to acquire a bride for a favoured son.[15] Despair seized the nation and the disasters that had befallen it were interpreted as omens of apocalypse.

Many of the rumours and fantasies that gained currency concerned Dinuzulu. At this time, he was still in exile but it was said that he would soon return and drive the whites from his land. At that point, the plagues would cease. The prevalence of these beliefs actually delayed Dinuzulu's return. His release had been agreed in Whitehall in 1896 when Natal's governor, Havelock, advised the Colonial Office by telegram: 'Unsafe to bring Dinuzulu back at this time. Loss and suffering may dispose natives to disorder, owing to despair.'[16]

The threat of unrest seems to have made the colonial authorities less, rather than more, sensitive to the natives' plight, for scarcely had native herds started to recover from the rinderpest plague than the government appointed a commission to examine how Zulu territory could be opened up to white settlement.

This body sat for two years, at the end of which it set aside some 40 per cent of the remaining area of Zululand for white occupation. This was a complete betrayal of the undertaking given by Wolseley as administrator after the war. It will be remembered that the Boers had already taken about a third of the former kingdom in 1884, as a payment for helping Dinuzulu against Zibhebhu. In short, by 1904 the land occupied by Zulus living in traditional style north of the Tugela had been whittled down in ten years by almost 70 per cent to just 3.8 million acres.[17] They were now in much the same boat as the Zulu-speakers of Natal, whose 'locations' covered about 2.3 million acres. The turnaround in land distribution was rapid and dramatic. In Natal and Zululand as a whole in 1904, each African occupied on average eight to nine acres. Each white, by comparison, occupied 184 acres.[18]

The Zulus were watching the extinction of their pastoralist heritage. After locusts, drought and disease, they were now being squeezed between wattle and sugar plantations arising suddenly on the coast, and the white farmers' herds which roamed the hills of the north.

One more blow hastened the process. In August 1905, the legislative assembly in Pietermaritzburg passed a bill imposing a poll tax of £1 on every black adult male not already paying the hut tax. This measure was aimed specifically at young men who had so far eluded the colony's revenue net – in spite of the fact that many young men were already working in order to pay the hut taxes incurred by their fathers. The accumulated grievances and resentment of colonial rule that had been festering for years were felt most acutely in the rural areas. By the end of the year, a mood of defiance united traditionalists on both sides of the Tugela.

Anxiety among Natal's whites was nothing new but, at the start of the new century, it intensified in response to what seemed the rebelliousness of blacks in much of colonial Africa. Uprisings by the Herero and the Nama in German South-West Africa, and the so-called Maji Maji rebellion in German East Africa, followed resistance to British rule in Uganda and Sierre Leone. Most disturbing of all, to the colonists' way of thinking, had been events in the Matabeleland province of Rhodesia.

The Ndebele kingdom, founded by Shaka's onetime ally, Mzilikazi, was a Zulu-speaking state with a warrior tradition. In 1893, an army raised by Cecil Rhodes's British South Africa Company invaded the kingdom and sacked Bulawayo, capital of Mzilikazi's successor, Lobengula. Matabeleland was thrown open to whites. Three years later, the Ndebele rose up in the night without warning and murdered dozens of settlers before being crushed. The same pattern of rebellion and retribution was repeated a few months later among the Shona-speaking people to the east.

The parallels of Matabeleland and Natal made many whites fearful of an African uprising after 1896. The susceptibility of white society to rumours did not help: after his return from St Helena, Dinuzulu figured largely in the public mind as a bloated and sensual revolutionary. Once again, a Zulu king was being invested with imaginary powers and ambitions for white destruction.

Africans were to be no less affected by rumour and speculation. The mutinous mood sweeping kraals on either side of the Tugela was encouraged by a belief that the king would soon call on Zulus to rise.

In January 1906, reports started coming in from magistrates' offices of defiant protests against the poll tax. Then, on 7 February, a group of men of the Fuze chiefdom, near Richmond in southern Natal, brandished their assegais at white officials and announced that they would not pay the tax. When a police detachment was sent the next day to arrest them, a scuffle broke out after two prisoners were taken and then set free by a jeering mob. Two policemen were stabbed to death.

Martial law was proclaimed and the militia placed under Colonel Duncan McKenzie, a Natalian who had fought in Matabeleland and believed he had learned a thing or two about how to deal with native insurgents. He saw his job as a 'golden opportunity' to instil 'a proper respect for the white man'. His methods rapidly won him the nickname, Shaka.[19]

Descending on the Fuze, McKenzie had two men shot out of hand, then rounded up a score more. Twelve of them were sentenced to death at the subsequent court martial and the remainder to twenty years' imprisonment. The Colonial Office requested that the sentences be delayed for further enquiries to be made but this provoked a mass resignation by Natal's cabinet and Whitehall quickly backed away. On 2 April, the twelve men were publicly executed by a firing squad at Richmond. Three others, including the supposed ringleader, Mjongo, who had announced 'We shall refuse our money for the poll tax,' were hanged in September after recovering from injuries sustained during their arrest.

By then, McKenzie and his force had trampled across the Midlands and south Natal, sniffing for any hint of opposition to the poll tax, seizing cattle as well as weapons, and burning kraals as they went. He was joined enthusiastically in this by another officer who prided himself on knowing 'the native mind', a former stock farmer named Colonel George Leuchars. Leuchars, who was later to be knighted, ordered a chief in the Mapumulo division in north Natal to surrender 300 men who had demonstrated in opposition to the tax and, when he prevaricated, shelled his kraal with artillery. In their vindictive and contemptuous attitudes towards blacks, men like McKenzie, Leuchars and Henry Winter, the secretary for native affairs at the time, prefigure the worst forms of white racism that Afrikaner nationalists were later to demonstrate.

Meanwhile, the disturbances had spread. The leading protagonist north of the Tugela was Bambatha ka Mancinza, chief of a faction of the Zondi clan whose homesteads were in the Greytown area. Bambatha was a pugnacious individual who had come into conflict before with his own people as well as colonial officials and was quickly associated with opposition to the poll tax. In March, a militia was sent to arrest him and he fled to Zululand, where he had an audience with Dinuzulu. Subsequently, Bambatha's followers used the war cry of the royal house, '*Usuthu!*' and he wore a charm which he said had been given to him by the king to turn his enemy's bullets to water. On 5 April, Bambatha's *impi* attacked a police patrol at Keate's Drift, killing four men. The body of one, a Sergeant Brown, was found to have been mutilated, the genitals being removed by a *sangoma* to make a *muti* effective against the whites.

This was the first act of aggression against the authorities and led to the poll tax disturbances being dubbed the 'Bambatha Rebellion'. With a following of around a thousand men, all armed and doctored for war in the old manner, Bambatha withdrew into the forests and gorges of Nkandla. From this rugged country north of the mid-Tugela, which had been the stage for rearguard actions since Shaka's time, he sent out appeals in Dinuzulu's name, urging other chiefs to take up arms and join him. One who responded to the call was a Tuli *induna*, Mangati ka Godide, a grandson of Dingane's military commander, Ndlela. An even more influential supporter was Sigananda ka Zokufa, the venerable chief of the Cube, who had sheltered Cetshwayo in his flight from Zibhebhu. Finally, Bambatha was joined by Mehlokazulu, the now-ageing fire-eater whose raid into Natal in pursuit of his father's adulterous wives had been the *casus belli* of the 1879 war, and who had fought with distinction at Isandlwana.

For two months, Bambatha conducted a series of guerrilla actions against McKenzie's Zululand Field Force, which pursued him through the Nkandla region. The ravines and forests were hard going everywhere and, in some places, impenetrable; McKenzie became infuriated at his inability to bring about a decisive confrontation. On 17 May, his men set fire to Sigananda's kraal and burned Cetshwayo's grave. Early successes in avoiding casualties made Bambatha reckless; the Zulu may have been convinced that the charms and *muti* had indeed turned the white man's bullets to water. But resistance was doomed from the outset. In the words of one African source, Bambatha,

. . . was very much like a beast which on being stabbed rushes about in despair, charges backwards and forwards and, it may be, kills someone that happens to be in his path.[20]

McKenzie caught up with Bambatha on 10 June. The Zulu were streaming through the Mome Gorge, one of the most remote and dense spots in Nkandla, when gunfire poured down on them. What followed was a pitiless massacre. The whites were using dum-dum bullets which inflicted horrific wounds and were not prepared to accept any surrender. Out of about 1400 men on the Zulu side, only half managed to escape from the gorge. Among the dead were Mehlokazulu and Bambatha – or so it was long assumed, after a head cut off from one of the bodies in the gorge was identified by a number of Zulus as that of Bambatha. However, Dinuzulu's biographer, C.T. Binns, found a number of African sources in the 1960s who claimed that Bambatha's followers had hood-winked the whites, and that he had escaped to Mozambique.[21] Whatever the truth of the matter, the troubles were over in Zululand.

A week after the Mome Gorge massacre, the chiefs in Mapumulo division, just south of the Tugela, rose up. Among them was Ndhlovu ka Timuni, who had once asked Stuart where the 'gate' lay to the white man's heart. In February, Ndhlovu announced his opposition to the poll tax and Leuchars had him and other chiefs in Mapumulo arrested and thrown in prison for six weeks. Men of lesser status were flogged. On 19 June, Ndhlovu's followers fell on a place called Thring's Post, killing a Norwegian storekeeper and a trooper.

Once again, McKenzie and Leuchars saddled up and rode out. Over the next three weeks, the slaughter continued as they scoured the south bank of the Tugela. Only one engagement remotely resembled a battle, at Insuze Drift on 3 July, when about 400 Zulus were killed for one trooper. Otherwise, the Zulu casualties were incurred in running clashes and 'mopping-up' operations that were no more than summary executions. By the middle of June, the Colonial Office was advised: 'Resistance is more or less over, rebels for the most part cowed and in hiding.'

If a rebellion it had been, there could be no doubt which side had come off worst. In five months of sporadic unrest, eighteen whites and six loyal blacks, had died at rebel hands; these included six civilians, but in spite of the hysteria that had gripped colonial society, no threat had been offered to any white women or children. Estimates of Zulu dead vary from 2300, in Stuart's original study of the disturbances, to up to 4000, according to Shula Marks. Almost 5000 men were in gaol. When the judicial process dealt with them, dozens, including Ndhlovu ka Timuni, were condemned to death. These sentences were subsequently commuted to long terms of imprisonment and exile to St Helena. Thousands received shorter terms, with lashes. Among the extra-judicial punishments, more than 30,000 people had been made homeless. Of the further impoverishment of traditional society, by loss of cattle and crops, no estimate can be made.

All this time, Dinuzulu had been observing events from the sidelines. His sympathies, we cannot doubt, were with the dissidents, but it would have been suicidal to show his hand. So when the government called on him to demonstrate his loyalty, he did all that was asked. He said the rebels who were using his name and the Usuthu war cry did so without his authority and he offered to raise an *impi* to assist the colonial force. In the meantime, the dissidents continued sending messages, urging Dinuzulu to throw his weight on their side. There is no evidence to suggest that he seriously contemplated such a step. But the dilemma of the man caught between action and passivity was nicely captured by Stuart, who dubbed him the Zulu Hamlet.

The authorities were also in a bind. Colonial society had decided that Dinuzulu was the puppet-master, guiding the forces of insurrection from his headquarters in Nongoma. However, official policy was founded on the principle that Dinuzulu was not a king, only a chief, with no more influence than any other. Thus, officials required his loyalty, but then were obliged to insist that it was of no great account. Secretly, they could not fail to recognize that at one word from him, virtually the entire country would have risen up. In the months following the rebellion, Dinuzulu's many foes gathered evidence of clandestine contacts between the king and the rebels.

Dinuzulu was not entirely without white friends, notably the indomitable Harriette Colenso and her brother, Francis, the last of the bishop's brood. Harriette, now greying and spinsterly, had adopted her father's campaigning role and was the *bête noire* of colonial society, an impassioned Usuthu partisan who had been so outraged at the injustices done to the Zulu royal family over the years that she was blind to fault within it. Her support for any cause doomed it in the public eye, but she was able to help Dinuzulu in practical ways. When the inevitable happened, and the king was arrested and charged with high treason, Harriette engaged the best available counsel to defend him.

The trial opened in November 1908 in the town hall of Greytown, a prosperous little municipality set in lovely country on the high, cool mist belt north of Pietermaritzburg. Dinuzulu tried to cut an imposing figure in pith helmet, khaki military dress and leather leggings, but the effect was spoiled by his physical grossness. He was adamant about his innocence. 'I am guilty only of being Cetshwayo's son,' he told his advocate, the prominent Cape liberal William Schreiner. 'Bambatha is made the pretext, whereas it is the old charge.'[22]

More than two years had passed since the disturbances and much preparation had gone into the prosecution case. This was aimed, in the first place, at proving that Dinuzulu had incited Bambatha to insurrection during the chief's visit to him in Nongoma. When that was rejected by the bench, the emphasis turned to demonstrating that he had succoured the rebels. Thanks to Schreiner's incisive cross-examination, Dinuzulu was acquitted on all but three of the twenty-three charges of treason. He was found guilty of sheltering Bambatha and his family, along with other prominent rebels. On 3 March 1909, he was sentenced to four years' imprisonment and taken to Pietermaritzburg gaol.

In the year after Dinuzulu's imprisonment, Louis Botha, a former Boer general, became prime minister of Britain's newest dominion, the Union of South Africa. Botha happened to have been a member of the Boer *kommando* which defeated Zibhebhu in Dinuzulu's name in 1884 and he had not forgotten the king. Soon after taking office, Botha ordered that he be released. But although Dinuzulu was settled comfortably on a farm in the Transvaal, he remained in effective exile and was never able to return to Natal. He drank heavily, and died in October 1913, aged forty-five. He was buried at Nobamba in the Emakosini, in a simple traditional grave, surrounded by stones.

Dinuzulu was succeeded by his son, Solomon, and he by his son, Cyprian. These were desperate years for the royal house. The South African government refused to grant recognition as the Zulu kings to Mpande's descendants and Cyprian, in particular, was a sad, wasted figure who drank to excess.

The monarchy was to be mobilized again as a political force, paving the way for a revival of Zulu nationalism. For the time being, however, the torch of resistance was passed to the section of society which had been evolving under the influence of missionary education, which could articulate its grievances on equal terms with the colonial authorities, and which was now to take up the struggle for political rights – the *amakholwa*.

16

CHRISTIANS AWAKE

We belong neither to the Europeans nor to the natives.
We are a people apart and without proper laws.

John Kumalo, Christian convert, to James Stuart,
December 1900

To me, it is rather strange that people feel proud that
their forefathers wore skins. Every nation has been
through skins. I have no attachment to the skin – I
even have a negative attitude towards it. If I go
anywhere I look at the churches, because that is the
nurturing I had.

Paulus Zulu, political scientist, to the author,
April 1992

The early converts might have been drawn from the pages of the
gospels as a parable for Christ's mission. They were the meek and
despised, the fugitives and outcasts and, sometimes, the plain bad.
There were missionaries who feared, as one put it, that they had
become 'refuges for characters of the worst description'.[1] But in
1895, sixty years after the arrival of the American mission to the
Zulu, there were more than fifty stations south of the Tugela and

around 40,000 souls had professed the Christian faith. Although the number of converts north of the river remained small, conquest of the kingdom had opened the way for a new generation of proselytizers.

The Christian message of love and forgiveness chimed powerfully with the African concept of humanism, *ubuntu*, while, in the eyes of their adherents, the 'teachers' made potent substitutes for chiefs. Missionaries were the first literate men to take a personal interest in African society, and were responsible for the early linguistic and anthropological studies on which later scholarship was based. In addition to his other work, Colenso compiled a Zulu dictionary and grammar. Alfred Bryant, the father of Zulu historiography, served in Roman Catholic stations all over south-east Africa before producing, in 1905, his Zulu–English dictionary and, in 1929, an historical survey, *Olden Times in Zululand and Natal*; both are still landmarks in their fields. Henry Callaway, an Anglican, collected folklore, published a study of Zulu religious beliefs and completed the first Zulu translation of the Bible.

There were other influences drawing Africans to the gospel. Missions were seen not just as refuges but as sources of work and income. Many stations controlled large tracts of land known as reserves, granted by the government and available to converts for commercial production. Above all, perhaps, the missions seemed to be the one gate that was open to the white man's world. Christianity was to be a stepping stone to status and advantage. To early converts it must have seemed that by turning their back on the 'barbarism' which the missionary deplored and embracing his way, they too might enter the heaven on earth which was so clearly the white man's lot.

They were soon to be disabused. Whites continued to keep them at arm's length, many making it clear that they were even more prejudiced against the *amakholwa*, with his quasi-European ways and ideas above his station, than against the traditionalist who, though an 'untutored savage', was a man for all that. Farmers in particular took against the *amakholwa*, especially when they started to prove themselves able competitors.[2] Even missionaries sometimes fell into the trap of treating members of their flocks as brothers in church, but strangers on the street.

Nevertheless, black Christians adopted European dress and European names, often the grand and resonant ones of biblical patriarchs. They abandoned the beehive-shaped *indlu* and built European-style dwellings. At first, they aspired to follow their patrons, many becoming ministers of religion and teachers. Fired with the ideals of progress and the dignity of labour, *amakholwa* also made industrious workers. They had discovered the reward system of modern capitalism and gradually they started to push their way into the commercial life of Natal, as traders, shop-owners, clerks and, above all, as farmers.

Kholwa farmers seized the opportunity granted by commercial growing with both hands. Some pooled their resources to buy private land, forming cooperative ventures. A few prospered sufficiently to become employers of black labour in their own right. The majority, though, dwelt on mission reserves near Pietermaritzburg or on the coast near Durban. The American missionary board was quick to encourage enterprise and the introduction of new crops. A few other benefactors also helped. Sir James Liege Hulett, a tea and sugar baron, took an interest in African agriculture in general and the American mission at Groutville in particular. Along with the Methodist station at Edendale, this was to be one of the most prosperous and influential *kholwa* communities, producing one early nationalist leader, Martin Lutuli, and his more famous nephew, Albert Lutuli, the Nobel Peace Prize winner. Another prominent protégé of the American missions was John Langalibalele Dube, the son of a refugee chief, who was a founding father of the African National Congress.

In spite of, perhaps because of, the strides taken by some *kholwa*, there remained a tendency among traditionalists to regard them as outcasts – miscreants who had fled tribal life over some allegation of theft or witchcraft. These misgivings were not always misplaced. Mission stations tolerated standards of conduct that were unacceptable in traditionalist society and a few had well-founded reputations for criminality. Sexual mores changed among the *kholwa*. Absalom Vilakazi, a Zulu sociologist, has noted how the Christian tendency to secretiveness in sexual matters led to the loss of *hlobonga* techniques except among traditionalists. Vilakazi wrote: 'When Christian young people meet and have sex relations, it is generally not intercrural sex play at all, but coitus.'[3] As a result, there was a striking increase in illegitimacy among *kholwa* communities. Many unwed mothers were cast out by their fathers and, forced into the cities for work, drifted into prostitution.

The rift between Christians and traditionalists widened during the 1906 rebellion. While 'heathen' communities in Natal and Zululand rose up against the poll tax, John Dube, already an influential figure, urged *amakholwa* to pay the tax and remain loyal. Vilakazi observed: 'They earned the label of *amambuka* – deserters from the traditional Zulu.'[4] Most Zulus would have echoed the old man who told Stuart ten years later:

Missionaries have asked me to convert, but I have refused on the ground that God created me as I am, told me to wear the loin-cover, and did not tell me to lead a life different to what I am leading. These *kholwas* talk a lot about Nkulunkulu [God] but they do not understand his affairs; they do not know them properly.[5]

Among the converts, the wiser spirits recognized the virtues of social cohesion in traditional society, and sought a middle path that combined the best of both worlds. Martin Lutuli, the Groutville chief, ran a community in which converts and traditionalists lived comfortably together. Stations like Groutville evolved into independent societies in which a Christian code was applied through a form of democracy involving a ballot for the senior men. Such *kholwa* communities formed a platform for modern political consciousness.

However, many *amakholwa* did not endear themselves to traditionalists by imitating white attitudes of superiority, calling them *amaqaba*, a derisive term meaning that they were ignorant and uncultured.[6] Drawn, as they were, from diverse cultural backgrounds, there was little to encourage converts to cherish anything of the past. As a result the traditionalists' devotion to his clan and chief were entirely alien. What united *amakholwa* was their colour and their faith.

Not all the missionaries' ideas proved acceptable. Two totems of traditional culture survived and have endured to modern times, defying the best efforts of the establishment church to eradicate them: a belief in witches, and polygamy.

At first, many missionaries tried to deal with polygamy by insisting that converts should give up all but the first of their wives – with little apparent thought to what would become of those who were discarded. Shepstone had recognized the fruitlessness of such a course. 'Of all the institutions among them, polygamy is the one they cling to with the utmost tenacity,' he wrote.[7] Colenso was among the few churchmen to turn a blind eye to the custom, so that Magema ka Magwaza, the historian and one of his earliest followers, could continue to aver devoutly after his own conversion: 'A man with but one wife is a poor fellow.'[8] It was the tolerance of a few farsighted early Christian missionaries like Colenso that opened the path to syncretism, which is the despair of orthodox theologians but also accounts for the church's continued strength in Africa today. The present Zulu king, Goodwill Zwelithini, is among many African traditionalists who have reconciled their Christian faith with polygamy.

The roots of the old spiritual beliefs have also proved durable. Many nominally Christian Africans continue to consult *izangoma*, who not only prescribe herbal remedies for physical ailments but who offer interpretations of dreams and troubling psychic manifestations. Some are traditional healers, as they are now called, who deserve to be treated seriously and provide services similar to herbalists elsewhere; others are outright charlatans. Many Africans have been bled of savings by *izangoma* claiming to be able to quiet the disturbed spirit of a departed relative, or secure some material gain. A belief in witches also survived, and has, on occasions, been a lethal ingredient in the strains of township life.[9]

One thing united both *kholwa* and traditionalist – a thirst for education. Learning, it was clear to Africans, was the one way out of their plight. Even Ndhlovu ka Timuni, a diehard traditionalist whose part in the rebellion earned him exile to St Helena, told Stuart of his desire that his children should be educated. Until the politics of anarchy in the late twentieth century appeared to offer an alternative means to the same end – empowerment – black South Africans of all language groups pursued education with a moving faith and dedication. Generation after generation of parents sacrificed themselves in menial labour that their children might escape the same fate. In many cases, these efforts were not in vain. But learning was won in spite of, rather than because of, the educational establishment in South Africa. We can but speculate how different the country's prospects might now appear had this yearning been channelled and encouraged. Instead, the hand of institutionalized racism saw to it that blacks were steadily and increasingly cheated of educational opportunity. When, in 1976, that lesson was confronted in the schools of Soweto, it ensured that the icon of learning would be replaced by the icon of revolution. Since then the chilling cry 'Liberation before education' was to prevail in the schools of the townships.

For many years, missions were the only places offering schooling to blacks in Natal. It followed that the *amakholwa* and their children were the first to benefit from the basics of reading and writing in Zulu and English and from arithmetic. Slowly, the colonial administration came round to accepting responsibility for African education. In 1885, the mission schools were brought under government control; by the turn of the century, there were around 200 schools for blacks in Natal and twenty in Zululand. The pioneering place of Zulu education, Ekukanyeni, Colenso's 'place of light', did not long survive its founder, but Anglicans and Wesleyans remained active in the education field. Most influential of all, however, were the Congregationalists of the American Board. The spirit of Newton Adams, the first of the American missionaries, who had decided that education should come before conversion, lived on: Adams College at Amanzimtoti, south of Durban, was the Eton of the Zulu world, producing successive generations of political leaders, from John Dube through Albert Lutuli to Mangosuthu Buthelezi.

Natal officials had no desire to instil a love of learning among the Africans, let alone a political sense. In 1906 the superintendent of education wrote:

The native education policy of this colony should aim rather at the leavening of the whole lump of heathenism and ignorance than at the raising of the few to a giddy height above their fellows.[10]

A spirit of learning had been planted, however, and was not to be denied. Christian missionaries have been the subject of much criticism in Africa, branded as cultural imperialists who did as much harm in their way as the soldiers and bureaucrats who followed them. This may be true. The assumption of superiority which underpinned the missionary attitude sits uncomfortably with what we understand of the Christian message today, although in their confused and bumbling way many missionaries loved their flocks no less than did Colenso. More importantly, they opened the eyes of African society to the peculiarly Christian qualities of compassion and mercy. However, it was as educationalists that missionaries really proved their worth, equipping a small minority to act as a new generation of leaders and, in the end, justifying the term by which they had introduced themselves to the Zulus, as 'teachers'.

How different it would have been if, after the conquest, Britain had extended the same protective wing over Zululand that it did to three other large ethnic groups in the region. The Tswana, the Sotho and the Swazi were insulated from the turbulence of modern South Africa by being enfolded in three High Commission territories. Bechuanaland, Basutoland and Swaziland were ruled directly – and by and large benevolently – from Whitehall until being granted their independence in the 1960s. Since then, as Botswana, Lesotho and Swaziland, they have survived in relative stability amid the turmoil around them. But in spite of a brief campaign, by the Aborigines Protection Society in London and a few Radical MPs for Zululand to be removed from Natal's control and placed again under direct imperial rule, the Zulus were to find themselves shackled to the ill-fated destiny of a united South Africa.

Around the turn of the century, the question facing enlightened white administrators was how a pre-literate and pre-industrial people could join the modern world without losing their identity or dignity. This debate had produced two models: on the one hand, Colenso's 'educate and integrate' argument; and on the other, Theophilus Shepstone's paternalistic separatism based on tribal reserves. Although both men had been regarded in their time as dangerous negrophiles, the Shepstone system had won acceptance and, in the end, acquired the status almost of holy writ. But while it enabled traditional culture to survive almost without interference, it also retarded any possibility of political evolution.

Constitutionally, Africans were in an ambiguous position. Whitehall's insistence in the early days of the colony that all men should be held equal under the law, left open the theoretical possibility of a government elected and ruled by 'natives'. The catch was that to have any chance of being given the franchise, blacks had to petition and win exemption from native law. The basis for requesting exemption was that a man had certain property and could read and write. In effect, this meant that he was a *kholwa*.

Shepstone had made no secret of his preference for traditionalist society. He told converts: 'The white people praise their spirits; you should praise your own.'[11] In the twenty years that he was secretary of native affairs, Shepstone did not issue a single certificate of exemption.[12] Thereafter matters improved slightly, but as *kholwa* numbers increased, so white pressure mounted on the authorities to limit the granting of exemptions and so restrict the number of black voters. Exemption remained an elusive goal and the franchise a grail. At the turn of the century, fewer than 2000 Natal Africans had been granted exemption certificates, and just six had won the right to vote.[13] In the Cape, by contrast, males of all races were entitled to vote provided they met certain criteria of income or property. On a visit to Natal, the renowned Cape parliamentary liberal, John X. Merriman, was appalled by its rugged frontier politics. He told his hosts:

You have not elevated the natives in Natal; you have not educated them; they are barbarous, and you have designedly left them in a state of barbarism.[14]

For all that, there were worse systems than Natal's, as was demonstrated in a vigorous correspondence between President Francis Reitz of the Orange Free State and Shepstone in 1891. Reitz, whose views foreshadowed the true spirit of Verwoerdian racism, denounced Natal's policy in an article in the *Cape Illustrated Magazine*, declaring that it was civilization's responsibility to stamp out chieftainship and the tribal system in order that blacks could be forced to serve whites. 'Immoral and degrading heathen rites' should be suppressed.

The Kaffir, as an individual, may be 'a man' and (under due reservations) 'a brother', but as a member of a tribe, and the subject of a fat, arrogant chieftain, he can never be such. He is divided by an impassable barrier from the laws and customs of civilized humanity, and there is no room for him in his tribal condition in our European system of political economy.[15]

That the attitudes of Reitz came to prevail in South Africa, rather than those of Merriman, or even Shepstone, was due to the long-delayed triumph of confederation and the formation of the Union.

The war provoked by Britain against the Boers in 1899 had as little moral justification as that instigated against Cetshwayo twenty years before. The reason, on this occasion, was that the discovery of gold in 1886 had made the Boer Republic of the Transvaal the richest province in Africa, and the Witwatersrand, in the words of Lord Selbourne, the colonial under-secretary, 'the richest spot on earth'.

On the brown, sun-burnished plains of the Transvaal, arose Johannesburg and its satellite cities – a new Babylon, as the social historian Charles van Onselen called it, that transformed sub-Saharan Africa and whose power was able to shake stock markets across the globe. Because of the helter-skelter pace at which this revolution occurred, and the numbers of people that it affected, the social upheaval was immense. Gamblers and gangsters, entrepreneurs and refugees, European industrialists and Jewish bankers, all joined the greatest gold rush of all.

The second Anglo-Boer war lasted until 1902 and was the costliest and bloodiest British campaign since the Napoleonic era. The aim was to break Boer independence and, that done, to impose the union of British colonies and Boer republics that Disraeli's Tories had first sought in the 1870s.

The details of the war need no repetition here. In the early stages, it was fought largely in northern Natal where one disaster followed another for the British side . . . Ladysmith, Colenso, Spion Kop. . . . Buller, the hero of the Zulu campaign, became the scapegoat for British incompetence in the face of a highly motivated guerrilla army. Then Field Marshal Lord Roberts came to the rescue, driving a great force like a steamroller up from the Cape front, into the Orange Free State.

Africans had been warned against any kind of interference. This was a 'white man's war'. That did not stop the British recruiting Zulu irregulars in 1901 to act as scouts in the Transvaal, which may have sparked the one act of war in which Zulus were involved. Following a Boer cattle raid, Sikobobo, chief of the arch-royalist Qulusi section, remonstrated with a Boer officer named Potgieter, who was in charge of the Vryheid *kommando*. Sikobobo had been provoked by the Boers before and when Potgieter replied, challenging him to come and take back his cattle, the chief sent an *impi* of 300 men which caught the Boers unawares at Holkrantz. The ensuing skirmish, in which fifty-six Boers and fifty-two Zulus were killed, caused outrage among the Boers, who compared it with

Dingane's massacre of the Retief party, and accused the British of using savages as mercenaries.[16]

This was one of the last acts of the war. The overwhelming superiority of imperial arms had prevailed, although not before one final and most disgraceful blot was revealed on Britain's stained South African record: between 18,000 and 28,000 people, Boers and blacks, women and children, had died of neglect and disease in concentration camps.[17]

The Afrikaner's defeat in war was to be the making of his political rise. In an act of contrition and reconciliation, Britain handed power in 1910 to a Union of South Africa government headed by two moderate Boer leaders, Louis Botha and Jan Smuts. To the original British colonies of the Cape and Natal were added the Boer republics of the Orange Free State and Transvaal, which was now the economic powerhouse of Africa. To maintain a semblance of geopolitical equilibrium, the administrative capital was sited at Pretoria, and the parliamentary capital at Cape Town.

Blacks who had hoped that union might bring an extension of the liberal Cape political system over the whole country were to watch with dismay as, instead, the reverse happened. Slowly at first, and then with gathering rapidity, the attitudes which fostered segregation and repression, and which had followed the Boers into the interior, filtered back down to the former British colonies, until the voices of liberalism, and even those of benevolent paternalism, were drowned.

As Natal would not provide opportunities for higher education, the brightest of the *kholwa* minds were guided elsewhere by their missionary mentors. Natal's first black graduate had returned from the United States as early as 1876 and around the turn of the century there were twenty Zulu-speakers studying in America. They included John Dube and another man who was to be the founder of the ANC, Pixley ka Seme.

Dube was born in 1871, the son of a minor chief who had fled to an American mission after his father's death at the hands of Dingane. The elder Dube so prospered as a farmer and trader that, after schooling at Adams, his son John sailed as a teenager for America with, it is said, thirty gold sovereigns. Important though his studies at Oberlin in Ohio were to his development, the main legacy of Dube's American education was the influence of Booker T. Washington, the black leader who was advancing the principle of self-help at a school in Tuskegee. Fired with the notion of spreading Washington's ideas in the Zulu-speaking world, Dube concluded his time in America with a lecture tour to raise funds for a similar venture in Natal. The Ohlange Institute for Christian Africans was opened in 1901 at Inanda, in the magnificent country of the Land of a Thousand Hills just north of Durban.

Dube was the outstanding member of a generation of comparatively wealthy and privileged *kholwa* landowners. They were upright, gentlemanly figures, who wore dark suits, black felt hats and white shirts that were spotless even if the collars were sometimes frayed, and who spoke with quiet dignity. From this nucleus, of Dube himself, the Msimangs of Edendale and the Lutulis of Groutville, sprang the intellectual foundation of African political development in Natal which, in turn, was to prove so influential in South Africa as a whole.

Another *kholwa* star, Solomon Kumalo, a product of the Edendale mission, edited the first Zulu-language newspaper, *Inkanyiso yase Natal*. The paper, founded with Anglican backing in 1889, led an outspoken campaign for a wider franchise for seven years, before it closed.

The white man refuses to bestow the franchise on us, even upon a few, not because he thinks we will make a bad use of our vote, but because he feels that we might make too good a use of it. Through our representatives we should secure for our people what in so many instances they have not now, viz. Justice.[18]

It was the editorials of *Inkanyiso* and its successor, *Ilanga lase Natal*, founded by Dube in 1904 and still published today, that first articulated publicly what many had long been saying privately. Here can be seen the earliest calls for political organization among blacks – 'a central body composed of those in whom the whole community has trust' – and the stirrings of an intellectual pride that recoiled from missionary paternalism:

It is lamentable that those who have a benevolent interest in our race too often express it with a kind of contemptuous pity, and regard our efforts at advancement much as they would a trick learned by a favourite animal, instead of the natural impulse of human beings like themselves.[19]

This new spirit of independence, it was clear to concerned officials, went beyond the familiar grievances over taxes and labour. Here was an educated and articulate élite demanding equality. Henceforth, as Zulu traditionalist society became increasingly alienated and overawed by the modernization going on around it, it was the westernized *kholwa* who took up the struggle for liberty and fair treatment for the Zulu as a whole.

Zulu traditionalists have remained wary of Christianity. Where the church has had an impact it has been in the separatist movements, in particular the Church of the Nazarites, founded by a one-time Baptist minister and polygamist named Isaiah Shembe. With its emphasis on traditional Zulu values and its nationalist core – it marked the anniversary of Dingane's defeat by the Boers as a day of mourning – the Shembe church appealed to tribal people desperately seeking substitutes for their fast-disintegrating culture. Shembe's apocalyptic message, that the world was shortly to come to an end and then would be recast and inherited by the Nazarites, marks him as one of a line of Bantu prophets born out the upheaval of the modern era. The movement grew rapidly after Shembe left the Baptist church in 1911, and survived his death in 1935. In his lifetime, according to the sociologist Vilakazi, he had a greater influence on illiterate Zulus than any political leader, although with no discernible result.[20]

Traditional society, as Vilakazi has noted, had become completely demoralized in the aftermath of the rebellion. Once-strong men were reduced to 'an army of kitchen boys', doing jobs which in their own culture would have brought them ridicule. Otherwise, men turned to work as nightwatchmen, police and labour gang 'boss boys'. They learned little and gained no skills in the cities that would serve them when they returned to their homesteads in the hills. Even the past, with its evocation of a glorious age, became a burden. As policemen, many Zulu traditionalists outstripped whites for cruel and overweening behaviour, showing 'their self-hatred in vicious treatment of their own people', as Vilakazi put it.[21] This attitude was to be the making of much subsequent manipulation by white authority.

For now it was the westernized, Christian African who had been identified by Europeans as the enemy. A sinister bond, it was clear, had been forged between religion and politics. This bond would strengthen and grow so that, in the apartheid era, South Africa evolved its own brand of liberation theology. Early in the century the authorities coined a new word for the supposed threat – 'Ethiopianism'. It was not long before the term 'Ethiopian' became applicable to almost any educated black man in Natal as a label of subversion.

17

ACTIVISTS AND NATIONALISTS

We have got to maintain the sense of paternal and
tribal responsibility – with all its obligations of courage,
honour, truth, loyalty and obedience – for all we are
worth.[1]

John Dube,
1928

In January 1912, a group of black leaders, including chiefs, lawyers,
teachers and clergymen, gathered at a community hall in the
brown, dusty town of Bloemfontein. The capital of the old Boer
republic of the Orange Free State might have been thought an
inappropriate place to launch a black political movement, but
the choice was partly symbolic. It had been in Bloemfontein,
almost three years earlier, that Britain had signed away control
over the Union of South Africa and abandoned the fate of
the blacks to a sovereign, exclusively white parliament. No
African had been consulted in that process. Now this group
had come to the same spot to form 'our national union for the
purpose of creating national unity and defending our rights and
privileges.'[2]

Such were the words of the man who had summoned this inaugural meeting of what was to be the African National Congress,
Pixley ka Seme. The son of a Natal *kholwa* farmer, Seme is the

most enigmatic of the ANC's early leaders. He concealed his humble origins – it was suggested by the journalist, Jordan Ngubane, that he was not Zulu at all, but came from a Tonga tributary group – and later claimed to have been the nephew of the Qadi chief, Mqawe.[3] Escape from the life of a peasant farmer was provided by a missionary of the American Board, the Rev S. Pixley, who sponsored him to study in the United States, at Columbia University. One of the earliest black South Africans to be educated overseas, Seme went on to take law at Oxford and practised at the Middle Temple, returning to South Africa as one of a tiny élite of black professionals. He sealed his glittering transformation by marrying one of Dinuzulu's daughters and, after setting up a legal practice in Johannesburg, was retained as legal adviser to the Swazi royal family. Here was living proof, if any more were needed, of the social magic of education.

Other Zulu-speaking lawyers had also been attracted to the new metropolis of the Rand. Richard Msimang, a member of a renowned *kholwa* dynasty, had come up via Dube's Ohlange Institute. Most prominent of all was Alfred Mangena, who was legal adviser to the Tembu chiefs. But it was Seme who took the initiative in bringing together African leaders from all over the country for the first time. In a manifesto drafted with three other lawyers from different tribal backgrounds he declared: 'The demon of racialism, the aberrations of the Xhosa–Fingo feud, animosity that exists between the Zulus and Tongas, between the Basotho and every other native must be buried. We are one people.'[4] The Zulu journalist Jordan Ngubane wrote: 'They were no longer to be narrowly Zulu or Xhosa or Sotho. They were going to be the African people.'[5]

Here in Bloemfontein, the first steps were taken towards this goal. According to one version of the legend, the assembly sang 'Nkosi Sikelel'i Afrika' ('God Bless Africa'), the grand and moving hymn that is the ANC's anthem today. Actually, they sang another Xhosa hymn, 'Fulfil Thy Promise, God of Truth' by Tiyo Soga.[6] John Dube was elected the first president of the ANC; the secretary-general was Sol Plaatje, a Barolong from the Free State and a most gifted man, a journalist, writer and linguist; Seme was treasurer. This Zulu dominance was offset by the election of Walter Rubusana, a Xhosa, as honorary president, and of vice-presidents from all the main cities. However, the decision of Tengo Jabavu, the giant of black politics at the Cape, also a Xhosa, not to attend, was an early sign of regional rivalries.

A comprehensive, dispassionate and up-to-date history of the ANC has yet to be written. (The otherwise excellent study by Peter Walshe stops in 1952 and Tom Lodge's work has been based on black nationalist politics since 1945.) Perhaps it is too early; often the nobility of the movement's cause, the qualities of outstanding leaders like Lutuli and Nelson Mandela, and the contrast with white racism, have blinded writers to the flaws that underlie any human endeavour. It is no part of this work to redress that balance, only to consider the Zulu part in the making of the ANC. This might seem invidious, as the organization is avowedly non-racial; still, there is a characteristic strand that runs through the Zulu contribution to the movement and which bears examination in considering why it is less significant today than it was. And the ANC's public disavowal of ethnicity, or 'tribalism', has not always been matched by the private conduct of its leaders.

The first big challenge to the ANC was the drafting by parliament of a bill that confirmed all the worst fears of blacks about the new South African state. The Native Land Act of 1913 was white power's response to the rise of black commercial farmers, the *ama-kholwa* of Natal and peasant producers in the Cape and Transvaal, who were turning the fruits of their toil into land ownership. Black producers had become a commercial challenge which the Native Land Act aimed to remove. In future, no black would be able to buy or rent land outside the so-called 'scheduled areas' – the mission reserves and those tracts already owned by blacks. The Act of Union had removed the hopes of educated Africans for the franchise. The Land Act, in effect, restricted Africans to less than 8 per cent of the land area of South Africa and was to drive what had been an increasingly self-sufficient rural population into the cities for work.

The Act had significantly less impact in Natal than elsewhere. Thanks, paradoxically, to the Shepstone system, almost 30 per cent of the land was still in African hands, in the form of tribal and mission reserves, compared with 3.5 per cent of the Transvaal and less than 1 per cent of the Orange Free State.[7] Still, Zulu speakers were roused by the implications of the Act no less than anyone else. Dube led an ANC delegation to London to protest against the bill, while Seme raised funds to buy up what land he could before it became law. The delegates came home empty-handed, but Seme's initiative on behalf of the Native Farmers' Association of Africa marked one of the few successful and enduring acts of resistance at this time.

In the district of Wakkerstroom, on the Natal–Transvaal border, Seme negotiated to buy land from three white-owned farms on which was settled a multi-ethnic community of Zulu, Swazi and Sotho. The Wakkerstroom experiment flourished, the population grew and, over the decades, schools and amenities were established. Then, in 1958, another piece of legislation was passed, the Group Areas Act, confining all black South Africans to their supposed 'homelands'. Here was the triumphalist spirit of apartheid in all its blind, crass cruelty. 'Black spots' like the Wakkerstroom community were to be broken up, the 1500 landowners dispossessed and around 30,000 inhabitants forcibly moved to their respective 'homelands'. Government efforts to disperse Wakkerstroom started in 1965 and culminated in the shooting of a community leader by police in 1983. Finally, they were abandoned.[8]

Racial policy between 1910 and 1948, the year of Afrikaner nationalism's accession to power, was based on a more *laissez-faire* system of segregation, but the principles were the same: the white parliament was to remain for ever the sovereign power, although Africans would gradually be allowed a degree of self-government to manage domestic affairs 'in their own territories'. In the meantime, the main area of government policy affecting urban blacks was job reservation. As the mining industry brought wealth and investment to the young dominion, white workers campaigned successfully for the exclusive right to skilled, better-paid jobs. Blacks were to be the drawers of ore-carts and hewers of rock. When they tried to organize resistance to this notion in 1913, they were dismissed *en masse*, and replaced.

Another source of grievance was the pass: a form of identity document. Although the full malignancy of the pass system was not to be felt until apartheid's heyday, urban Africans had their movements and abode restricted by a range of permits which they detested. Organized opposition took some years to emerge and, in finding their feet, Africans were inspired by the methods of a remarkable and unlikely ally, Mohandas Gandhi.

Indians had been brought to Natal in the first place because of the reluctance of Zulus to labour on sugar plantations. They were indentured for five years, with the option to stay. By 1875, Natal's

Indian population numbered some 10,000, mainly Hindus from Madras but also Gujarati Muslims. The majority stayed, so by the time of union there were around 130,000 people of Asian origin in Natal.[9] They contributed a flair for trade and a culture of industriousness that set them awkwardly apart. As shop-owners, they worked longer hours than whites, and they were shrewder with money than blacks; legislatively, they were also on uneasy ground, being neither as privileged as whites nor so restricted as blacks. Unsurprisingly, they were unpopular with both.

Gandhi arrived in South Africa in 1893 as a young lawyer to assist in a case involving an Indian businessman in Pretoria. He stayed twenty-one years, during which the groundwork was laid for his later career. He helped found the Natal Indian Congress, which the Natal *amakholwa* took as a model for their own political organization; he also established a commune-like settlement called Phoenix near John Dube's Ohlange institute, although it seems that the two great campaigners for African and Indian rights never met; like Dube, too, he founded a newspaper for his community, *Indian Opinion*; and he deployed the strategy of *satyagraha*, or passive resistance – most successfully in challenging the government on a series of petty taxes and restrictions on Indians. He returned to India in 1914, to carry on the struggle for political rights there.

Africans noted and absorbed these methods; passive resistance was used in anti-pass demonstrations in the Transvaal, for example; but the aim of African unity was to prove elusive – indeed, it could be argued that it was never fully achieved. Communication was one difficulty in so large a country, 'especially since many of us do not belong to the travelling classes,' as Albert Lutuli put it. Another factor telling against joint action was the smallness of the black leadership class, the literate, westernized men known in Natal as the *amaRespectables*. The principal obstacles arose from regional and ethnic diversity, however.

The Xhosa-speakers of the Cape were the most politically aware Africans in the country, having grown up within a relatively liberal environment in which a qualified franchise had long been available. (At the time of union, there were some 12,000 black and coloured [mixed race] voters on the Cape roll, compared with three in Natal.) Zulu-speakers were conservative, even parochial, by comparison, having had relatively little exposure to political affairs and remaining more responsive to traditional authority. These were the two largest ethnic groups in South Africa, but the Cape and Natal had now been surpassed by a third region, the Transvaal Rand, as the political and social focus of new ideas, the melting pot where African nationalism was to take root.

Tribal jealousies were never far below the veneer of unity that the ANC sought to foster and the movement was often in the hands of one faction or another. At first, the Zulu contribution to the movement was disproportionately large because the Xhosa were divided by the rivalry between their two main leaders, Jabavu and Rubusana. The Zulus appear to have alienated others, partly because of Dube's conservatism but also because pride in the richness of their past sometimes crossed the line into arrogance. Seme, in particular, was guilty of this kind of ethnic superiority. 'The Xhosas are useless, as you know,' he once wrote to a colleague.[10] Sol Plaatje, a journalist from the Free State and the ANC's first secretary, lamented that 'the demon of tribalism is the great stumbling block to our unity'.[11] In all fairness, though, it is hard to see how it could have been otherwise when, however dedicated they were to eradicating tribalism, African leaders were at this time invariably dependent on regional and linguistic power bases which pulled them the other way. Dube, for example, might be the national leader of the organization, but he was little known to the membership outside his home region of Natal.

The ANC's wilderness era is easily overlooked. The years between its formation in 1912 and the Second World War left few golden moments on which later generations could draw for inspiration or mythology. Only a student of South African history would know the names of the first six ANC presidents. In 1917, Dube was ousted as a more militant mood gripped the movement and the centre of power moved to the Rand. Amid the rise of organized labour and the spread of communist influence during the 1920s, a Leninist faction took the helm until the old guard reasserted their control and Seme – by now a dapper figure with a fondness for spats – was elected president in 1930. It was a mistake: Seme had lost his faith in an inclusivist Africanism and directed most of his energies to trying to revive the Zulu royal house. He was succeeded by another affluent professional, Dr Alfred Xuma, a peppery physician and a Xhosa, who revived the ANC and shook out the corruption that had gathered in some quarters. But he too was a conservative and too much of the old school for the younger men coming through the ranks at a time when the end of the war heralded a new era in South Africa no less than in Europe.

Dube, Seme and Xuma were of a similar stamp: educated and relatively prosperous men – some have said élitists – who accepted that the African's progress to full political rights was bound to be slow. They were cautious and conservative, with an instinctive grasp of what they were up against and without false bravado. A kind and gentle soul, Dube in particular did not shrink from tugging the forelock, from *konza*'ing in the old manner, if it would serve his purpose. One of his appeals for English benefactors on behalf of the Ohlange Institute, 'The Zulu's Appeal for Light', was couched in terms that recall an unreconstructed version of the White Man's Burden:

My people are thirsting for knowledge, are hungering after enlightenment, are ashamed of their nakedness and their empty minds. Our ignorance crushes us down. We cannot rise, even to be helpful to those that rule us, so long as this impotence lies so heavily upon us. Relieve us of it. Help us to rise to those better things which we hoped for on your coming. That is what we pray; that is England's duty.[12]

Reading such tracts today, it is difficult to comprehend that Dube was once regarded in Natal as a dangerous 'Ethiopian' who had to be kept under surveillance and whose political views landed him in detention, albeit briefly. He could, however, be outspoken, especially in denunciation of the Land Act and in his editorship of the Zulu newspaper *Ilanga*. The truth is that, like any other African leader of the time, he was in an impossibly ambiguous position. To endure, to persevere and, finally, to survive became the art of what Shula Marks called 'the politics of the tightrope'. After losing the ANC leadership, Dube turned to the affairs of Zulu-speakers where he discovered a rival who was to be an even more adept practitioner of that art, Allison Wessels Champion.

Champion was among the most intriguing and certainly the most raffish of modern Zulu leaders – for a Zulu he was first and foremost. The European name – his parents christened him after the American missionary – was only one of the ambiguities surrounding him. He was as comfortable hunting with the hounds as running with the hares; he could rouse the masses to storm the barricades one minute, and join the plutocrats in robbing them blind the next. The journalist, Jordan Ngubane, called him 'a rogue elephant',[13] while Rowley Arenstein, a white communist lawyer in Durban, thought him 'a real gangster'.[14] With Dube what you saw was what you got: an Edwardian gentleman complete with frock coat and handlebar moustache, somewhat didactic and certainly fallible, but a man of high principles and selfless ideals. Champion was quicksilver – the scion of a *kholwa* family – who had been a policeman before his instincts led him to make his mark in the Chicago school of trade unionism.

While the concept of the vote was still novel, the growing ranks of urban Africans were readily mobilized by the ideas of fair pay. Leading the way was the Industrial and Commercial Workers' Union, which was founded in 1919 among the dockworkers of Cape Town by a flamboyant Nyasalander named Clements Kadalie. Six years later, the young Champion arrived in Durban as the first secretary of the ICU in Natal.

The ICU was a general union, open to the rank and file of the black workforce, from dockers to sharecroppers. At first, there was some reluctance among traditionalists to accept the leadership of a man who was not a chief, but Champion was an imposing figure as well as a populist. As a young man, he was tall and slender, and his praise name, Mahlathi Mnyama or black forest, represented him as a refuge for the Zulu people, as the Nkandla forest had been in the days of old. When he rose to speak in Durban the crowd would call: 'Oh, speak, dense forest.' His appeal was direct, pitched to the Zulus' profound sense of land loss. 'Come to the ICU and we will buy farms for you,' he cried.[15]

The spread of the ICU was electrifying. Champion had officials out on the streets, in the labour hostels, at the docks, selling membership cards at two shillings and sixpence a time. Two years after his arrival in Durban, Natal was the union's most successful branch, with a reported membership of 26,000 out of a working African population in the city of 35,000. In the province as a whole, it claimed 50,000 members.

It was Champion's ambition to buy land to resettle the Africans who were streaming into the city for work after being evicted as tenant farmers and sharecroppers on white farms in the wake of the Land Act. In fact, this scheme never came to fruition, and the object of his intention at one time to charge members a levy of £1 to 'buy farms' which, in terms of the Act, could only have come from other African owners seems to have been mighty dubious if not downright fraudulent. His popularity endured thanks to a series of spectacular and successful challenges to the municipal authorities which at last gave Durban's black population something to cheer about.

When Champion launched the ICU in the city, Africans were still subject to a 9 p.m. curfew and were forced to carry a pass that authorized their presence in Durban. They also had to keep about them a character reference from their employer; this gave whites a coercive hold over their workers which some used to intimidate and to punish. On top of this, Africans were prohibited from renting rooms in town, or trading outside the 'native market'. All these edicts Champion took to the courts where they were argued by a white attorney, Cecil Cowley, who was to remain a lifelong ally. In each case, they were victorious.

What was perhaps Champion's finest hour occurred after the threat of a typhus epidemic in 1926 led to Africans being subjected to a disinfectant bath. This, too, Champion challenged. His arch-enemy, C.F. Layman, the manager of native affairs, was obliged to immerse himself in the tank a number of times in a publicity exercise intended to dispel the sense of insult felt by blacks that they were being dipped like cattle. The gesture was in vain. Africans continued to oppose the practice and it was abandoned. Champion had taken on the city boss, and not only won but contrived his public humiliation. His star had reached its apogee.

By now Champion was a national figure, while the ICU's 100,000 members nationwide gave it a following that no African movement would rival again until the ANC of the 1950s. When Kadalie was delegated to attend an international labour congress in Geneva, Champion took over the head office in Johannesburg. Here his weakness started to show. The ICU had sufficient resources to afford reasonable expenditure, but money – for office cars and other extravagances – ran through Champion's hands. When Kadalie returned, the two men clashed. The ICU's founder was acutely aware that he had a formidable rival on his hands, and his accusation of embezzlement against Champion might have been no more than an attempt to discredit him; but rumours and whispers of chicanery tended to follow Champion around. In any event, this personal rift divided the movement. Champion flounced off, with his devoted local following, to form the ICU yase Natal.

The break came at a critical time. The rise of political consciousness among urban blacks and its channelling into the union movement, combined with the introduction of Marxist ideas, had given white politicians a new label to attach to an old bogey. The Hertzog government rallied Afrikaner voters against the perceived threat of the 'swart gevaar', or black peril, and passed legislation consolidating segregation.

White farmers watched the spread of ICU membership through areas like the Umvoti district around Greytown and reported with alarm how their black sharecroppers were organizing to demand higher pay. The Greytown branch secretary, Zabuloni Gwaza, was a true firebrand who declared 'a fire has been set burning which will drive the whites from the country'. One night he defaced the grave of a policeman killed in the 1906 poll tax rebellion.[16] Gwaza was arrested and almost lynched by a mob which stormed the jail, while the ICU offices in Greytown and Kranskop were torched. Local farmers responded to the demands of their croppers by evicting ICU activists and burning their homes.

Champion was tough but he was no martyr and his natural inclination was to avoid confrontation. By now, however, the ICU was firmly fixed in the mind of the white public as a hotbed of wild-eyed agitation. This, as much as anything else, led to Champion's downfall. It occurred in 1929, when what was merely one of a line of bafflingly insensitive measures to be introduced by the Durban corporation sparked the first racial rioting in the city.

Durban's African population (of about 35,000 people) lived in a belt of formal and informal shanty settlements that ringed the city; some years were to pass before the first township was established at Umlazi, on a former mission reserve. The small class of amaRespectables included around a hundred teachers, perhaps eighty artisans, sixty clerks, and a couple of hundred traders. Among the truly well-to-do were Martin Lutuli, the editor of Ilanga, and Charles Dube, the brother of John, who owned a hotel and eating-house in town. There was very little by way of entertainment for Africans. The main social gathering spots were municipal beerhalls and the illicit drinking dens known as shebeens.

The distinction between beerhalls and shebeens is critical. Shebeens were African enterprises, usually run by women known as 'shebeen queens' who brewed the traditional *tshwala*, the maize or sorghum beer that had been made since long before Shaka's time. The beerhalls were bleak municipal caverns which provided an insipid, mass-produced substitute. This legal monopoly of the liquor trade was widely resented, but it was not until early 1929, when the Durban authorities tried to stamp out 'home brewing', and the monopoly system was extended into the reserves, that trouble broke out. Women brewers, faced with the loss of their livelihood, held protest marches in a number of towns, carrying fighting sticks and chanting war songs; in some cases, women raided beerhalls and assaulted drinkers.

Champion called a boycott of the beerhalls in the name of the ICU. A series of marches in Durban went off without serious incident, but tension in the city was high and on 17 June rioting broke out. A white mob attacked the ICU headquarters in Prince Edward Street. On hearing this, hundreds of dockworkers, the most militant group in the ICU, charged through the city to relieve the hall, and ran headlong into the whites. For some hours, a racial mêlée flickered as Champion tried to calm the crowd and police sought vainly to intervene. Five blacks and two whites were killed.[17]

The beerhall riots of 1929 marked a watershed. Champion's efforts to keep the peace were not enough to save him from being banished from Natal under the Riotous Assemblies Act, and the local ICU went into a rapid and terminal decline. Four years later, Champion was allowed to return to Durban, where he picked up the threads of political life. He remained prominent in African affairs, following his old rival, Dube, as leader of the ANC in Natal, and wrote a regular opinion column in *Ilanga*, but he suffered the fate of becoming a part of the system he had once opposed. It is fairly clear that in later years he used his position to line his own pockets. He continued to hold court in flamboyant and imperious manner until his death in 1975 at the age of eighty-two. In one of his columns he once wrote with engaging candour: 'I admire this organization, the ICU, because it is the one that brought me to the notice of the public which knows me so well.'[18] It might serve as his epitaph.

It was not just the white bosses who had opposed the ICU. Dube, the grand old man of African politics in Natal, and other *amakholwa* leaders were also uneasy. Trade unionism and the spread of radical socialist ideas from the Reef were inimical to the *hamba gahle*, or 'go carefully' school of political protest espoused by these stalwarts, characterized by some academics as a new Zulu petit bourgeoisie.[19] Moreover, urbanization and the labour movement seemed part and parcel of a continuing cultural erosion that by now bothered the *kholwa* as much as the traditionalist. Many of the *kholwa* who had once railed against 'primitive' heathen customs now spoke up for the virtues of traditional life. Dube himself denounced the 'misleading and dangerous propaganda' of communism, and its 'absurd promises'. If victorious it

... would mean the breaking down of parental control and restraint, tribal responsibility and our whole tradition – the whole structure upon which our Bantu nation rests.[20]

Chiefs saw the union as yet another attack on their already reduced status, while Dinuzulu's son and heir, Solomon, had no doubt what socialism betokened for the monarchy. Through Dube's newspaper, *Ilanga*, he urged chiefs to 'kill this thing in all your tribes'.[21]

A further symptom of the trend bothering both traditionalist and *kholwa* was the appearance of a new urban sub-class, the *amaqhafi*. Here was the antithesis of the *amaRespectables*. The *amaqhafi* were among a generation which had grown up without the beliefs or codes of the past and, at the same time, had been excluded by law from the opportunities of the future. Absolom Vilakazi, a sociologist, described them as 'misfits' and 'cultural driftwood'. This may have been unfair, but they undoubtedly represented a new cultural strand. While the traditionalist loved the land, and the *kholwa* desired education, the *amaqhafi* thirsted for European wealth.

Although they were without traditions or education, the *amaqhafi* did not lack style. They dressed flamboyantly in the western manner, had a racy argot of their own and were fond of all things American, especially flashy limousines and jazz. Their elders threw up their hands in horror but they were a colourful and, by and large, harmless group. However, the condition of social dislocation they represented was not. Fostered by the policies of oppression, nourished by hopelessness and denied access to the material wealth that was to be increasingly flaunted around them, the rootlessness of young and deprived urban blacks was to mutate into social hostility. Its incarnation was to be seen at its earliest in the *amaleita* gangs which intimidated and harassed Africans in Durban and, later, the *tsotsis*, the gangsters who preyed on the townships in the 1950s and 1960s. The most pathological case, however, is to be seen in the lost generation – the children of violence – of the townships today.

Women, too, had been drawn to the towns by work. Between 1921 and 1936, the urban male African population of Natal doubled to 90,000, while that of females increased almost five-fold to 37,600. Many women were independent spirits who proved extremely capable and shrewd at running small entrepreneurial ventures like stores. However, many others turned to prostitution. Venereal disease, unknown in Shaka's time (it was to be called *isifo sabelungu*, the white man's disease[22]) became rife. So did premarital pregnancy, especially among girls from *kholwa* families. The problem was serious enough for some women to be galvanized into taking action. One of the most outstanding figures of the period, Sibusisiwe Makhanya, a relative of Dube, founded an organization called the Bantu Purity League, to foster sexual morality among women.

These forces of confusion and dislocation at a time of great social change in the aftermath of the First World War combined to produce a spirited revival of Zulu nationalism. Its sponsors were an unlikely alliance of *kholwa* grandees like Dube, Seme and Selby Msimang, a new generation of Zulu intellectuals who included the young Albert Lutuli, and the royal house itself. This turning away from the white culture that had spurned them was encouraged by the Smuts government, whose segregationist policies it suited admirably. From the Pongolo to the Mzimkulu, a revival was felt, focused on the living incarnation of the age of Shaka and Cetshwayo – Solomon ka Dinuzulu.

Solomon had been born on St Helena during Dinuzulu's exile and grew up in the shadow of his father's tribulations. Much of his life was spent trying to win official recognition, for although the Union government had acknowledged the paramount chiefs of the Xhosa, the Tembu and other major South African tribes, the

Zulu royal house was still ignored. Educated and intelligent, the young Solomon was a baptized Christian and attracted *kholwa* support as his father had never done.

The first manifestation of the new mood were moves in 1921 by Samuel Simelane, a clergyman, to found a body that would be the forerunner of the modern Inkatha movement. The previous year the government had passed a Native Affairs Act, which provided for the creation of elected African councils to administer rural communities. Smuts, who had succeeded Botha as prime minister, averred that while the white parliament would always be South Africa's sovereign power, Africans should be able 'to attend to their own domestic affairs . . . in their own territories'.[23] The Act was welcomed by Dube and the *kholwa* establishment, including Simelane, who made preparations to establish a Zulu National Congress in response to it.

African politics in Natal, meanwhile, was being convulsed by the emergence of a radical faction within the regional branch of the ANC. Dube's *hamba gahle* methods were scorned by this group, which was led by Josiah Gumede, formerly a Natal farmer. Gumede was an acolyte of the militant black American leader, Marcus Garvey, and an apostle of Soviet Communism. A fiery speaker who inspired his radical followers with the cry 'Africa for the Africans', Gumede established a personal ascendancy over the ageing Dube, and beat him in elections for the regional presidency in 1924. Gumede went on to win the national presidency of the ANC in 1927 but eventually alienated traditionalists with the rhetoric of class war. Even at this stage he would argue passionately that Africans had to unshackle themselves from the influence of chiefs, but was pragmatic enough to recognize the importance of the Zulu monarchy.

Thus it was that in the mid-1920s, Solomon was being wooed both by the new radicals and the old *kholwa* establishment. The young king was initially leery of politics. His main concerns were healing old wounds within the royal house, specifically the enmity between his Usuthu faction and the Mandlakazi, regaining official recognition of the monarchy and re-establishing Zulu national unity.

The struggle between conservatives and radicals for Solomon's support was resolved by a meeting at his residence, Mahashini, in October 1924, which led to the formation of the first Inkatha organization. The name was taken from the sacred grass coil, symbolizing Zulu unity, which had been destroyed by the British in 1879. Inkatha ka Zulu was intended to advance the welfare of Zulu-speaking people, mainly by the purchase of land, and to win recognition for the royal house. Dube was elected joint chairman with William Bhulose, another moderate ousted by the radicals from the regional ANC. As the historian Nicholas Cope has pointed out, Inkatha was thus the 'old guard' of the Natal ANC, in a potentially more influential form. For his part, Solomon had forged an alliance between the royal house and the *kholwa* intelligentsia, the first time this had been done.

Neither Solomon, nor his successor, Cyprian, was an impressive figure; both were reduced by alcohol, while Solomon was given to wasteful extravagance and Cyprian was intellectually dull. Like the clergy, though, it was not the individual but the office that mattered. As one native commissioner admitted in a despatch to Pretoria, it made no practical difference whether the government recognized the monarchy or not; the position of Mpande's anointed descendant was still 'such as to command the involuntary respect of the Zulu people'.[24] The near-mystical hold that the monarchy retained was vividly demonstrated during a visit by Edward, the Prince of Wales, to Zululand in 1925.

It was the first time that the people had come face to face with an heir to the conquering power of 1879 and Solomon had gone to infinite pains to make the visit a success, equipping a hunting expedition to East Africa to procure a suitably large pair of elephant tusks to present as a gift. Now he was drawn up with his chiefs at the old British administrative capital of Eshowe. Gone were the skins and cow tails of the past. Solomon was dressed in a dark military uniform edged with leopard skin and white sun helmet, while his chiefs were in khaki with leather leggings and Sam Brownes. They stood at the head of about 60,000 Zulus. As Edward arrived on a royal train, the crowd roared out the royal salute, '*Bayete*!' Later, Solomon and Edward retired to the carriage of the train for a private consultation as, it seemed to the beholders, brother monarchs.

All this was in stark contrast to the visit five years later of the Earl of Athlone, who, as governor-general, was the British Crown's representative in South Africa. On this occasion, Solomon scandalized the white authorities by making it plain that he thought the earl a very inferior envoy. The king admonished white officials, talked to his aides while the earl was reading his speech, and then made his feelings plain in his reply:

It is a pleasure to welcome you here for I am also a person of royal blood. The people at my back recognize me as a chief of the royal house of Zulus. Each country has its own king. We are loyal to the king of England but he has many countries to rule and it is difficult to understand how he can administer them all. Some people think they can rule a country by their cleverness, but we know that only people of royal blood are fitted to rule. Things in this country will never be right until I am recognized as the head of the country. It is regretted that you visit us only at the close of your term of office. However, we wish you God-speed. We trust that you will convey to the royal family in England the unsatisfactory treatment meted out to the natives of this country. Farewell.[25]

Solomon's 'insolence', as local white officials termed his behaviour, caused a tremendous stir and there were immediate calls for him to be disciplined. He somewhat spoilt the defiant pose he had struck by writing an official apology in which he claimed to have been drunk at the time. In the end, half his annual stipend of £500 was withheld.

None of this altered the tonic that had been given to Zulu nationalism. Even the Mandlakazi leaders who, under Zibhebhu, had denied the paramountcy of the royal house, had returned to the fold. Solomon raised new *amabutho* of young men, some 6000 in all, who tended his herds and built him a new royal *umuzi* at Nongoma, about thirty miles north-east of Ulundi; this site has been the residence of the kings since Dinuzulu. Inkatha, following the example set by the state, raised taxes from the Zulu population via a network of chiefs and became a quite wealthy organization. The money was to have been used to acquire land on the nation's behalf. Some went towards the erection in 1932 of the Shaka memorial at Stanger, 'by his descendant and heir, and the Zulu nation'. Much of it, however, was spent on Solomon's lavish living.[26]

Solomon never did gain official recognition. His drinking became an increasing problem until, in March 1933, he collapsed and died, aged only forty. None of his sons was of an age to succeed him and for fifteen years Arthur Mshiyeni, another of Dinuzulu's sons, acted as regent. A forceful and somewhat forbidding man, Mshiyeni was, in fact, more capable than either of the kings whose reigns he straddled, and he kept the flame of nationalism burning. When Inkatha fell into decline, he was a leading supporter of the establishment in 1937 of its successor, the Zulu Cultural Society, by Albert Lutuli, then a teacher at Adams College and the recently elected chief of the Groutville community.

Like Inkatha in its time, the Cultural Society was dedicated to gaining state recognition for Mpande's line as the Zulu paramounts and attracted virtually every prominent Zulu-speaker of the day, from the old political rivals, Champion and Dube, to the finest of modern Zulu poets, Benedict Vilakazi and Rolfes Dhlomo. Amid a vigorous debate about the direction of African nationalism, one of the society's principles was a trenchant statement of ethnic identity:

It is plain that responsible opinion is unanimously in favour of the Zulus being established always, retaining what is of good repute in the heritage that was given them by the Great Owner of Nations to distinguish the Zulus from other nations. Thus the Zulus may appear with their own traditional sacred anthem, not an anthem borrowed from other peoples.[27]

It was not until 1951 that Pretoria at last granted the recognition that had so long been withheld from Mpande's descendants, and then it was for the government's own purposes. Mshiyeni acted as regent until Solomon's son, Cyprian, was old enough to take his place at the head of the house of Zulu, aged twenty-four. By then, however, what was to be the gradual but steady compromising of traditional authority was already advanced.

Max Gluckman, an anthropologist who did valuable fieldwork in Zululand during the 1930s, noted how chiefs had been drawn into collaboration with industry and, in particular, the mines. 'Zulu princes are employed as compound *izinduna* and police by the Rand mines and Durban barracks ... The chiefs have no legal status: the legal authorities are white. The chiefs plead for better treatment and higher wages for Zulu workers, yet at the same time, they are constantly urging their men to go out and work.[28]

Gluckman also noted the destabilizing effect that magistrates had on traditional authority as, by the exercise of power, they became, in effect, substitute chiefs:

The people turn to [the magistrate] when they are opposed to the chief. Individual Zulus transfer their allegiance from chief to magistrate and from magistrate to chief according to the advantage they desire ... A man uses the existence of different groups to escape from difficulties in one of them. In doing this, he may even act against what he considers to be the interests of a group of which he is a member, without perceiving the contradiction in his behaviour.[29]

The penny had finally dropped: white administrators had come to see that the best way of controlling African society was not to deny the existence of the traditional systems of authority, but to penetrate, subdue and ultimately control them. It had been the way of Boer leaders during the Great Trek to divide their powerful black opponents, to play tribes and factions off against one another. As Afrikaner nationalism came into its own in the aftermath of the Second World War, this same strategy would be used to counter the political activists seeking to mobilize African society.

18

'SEPARATENESS'

> When the white rulers resort to wholesale
> indiscriminate violence – as they surely will do – it
> will be the sign that their end as a master-race is
> beginning.[1]
>
> Albert Lutuli,
> 1962

Modern South Africa was spawned on a late autumn May day in 1948. The winter that followed was to be more harsh and bitter than anything that had gone before.

On that day of 26 May, white voters exercised their five-yearly right to elect a new government. The choice was between the ageing Boer War leader, Jan Christiaan Smuts, now the darling of the British Empire, a world figure more at home on the international stage than among his *volk*; and a burly, hard-faced former clergyman, Daniel François Malan, who represented an assertive new strand of Afrikaner ethnicity. Malan's Nationalist Party and various affiliated cultural organizations had sympathized with Hitler's Germany during the war and now desired to distance South Africa from Britain and the other white dominions. At bottom, however, Nationalist policy was founded on the principle that the *volk* should never again lose control of their destiny. The means by which they were to retain political and economic dominance was called *apartheid*. Like most of the phrases and terms which have acquired a particularly malevolent force in our time, the word was a euphemism. Translated, it meant 'separateness'.

The story of modern South Africa is, in one sense, the story of Afrikaner politics. The leathery-faced nomads and farmers of the nineteenth century had become an electoral majority, one which burned with a fierce sense of grievance towards British colonialism and was filled with a dread of being overwhelmed by the black majority. To the injustice of the Boer War had been added the suffering of the Depression, which forced tens of thousands of Afrikaners off their land and into the cities where many were as ill-equipped to earn a living in a modern industrial state as the blacks they had so long treated as menials. The Afrikaner found himself without skills, trapped between, on the one hand, the English and Jewish financiers who controlled the economy and, on the other, a black proletariat able to provide the labour for which industry clamoured. The experience burned itself into the Afrikaner soul and it is not to be wondered at that, during Hitler's ascendancy, many Afrikaners were inspired by National Socialism, both for its ideas of racial purity and as evidence of how a defeated people might rise triumphant from the ashes. During the 1930s, Afrikaner history and culture were fostered as never before by a new breed of academics and intellectuals. The same spirit infused the openly pro-Nazi views for which a number of Afrikaner extremists were interned at the start of the Second World War. Now, in 1948, white South Africa was going to the polls again for the first time since the end of hostilities.

Afrikaners had this one priceless weapon, the vote. Smuts had survived in office thus far because his United Party was the political home of most English-speakers and had some residual Afrikaner support. But Afrikaans-speakers formed the larger voter group, and when the ballots were counted Malan had won a small majority. From then until 1990, when Frederik de Klerk announced that he would negotiate with the ANC on multi-racial democracy, Nationalist Party governments steadily accumulated both white supporters and authoritarian powers – so that South Africa became that most grotesque of political hybrids, at one and the same time a democracy of sorts, and a totalitarian state.

Many white South Africans were initially dismayed to see the government of their country pass from the urbane and worldly

Smuts to what seemed, even at the time, a clique of dour and resentful xenophobes, at sea with the English language and at odds with the modern world in general. But the country was passing into a period of unprecedented economic growth and industrialization from which the English-speaking business community, in particular, benefited, and which purchased its acquiescence in most of the deeds of Afrikaner nationalism. Malan was succeeded by Johannes Strijdom, a strident advocate of ethnic purity, and he by the even more fanatical Hendrik Verwoerd, the high priest of apartheid. After Verwoerd's assassination by a demented parliamentary messenger in 1966, power passed first into the hands of John Vorster, who had been interned as a pro-Nazi, and then to an ill-tempered bureaucrat, Pieter Botha, known by colleagues as 'die Groot Krokodil' because of his penchant for snapping heads off. The first used the police, and the second the army, to transform 'the beloved country', as the author Alan Paton called South Africa, into an international symbol of hatred and oppression.

The initial response of Africans to the Nationalist victory of 1948 was less one of dismay than uncertainty. One man who observed it with mild suspicion was the middle-aged Zulu chief of the Groutville mission reserve in Umvoti district. Recently elected to the Natal executive of the ANC, Albert Lutuli had found Smuts's United Party 'willing at times to give half an ear to the African voice'. Now, he recognized, 'there would probably be an intensification of the hardships and indignities which had always come our way.' But, he added

I think that it is true that very few (if any) of us understood how swift the deterioration was destined to be. I doubt, too, whether many of us realized at the time that the very intensity of Nationalist oppression would do what we had failed to achieve – awake the mass of Africans to political awareness.[2]

The legislation of apartheid followed thick and fast. The Mixed Marriages and Immorality Acts prohibited first marriage, then sexual intercourse, between whites and 'non-whites' – blacks, coloureds and those of Indian origin. The Population Registration Act required that all people should be classified by race, while the Group Areas Act defined where they might and might not live. In that same year, 1950, the Suppression of Communism Act was passed. This empowered the government to restrict, or 'ban', any supposed communist, although that term rapidly became interchangeable with 'non-whites' seeking political rights.

It was not simply the ugliness of the legislation that quickly started attracting international opprobrium, but the manner in which it was implemented. Required to enforce racist laws, the South African Police force attracted men who were themselves virulent racists. My own memory of childhood in the rural southern Transvaal of the 1950s is marked by incidents involving bull-necked local *konstabels* with names like 'Blackie' Swart, men who might suddenly appear out of clouds of dust in a rattling blue Ford van on a dirt road across the veld to descend on a few Africans, making their way perhaps to a beer drink. The van would crunch to a halt on the stony road surface, and the police leap out with the rapid swagger of men who are about to join a brawl. The Africans shrank. '*Kaffir, waar's jou pass*?' a *konstabel* would shout. From jackets or trouser pockets some drew the pathetic, tattered pieces of paper that authorized the bearer to be on the white man's veld. Those so favoured were sent on their way with a curse and a cuff. Those without passes were manhandled into the meshed-off rear of the van, which then disappeared in another cloud of dust.

The ANC was initially caught off balance by the speed of the government's action. The movement had passed through a lack-lustre period, but the challenge of apartheid aroused a spirited and unified response from a new generation of leaders and, for the first time, from the broad mass of urban African society. The 1950s were the ANC's golden age, up to its accession to government.

The seeds of the revival had been planted a decade earlier, when the son of a Zulu farm worker, Anton Lembede, founded the ANC Youth League. Lembede was a man of great organizational and intellectual gifts, a Roman Catholic who had educated himself sufficiently to win a bursary to Adams College – where he was taught by Lutuli – and then gained a legal degree by correspondence. He was joined in forming the Youth League by another young Zulu intellectual, Jordan Ngubane. Like Dube before them, both were hostile to the ideas of communism that were becoming fashionable with opponents, mostly white, of apartheid. 'Africans do not suffer class oppression,' Lembede wrote, 'they are oppressed as a group, as a nation.'[3]

Lembede died from an undiagnosed illness, aged only thirty-three, in 1947, but by then the Youth League had attracted other men who were to play yet more prominent roles in the ANC. Two inseparables stood out, even then. Nelson Mandela was a lawyer, a scion of the paramount house of the Tembu, a Xhosa sub-group in the eastern Cape. His closest friend was Walter Sisulu, also a Xhosa-speaker, but of mixed parentage. With Oliver Tambo, another Xhosa lawyer, Mandela and Sisulu were to rejuvenate the ossified ANC leadership. A year after Malan's Nationalists came to power, Xuma was replaced as president by James Moroka, a doctor from the Free State. But it was this triumvirate that constituted the core of the leadership, with Sisulu as secretary-general and Mandela and Tambo on the national executive. No longer could anyone say, as Seme once had, 'the Xhosas are useless'. The point was established once and for all by the Defiance Campaign of 1952.

In January of that year, Moroka and Sisulu sent an ultimatum to Malan, demanding the repeal of six 'unjust laws'. This was rejected, and in May the ANC called for mass civil disobedience by Africans. The instruction was to defy the laws of apartheid, to refuse to carry passes, to use 'whites only' entrances to public buildings and ignore curfew regulations.

The campaign began in the centres of the Rand on 26 June. It was only to be expected that strong support would come from the mining and industrial heartland. What no one could have foreseen, however, was the fervour with which the campaign was taken up in the eastern Cape. The port cities of Port Elizabeth and East London were the new manufacturing centres, with Xhosa-speaking workforces drawn from an impoverished rural hinterland. Communist and trade union recruiters had found fertile soil here during the 1940s and in the Defiance Campaign an alliance was forged between these groups and the ANC which bore fruit in spectacular fashion. Figures collated by the political historian, Tom Lodge, show the eastern Cape to have been far and away the most vigorous centre of opposition to the apartheid laws. By the time the campaign had run its course, five months later, 5941 resisters had been arrested in Port Elizabeth, East London and smaller towns, compared with 1578 in the Transvaal. In the small rural *dorp* of Peddie alone, 669 had contrived to get themselves arrested. The eastern Cape had established itself as a focal point in the coming struggle.

In Natal, on the other hand, the Defiance Campaign was a

failure. The local ANC was still traumatized in the aftermath of an inter-racial bloodbath and not even the emergence of an influential new leader had been able to galvanize a strong local response. The call was heeded only in Durban, and even then only 192 resisters were arrested, against 2007 in Port Elizabeth, a city of comparable size.[4]

Reduced to a crude but illustrative ethnic shorthand, the torch of resistance had passed for the time being from the Zulu to the Xhosa.

※

For all its horrors, apartheid was able to offer its opponents, if not its victims, a curious form of reassurance, even comfort. Because it was so transparently wrong, it could be made culpable for all the social ills that occurred within its poisonous lifespan. It excused everything that was done to oppose it and explained all the other human shortcomings of the oppressed. Taken to that extreme, this had the patronizing effect of denying Africans responsibility for their own actions. Nowhere has this tendency been more common than in the diagnoses of violence in South Africa.

That apartheid brutalized its victims and fostered ethnicity is beyond doubt. But factionalism has been an almost constant characteristic of Zulu life. At bottom, traditional Zulu society was still composed of the clans controlled by Shaka and, while the kingdom had been capable of a unified response to an outside aggressor, as in 1838 and 1879, it had always been liable to splinter and fragment. The cumulative effects of land shortage and a steadily increasing population, on top of these other social factors, created conditions ripe for instability. While other parts of the country were in the grips of what was termed proletarian revolt against white oppression, the rage of Zulu-speaking people was often turned inwards.

The phenomenon used to be known as 'faction fighting'. A typical press item in, for example, the *Natal Mercury*, would consist of a cursory paragraph reporting that a beer drink at a rural location had ended in a faction fight in which five Zulu men had been killed and ten injured. The curt facts, the bland absence of explanation in these reports, foreshadowed their modern equivalent, the daily unrest briefings issued by the police: another night in the townships, another seven dead. There is a difference, however. Now the catch-all category into which such items fall is political unrest. Then it was faction fighting.

Faction fighting had, in fact, been going on in various forms since before the turn of the century and, in some instances, could be traced back to the civil war of the 1880s. In most cases, a dispute over land was the discernible original cause, but once blood had been shed vendettas quickly became established. As a result, the same areas tended to crop up repeatedly in reports of faction fighting – Port Shepstone . . . Ixopo . . . Umbumbulu. Most were south of the Tugela, where land tenure was more subject to dispute because of the Shepstone location system than in the traditionalist heartland.

Of all the blood feuds, the most enduring were those of Msinga, a desolate rural location of some 350 square miles, just south of the Tugela in northern Natal. Six main clans lived in this district, the Cunu, the Tembu, the Bomvu, the Mabaso, the Sithole and the Majozi. Being the largest, the Tembu had a tendency to encroach on the territory of their neighbours and to colonize outlying kraals of their adherents. As the population grew, overburdening the capacity of the district to support life, this Tembu expansionism became more marked.

Clan boundaries had been a matter of uncertainty since Shaka's time, when both the Tembu and Cunu had temporarily abandoned the region. In 1922, a magistrate's ruling on a running boundary dispute between the Tembu and the Mabaso triggered a short, sharp conflict in the old manner, with shield and assegai, in which the Mabaso chief, Gqikazi, was among those killed. This drew in the Majozi, old allies of the Mabaso, who attacked outlying Tembu groups, burning their huts. A board of inquiry found the Tembu to have been the aggressors and they were punished by forfeiting lands to surrounding chiefs.

Although it is clear that land was often a factor in disputes, it is too simple to explain all the Msinga 'wars' as a consequence of over-stretched resources. After 1926, the Tembu fought a series of battles with their largest rivals, the Cunu, in the most serious of which two *impis*, each of roughly 3000 men, confronted one another near a mountain called Ngongolo in northern Natal in September 1944. When the dust cleared, forty-nine Tembus and eighteen Cunus were dead. It is unlikely that either side recalled the origin of their enmity. Msinga's troubles had become old-fashioned blood feuds, in which a group identity required collective response to erase an insult or avenge a killing. A Zulu proverb vividly captures this spirit: *iva likhishwa ngelinye*, or 'a thorn [in the foot] is removed by another thorn'.[5]

An anthropologist and musician, Jonathan Clegg, has recorded another proverb of the Msinga blood feud, *ukubuyisa isidumbu*, 'to bring back the body'. A death can only be redeemed by killing an enemy. Groups would keep tallies of the state of their feuds, noting which of their enemies 'owed' them bodies, and how many. This constant renewal of feuding gave rise to the equivalent of mafia assassination squads, a core group of the hardest and toughest men, *amashinga*, who could be relied upon by the clan to uphold its honour and ensure that it stayed ahead of its enemies in the body count. The *amashinga* were supported by a levy on clan members working in the towns or on the mines.

Feuds carried from the blood-red earth of northern Natal to the Rand and back. The old scars were easily opened in the cramped and squalid mine compounds, where a careless remark, a flash of ill-temper, could trigger an outbreak of fighting. News of such a clash would be sent back to the combatants' homesteads, often to be translated into trouble there. Equally, when a confrontation was brewing in the district, messages were sent to the distant migrant workforce to come to the support of the group. Men would abandon their compounds and travel home in bus and lorry loads to their homesteads before mustering at an appointed place to refresh their feud.

Nothing seemed to stop it. White administrators resorted to extreme methods. First, an edict was passed that if it could be proved that a member of a particular clan was in an area when an affray took place, he could be held to account; his mere presence was taken to be participation. Judicially, the principle may have been grotesque, but it had a certain commonsense. A former magistrate at Tugela Ferry in Msinga told me how once, in the 1930s, he had been approached at the courthouse by an elderly Tembu who wanted someone to defend him on a charge of murder. My informant started to question the man, and had established from him who the victim was and where the murder had taken place before it dawned on him that no offence had yet occurred – the old Tembu was speaking in the future tense.[6]

Blood feuding in Msinga continued, but with an even more

lethal component – modern firearms. As recently as 1979, sixty-eight members of the Sithole and Zwane sections died over a nine-month period. One of the protagonists in this round of bloodletting was a white *umshinga* named Johan Verster who was in the pay of the Sithole. Four years later, another of the district's vendettas resulted in dozens of deaths in distant Soweto, the vast black township south-west of Johannesburg.[7] By then, similar patterns of violence were starting to appear elsewhere in Natal.

Traditionalist society in Zululand was less susceptible to feuding because chiefs, notably in the royalist heartland of Nongoma and Mahlabatini districts, channelled the energies and loyalties of their young men into a ritual of strength-testing known as *umgangela*. In the time of the kingdom, stick-fighting had been the sport of warriors; a stout stick was carried in each hand, one to strike, the other to parry. Now chiefs cooperated in organizing large scale stick-fighting tournaments between districts. The fact that *umgangela* was a form of play did not make the participants any less vigorous or determined: fatalities did sometimes occur. But the process was governed by rules, enforced by the chiefs and their *umpathis*, or team captains, to uphold fair play and ensure that district rivalry did not turn to enmity.[8] Stick-fighting is still practised in some districts north of the Tugela.

Against all the odds, whites remained inviolate. They might have bemoaned declining standards of honesty, of the passing of a time when it was possible to leave a bicycle beside the road and be sure that it would still be there even days later. But while white materialism became ever more insatiable, Natal and Zululand were notable in the apartheid era for an absence of overt race hostility towards whites, such as became increasingly common in the Transvaal. The region's worst post-war racial explosion occurred in 1949, and involved not Europeans but Asians.

Relations between Zulus and the substantial Indian urban population were uncomfortable, for reasons that we have seen. Although also categorized by apartheid as 'non-whites', Asians were less restricted in a number of ways, notably in their movements and in commercial activity, at which they had prospered. It was widely held that Asian shop-owners exploited the unworldliness of African customers and, whether true or not, this belief fed black resentment towards Asians. So did the fact that almost half of Durban's black population lived as tenants of Asian landlords in shanty slums such as the inaptly named Cato Manor.

The depth of the frustration became apparent following an incident at the Indian market in Durban on 13 January, when an Asian trader struck an African teenager. Blood flowed, and word spread among Africans in bus queues nearby that the boy had been killed. Asian traders were attacked and, in the night, rioting spread to residential areas, where murder, arson, looting and – most unusually – rape, occurred. Three days later, when the security forces had restored order, fifty Asians were dead and more than 500 had been injured. About 1500 homes and 700 stores had been destroyed or damaged. Eighty-seven Africans were also dead, most of them shot by police and army units quelling the disturbances.[9]

A commission of inquiry later found that once the violence started, certain whites actively incited and fomented trouble by transporting blacks to Asian areas. At a less active level, many whites took the blacks' part because they were galled by the Asians' commercial success and social aspirations. There is no reason to suppose that these same whites would have disagreed with the Nationalist MP who declared that all the affair proved was the justification for apartheid.

Champion, who at this stage was still Natal's ANC president, brought his career with the movement to an inglorious end, stating that the Indians had got too big for their boots and deserved a lesson. Fortunately for all concerned, Asian community heads responded with sensitivity and wisdom, while from the African side now emerged a man of humanity and courage.

The greatest of modern Zulu leaders was not born in South Africa at all, but in Rhodesia. His father was a clergyman who, because of the similarity of the Zulu and Sindebele tongues, had been sent to Bulawayo to minister to the Ndebele descendants of Mzilikazi's kingdom. Albert John Lutuli, also known by his Zulu name, Mvumbi, meaning constant rain, was born there in 1898.

His father died while Albert was still an infant and, in due course, the young Lutuli returned to the family home at Umvoti mission reserve, just south of the Tugela, where his uncle, Martin Lutuli, was the chief. After preliminary education at the local mission school, Albert attended first Dube's Ohlange Institute and then Adams College.

Lutuli was called both to teaching and the church before becoming involved in politics, but he might as easily have been an academic. He was offered a bursary to Fort Hare, the sole African university, but declined it in order to support his mother, who had sacrificed herself for his education. Staying on at Adams as a teacher, he fell under the spell of its principal, Professor Zachariah Matthews, the leading African academic to be produced by South Africa and the intellectual spirit of the ANC in the 1950s. It is to Matthews that much of the credit falls for the ANC's Freedom Charter, a high-flown statement of principles.

Lutuli was the obvious choice to succeed his uncle as chief and, in 1936, he left Adams to take up his duties at Umvoti. Respectful of the past without being enslaved by it, intelligent but without guile, he was able to straddle, as none had to quite the same extent before, the gulf that separated the traditionalist and the urban sophisticate. As a chief he had an immediate impact, rejuvenating African commercial agriculture and bringing prosperity not only to his own people but to their neighbours. As a Methodist lay preacher, he attended missionary conferences in India and America, gaining insight into racial politics in those great ethnic cauldrons. In the process, he became a compelling public speaker. Charles Hooper, the ghostwriter of his autobiography, *Let My People Go*, said he had 'assurance without arrogance, and the humility of a man who cannot be humiliated'. Above all, though, the respect and love that he inspired derived from the fact that he was a man of peace. If John Dube was the Booker T. Washington of South Africa, Albert Lutuli was its Martin Luther King.

For more than ten years after moving to Umvoti, he confined himself largely to tribal and church affairs. Then, inspired by the example of Dube, he was drawn to politics and was encouraged in the aftermath of the Durban riots to challenge the discredited Champion for the Natal presidency of the ANC in 1951. Lutuli's victory came too late to invigorate Natal's response during the Defiance Campaign, but a start was made to rebuild the movement locally and the low number of arrests in Durban during the campaign was partly due to the fact that the local police were more tolerant than those in many other parts of the country. Nevertheless, Lutuli managed to get himself arrested with the Indian congress leader, Dr G. Naicker, which helped restore a degree of Afro-Asian solidarity.

Soon afterwards, Lutuli came to his personal Rubicon. He was summoned to Pretoria and told that political activity was incompatible with his status as a chief; either he must quit the ANC or he would no longer be recognized by the government as chief at Umvoti. He refused to resign from the movement and soon afterwards was deposed as chief. Initially, the Umvoti people held firm, telling Pretoria's representative at an *indaba* that they would elect another ANC man. But within weeks what Lutuli called 'the usual resignation' that now afflicted tribal society had set in, and the reserve eventually surrendered to pressure and elected a more pliable chief. He was bitterly disappointed. Although he had always been proud of his heritage, having founded the Zulu Cultural Society, he was now to cut himself off from tribal affairs.

It was against this background that Lutuli arrived in Johannesburg at the end of 1952 for the ANC national conference. He was completely unknown to ANC members outside Natal, having never had a chance to visit another branch of the organization. Extraordinarily, however, he was elected national president on 16 December.

Lutuli replaced Dr James Moroka, the Free State leader who had discredited himself by buckling under pressure during the Defiance Campaign. There was a new militancy in the air. Africans had tested themselves and found they were capable of strong, united action. One activist captured the mood, declaring that the ANC had purged itself of 'pleading, cowardly and *hamba gahle* leaders'.[10]

Lutuli's appeal in these circumstances is clear. Here was a man of presence and proven principle, who detested apartheid with his every fibre and had captured the African imagination by his refusal to compromise with the oppressor. It is unlikely, however, even at this stage that Lutuli was seen as a natural ally by Mandela, who had been elected his deputy, or the other members of the triumvirate, Sisulu and Tambo, who were now the leading lights of the ANC in the Transvaal. As Tom Lodge has written: 'Lutuli saw the ideal future in terms of African "participation" in government rather than absolute control of it, and his nationalism was of a considerably gentler quality than that of the Africanists who had supported him originally.'[11] Lutuli shared, rather, Gandhi's conviction that passive resistance and the sheer moral superiority of the

African nationalist position could bring about a change of heart among whites and so gain a partnership in the government.

He may even have been right, but white South Africa had set off into the black night of its soul and there was to be no turning back. Inevitably, it was the militants who won the debate.

Barely had Lutuli returned from the conference than he was restricted under the Riotous Assemblies Act. In effect, he was banned from visiting larger towns, and from public gatherings. Mandela and Sisulu were also banned in this first official crackdown on the ANC, but because their homes were in Johannesburg they were better able to get round their restrictions and remained active among the ANC's growing membership, estimated at 100,000 nationwide in the aftermath of the Defiance Campaign. Two years later, soon after Lutuli's first banning order expired, a new one was imposed, this time confining him to the Stanger magisterial district.

Now the momentum of repression gathered pace. Two new pieces of legislation revealed the full extent of the Nationalists' ambitions for social engineering. The Bantu Authorities Act laid the foundations for the removal of blacks from white areas to their supposed 'homelands' where they were to be placed under chiefly rule. This might have had a superficial appeal for traditionalists, but the principle was quickly to be betrayed by the practice. The Nationalists had recognized in the traditional model a basis for rule by proxy and the homelands were to be no more than labour dormitories for white-run industry. Chiefs were to be rewarded for carrying out government policy, usually against the will of their own people. It was divide and rule carried to its most refined state.

The second piece of legislation caused more immediate recrimination. The Bantu Education Act aimed to ensure that Africans were educated only to a level appropriate to their enforced status as labourers. As Verwoerd, then minister for native affairs, put it: 'Good racial relations cannot exist when education is given under the control of people who create wrong expectations on the part of the native.'[12] To this end, all African schools, including the liberal, missionary-founded institutions typical of the Natal reserves, were placed under the control of a single Orwellian department in Pretoria.

Verwoerd's belief that 'there is no place for him [the black man] in the European community above the level of certain forms of labour,' struck at everything for which Africans had striven. Men like Lutuli, products of the liberal schooling that the Nationalists were now determined to destroy, were chilled to their marrow. 'The new education,' Lutuli wrote, 'was intended to *create* Africans anew after [Verwoerd's] image of the "real native"'.[13] Women, who saw hopes for their children dimmed, were equally mortified. 'My womb is shaken when they speak of Bantu education,' said one.[14]

The underlying thrust of all apartheid legislation, as Lutuli saw, was to subvert any African leadership that was not submissive. Part of the same programme was 'that we should return to the primitive'. The upshot was that the political unity of Zulu-speakers established in the 1930s was destroyed. Traditionalist authority was again compromised in the eyes of the African élite, not because of the values it represented, but because it was being manipulated by the government. Lutuli, who had once seen traditional culture as a bulwark for Zulus against the impact of industrial society, started to reflect this ambivalence. 'Guardians of great herds of cattle have, with the theft of our land, become keepers of a couple of bony cows,' he wrote. Tribal life now resulted in an 'unproductive stoicism', which made men fatalistic and resigned, directing their best efforts, as he saw it, at polygamy rather than self-improvement. 'No wonder that the oppressor is going to fantastic lengths in a futile effort to preserve it,' he added.[15]

Pretoria's embrace of traditional authority imposed a heavy responsibility on the new Zulu king, who was sadly ill-equipped to cope with it. Solomon's son, Cyprian, had been installed in 1948 after a fifteen-year regency by Prince Arthur Mshiyeni. Four years later, the government extended the official recognition of the Zulu monarchy that had been withheld since Cetshwayo's death in 1884.

Cyprian actually made a promising start, resisting pressure from Verwoerd to denounce the Defiance Campaign and to accept the provisions of the Bantu Authorities Act. However, he was not a strong personality and was already showing signs of the alcoholism that was to dog him. Two years later, he summoned Zulu chiefs to Nongoma and announced that he had decided to accept the Act.

Cyprian was to become, as Lutuli noted without rancour, 'a

supporter of apartheid even when this has not been incumbent upon him'. Yet as a chief himself, Lutuli had once paid court to Cyprian and he would never attack him outright. 'Respect for the Paramount is in my bones,' he wrote. Of Cyprian's dilemma, he said: 'He has had our sympathy throughout. His position is unenviable.'[16]

Legal, united opposition to the Nationalists reached its high point at an open space outside the coloured township of Kliptown, south of Johannesburg, on 26 June 1955. The Congress of the People brought together about 3000 people of all races, representing the ANC, the Indian Congress, the Coloured Congress, and white communists and trade union leaders. Mandela was not able to attend, because of his banning order, but watched proceedings from a house nearby. Lutuli, however, was confined to Umvoti 400 miles away.

Remarkably, the ANC president had not been shown a draft of the document the meeting had been summoned to approve, the Freedom Charter, although this may be partly explained by the fact that Lutuli had been in hospital after a stroke, the start of the decline in his health. When he did finally see it, he had some objections, notably to the section dealing with nationalization. Mandela, on the other hand, believed at this time that monopolies, such as the mining industry, should be 'smashed up and the national wealth of the country turned over to the people'.[17]

The Charter, which was to become the movement's statement of constitutional principle, affirmed that South Africa belonged to all its people, black and white; it demanded that the country should be ruled by a non-racial, democratic system of government, and that all people should be held equal before the law; it declared that the mines, banks and other monopoly industries should be nationalized; and it concluded that there should be houses, security and comfort for all. The charter was adopted by a show of hands, on a baked strip of veld where Soweto now stands.

All this was too much for the authorities. On the afternoon of the second day, police carrying light machine-guns swooped on the platform, seizing documents and announcing that they believed treason was being plotted. By the end of the year, forty-two ANC leaders had been banned, including Lutuli and Mandela for the second time. The following year, in a series of dawn raids, 156 leading Congress figures were arrested.

Lutuli was roused at 4 a.m. by police, one of whom announced portentously, 'Yes, the day has come!'. That afternoon he was flown to Johannesburg in a military plane and taken to the Fort, the city's oldest prison, where the rest of what were to be the Treason Trial defendants were being held, including Mandela, Tambo and Sisulu. The trial began in December 1956 and was to be one of the longest in legal history, continuing until March 1960, when the last thirty-one accused were acquitted. Lutuli regretted that he was among the sixty-one whose charges were suspended without explanation in 1957. Not one of the 156 defendants was convicted of the charge of involvement in a communist-inspired conspiracy to overthrow the state. (The independence of the judiciary, and of the English-language press, were repeatedly to frustrate the government's authoritarian instincts; its efforts to bring each to heel in the manner required by the modern totalitarian state were to be belated and botched.)

If the state's case of treason was unproven, it was undeniable that Soviet-inspired communism had gained a strong influence on the nationalist movement through white activists like Bram Fischer and Solly Sachs. In Natal, the most influential figure of this persuasion was a lawyer, Rowley Arenstein. Lutuli tolerated the communists as allies against a common foe, while rejecting their ideology. Under his leadership, however, white communists made significant advances within the ANC, a trend that alarmed a militantly Africanist faction.

The Africanists' leader was Robert Sobukwe, a disciple of Lembede from the Cape. Sobukwe rejected the non-racial character of the Freedom Charter, on the grounds that whites could not identify fully with either the black cause or a complete overhaul of South African society, because they were its beneficiaries. The Africanists also disregarded the Asian and coloured opponents of apartheid. Lutuli battled against these tendencies, warning that racism was appearing within the ANC in the guise of nationalism. But, in April 1959, Sobukwe led a breakaway to form the Pan-Africanist Congress, of which he became the first president.

Even as the Treason Trial continued, more and more ordinary Africans were being caught up in the snares of apartheid. Arrests under the pass laws were running at something like 300,000 a year – roughly 10 per cent of the black population – offenders generally serving sentences at prison farms of notorious brutality. Meanwhile, residential apartheid was being rigorously enforced. Sophiatown, a bohemian black suburb west of Johannesburg, where writers, musicians, gangsters and herbalists rubbed shoulders, was only the first of a series of townships which had evolved in a more tolerant age and were now to be destroyed. Residents were shipped off to impoverished tribal 'homelands' or moved to great geometric urban sprawls that were to become synonymous with misery and disorder: Soweto, south of Johannesburg; Daveyton and Katlehong, on the east Rand; Sharpeville and Boipatong, on the south Rand.

In Natal, the process of forced removals was repeated at Cato Manor. Erasure of the old slum would have been mourned by few, but demolitions began in 1959 before any accommodation became available at the new township of KwaMashu, being built north-east of Durban. This coincided with a police drive against illegal brewing by the shebeen queens and, together, these actions produced the most sustained local resistance since the beer riots thirty years earlier. Once again, women were in the forefront of protest, marching on beer halls. The mood of defiance spread to the countryside. Here, women were resentful of certain duties imposed on them by farmers, such as the filling of cattle dipping tanks, for which they received no pay. Dozens of tanks were smashed and cane fields set ablaze. An estimated 20,000 women were involved in urban and rural protests, and more than 1000 were arrested.

In Durban, matters came boiling to a head in January 1960. Searing temperatures and soaking humidity have always made the high summer months a time of volatile tempers and now it took only a minor incident to trigger a bloodbath. During a shebeen raid, a policeman stood on a woman's toes. An altercation followed and, suddenly, a mob was out of hand. Nine policeman got cut off from their colleagues in the riot and were beaten to death.

All eyes were thus on Natal when a new anti-pass campaign began that was to throw the spotlight back on the Transvaal, with consequences which echoed around the world. The PAC had been recruiting vigorously and on 21 March a crowd of 5000 gathered in the township of Sharpeville. Around noon they descended on the police station, where reinforcements started arriving, boosting the standing strength from twelve to 200. The crowd pressed in on the fence and as tension rose the police arrested three ring-leaders. A scuffle developed at the gate to the station and, according to police, stones were thrown. A few shots were fired. Then, with the crowd already in flight, a volley of fire erupted. Of the sixty-nine people killed, the majority were shot in the back; ten were children and eight women. Later that day, police arrived at a hospital where about 140 people were being treated for gunshot wounds and announced that they were all under arrest.

Lutuli was still under a banning order but had been called to give defence evidence at the Treason Trial and was in Pretoria when he heard of the massacre. He promptly called a day of mourning and prayer, in effect a one-day national strike, which was widely heeded. On 26 March, he publicly burned his passbook before press cameras and urged others to follow suit.

Four days later, the government declared a State of Emergency, giving the police sweeping new powers to detain without charge. Lutuli was arrested at the home of the Afrikaans couple in Pretoria with whom he had been staying, was assaulted by a white police-man and placed in isolation. The ANC and PAC were declared banned organizations and thousands of their members were rounded up in police sweeps around the country, including Mandela. One important figure evaded arrest, Oliver Tambo, who managed to slip across the border into Bechuanaland (Botswana).

The Sharpeville crisis, as Tom Lodge has written, represented a turning point in the history of African nationalism, when protest finally hardened into resistance. Black leaders started to think of a revolutionary strategy. From this watershed were to emerge the ANC's armed wing, Umkhonto we Sizwe, and the PAC's Poqo, with its slogan of 'One settler, one bullet'. Young Africans started leaving the country clandestinely for training in guerrilla warfare in the Soviet Union, China, and the emerging black states to the north.

The revolutionary shift within the ANC is perhaps the least adequately researched area of the movement's history. The 'armed struggle' contributed to the reduction of parts of South Africa to a state of ungovernability. But, as the present ANC leadership has acknowledged, it failed to win military victory. Apartheid was defeated, as it was always bound to be, by economic pressure, mainly from outside the country. By then it was evident that the burden of a policy of violence had been borne largely by those it was designed to free. It is still by no means clear that the wounds will heal, or that the condition will not deteriorate further. Once achieved, a state of ungovernability is not readily responsive to treatment. Mandela himself acknowledged as much in 1992, in Port Elizabeth, when he said it was difficult to make young ANC members understand a need for change after they had been 'told to make the country ungovernable'.[18]

The critical decision to begin armed struggle stemmed from a national executive meeting in June 1961. The State of Emergency had been lifted the previous year and Lutuli, Mandela and other detainees freed. Now Mandela put before the executive a proposal to use violent tactics. His view was that, 'as violence was inevitable, it would be unrealistic and wrong for African leaders to continue preaching peace and non-violence when the government met our peaceful demands with force.'[19]

Lutuli was not present, being restricted to Stanger, and it was not until the following year that the Transvaal militants sent a delegation to Natal to apprise him of developments. Although this can in part be ascribed to problems of communication, moderates suspected that the president was being bypassed. By then, the decision had already been taken: as a movement, the ANC would continue to seek change by peaceful means, but would not discipline members who engaged in violence.[20] The way was open for the formation of Umkhonto we Sizwe, the Spear of the Nation, the ANC's armed wing. Mandela was its first commander-in-chief.

A tactful attempt to influence the rapidly deteriorating situation in South Africa was made by the Norwegian Nobel committee, which announced in October that its 1960 Peace Prize had been awarded to Lutuli. Although he was still banned, and now in declining health, the government had little choice but to allow him to travel to Oslo for the awards ceremony. Africa's first Nobel winner accepted his prize 'on behalf of the freedom-loving peoples of South Africa, and on behalf of all the peoples of Africa, irrespective of their race, colour or creed.'[21]

Against this, the white leadership of the South African Communist Party was now lobbying forcefully for the armed struggle. Joe Slovo, a white Johannesburg lawyer, and Arthur Goldreich, were influential in forging contacts with the Soviet Union. Gradually, the communist voice became more dominant within the ANC, especially after it became the Soviet Union's officially designated liberation movement in South Africa. In this category, it joined Zapu of Rhodesia, Frelimo of Mozambique, Swapo of Namibia, and the FNLA of Angola as the recipients of Soviet military aid in those territories.

Not all the communists were in favour of violence. Rowley Arenstein, an activist and trade unionist in Durban, was convinced, as was Lutuli, that the means to destroy apartheid lay within the economy. Arenstein, who was to be detained or restricted in various forms for twenty-four years, recalled the clandestine meeting in June 1962 when Sisulu came to brief Lutuli and other ANC leaders in Natal. Six months earlier Umkhonto had announced itself with a series of bombs that had gone off harmlessly at government buildings.

We asked Sisulu: 'What is this Umkhonto?' He replied: 'We have connections with Umkhonto. If employers are reluctant, Umkhonto will step in.' We said: 'Who decides to deploy Umkhonto?' Lutuli was chairman. He was opposed to violence. But Sisulu was hardline. We said all it will do is bring disaster and it did. Because I would not agree with the armed struggle I became a traitor, a sell-out.[22]

Lutuli, whose pacifism was informed by his devout Christianity, had always believed that political activity should be guided by moral conviction. The road to freedom, he once wrote, was 'sanctified with the blood of martyrs – in other words, no cross, no crown'.[23] Beyond such statements, we know little of his thoughts on the crisis within the ANC at this time as he kept them to himself and, in his autobiography, drew a veil over the subject. It has been argued by two American academics, Tom Karis and Gail Gerhart, that by failing to insist on expelling Mandela and others who embraced violence, or by resigning himself in protest, Lutuli gave tacit consent to Umkhonto's early acts of sabotage.[24] However, it is difficult to see how, confined and isolated as he was, the president could have acted against the powerful Transvaal militants without splitting the ANC again, and unity had always been his paramount concern. He may also have felt that he could turn a blind eye to Umkhonto, as its overt links with the ANC were not publicly established until 1963. It is not possible to claim that he accepted the revolutionary use of guerrilla violence to which Umkhonto became committed. Indeed, the gap which had existed before between the ANC's president and his colleagues on the Reef had widened. Mandela's view at this time, that Lutuli was too much of an individualist for a leader, reflects this distance.[25]

The crisis in the movement was resolved by the authorities. In August 1962, Mandela was arrested after a secret visit abroad and imprisoned for inciting a strike. A year later, police arrested others in the Umkhonto high command, including Sisulu and Govan Mbeki, at a farm in Rivonia, north of Johannesburg. They were brought to trial with Mandela, charged with sabotage. Facing death, Mandela was magnificent in defiance. In a ringing address to the court, he declared that he had sought only a democratic and free society in which all people lived in harmony and with equal opportunity, and for this he was prepared to die.

Instead, he and his fellow defendants were sentenced to life imprisonment and, in July 1964, they were ferried out from Cape Town to Robben Island where, 150 years earlier, Shaka's intermediary, Jakot, had been confined. Mandela was to remain there until 1982, when he was moved to a mainland prison, where he served another seven years before his release in February 1990. His conduct throughout this time won the respect of captors and the devotion of fellow prisoners. The Mandela legend became a far more potent weapon in the ANC's hands than all the East bloc arms and explosives that started filtering into the country, or the growing army of cadres undergoing military training abroad. Lutuli's dictum, 'No cross, no crown', was to have its ultimate vindication in the subsequent career of Mandela himself.

Lutuli responded to the imprisonment of the Umkhonto high command with a statement that 'no one can blame brave just men for seeking justice by the use of violent methods'.[26] But from now his own tactics were to be directed at persuading the international community, in particular Britain and the United States, to impose economic sanctions on South Africa to 'avert what can become the greatest African tragedy of our times'.[27] He did not doubt, he said, that a boycott would entail hardship for Africans. 'But if it is a method which shortens the day of bloodshed, the suffering to us will be a price we are willing to pay. In any case, we suffer already, our children are undernourished, and on a small scale (so far) we die at the whim of a policeman.'[28] It would be another twenty years before the West accepted the challenge of sanctions. The steep economic decline that followed, and the consequent collapse of apartheid, were a belated justification of Lutuli's position. By then, however, South Africa's political condition was pathological.

As it was, South Africa was already well on its way to becoming an international pariah; with Verwoerd as prime minister, and the neo-fascist Vorster as justice minister, the scale of repression was increasing all the time. Verwoerd had cut the last constitutional ties with Britain, declaring the country a republic in 1961 and withdrawing from the Commonwealth. But the economic lure for foreign investment capital remained strong.

The torch of ANC leadership had passed out of the country with Tambo, who, operating from London, was to prove an able organizer and lobbyist. A diffident figure with a gentle manner, Tambo seemed the antithesis of the exiled insurrectionary leader and was the ideal foil for the Mandela legend that burned ever more brightly. But although less conspicuous, the hardline communists in the organization, such as Joe Slovo, and the guerrilla leaders, Chris Hani and Joe Modise, were to become increasingly influential.

Internally, the ANC was, to all intents and purposes, defunct. Although Lutuli's prestige remained intact, his ability to provide forceful leadership was reduced by his continued banning order, poor health and failing eyesight. Through the 1960s, another figure came to the fore in the affairs of Zulu-speakers. He was Mangosuthu Gatsha Buthelezi.

Buthelezi's political credentials were formidable: one of his grandfathers was Dinuzulu, the other was Mnyamana, who had been Cetshwayo's chief adviser. His uncles included King Solomon and Seme, the ANC's founder, and he himself was an activist within the ANC Youth League. In 1957, he succeeded his father as chief of the Buthelezi, one of the aristocratic inner circle of Zulu clans. For a patrician, he was unusually well educated, having matriculated at Adams and gone on to Fort Hare University, where Professor Matthews, inspiration for the Freedom Charter, was a tutor, and Sobukwe, the PAC founder, a classmate.

The relationship of Lutuli and Buthelezi was that of mentor and protégé. Buthelezi's later rift with the ANC would generate a propaganda campaign aimed at disproving this, but the evidence is not persuasive. Buthelezi had been aware of Lutuli since his childhood and frequently sought the old chief's advice, visiting him at Groutville towards the end of his life. He revered Lutuli and, for his part, was held in sufficiently high regard by the family for Lutuli's widow, Nokukhanya, to ask Buthelezi to give the address at his funeral.

On 21 July 1967, Lutuli was walking to his home at Stanger across a railway bridge when he was struck by a train. He died later that day in hospital, aged sixty-eight. Ignored by the great majority of white South Africa, his passing was noted in a substantial obituary in *The Times*. His own final words were the creed he enunciated in the last pages of *Let My People Go*, composed at a time when hopes for multi-racial evolution were still high and which foreshadow the civil rights addresses of Martin Luther King some years later.

Our history has been one of ascending unities, the breaking of tribal, racial and credal barriers. There remains before us the building of a new land, a home for men who are black, white, brown, from the ruins of the old narrow groups, a synthesis of the rich cultural strains which we have inherited. There remains to be achieved our integration with the rest of our continent. Somewhere ahead there beckons a civilization, a culture, which will take its place in the parade of God's history beside other great human syntheses, Chinese, Egyptian, Jewish, European. It will not necessarily be all black; but it will be African.[29]

Five years after his death, a memorial stone to Lutuli's memory was unveiled at Groutville. Buthelezi gave the address. Realization of Lutuli's vision seemed further away than ever: the ANC's leaders were all in prison or in exile, apartheid was triumphant. But in one sense, he was soon to be proved right.

On 16 June 1976, black schoolchildren took to the streets of Soweto in protest – nominally against the enforcement of Afrikaans as a language of instruction but, in reality, against the entire system of Bantu education. Two children were shot dead and within hours Soweto was ablaze. In the weeks that followed more than 500 Africans died, most of them under thirty, and a large number in their teens. A pattern of youthful rebellion had been established on the south Rand. All the black arts of totalitarianism were now to be employed by the security forces, from the systematic use of torture to death squads.

As Lutuli had said: 'When the white rulers resort to indiscriminate violence, as they will surely do, it is a sure sign that their end as a master-race is beginning.'

19

BUTHELEZI AND INKATHA

In our history, Zulus went to war for spoils. It was
very clear to us that any war with the South African
Defence Force would be a war without spoils, just
ashes.

Chief Mangosuthu Buthelezi, to the author,
March 1992

The most famous political prisoner in the world walked free on 11
February 1990, under the eyes of television cameras that carried
the moment by satellite instantly to Europe and America: the tall,
grave man with a slight stoop, waving to the crowd outside Victor
Verster prison, had not been seen in public for more than twenty-
five years. Nine days earlier, President Frederik de Klerk had
announced the release of Nelson Mandela and unbanned the ANC,
the PAC and the South African Communist Party. The apartheid
era was over, and the whites were in the process of surrendering.
Only the terms of peace had to be agreed.

One note jarred on black South Africa's moment of triumph: in
Natal, the worst violence of recent times was in progress. While
Africans as a whole seemed to be united in resistance, Zulu-
speakers were more divided than at any time since the ruinous
civil war a century earlier.

Once again, the Tugela marked a fault line. To the north, in the old kingdom, Zulu nationalism was resurgent in the form of the Inkatha movement, revived in 1975 by Mangosuthu Buthelezi, now chief minister of the self-governing territory of KwaZulu where traditional authority had been formally reconstituted. Zulu ceremonial was being celebrated under King Goodwill Zwelithini as it had not been since before the conquest.

South of the Tugela, a ferocious struggle for territory had been growing year by year since 1985, mainly in the townships of Durban and the rural locations around Pietermaritzburg, where, by mid-1990, some 3500 people had died. It was essentially a political conflict, between Inkatha and a body known as the United Democratic Front, formed as a surrogate for the ANC and other illegal groups in 1983. But, as many of those caught up in the confrontation had no overt political affiliation, being resigned to accept the leadership of whichever side offered better security, it was also a battle for territory and followers.

At the cutting edge of the UDF side was a generation of young activists, responding to an ANC campaign to make the townships, including those in KwaZulu, 'ungovernable'. At the softer end were Zulu-speakers in the *kholwa* tradition, churchmen and professionals who recoiled from what they saw as the ethnic retrogression represented by Buthelezi and Inkatha. By 1990, the old nineteenth-century cleavage had returned, of a royalist Zululand and a divided Natal.

In terms of brutality, there was little to distinguish the Inkatha 'warlords', as they were known, from the UDF 'comrades'. Rampaging Inkatha *impis* had undoubtedly killed more people in their surges through supposed enemy settlements. The comrades, on the other hand, employed stealth. Inkatha leaders were liable to be shot on answering their doors, or to be set upon and then placed in the embrace of a car tyre doused in petrol and set alight. If warlords used terror and patronage to keep their communities in line, so too did comrades.

Still, the Natal conflict had acquired for many onlookers, especially liberal whites, something of the quality of a crusade. For one thing, it was quite clear that the loathed South African police, fighting their own covert war against the UDF, had been actively assisting the Inkatha side, turning a blind eye to violence against the UDF and even recruiting and training Inkatha members to act against those the state referred to as 'terrorists'. That alone seemed enough to define the conflict as one between the forces of progress and reactionaries threatening a medieval African night. But there was also the factor of Mandela himself, a noble, gentle figure, free at last and apparently decreed by destiny to become the first leader of a non-racial, democratic South Africa.

It was, however, legitimate to ask what the prospects were for a non-racial, democratic South Africa. It was becoming clear that once the cement of apartheid, which had bound together the foes of white domination, was lost, the ethnic bricks that made up this diverse and complex nation would be exposed. The South African state formed in 1910 was a British empire in microcosm and, without apartheid, was always likely to show the same fissiparous tendencies of the Russian empire without communism. Although there was reluctance to accept this proposition at the dawning of that for which so many had yearned for so long, the signs had already started to show. Ethnic politics, so long obscured or concealed, suddenly mattered a great deal.

The control of the ANC's hierarchy by Xhosa-speakers was glaringly obvious. In addition to the freed prisoners and returned exiles – Mandela, Tambo and Sisulu – the two newest stars of the movement, Chris Hani, chief of staff of Umkhonto we Sizwe, the armed wing, and Thabo Mbeki, the foreign affairs spokesman, were Xhosa-speakers. This dominance disturbed not only Zulus – who were now unrepresented in the ANC leadership – but members of two other large black groups too, the Sotho and the Tswana. Among the Tswanas of western Transvaal, there was even talk of reunion with their kin in neighbouring Botswana.

As well as the black components, one strand of white ethnicity was clearly visible in the new equation. This was an Afrikaner nationalism that had been bypassed in the slow but inevitable drift towards reform of the more sophisticated Afrikaner establishment in the 1980s. The diehards still spoke of themselves as a *volk* and, like the Zulu nationalists, drew strength from the traditions and symbols of their past, from the Great Trek to the Boer War. Among them were figures from the neo-Nazi right, like the malevolently buffoonish Eugene Terre Blanche and his Afrikaner Resistance Movement, but they also included serious right-wing politicians with connections in the military.

Twenty years before, it had all seemed so simple. The goal then for all Africans was political rights, the obstacle white power. Now competing fears and ambitions swirled around elusively. Even before negotiations started, however, one thing was clear: De Klerk had gambled all on an agreement with the ANC – an alliance of the white political and business establishment, on the one hand, and the black party best able to deliver the African majority, on the other.

That left Zulu and Boer nationalists out in the cold. Both feared reprisals, and both were determined to secure for themselves a measure of self-rule within the new dispensation. Extraordinarily, the way was open to an alliance between white and black conservatives, Boer diehards and Zulu royalists, between the foes of Blood River.

❋

In October of 1955, Hendrik Verwoerd, then minister for native affairs, addressed an *indaba* of King Cyprian and 300 of his chiefs at Nongoma. The Zulu nation, he announced, was to be handed back its land, and the Zulu people were once more to be ruled by their hereditary chiefs.

The Nationalist notion of tribal 'homelands', or Bantustans, dated from the Bantu Authorities Act, when Verwoerd announced that he was, 'training the Bantu for possible forms of self-government, based on their own traditions'. In the Nationalist vision, this never went beyond parcelling out small and impoverished strips of land, and the concept was naturally loaded with other benefits for apartheid. By allocating territory for blacks to rule themselves, the government gained a dumping ground for those who were surplus to labour requirements in the white domain and, by opening up another channel for black political activity, it theoretically redirected the demand for full rights in South Africa.

However tawdry, the proposal for a Zulu homeland played upon a deep yearning among rural Zulus. Of all the black ethnic groups, it was the Zulus whose culture remained, even now, most deeply rooted in the land, in a symbiosis between man, homestead, cattle and pasture. Allied with this was a continued loyalty to the institutions of traditional authority: the pyramid of the royal house, the king, the *abantwana*, the dozens of princes descended from Mpande, and the chiefs who gave them allegiance.

To the urban black intelligentsia of Natal, however, the concept was anathema. While Lutuli acknowledged that loyalty to chiefs was 'real and a force to be reckoned with', his view was that their influence tended to retard political progress, especially now that the government was dismissing those who showed signs of dissidence, and replacing them with puppets. Declaring that the proposed Zulustan amounted to 'government by stooge', he wrote:

Inside this close world there is no hint of democratic rule. There is provision only for the march back to tribalism – but in a far more dictatorial form than Shaka dreamed of. The modes of government proposed are a caricature. They are neither democratic nor African. The Act makes our chiefs into minor puppets of the Big Dictator.[1]

There was always bound to be an historical parting between the old ways and the new. It is easy now to see that Lutuli was right in fearing that Bantustan rule would open up all the old divisions in Zulu society: traditional authority, in decline and perhaps doomed, would enjoy a revival but would eventually be compromised by the oppressor's writ and, inevitably, find itself in confrontation with aspirations for full political rights. But it is hard, too, not to be moved by the instinctive response of those who, having lost all, simply longed for the past to be restored to them.

The ambiguities and complexities of the man who succeeded Lutuli as the dominant voice in Zulu politics derive at least in part from the fact that he fell in both camps. It was no political trick that made this so. Mangosuthu Buthelezi, like Lutuli, was a Christian. Moreover, he had a university degree from Fort Hare. But like his cousin, King Cyprian, he was also a Zulu aristocrat, with his own large tribal constituency in the Mahlabatini heartland between the White Mfolozi and the Mhlatuze. In 1953, aged twenty-five, he became acting chief of the 30,000-strong Buthelezi clan, a position confirmed four years later.

Great expectations were invested in him from the outset. As Cyprian's chief adviser, and a confidant of Lutuli, Buthelezi saw his role as a mediator between tradition and modernity, country and town, and a representative of both before an unresponsive white power. It was a thankless task, and perhaps an impossible one, but it would have been less burdensome had Lutuli lived, or Cyprian been a stronger man. As it was, the responsibility fell on Buthelezi, and the load left its mark. Conservative by nature, he was to show an increasing tendency towards impatience, authoritarianism and hypersensitivity to criticism. When, at last, he had to choose between his constituencies, there was little question which it would be. Whereas Lutuli was an African nationalist first, and after that a Zulu, Buthelezi was always a Zulu first.

Naturally cautious, he decided early on to operate against the system from within. In the 1950s, he had met Mandela on a number of occasions at his home on visits to Johannesburg with Cyprian. Buthelezi has since made a good deal of his early connections with the ANC, but although a member of the Youth League at one time, he appears not to have been active in the organization after leaving university. His meetings with Cyprian and Mandela in Johannesburg may have been more in the nature of courtesy calls between tribal aristocrats: Mandela was a prince of the Tembu house, a Xhosa sub-group. In any event, the ruthlessness of the apartheid crackdown on African nationalism decided Buthelezi to work against the government within the law. Indeed, unlike the vast majority of blacks, he harboured no resentment against Afrikaners. He always took the view that the Zulus' real foe had been Britain; the Boers were a white tribe with whom he could rub along. As long ago as 1971, he told Afrikaans students that they, 'just like my own people, were victims of colonization for a very long time.'[2]

According to Hermann Giliomee, professor of political studies at the University of Cape Town: 'The ANC took the position that Africa's liberation wars were paradigms for South Africa. Buthelezi's position was the opposite. South Africa is *sui generis*; it could not be defeated militarily, therefore negotiation was necessary.'[3]

With Mandela in jail and the ANC and other black political organizations silenced, Buthelezi emerged in the 1960s as apartheid's most forthright and effective African critic. Blacks across South Africa, yearning for heroes, gradually came to see him less as a Zulu chief than as the only African leader who was prepared to tackle the government publicly. Although a poor public speaker, he developed an effective language of allusion and veiled threat in warning of the consequences of oppression. His basic premise was that blacks could win their liberation through exerting incremental leverage on the system. He won the support of white liberals. Alan Paton, the author, and Helen Suzman, the MP, became friends and confidants. At the same time, his conservative economic views made him welcome in the boardrooms of great corporations, such as Harry Oppenheimer's Anglo-American mineral empire.

Deprived of his passport from 1966 to 1971, Buthelezi then travelled abroad and consulted such figures in Pretoria's pantheon of demonology as Julius Nyerere of Tanzania and Kenneth Kaunda of Zambia. His meeting with Nyerere convinced him that he had undertaken the right strategy. 'He told me that no African state, or combination of African states, could take on South Africa militarily,' he recalled.[4]

Moreover, Buthelezi made no secret of his contacts with ANC exiles such as Tambo. Gradually, but undeniably, the profile of the tribal chief from Mahlabatini was transformed into that of an international figure. When no government leader could get so much as a tea invitation from a Western democracy and white South Africa longed for outside approval, Buthelezi found a hugely enjoyable way of embarrassing Pretoria: he secured any available spot with a little limelight – a prayer breakfast with Richard Nixon, an audience with the Pope – and then relayed this to the South African press. These experiences gave him a grasp of the modern political skill of media manipulation.

One other early lesson was to prove valuable. In 1964, a British crew arrived in Natal to make a film about the Zulu war, and Buthelezi was offered the role of his great-grandfather, Cetshwayo. His screen appearance was brief, and Pretoria then committed one of its customary gaffes by refusing to let the film be shown in black cinemas (evidently fearing that the subject matter might inflame Africans, even though the film's concern was not the Zulu victory at Isandlwana, but the defeat at Rorke's Drift). It made no difference. *Zulu* made a big impact on world cinema screens. Perhaps it was at this point that Buthelezi recognized the atavistic appeal that the warrior image still had for industrialized man, and the fillip such displays gave to Zulu self-esteem. It was a card he was to play with characteristic shrewdness and toughness.[5]

The path to KwaZulu's self-government began with the establishment of a series of territorial authorities within the scattered fragments of tribal reserve north and south of the Tugela. On this issue, Buthelezi held the line between his two constituencies in a way that even his severest critics acknowledge. He could do nothing to quell the royal house's enthusiasm for a Zulu homeland. But, at the same time, he indicated his own opposition by refusing to accept the legitimacy of a tribal authority in his Mahlabatini district for six years. Once the government made clear it would impose tribal self-government, however, he gave in. 'We have to obey the government,' he said. 'The alternative is revolution, which is out of the question.'[6]

In the transition to self-rule, Buthelezi's ascendancy became all the more marked as a result of Cyprian's decline. The king died of cirrhosis in 1968 and, until the installation of Goodwill Zwelithini three years later, the regent was Prince Israel Mcwayizeni, whose ardour for a Zulu state was, if anything, even greater than Cyprian's and who felt Buthelezi had risen above his station. An arch-royalist faction, resentful of the chief's position, mustered around the new king and was quickly exploited by Pretoria.

King Goodwill was a good-looking but immature young man who, against Buthelezi's wishes, had received only a perfunctory education and taken his first wife by the time he was twenty-one. (He has since acquired four more, including a Swazi princess.) He became king at the age of twenty-three, having been encouraged by the government and the royalists to believe that he could challenge Buthelezi for executive powers in the KwaZulu assembly. Prince Israel was involved, but the government had also invested hope and money in two pliant political organizations, the Zulu National Party, led by a businessman named Lloyd Ndaba, and Shaka's Spear, founded by Chief Charles Hlengwa. Both men had connections in the royal house; Hlengwa had, in addition, been sponsored by the Bureau of State Security (Boss) to recruit the king to Shaka's Spear.[7]

Under the constitutional model for KwaZulu proposed by Pretoria, King Goodwill was to be given the power of legislative veto. A white official closely connected with the manoeuvrings at this time, said: 'Our department [Bantu Affairs] was trying to invest the king with as much power as possible, partly because they thought the king would ultimately be the most powerful voice in Zulu politics, but also because they wanted to undermine Buthelezi.'[8]

KwaZulu came into being on 31 March 1972. The self-governing territory relied on Pretoria for about three-quarters of its revenue, consisted of forty-four separate pockets of land north and south of the Tugela, and covered perhaps 10 per cent of what had been Shaka's domain. It is a measure of the ludicrousness of this patchwork state that the most hallowed of all Zulu lands, the Emakosini valley, burial ground of the kings, was excluded because it fell across a series of white farms. The symbolic resurrection of a Zulu state was limited to the building of a legislative assembly at Ulundi, site of Cetshwayo's *umuzi*.

Subsequently extended, the territory reached from Transkei in the south to Mozambique in the north. Like other homelands, it was populated largely by women and children, the majority of men being away at work in the white areas. The land was grossly overworked, poverty as widespread as anywhere in South Africa and malnutrition high. And yet, for all its pathos and absurdity, KwaZulu managed to acquire a certain dignity. Like Buthelezi himself, it was disciplined, authoritarian and desperately keen to succeed, a would-be African Singapore. Its civil servants were polite and dedicated and education was pursued with dogged determination. Enterprise was encouraged and a generation of African businessmen and small-scale entrepreneurs arose, many of whom attributed their success to the support of Buthelezi.

The early years of self-government were the high-water mark of Buthelezi's fortunes. Pretoria had been reduced to helpless rage by his refusal to accept full 'independence' for KwaZulu. Buthelezi rejected with contempt what he called a 'polka-dot state', while indicating that a consolidated Zululand might be another thing. The fact that the largest and most unified of South Africa's ethnic groups had thrown back the Bantustan scheme in the government's face deprived the system of the international credibility that Pretoria so desperately sought. Meanwhile, Kaiser Matanzima, a Tembu chief once close to Mandela, accepted the presidency of the Xhosa-speaking Transkei, a nominally independent state, in 1979. Other independent 'homelands' were to be the Tswana-speaking Bophuthatswana under Lucas Mangope (1977), Venda (1979) and Ciskei (1981).

Buthelezi's reputation as apartheid's doughtiest opponent still at liberty was further enhanced by his open calls from 1973 for 'the release of Nelson Mandela and other black leaders on Robben Island' and for the granting of immunity for Tambo to return from exile.[9] His position was also strengthened by confrontation with opponents in KwaZulu. In 1974, Buthelezi dealt with Chief Hlengwa by publicly divulging that Shaka's Spear had been funded by Pretoria. More controversial was his disposal of Barney Dladla, a member of the KwaZulu cabinet responsible for labour affairs. An independent spirit, Dladla sided with workers against white employers in a number of wage disputes, apparently without first obtaining cabinet approval, at a time when Buthelezi was trying to win investment in KwaZulu. That same year, 1974, he secured Dladla's dismissal through the KwaZulu assembly.

Although this episode signalled what was to become Buthelezi's marked aversion to strikes and boycotts, which to many Africans were the only available means of expressing dissent, now more than ever he was seen as the ANC's strongest ally within South Africa. However, as the march towards totalitarianism continued, the stakes were raised – and with them the risks. From 1975 his balancing act started going wrong.

Buthelezi has said that he got the idea of reviving Inkatha from Kaunda of Zambia, who told him he needed his own constituency. Just what that constituency was, however, has been a matter of confusion. Buthelezi was by now constantly pulled between the regional and national stage and the ambiguity of his position was reflected in the new movement.

In March 1975, Inkatha ya KwaZulu was reconstituted as a 'cultural liberation movement' at a ceremony in old Zululand. The emphasis initially was on the Zulu character of the organization. This was natural, as any overt appeal to a broad African membership would almost certainly have brought government intervention. As it was, Buthelezi was later summoned to Pretoria by Jimmy Kruger, the law and order minister, and warned to confine himself to a Zulu following.[10] Oscar Dhlomo, Inkatha's secretary-general for the next fifteen years, recalled later: 'There had been no mass black political party since the banning of the ANC, and we had to be cautious.'

Initially, too, Buthelezi would have seen a Zulu-based Inkatha as a means of binding in the more fractious royalist elements. King

Goodwill still aspired to executive power and Buthelezi was being sniped at by the arch-royalists who questioned his aristocratic credentials. His entitlement to be called *mntwana*, or prince, was dismissed by some who called him 'son of a princess', as he was descended from Dinuzulu through his mother rather than his father. Buthelezi responded to such assaults on his suitability for high office by claiming that the Buthelezi clan had traditionally acted as the kings' 'prime ministers'. He gained credibility for this view, although it is not sustained by history. (Cetshwayo's chief adviser was a Buthelezi, but those of Dingane and Mpande were not.)

That Buthelezi was actually preparing himself for a wider political role became apparent in the months after Inkatha's initial relaunch, when its title was changed to Inkatha ye Nkululeko ye Sizwe, a subtle change of emphasis from 'ring of the Zulu' to 'ring of the nation'. It was clear that Buthelezi was creating a platform from which he intended to regain the Zulu place in the ANC, vacant since Lutuli's death. At the same time, he would necessarily be adopting policies that stopped short of the ANC's insistence on a non-racial South African state based on universal adult suffrage. It was a bold strategy, but also a dangerous one.

The new Inkatha drew heavily on the traditions and symbolism of the ANC, and its constitution had echoes of the Freedom Charter. The chief aim was 'fostering the spirit of unity among the people of KwaZulu throughout southern Africa, and between them and all their African brothers'. To this end, Inkatha would 'co-operate with any movement or organisation for the improvement of the conditions of the people . . . and for the eradication of all forms of colonialism, neo-colonialism, racialism, imperialism, discrimination and to strive for the attainment of African unity'. Buthelezi told a press conference: 'Inkatha plainly declares itself to be an instrument of liberation. The business of black liberation is our business.'[11]

In Natal, almost every member of the old ANC establishment joined Inkatha, from Selby Msimang, one of the founding fathers of 1913, to Jordan Ngubane, the fiery co-founder of the Youth League who had broken with the ANC over its communist links and who was to be the new movement's leading intellectual. Alphaeus Zulu, the much-loved Bishop of Zululand and a longtime ANC sympathizer, also joined. So did a number of former Robben

Island detainees. Buthelezi had received the blessings of Mandela from prison and Tambo from exile for the move.[12] Lest anyone should have missed the point, Inkatha's colours were the green, black and gold of the ANC.

The success of Buthelezi's strategy seemed to be confirmed when, in March 1976, he received a tumultuous reception at Jabulani stadium in the heart of Soweto and proceeded to deliver his most outspoken address. The hour was late, he said, but not too late, if the country started promptly to move towards majority rule. At that moment, Buthelezi had won the respect of even radical Africans. Steve Biko, the Black Consciousness leader who was beaten to death in his prison cell the following year, wrote of him as 'a man who could easily have been my leader' if only he had given up his homeland role.[13]

Three months after Buthelezi's Jabulani speech, Soweto exploded.

Books, reports and theses have been written about the Soweto uprising of June 1976. Like February 1990, it marked a point in South African history from which there could be no return. The spark was the system of Bantu education and the teaching of Afrikaans to African children. On 16 June, a student march in Johannesburg's southern township was stopped by police bullets. Within days, Soweto was in flames.

In the months that followed, young blacks cast their bodies against the steel machine of oppression and died in their hundreds as police responded with unprecedented savagery. Disturbances spread to other parts of the country, and continued for more than a year – indeed, it might be said that they never really ceased. In that first year, however, about 700 blacks died, more than 100 of them under the age of seventeen and the vast majority under twenty-five. A martyr generation had been created.

But in 'taking the township almost entirely into their own hands', as a Soweto resident put it, young Africans had crossed a dangerous psychological line. The bloody, heady victory of youth had discredited the politics of negotiation, and the victors were to hold an entire older generation up to ridicule. In all the tracts written about the uprising, nothing gets closer to the heart of the matter than the brave and poignant words of Aggrey Klaaste, a black journalist, written nine years later when the legacy had started to sour:

The first time I saw schoolgirls in their tunics marching on police vehicles, I could have wept. I could have wept to see their clean courage and wept at our desperate attempt to articulate that which, to them, is incomprehensible.

Now we are reaping the whirlwind. In 1976, we turned boys and girls into revolutionary heroes and heroines. We gave them power with a pat on the back and a fearful hug of courage that was not in us. They have got that power, grown cancerous because of what we did and are still doing to these children.[14]

While attention was concentrated on the courage of the student protesters and the brutality of the police, one episode was largely overlooked. That September, the young militants used intimidation to prevent Zulu hostel dwellers in Soweto from going to work. The enforced strike or boycott was to be a key weapon in attempts to disrupt the white economy. However, when calls were issued the following month for another stoppage, the hostel dwellers responded that they could not afford to lose wages again. They were attacked by activists on their way home from work, triggering a violent reaction as Zulus from the Mzimhlophe hostel turned on the local community. Police stood aside and allowed a number of young men to be killed. At the time it was an unusual occurrence, but it set a pattern for the shape of things to come.

Buthelezi flew to Johannesburg, and by meeting hostel dwellers and students managed to calm both sides for the time being. But after 1976 nothing could be the same. As an 'internal leader' working within the system for change, Buthelezi and his supporters were suddenly far more vulnerable to the accusation of collaboration.

Others had also lost ground. ANC exiles such as Tambo had no inkling that Soweto was on the brink of revolt, and were desperately seeking to re-establish their connections in the townships. Tom Lodge, the political scientist, has posed the question whether, in its subsequent calls for the townships to be made 'ungovernable', the ANC was taking a lead or, rather, trying to stay in touch with the militancy on the Rand.

For the meantime, Buthelezi's caution was matched by the mood in Natal and KwaZulu, which were to remain beyond the flames of unrest for another ten years.

In October 1979, Buthelezi led an Inkatha delegation to London for a meeting with Tambo and other members of the ANC. The two leaders had met many times before and their dealings had always been warm. Now, though, more than good personal relations were at stake.

Three years after the uprising, Buthelezi appeared in some respects to be closer than ever to the ANC. He affirmed that his goal was majority rule and now claimed open identification with the liberation movement. Inkatha, he said, had 'taken up the struggle where the ANC left it after it was forced into an exiled position.'[15] A month before leaving for London he told a meeting in Soweto: 'From jail I hear a message from Nelson Mandela and Walter Sisulu telling me to go on doing what I am doing on behalf of millions of black people.'[16] Four years after its revival, Inkatha's membership was 250,000, although by independent estimates more than 90 per cent were Zulu-speakers.

At home in Natal and KwaZulu, Buthelezi was now unassailable. Only three months earlier he had finally succeeded in imposing his will on King Goodwill. Strains between the two men had come to a head in August when Buthelezi subjected the king to a public tongue-lashing in the legislative assembly over his continued dabbling in political matters. KwaZulu MPs joined in the criticism and Goodwill fled the chamber.[17] Buthelezi had handled his difficulties with the royalists in imperious fashion, leaving Zulus in no doubt who their strongest leader was. Henceforth, Goodwill appeared to reconcile himself to the role of constitutional monarch. With maturity he became an effective figurehead with a transparent desire to achieve the best for his people, but Buthelezi remained the power behind the throne.

Outside Natal, however, Buthelezi was increasingly taxed with the charge of being a government 'stooge'. With the acceptance of further powers of self-government for KwaZulu in 1977 and the homeland's first general election the following year, he became chief minister of a cabinet responsible additionally for the police force and justice. Already dependent on the government for funding, the ties binding Ulundi and Pretoria were inevitably strengthening. Notwithstanding his occasional flourishes of radical rhetoric, it was clear that Buthelezi's political views had diverged from those of the township militants, and were coming closer to those of reformist, or *verligte*, ministers in the Nationalist government, who were at last looking to build bridges with moderate blacks. All the time, too, it was apparent that Inkatha had benefited from the ban on more radical African movements.

Shortly before leaving for London, Buthelezi was publicly denounced for the first time by an important figure in the Rand townships. Nthato Motlana, chairman of a group known as the Soweto Committee of Ten, challenged his claim that he was working with the ANC, saying that the organization would not 'collaborate with traitors'. It was an unfortunate remark, but Buthelezi only made matters worse with an unedifying display of spleen, describing Motlana at a public rally in Soweto as a 'political skunk', a baboon and a leper, and warning his associates to 'abandon Motlana before they are destroyed with him'.[18]

Despite these omens, both sides came to the Inkatha–ANC meeting in London on 30 October with hopes of mutual cooperation. The ANC had decided it could not afford to ignore Inkatha and still saw Buthelezi as a potential ally. For his part, Buthelezi by now badly needed ANC recognition for Inkatha in order to counter the charge that he was a stooge.

Tambo proposed that Bishop Zulu of the Inkatha delegation chair the meeting and the talks were held in a cordial atmosphere. But a distance separated the sides culturally as well as ideologically: the Inkatha delegates were shocked to find that Tambo's children, raised in exile, spoke no African language;[19] and when they all sang the liberation anthem, 'Nkosi Sikelel'i Afrika', the ANC members raised clenched fists, while Inkatha stood stiffly to attention.[20]

On matters of substance the differences were more fundamental. Tambo started with a review of the 'armed struggle'. Guerrillas of the ANC's armed wing, Umkhonto we Sizwe, were infiltrating South Africa from Mozambique, and the remote and marshy west of KwaZulu offered a similarly promising wilderness for penetration. Buthelezi was explicitly opposed to the armed struggle. He has always stated this as a matter of principle, citing the policy of passive resistance espoused by Lutuli, the last elected ANC president. However, pragmatism rather than principle has been the dominant feature of his make-up; Rowley Arenstein, the lawyer who has been, over the years, probably his closest white confidant, said: 'Buthelezi simply could not have acceded to ANC requests for help with the armed struggle. Inkatha would have been destroyed.'[21]

Buthelezi then put to the ANC a series of requests that it publicly acknowledge Inkatha as 'a vital force in the struggle', cooperate with it on matters of shared information, and warn the new militant township groups, such as Azapo, that it was not in black interests to attack Inkatha. The ANC side agreed to discuss these points before responding. According to Tambo, the meeting 'ended up nicely'.[22]

Harmony in private could not conceal the fact that the interests of the two groups had fatally diverged. It was becoming increasingly difficult for the ANC to embrace Inkatha publicly when it was itself in danger of being outflanked by more radical groups. Furthermore, many ANC officials were by now certain that Buthelezi was not an ally but a rival, intent on hijacking 'the struggle'. Buthelezi would not allow ANC guerrillas to launch raids from KwaZulu, or use it as a haven. He and colleagues like Oscar Dhlomo now claimed Inkatha to be the true custodian of the ANC tradition. As political conservatives, they were uncomfortable with the prominence of Moscow-orientated communists in what they now termed 'the exile wing of the ANC'. And with their own paid-up membership larger than any in South African history, Inkatha leaders were inclined to think their organization the ANC's equal, if not its superior.[23]

Buthelezi returned home in a blaze of publicity, declaring that all problems between the ANC and Inkatha had been resolved. The ANC took immediate offence at what it saw as a breach of confidentiality. Tambo never did respond to Inkatha's requests. The following June, Alfred Nzo, the ANC secretary-general, made an ugly attack on Buthelezi in London. Four weeks later in Zambia Tambo pronounced that Buthelezi had 'emerged on the side of the enemy against the people'.[24] The rift was complete.

The ANC's decision to confront Buthelezi started with a campaign to marginalize Inkatha nationally, and broadened into a confrontation on its home ground in Natal. From 1980, the message was spread by Radio Freedom broadcasts beamed into South Africa: Buthelezi was 'the major political foe of the ANC inside South Africa'; the 'snake poisoning the people of South Africa – it needs to be hit on the head'.[25]

The shift in mood among Africans now started to undermine Buthelezi's position closer to home. Although for long the dominant voice in Zulu politics, there was never a point at which it could be said that he spoke for Zulu-speakers as a whole and, after 1980, the tide started to go out. North of the Tugela he remained unchallenged. But in the urban areas of Durban and Pietermaritzburg, new forces were coming into play. In 1983, the United Democratic Front emerged as a nationwide movement, a surrogate ANC challenging the government's writ in the townships of the Transvaal and Cape. In laying out their stall, UDF leaders announced they would work with any black political organization besides Inkatha. The lines had been drawn for battle in Natal.

The name of Mandela was working its magic from prison on Natal's black intelligentsia while Buthelezi had become tainted by association with the ruling regime. As campaigns for Mandela's release gathered pace around the world, by 1985 opinion polls in Durban were showing more support for Mandela, a Xhosa-speaker, than Buthelezi. Here might be seen evidence that political conviction could overcome narrow ethnic loyalty. According to Paulus Zulu, a political researcher: 'People started turning against Inkatha for failing to deliver services they thought were due to them, while the ANC still enjoyed symbolic cleanliness.'[26]

Gradually, Buthelezi was thrown back on to his traditionalist following. Inkatha retained in its hierarchy men of the old ANC school, dignified patricians like Bishop Zulu, Frank Mdlalose and Oscar Dhlomo. However, it also became increasingly dependent on rural chiefs, whose instincts were decidedly undemocratic, and urban racketeers, who infiltrated the movement for their own purposes and used it to build power bases.

Meanwhile, Buthelezi's own position on ethnic identity hardened and the symbolism that underpinned Inkatha became more strident. Shaka Day celebrations took on a theme celebrating Zulu might and pride. Buthelezi and King Goodwill would appear in full regalia, leopardskin headbands and feathers. Ceremonial and tradition focusing on the royal house were cultivated. The emphasis was not invariably militaristic; revival in 1984 of the reed dance, performed by unmarried women before the king, was intended to counter the rising incidence of venereal disease and, later, Aids. However, the overall effect was to nurture the conservative values of the past and set traditionalists against the challenge of the young.

A landmark incident occurred in October 1983, when students at the University of Zululand staged a protest against an appearance by Buthelezi, its chancellor. Inkatha supporters, outraged at this insult by 'children', formed an *impi* which invaded the campus at Empangeni and set about the students. Five died and many more ended up in hospital.

The deaths seriously affected Buthelezi's standing. Every parent who had made sacrifices to educate a child could identify with those who grieved. What made it particularly galling, in the eyes of professional people, was that the onslaught on the student body had come from uneducated *amaqaba*. Buthelezi followed this by issuing a warning: 'The abuse of me must now cease. Continuing to label me a sell-out is going to have ugly repercussions.'

From 1983, the UDF became increasingly active in the Durban and Pietermaritzburg areas. Brandishing the slogans of radical populism, activists denounced the twin evils of white capitalism and black collaboration. In challenging the latter, 'the masses' were to be mobilized against administrative stuctures – such as local councils – run by Inkatha. Early troublespots were two Durban townships, Lamontville and Hambanathi, where running street battles between Inkatha and UDF groups occurred. Here a question of ethnicity came to the fore for the first time. The UDF activists included the Rev. Mcebisi Xundu, a minister from Port Elizabeth, and Victoria Mxenge, both Xhosas; Asians were also prominent in the UDF. Buthelezi showed his teeth, issuing veiled threats against 'the non-Zulus who are dividing us'. Xundu he described as 'a Xhosa priest and troublemaker'. Asians who had called him a 'puppet on a string' were reminded of the events of 1949.

The following year Mrs Mxenge was shot dead outside her home in Umlazi, south of Durban. The crime remained unsolved.

In 1985, South Africa came to the Rubicon – or so President Botha put it in a series of speeches that raised local and international expectations of far-reaching reform. Instead, having reached the water's edge, he withdrew by announcing measures amounting to no more than a refinement of the old formula, and which still offered no empowerment for blacks outside the homelands. Deflated expectations triggered unrest and boycotts on the Rand and in the Cape. The government declared a state of emergency in July, giving the police almost unlimited powers of restriction, along with a blanket indemnity.

Despite the unrest, the final phase of the South African power struggle was decided not on the streets but in the boardrooms of international business and finance. Economic sanctions, first proposed by Lutuli after the Sharpeville killings in 1960, gathered momentum after 1985. The European Community, the United States and the Commonwealth tightened the screw on South African trade while international firms disinvested in South Africa in droves. Although Britain under Margaret Thatcher declined to join in, the impact was decisive. The currency, the rand, plummeted to a third of its 1981 value, and foreign debt spiralled to the point where the country's financial managers came close to reneging on repayments to international institutions.

At this point, Buthelezi committed a cardinal blunder. He toured western capitals, arguing against sanctions and disinvestment on the ground that it would cause hardship to the very blacks it was intended to help. However sincere he might have been, by embracing Western conservatives like Thatcher and Ronald Reagan, Buthelezi demonstrated his distance from the mood of the townships. Moreover, while he still claimed to be following in Lutuli's footsteps, he had abandoned the cornerstone of his mentor's policy.

Although compromised, Buthelezi still had one big card to play. Two months before the declaration of a state of emergency, he opened a conference in Durban known as the KwaZulu/Natal *indaba*, to explore ways for white and black in the region to peel off from South Africa and legislate for themselves. To Buthelezi, the *indaba* represented another step towards a goal that he had outlined at Inkatha's founding in 1975: 'Shaka's country is the whole of Natal. We see the autonomy of such a state as a unit of one federal multinational state of South Africa.'[27] For the first time, however, Buthelezi, Inkatha and, by extension, King Goodwill, had staked a claim for a reconstituted Zulu state, albeit one with a large white population and with constitutional links to South Africa.

The idea of a province breaking away from Pretoria's control could only have been taken seriously in Natal. A secessionist tendency had been close to the surface of white politics since 1910, when English Natalians had to be brought kicking and screaming to the Act of Union. Now a conviction was growing among whites that conservative Zulu nationalism was the best available port in a radical storm. The author Alan Paton, a longtime friend of Buthelezi's and leader of the defunct Liberal Party, saw the *indaba* as representing 'the moderate, peace-loving, conflict-hating, middle-of-the-road people of KwaZulu and Natal'.[28] Businessmen recognized in Buthelezi a leader committed to capitalism, as opposed to the ANC's declared policy of nationalization.

The *indaba* was the first multi-racial debate to seek a new political consensus for South Africa. In the chair was Desmond Clarence, principal of the University of Natal, and with him John Kane-Berman, director of the South African Institute of Race Relations. Buthelezi set the tone. President Botha, he said, was 'blundering into a political abyss'.

Eight months later, the *indaba* was wound up with a blueprint for non-racial regional government covering Natal and KwaZulu which would legislate on all matters with the exception of foreign affairs, defence, police, transport and communications. Buthelezi, it was clear, would be elected the first premier, but in a two-chamber legislature whites would retain a veto. In 1987, the plan was presented to the Botha government, which rejected it out of hand. By this time, the violence now endemic in the Transvaal and the Cape had engulfed Natal.

A modern *impi* on the move is often heard before it is seen. It starts with a murmured chant which grows louder as the first ranks jog into view over the brow of a hill or around a street corner. They brandish sticks and wickedly sharpened lengths of metal rod. Some hold oddly small cowhide shields. Naked feet and cheap trainers slap the ground in unison as they jog to the rhythm of their chants, the war songs of the old days and the rallying cry of '*Usuthu*!' It is a fearsome and ugly sight, for the mob is intoxicated by male ascendancy and any challenge, any perceived foe, will surely be attacked. It is also curiously pathetic. For, pursuing a phantasm, a memory of a time when they were a powerful people, these dishevelled twentieth-century warriors are flaunting their aggression against what they perceive to be the scorn of other social and tribal groups.

Such images have made Inkatha *impis* feared and hated from the townships of central Natal to the east Rand. They make terrifying viewing on television and are, consquently, much shown. Since 1987, marauding groups like these have been responsible for many hundreds of deaths.

But there have been other protagonists too. UDF activists were generally less visible and operated on a more subtle level than Inkatha. They would start by exploiting grievances against a local council in Inkatha hands, then target the leadership. Sometimes Inkatha officials were coerced into switching sides. Those who refused were likely to be assassinated or driven away. One UDF tactic, the tyre-and-petrol 'necklace', was a specially effective, if fiendish, instrument of intimidation.

Bishop Stanley Mogoba, the Methodist Bishop of South Africa, who was a close observer of the Natal wars of the 1980s, said:

There were no angels here. Both sides worked on the basis of spheres of influence. They would say, 'Here is our area and it is a no-go area for the others. Those who live here must think like we do, or they will be destroyed.'

We saw the division of communities, the division of families – of schools, of churches. Almost every institution was affected.[29]

On the one hand were Inkatha 'warlords', such as David Ntombela and Winnington Sabelo, known killers who were seen to be instigating violence against communities of suspect loyalty. On the other was the UDF youth, fired with the rhetoric of armed struggle and determined to confront the KwaZulu administration at any opportunity. Gavin Woods, director of an Inkatha research group, said: 'They will attack an entire community as "sell-outs" and then be unable to say what they mean by that, other than that by getting rid of them they are one step closer to freedom.'[30]

In 1987, 413 people died violently in the Natal Midlands, the following year the toll rose to 691 and, in 1989, it topped 700. Roughly twice as many known UDF supporters were killed as known Inkatha supporters. But the violence had a malignant, spontaneous force of its own, and perhaps half the dead had no known political affiliations of any sort. Indeed, many of those who claimed to act on behalf of one organization or the other had no formal connection with either. Outright criminals exploited the situation. So did the police and the government.

Intra-black conflict was gleefully stoked by the security forces wherever it occurred. Nowhere was the process more visible, however, than in Natal, where police either stood passively by or joined in on Inkatha's side. With the darkening of the conflict, Buthelezi and Inkatha were drawn deeper into Pretoria's fatal embrace. At this time, it has since emerged, individual Inkatha supporters were selected by the South African Defence Force and sent to secret bases for training in 'counter-terrorism', including political assassinations. The KwaZulu police, responsible for law and order in territory administered by Inkatha, became an overt tool of the movement, and were involved in taking action against its rivals. Pretoria, it is also known, channelled funds to Ulundi to organize rallies and help Inkatha form the conservative Uwusa trade union, which was intended to rival the UDF-affiliated Cosatu. Uwusa intimidated radical opponents and in one known instance three rival organizers were murdered.[31]

Much of this activity was invisible at the time, but it was nevertheless clear that Buthelezi could no longer credibly maintain that he was resisting Pretoria. He was a compromised figure. Liberals were saddened or dismayed, while a clique of white academics in thrall to radical populism joined in excoriating the man who had once been seen as the best hope for defeating apartheid. Buthelezi became the easiest and safest of Aunt Sallys, derisively called 'Gatsha', the name by which he had been known informally by white friends. It made a curious and unedifying spectacle. The English-speaking intelligentsia had always found it painfully difficult to acknowledge fault in African society. Here, at last, was a black man at whom it was socially acceptable to jeer.[32]

Buthelezi did little for his own cause. Always thin-skinned, he had become short-tempered and belligerent, given to hectoring and interminably self-justifying speeches. A victim by now of his own personality cult, his insistence that rival parties in KwaZulu were 'a luxury that we cannot afford', sounded more the refuge of authoritarians down the ages than the creed of a man who was supposed to have spent his life fighting for multi-racial democracy. Although he declared that Inkatha deplored violence, no visible steps were taken to exclude or discipline those known to have been involved in it.

What the critics missed was the devotion in which Buthelezi was held by his reduced but still formidable constituency. South of the Tugela, his support was down, by most estimates, to well below half the black population; to the north, he was supreme. Here he was to be seen at his most effective: 'Shenge', the chief, working his way among his people, affable and approachable, remembering a family history here, offering help with a personal problem there. Political tribulation had strengthened the bond between leader and his core following. The more outside critics blamed Inkatha for violence while turning a blind eye to the excesses of others, the more it drove an aggrieved Zulu establishment into a corner, convinced that it had never been understood by Europeans; and, moreover that, not for the first time, it was under attack because it would not respond to white dictates on political culture.[33]

As the decade drew to an end, there was little to indicate that South Africa would not simply continue hurtling down the same road to perdition. Then, in August 1989, with the country in chaos, the economy in ruins and the Nationalists facing a new challenge from the far-right Conservative Party, the discredited Botha resigned. His successor was a relative outsider, the Transvaal Nationalist leader, Frederik de Klerk. Analysts predicted that De Klerk would be no reformer but, six months later, he stunned the world by unbanning the ANC, the PAC and the Communist Party, and releasing Mandela.

Like all great reformist moves, De Klerk's step forward was taken into the unknown. It was nevertheless certain that an alliance with the ANC had to be his paramount objective. All deals with old allies were off. Inkatha would, if necessary, have to be dumped.

So it proved. As negotiations began on a new constitution, ANC officials were adamant that Buthelezi merited no place at the top table with De Klerk and Mandela. Rebuffed, he retreated, brooding resentfully. Although in the talks that followed, De Klerk's negotiators emerged from time to time making hopeful noises about a federal dispensation that would concede a considerable degree of autonomy to regions such as Natal/KwaZulu, the ANC was having none of it.

It took a year following Mandela's release for the ANC to consent to his meeting Buthelezi, a year in which another thousand people were killed. An early joint appearance by the two leaders at Taylor's Halt, one of the worst trouble spots in the Pietermaritzburg area, was proposed by Inkatha and preliminary agreement seemed to have been reached. Then the ANC withdrew, on the grounds that Buthelezi would try to make political capital out of the meeting.

Instead, on 25 February 1990, as the death toll mounted, Mandela appeared on his own in Durban. He received a hero's welcome from tens of thousands of Zulu-speakers down on the foreshore. The ANC leader proceeded to deliver a typically dignified and statesman-like address, ending with a ringing exhortation to his followers: 'Cast your weapons into the sea.' It made no discernible difference at all.

Three months later, Zulu hostel-dwellers in Sebokeng, east of Johannesburg, were roused by Xhosa-speaking youths who taunted them as 'Gatshas' and 'Shakas'. *Agents provocateurs*, possibly instigated by the police, meanwhile spread rumours that Zulus working on the Reef were to be sent home and their jobs and accommodation given to returning ANC exiles. The hostel-dwellers attacked local residents, killing twenty-seven. It was the start of overt ethnic violence on the Rand. The pattern was to be repeated with terrible frequency.

EPILOGUE

> If Britain is at war, her people unite under their
> queen against the enemy. How could we face the
> problem here, when we are enemies among
> ourselves?
>
> King Goodwill Zwelithini,
> to the author, March 1992

In the two years after De Klerk's bold stroke, I twice visited Natal
and Zululand. Then, in April 1994, I returned again during South
Africa's first all-race election. Over that four-year period, negotiations continued for a new constitution while the country plunged
and bucked on a perilous rollercoaster ride towards democracy.
Often the carriage seemed about to fly off the rails altogether but,
whenever catastrophe appeared imminent, it slowed and steadied
before resuming again at helter-skelter pace. About 14,000 people
were killed during that time, almost 10,000 of them in Natal/
KwaZulu, where the power struggle between the ANC and
Inkatha was fought over the bodies of Zulu-speaking people.
Somehow, at the end of it all, a form of stability was arrived at.
However transient this may prove to be – and there are plenty
who believe that a war to the death between Inkatha and the ANC
will resume sooner or later in Natal/KwaZulu – such an outcome
was sufficient reason for thanksgiving.

The proximity of violent death to life is something with which black South Africans had become familiar but which outsiders such as myself found unnerving. I felt it particularly acutely one warm March evening, drinking beer in a steamy, slushy warren of shacks some twelve miles south of Durban, known to its inhabitants as Uganda. The name along with others like Cuba and Maputo, proclaimed its supposed radicalism and adherence to the ANC. The night before, armed men had surged out of a little valley that separated Uganda from an Inkatha-controlled section of Umlazi township, firing pistols and swinging the cane-cutting machetes of Natal called pangas. Most Uganda residents fled, but sixteen of them, including eight women and a child, were not swift enough. Their bodies, hacked or shot, were discovered later scattered around the camp.

Now it was just another sultry African evening, with conversation, laughter, pots cooking on open fires, the smell of paraffin and wood smoke. Uganda's leader was an unlikely figure, a slight man of fifty-five named Elliott Daniel, originally from the southern coastal region of Pondoland, who worked by day as a waiter at the Amanzimtoti Country Club. Here he was known as 'Mandela', or with jaunty irony, 'comrade-president' by the men clustered around in a circle. As they exchanged animated talk, those who had shared this life until twenty-four hours before and who now lay in a police mortuary might never have existed. There was no sign of mourning. Just a few paces away was the spot where a woman and her baby had been found, killed by one bullet which passed through both their bodies.

If there were an ideological basis for the violence few were aware of it, and whatever policy differences existed between Inkatha and the ANC no one here could explain them. Shack settlements such as Uganda tended to be composed of displaced people, or economic migrants drawn to the city by the hope of jobs. Most people at Uganda said they supported the ANC because local party officials held out the prospect of protection and promised a time of plenty and prosperity under an ANC government. The local hero was Harry Gwala, the hardline Stalinist leader of the Midlands, who revelled in what he called 'the militancy of the masses' and openly advocated the assassination of Inkatha leaders. 'The people are exercising their legitimate right to get rid of warlords,' he told me blandly at his headquarters in Pietermaritzburg.

Similarly impoverished communities elsewhere clung to Inkatha's patronage, distinguished from ANC areas only by an accident of geography. A man finding himself in an Inkatha neighbourhood would be required to adhere to its communal loyalty, just as ANC sympathies would be demanded of the inhabitants of an ANC area. Such imperatives only intensified the conflict, as force and intimidation rather than any appeal to reason became the way by which each side won adherents from the other. These residential blocs of ANC and Inkatha loyalty, often living within a stone's throw of one another, brought to mind the words of Allen Gardiner, the first missionary in the region, more than 150 years earlier. Of the Natal 'natives' living south of the Tugela, he wrote then: 'Their very existence depends upon their continuing to defend the asylum they have chosen.'

Equally binding chains of allegiance could be established by work. Industrial workers were coerced into joining the ANC-affiliated Cosatu trade union organization. Other avenues were exploited by Inkatha. Travelling near Ulundi once, I struck up an acquaintanceship with a strapping young man named Innocent. Although guarded at first, he eventually confided that, like many other younger Zulus, he was an ANC supporter. Now, however, he was just back from being interviewed for a job with the KwaZulu Police, which was under Buthelezi's control and hostile to the ANC. If recruited, Innocent might be required to take action against his own side, a prospect which he accepted without resentment.

While slow but inexorable progress in negotiations towards democracy held the country in thrall, the power struggle in Natal caused many to become disillusioned with politics. Their opinion echoed a common African response to multi-party conflict. 'It would be better if there was just one party, then there would be no fight,' said one man on a bus, as if enunciating a self-evident truth.

It was a view shared by many of the victims of conflict. When I met Sydney Cile he was acting as a 'cultural guide' to one of the thriving enterprises packaging Zulu culture for tourists; a couple of years earlier he had been a small but successful businessman, with a fast-food shop in Inanda. In those days, he had paid protection money to the young men who claimed to represent the ANC locally, but who were no more than racketeers. One day the protection ran out, and his premises – uninsurable in a trouble zone –

were burned to the ground. He lost everything and was unemployed for a year, before getting a job that wasted his talents. He was biding his time, waiting for an election to decide the victor, before starting another venture.

'I've read about it in books,' he said. 'It is always like this – that you have violence until in the end you have a winning party. Then things will get better.'

❋

Throughout 1992, the troubles intensified, reflecting the crisis in negotiations between political leaders. The previous year had ended with the start of a convention to draw up a new constitution. Inkatha, advised by Albert Blaustein, a professor at Rutgers University, staked its claim for a federal constitution, with a large measure of regional autonomy. At the same time, the role of King Goodwill came to the fore as Buthelezi insisted that the monarch's special status required his presence at the convention, representing the Zulu people. De Klerk was amenable to the king's attendance and the Nationalists were at least partly persuaded of the merits of devolution themselves, but the ANC leadership was obdurately opposed to both and, as De Klerk was banking on a deal with the ANC, the Inkatha demands were dismissed.

Buthelezi retired to Ulundi, deeply embittered. Over the next two years his belligerent demeanour attracted much criticism, and he was widely blamed for the violence of Inkatha supporters. However, the triumphalism of individual ANC leaders only aggravated the wounds of ethnic pride. Buthelezi was persistently disparaged and dismissed as irrelevant, despite the contrary evidence provided by the spiralling death toll. Joe Slovo, for example, the white lawyer who had been a leading light of the 'armed struggle' predicted that Buthelezi 'will soon be a smell in history'. There was also a provocative tendency within the ANC to dismiss King Goodwill as a weak and venal puppet. Many of the attacks on ANC communities were triggered by the insults hurled at Inkatha supporters by young militants. 'They say that Mandela will be king, and Buthelezi and Goodwill will be his houseboys,' said one 'warrior' after a rampage by Inkatha hostel-dwellers.

By now the ethnic aspect of the conflict was inescapable. Although Buthelezi retained a following among conservative whites and a minority of Asians in KwaZulu/Natal, his true powerbase, more than ever, was in the Zulu heartland. Equally, while the ANC was able to appeal to a wide ethnic spectrum, thanks largely to the statesman-like and charismatic Mandela, its heirarchy remained largely Xhosa-speaking. To the ANC's credit, an attempt was made to remedy this imbalance in long-delayed elections for the national executive. Cyril Ramaphosa, an able and pragmatic union leader of Sotho extraction, replaced Alfred Nzo as secretary-general. The absence of any Zulu office-holder was addressed by the election of Jacob Zuma as a vice-president. This was a positive step in one respect as Zuma had established good relations with Inkatha: he proclaimed his pride in being a Zulu, and acknowledged Goodwill as his king. However, his transfer to Johannesburg left the baleful Harry Gwala as the most influential ANC figure in Natal. Moreover, the move failed to appease Zulu nationalists or dispel the impression that the ANC had a preponderance of Xhosa-speakers in its heirarchy.

Urban and educated Zulus were left in a dilemma: on the one hand alienated from Inkatha's raw traditionalism; and on the other pulled by a lingering sense of ethnic and cultural affinity. Nomavenda Mathiane, a woman whose wry and honest commentaries were among the best journalism to come out of the Rand townships, captured the mood:

One of my sisters was told by a guard at the hospital where she works that the Zulus were going to clobber Soweto people for holding them, Zulus, in contempt.

Most Zulus in the townships have no interest whatsoever in Inkatha and, in fact, most of us have been scornful of Inkatha because they collaborated with the government while the ANC was fighting for full-scale liberation. That factor is not quite the same any more, but even so there is much dislike for Inkatha and KwaZulu.

If the truth be known, it is that many of us in Soweto – and particularly the people who speak English and have good jobs – have considered ourselves the 'upper-class Zulus' and we see Inkatha as 'lower-class Zulus'. When that guard complains of Soweto people showing contempt for the Zulus I feel I know what he means . . . We township people, Zulus and non-Zulus alike, have looked down on hostel people. Now I think some of us feel guilty, and perhaps the Zulus among us more than others.

The turning point of the negotiation period occurred in June 1992 when marauding Zulu hostel-dwellers hacked to death forty-two people, mainly Xhosas, in the east Rand township of Biopatong. At this stage, the constitutional talks had made little progress and De Klerk's Nationalists were beset by ANC claims that they were being deliberately obstructive at the negotiating table, while secretly fomenting instability through a 'third force' of right-wing police and army officers. The Boipatong killers were said by local ANC supporters to have been transported to the scene in police vehicles.

It is clear that senior security force members were indeed encouraging and even instigating violent incidents. It is equally certain that the ANC exaggerated the extent and significance of 'the third force' and did De Klerk a great wrong by associating him with it. A week after Boipatong, Mandela withdrew from talks, claiming that the government 'pursues a strategy which embraces negotiations together with systematic covert actions, including murder, involving its security forces and surrogates'. The ANC, he added, was prepared to call for 'mass mobilization' in pursuit of its objectives.

Behind the scenes, a radical faction within the ANC was influencing events. In September 1992, the militants organized a march on Bisho, the capital of the nominally independent homeland of Ciskei, with the aim of overthrowing an administration hostile to the ANC. Ciskei army troops opened fire, leaving twenty-nine ANC demonstrators dead. The ANC radicals were temporarily discredited, while minds on both sides were concentrated by the anarchy that was threatening to envelop further areas of the country. Mandela and De Klerk were able to resume talks.

The following year saw no diminution of political violence but real progress was at last made in negotiations as both the key groups made concessions. The government gave way on the ANC's demand for the election of a 400-seat assembly, empowered to draft a new constitution with a framework of general principles already agreed. The ANC allowed the assembly to be elected by proportional representation and agreed that a two-thirds majority would be required to enact legislation. Following the election, a transitional government of national unity would be formed while the constitution was drafted.

In the face of these proposals, Buthelezi remained obdurate, standing by his federalist demands and insisting that Inkatha would not participate in any electoral process devised by the two main parties. When an election date of 27 April 1994 was set, he announced that Inkatha would boycott it.

Not all Buthelezi's colleagues supported him. How, it was argued, could the organization boycott an election based on universal suffrage, for which black South Africans had so long strived, especially as Inkatha was on paper the third-largest political party in the country, after the ANC and the Nationalists. If the opportunity was missed now, Inkatha would be consigned to oblivion; political violence would continue to spiral until, inevitably, the army would be sent in to crush whatever opposition existed to the new government. Ultimately, Natal/KwaZulu stood to relive the ghastly precedents of Katanga and Biafra. Faced with this prospect, dissension started to show in the organization between, on the one hand, Buthelezi and a clique of white Natal hardliners who had gathered around him and, on the other, the older *kholwa*-liberal faction of the party.

However, the crucial figure in Natal/KwaZulu during the final run-up to the election was neither Buthelezi, nor his internal opponents, but the Zulu king, who was once again to play a crucial role at a turning point in the region's history.

For years King Goodwill had been content to observe the limits on his authority, pursuing pet projects such as a college which taught agriculture and stockbreeding. Gradually, however, he was emerging from Buthelezi's shadow. He was easily dismissed by outsiders, since he expressed himself poorly in English, although a striking-looking man of fine bearing, whether in traditional or Western dress. Radical blacks heaped scorn on the monarchy, suggesting that it be abolished as a corrupt anachronism. However, even in the late twentieth century, Goodwill was, for a majority of Zulu-speakers, a cornerstone of their secular and sacred identity.

It was not only Zulus who were turning to their traditional leaders. Those who spoke so blithely of abolishing the monarchy might have reflected on the lesson of Uganda, where the socialist government of Milton Obote had deposed the monarch of Buganda, the Kabaka, in 1966. A few years later Obote was overthrown himself by his army commander, Idi Amin and, as in other parts of Africa where ancient systems of government were suppressed, Uganda slipped rapidly into chaos. Finally, in 1993, with

Obote and Amin in exile, a new Kabaka was summoned home from Britain by his people and received with joy and acclamation.

Around the end of 1993, Goodwill was approached by an inner circle of the royal family. For some time a feeling had been growing that Buthelezi's confrontational style had failed to achieve its objectives. Goodwill's view, expressed to me at an interview in 1992, was: 'KwaZulu and Natal are one. No other black race group originated here besides the Zulus.' At the same time, he rejected the idea of a Zulu state independent of South Africa. 'It's useless, we have been together for so many years. We are South Africans, but we are also Zulus in South Africa.'

Historians and academics could argue, and did, that Goodwill's claim to the whole of Natal as Shaka's domain was flawed and that since 1828 the kingdom had been confined to the steadily shrinking band of territory north of the Tugela. But his call for a Zulu right to self-determination – issued at a series of *mbizos* attended by tens of thousands of Zulus in the second half of 1993 – struck a deep chord. In January 1994, with the elections less than three months away, the king sent a memorandum to President de Klerk stating: 'I, the royal household, the *amakhosi* and all who are genuine Zulu subjects, cannot accept that any majority in the rest of South Africa has the right to decide on our future.' That same month, 25,000 Zulus marched on Pretoria in support of the king.

At the climax of this series of demonstrations, Goodwill proclaimed a sovereign Zulu kingdom with Ulundi at its heart. 'We the Zulu nation convene on the battleground which subjugated the freedom of our forefathers. We here today proclaim before the world our freedom and sovereignty, and our unwavering will to defend it at all costs.'

Such talk was music to the ears of the white right, mainly Afrikaners searching for their own independence in a *volkstaat*. From this shared concerned emerged a short-lived marriage of convenience between white and Zulu conservatives, the Freedom Alliance. The far-right dreamed with increasing confidence of an Africaner–Zulu partnership in a new 'liberation struggle'. It was always clear, though, that in the whites' scheme of things it was to be the Zulus who would bear the brunt of any fighting, and that in their own bellies there was more beer than fire.

There were plenty in the ANC who relished the prospect of such a confrontation, especially after street clashes finally brought down the homeland governments of Bophuthatswana and Ciskei. Slovo gloated: 'Two down, one to go.' A few days later, the tempo of violence increased when Inkatha marchers in the streets of Johannesburg were fired upon from ANC headquarters. The police intervened, using live ammunition to break up the demonstration, and dozens of Inkatha supporters were killed. With the election now less than a month away, apocalypse loomed.

Fortunately for South Africa, Mandela was emerging as a leader of greatness. Long before the election it was obvious that the ANC would win, and that – barring the intervention of illness or an assassin's bullet – he would be the country's first black president. It still took magnanimity and vision to write to Goodwill, asking for a meeting 'with your majesty's permission' to discuss his concerns.

Suddenly, sensing an opportunity to influence the king and perhaps draw him away from Buthelezi, the ANC was wooing Goodwill with fervour. Ramaphosa, its chief negotiator, let it be known that the king's status and salary would be guaranteed by an ANC government. The logjam was starting to break up.

Buthelezi had previously demanded a federal system of government which allowed entrenched regional constitutions and local powers of taxation. On this the ANC was immovable, but it was prepared to concede two of his other conditions for participating: recognition of King Goodwill as the constitutional monarch of the territory to be known as Natal/KwaZulu; and a two-ballot election, the first for the constituent assembly and a second, separate vote for regional assemblies. Under pressure now from the king, and seeing the last opportunity for peace and a future role for himself, Buthelezi changed the habit of a lifetime and backed down.

In a flurry of eleventh-hour meetings, a deal was done. The constitutional role of the Zulu monarch was to be written into the draft of principles. Inkatha would participate in the election.

Almost twenty million South Africans cast their ballots between 26 and 29 April. Of those, 4.6 million were in Natal/KwaZulu, where voting had to be extended by a day because of chaos in the initial stages. Among these was Mandela, who chose to cast his vote symbolically at Ohlange Institute, just north of Durban, the college founded in 1901 by John Dube, the ANC's first president.

The election itself was a bizarre combination of miracle and farce.

Nobody who witnessed it could fail to be moved by the drama and dignity of a cathartic ritual which represented the triumph of Everyman. The violence ceased – completely. In areas where, until a few days before, the factions had been fighting, men and women queued peacefully and patiently to vote, often for between six and eight hours. Not so much as a punch was thrown at polling stations from the ANC stronghold of Edendale to the Inkatha domain of Mahlabatini. But, at its heart, the election in Natal/KwaZulu was deeply flawed.

The ANC was assured of victory in all but two of the nine electoral regions – the Western Cape, where the Coloured majority associated more closely with De Klerk's Nationalists, and Natal/KwaZulu. It was nevertheless confident of victory in the latter, where opinion polls gave it a lead over Inkatha of between 52 per cent and 33 per cent. Inkatha's late entry had left it no time for campaigning; it was short of funds; and it had never had the ANC's organizational sophistication. The ANC, moreover, had managed to place activists within the Independent Electoral Commission, the agency responsible for supervising the election and ensuring that it was 'substantially free and fair'.

The commission proved itself hopelessly inept. On the first day of voting polling stations everywhere were missing items of essential equipment, or experienced shortages of ballot forms. Long delays resulted. In Natal/KwaZulu, with so much at stake, what were merely inconveniences elsewhere had more sinister connotations. North of the Tugela, a number of polling stations failed to open at all on the first day: worse was to follow.

Inkatha's late entry meant that stickers with the party's name had to be separately printed and attached to ballot forms which listed the other parties. On the second day of voting, reports came in from dozens of polling stations of ballot forms without Inkatha stickers. Presiding officers were telling voters to simply write Inkatha on the ballot form – or to pick another party. Irregularities at this stage were particularly common at polling stations in ANC-supporting areas. In the south, the ANC admitted that it had systematically bussed voters into Natal from the Transkei and Eastern Cape regions, where Xhosa-speakers were to give the ANC 84 per cent of the vote. By the end of the day, Inkatha officials had denounced the election as a fix, and Buthelezi was demanding a new poll. Hastily, the commission agreed that voting should be extended by a further day in Natal/KwaZulu to make up for the lost first day.

Irregularities that had favoured the ANC in the south were matched, if not exceeded, over the next two days by others that favoured Inkatha in the north. Procedural controls at polling stations in the Zulu heartland were virtually abandoned, so that youngsters clearly not yet of voting age were issued temporary voter cards. Some chiefs were reported to have established polling stations under their own auspices and when ballot boxes from these areas arrived at counting offices they were found to contain neatly stacked piles of Inkatha votes.

In the aftermath of voting, a façade of normality was projected by all sides in an effort to conceal the fact that something had gone badly wrong in Natal/KwaZulu. De Klerk conceded defeat with rare grace and dignity. Mandela acknowledged the international acclaim that greeted his victory. Meanwhile for more than a week ANC and Inkatha officials wrangled with election officials behind closed doors over the validity of dozens of ballot boxes at counting stations in Durban and Empangeni. The outcome was crucial, for it was evident that Inkatha had gained far more votes than the analysts had been predicting – enough to win an overall majority in the Natal/KwaZulu regional assembly, and enough to deny the ANC the two-thirds majority in the national assembly that would empower it to draft a new constitution without reference to other parties. All of a sudden, it was the ANC which was demanding that the Natal/KwaZulu vote be declared invalid.

The precise extent to which voter fraud by Inkatha north of the Tugela, and by the ANC south of it, affected the outcome of the election will never be known. This was a tragedy, for the IEC's failure to administer the vote properly left the result open to further dispute. A formula devised by the IEC for reconciling disputed ballots was accepted by all sides, but it rapidly became an article of faith within the ANC that it had been cheated of victory in the province. In fact, the margin of victory by Inkatha was sufficiently large – 50.3 per cent against the ANC's 32.2 per cent of the vote – for it to claim a legitimate majority.

Whatever the flaws, the result was good for peace. There can be no doubt that conflict on a larger than ever scale would have ensued if Inkatha had been denied its victory in the regional assembly. As it was, the avuncular and conciliatory Frank

Mdlalose, Inkatha's vice-president was sworn in as Natal/Kwa-Zulu's first premier. The prospects for peace were enhanced by Mdlalose's good working relationship with Zuma, who had been the ANC candidate, although the capacity of the belligerent Gwala to cause harm could not be under-estimated.

Inkatha had also gained 10.5 per cent of the vote for the national assembly, winning 43 seats – against 252 for the ANC and 82 for the Nationalists – and ensuring that the federalism debate would remain on the parliamentary agenda. This, too, should be no bad thing: in recent history unitary constitutions have proved poor remedies for divided societies. South Africa has joined India as the last great testing ground for multi-ethnic democracy, and it would do well to learn the lessons of the secessionist movements in Punjab and Kashmir.

Although Inkatha was thus destined for an opposition role, Mandela, in another magnanimous gesture, acknowledged the importance of Buthelezi's role in the battle for democracy and invited him into the cabinet as minister of home affairs. Having insisted all along that he would not serve in a government of national unity, Buthelezi accepted.

Only a future history will be able to answer the question posed by this turning point: whether Zulu nationalism will persist or start to dissolve, to be replaced by something like a spirit of national conciliation and compromise, a process not so much of ethnic submission as ethnic submersion.

The odds are not favourable. Efforts to explain away tribalism as an archaic political phenomenon or, alternatively, as a construction of colonialism, should, as has been said by many commentators, have expired long ago and been laid to rest on the streets of Sarajevo or Kabul. In Africa, it scarcely bears repeating, ethnicity has prevailed in virtually all formal political activity.

According to a recent, comprehensive survey, South Africa has around 8.48 million Zulu-speaking people. (By comparison, Xhosa-speakers number about 6.58 million, north and south Sothos 6.3 million, and Tswanas 3.3 million. There are 5.8 million Afrikaners, and 3.5 million English-speakers.) Probably less than half have any strong connection with the original north Nguni clans from which Shaka fashioned his kingdom. Many would disdain the Zulu royal house. But ethnic identity has a history of flexibility in South Africa and it would be unwise to under-estimate again the capacity of people to mobilize around the symbols and images of Zuluness which appeal to them.

Ethnic diversity has its positive side. People everywhere, confused and distressed by the spread of a stifling uniformity in the technological age, are entitled to seek an identity in what distinguishes them as much as what joins them. The stubborn survival of custom and culture indicates man's desire to resist reductionist pressures in an increasingly complex world. It identifies the individual as part of an enfolding and supportive tribal family.

Equally, it is evident that this yin has a negative yang. As the anthropologist, Harold Isaacs, noted more than a decade ago: 'If tribal separateness and its life-giving qualities are here to stay, so are inter-tribal hostility and its death-dealing consequences.' In an incisive summary of this duality, Isaacs went on:

We are fragmenting and globalizing at the same time. We spin out from a centrifuge, flying apart socially and politically, at the same time that enormous centripetal forces press us into more and more of a single mass every year.

While it would be foolish to ignore the dangers ahead, it would be perverse to regard the future without a sense of hope. Looking back just five years, the distance travelled by the inhabitants of this magnificent, tragic and baffling country, seemingly doomed and yet blessed, redeemed by its perseverence and often unsuspected humanity, defied comprehension.

Just such a sense of hope infuses the words of a young Zulu girl at the Inanda mission who wrote, more than a century ago, an end-of-year essay, regretful over the lost liberty of her people and yet anticipating optimistically the era at which her descendants have now arrived.

We often wonder if the English and Dutch did right to take the country away from us. It was right to help us to be better but it was not right to take our land and give us nothing but English government and taxes. I think they did right a little but much more wrong. If a man from the North Pole should come here, they would say that this land is the land of white people.

By and bye there will be no difference between white and black people.

Bye and bye when the people have learned to read the papers and under-stand the laws, then they will want to become citizens. We may have a Zulu for our magistrate, Zulu teachers, and why should we not have Zulu lawyers as well. Then will come Zulu newspapers and Zulu history.

When I think of all these things it makes me feel as if I had been born a hundred years too soon and that the good times are coming after my time is gone.

GLOSSARY

Zulu orthography is a study in itself and often a source of confusion and inconsistency. I have followed the usages favoured in the James Stuart Archive, which have the virtue of simplicity and are more easily read than some versions – Shaka rather than uTshaka, for example. Similarly, I have dropped the soft vowels sometimes employed at the start of proper names, as in uMzimvubu river or uDloko regiment.

The reader may still have difficulty absorbing Zulu names, which often heap unfamiliar combinations of consonants on top of one another. It may be helpful to read over a difficult name and formulate a personal pronounciation which then becomes a basis for further recognition.

The singular and plural of collective nouns are defined in Zulu by a prefix: thus **sangoma**, the singular for a spirit medium or diviner, becomes **izangoma** in the plural.

The following is a glossary of Zulu words appearing in the text.

giya: war dance
hlobonga: external sexual intercourse
hlonipha: system of respectful speech and behaviour shown by women towards senior males, especially of her husband's line
ibutho (plural **amabutho**): military regiment
ikhanda (plural **amakhanda**): military kraal, similar in concept to a regimental barracks
imbongi: praise-singer, employed to declaim the king's deeds
impi: army, military force
induna (plural **izinduna**): a man of authority, either civic or military
inkatha yezwe: sacred grass coil, symbolising the unity of the Zulu kingdom
isibongo (plural **izibongo**): praise poem
isicoco: fibrous headring worn by mature men
isigodlo: royal enclosure, including the quarters of the women of the king's household
isijula: stabbing gear
izinti: throwing spear
kholwa (plural **amakholwa**): Christian; convert

konza: pledge allegiance
lobola: system of bridal exchange, normally involving cattle
nkosi (plural **amakosi**): king; chief
sangoma (plural **izangoma**): herbalist; doctor
thakathi (plural **abathakathi**): a person possessed by evil; witch
tshwala: maize or sorghum beer
umuzi (plural **imizi**): homestead; kraal
uxoxa impi: to talk of war; to praise heroes

NOTES

The abbreviation JSA refers to the four volumes of the James Stuart Archive of oral testimony mentioned in the bibliography. Each reference includes a volume as well as a page number, e.g. JSA v.1, p.270

PROLOGUE

1 Hamilton, 'The Character and Objects of Chaka', paper presented at the University of Cape Town, May 1991, p.23
2 Thompson, *Travels and Adventures in Southern Africa*, p.248
3 Isaacs, *Travels and Adventures in Eastern Africa*, v.1, p.275
4 Thompson, *Travels*, p.168
5 Martin, S. J. R., British Images of the Zulu, 1820–1879, Ph.D. thesis, Cambridge, 1982, p.90
6 Trollope, *South Africa*, p.228
7 Etherington, *Rider Haggard*, p.72–3

1 TIME OF MOVEMENT

1 Shaka's career has invited comparisons with Alexander, Genghis and Napoleon. The culmination of such portrayals of nation-building are found in two very different works, E. A. Ritter's semi-fictional *Shaka Zulu*, which has reached a wide general readership, and an academic work, *The Zulu Aftermath* by J. D. Omer-Cooper, published in 1966. More recently, however, the trend among South African scholars has been to reduce the extent and impact of the Zulu empire. See the papers by Julian Cobbing cited in the bibliography and 'Shaka and the Modern Zulu State' by Dan Wylie in *History Today*, May 1994. See also Note 1, Chapter Two, and Note 3, Chapter Three, on the *mfecane*
2 Oliver, 'The Problem of the Bantu Expansion', *in* Fage & Oliver, *Papers in African Pre-history*, p.153
3 See Oliver, 'The Emergence of Bantu Africa', *in The Cambridge History of Africa*, v.2; and Oliver & Crowder, *The Cambridge Encyclopedia of Africa*
4 Gluckman, *Analysis*, p.22

5 Hedges, Trade and Politics in Southern Mozambique and Zululand, Ph.D. thesis, p.6
6 Bird, *Annals of Natal*, v.1, p.25
7 Ibid., p.35. See also p. 31: 'The natives are friendly, compassionate, obliging, strong, ingenious.'
8 Gray, p.125
9 Author interviews with Ian Player, 4.12.91
10 See Hedges' thesis, an absorbing exposition on the role of trade in the evolution of political structures in south-east Africa
11 Bird, v.1, p.47
12 The clan regimental system in south-east Africa is often mistakenly attributed to Shaka. See Wright, 'Pre-Shakan age-group formations'

2 SHAKA ZULU

1 The place of Shaka as a theme in literature has been explored in *Shaka: King of the Zulus in African Literature* by Donald Burness, and M. Z. Malaba in a Ph.D. thesis, Shaka as a Literary Theme, Centre for African Studies, University of York, 1986. For Shaka as film hero see Carolyn Hamilton's article 'A Positional Gambit: "Shaka Zulu" and the Conflict in South Africa'
2 The term 'Nguni' has long bothered anthropologists and historians. This summary is based on Stuart's views, outlined in his notes in the Killie Campbell Library. He would seem to have agreed with modern opinion that it cannot be used as an ethnic label and needs to be seen as a flag of convenience. Nguni, he wrote, was 'one of the profoundest and most reverential salutations to the Zulu kings . . . Shaka was the first to appropriate it'. (JSA v2, p97) See also Marks & Atmore, 'The Problem of the Nguni', *in* Dalby, *Language and History in Africa*; and Wright, *Politics, Ideology and the Invention of the 'Nguni'*
3 JSA v.4, p.290–300 has an account of *hlobonga* technique
4 Most of Stuart's sources agree that Senzangakona and Nandi never married, and that Shaka was a bastard: see JSA v.1, p.188; v.1, p.200; v.3, p.199; v.3, p.218; v.3, p.248
5 Accounts of bullying of Shaka are found in JSA v.1, p.16; v.1, p.180; v.1, p.191; v.2, p.107
6 A. T. Bryant (1865–1953), a missionary priest, was the first great researcher into the Zulu past and was long the standard authority. The flaws of his work have been brought to light by modern research but it is unlikely that his masterpiece, *Olden Times in Zululand and Natal*, which is perhaps as great a work of literature as it is of history or anthropology, will ever be surpassed
7 Stuart papers; also JSA v.3, p.15; v.2, p.181
8 JSA v.3, p.198–9
9 JSA v.2, p.187
10 JSA v.1, p.290

11 Shaka's appearance is cited in JSA v.1, p,8; v.1, p.57; v.2, p.232. For his stutter, see v.1, p.195

12 JSA v.1, p.190

13 JSA v.1, p.116

14 JSA v.1, p.181

15 JSA v.1, p.35. In another account of Shaka's military methods, Mayinga ka Mbekuzana recalled: 'Shaka said the old system of hurling assegais was bad; it caused cowardly behaviour. Shaka told the men to carry their shields under their arms and only to bring them out when they got in among the enemy. In the attack they would run in a stooping position and at a great rate.' (JSA v.2, p.247)

16 Bryant, *Olden Times*, p.641

3 SURVIVAL AND CONQUEST

1 Synthesis of JSA v.4, p.205 & p.227

2 Use of the term *'mfecane'* has been the subject of a vigorous academic debate in recent years. Julian Cobbing, of Rhodes University, has argued that the source of instability radiating from south-east Africa at this time was not African political development at all, but a slave trade emanating from Delagoa Bay and the eastern frontier of the Cape. See Cobbing, *The Mfecane as Alibi: Thoughts on Dithakong and Mbolompo*. The debate was comprehensively covered by a conference at the University of the Witwatersrand in September 1991, proceedings of which are to be published in a book, *The Mfecane Aftermath*. However, Cobbing has failed to convince most of his colleagues. See the conference papers by Elizabeth Eldredge, Jeff Peires and John Omer-Cooper

3 JSA v.1, p.182

4 JSA v.1, p.183

5 JSA v.3, p.226. For other accounts of this crucial episode, see JSA v.2, p.180; v.3, p.214

6 JSA v.4, p.3

7 JSA v.2, p.162

8 JSA v.4, p.73–7

9 See Keegan, *A History of Warfare*, especially 'War and the Anthropologists', p.84–94

10 JSA v.1, p.17; v.1, p.102; v.1, p.284; v.2, p.181; v.2, p.209

11 JSA v.1, p.284

12 JSA v.3, p.223. Komfiya was also one of the few people able to stand up to Shaka. Mandhlakazi ka Ngini tells how Komfiya remonstrated with the king when he ordered that two of the Qwabe's brother be put to death: 'Hau Nkosi! Why did I come here to the Zulu country? Why, when the people with whom I came from the Qwabe country are being killed?' Shaka said, 'Sit down Komfiya, you have spoken. Let them go.' (JSA v.2, p.188)

13 The conquest of the Natal clans is described by, among others, Maziyana ka Mahlabeni, in JSA v.2

14 For accounts of cannibalism, see JSA v.3, p.26–7; v.1, p.201; also Bird v.1, p.138

15 JSA v.1, p.287. This source, Lugubu, gives a full account of the Tembu assimilation

16 Evidence of Henry Fynn, Bird, v.1, p.103

17 Stuart & Malcolm, Diary of Henry Fynn, p.10

18 Guy, Destruction of the Zulu Kingdom, p.37

19 JSA v.2, p.55

20 JSA v.3, p.158

21 JSA v.3, p.44

22 JSA v.3, p.80

23 JSA v.2, p.296; See also Hamilton & Wright, The Making of the AmaLala

24 See Hedges, Trade and Politics in Southern Mozambique and Zululand

25 JSA v.2, p.53

26 JSA v.1, p.9

27 JSA v.2, p.54

28 JSA v.3, p.184. For Shaka's use of language as a unifying force, see Mageza ka Kwefunga: 'We [Mthethwa] were laughed at by the Zulus because of our dialect. The Mthethwa would have changed their language for fear of ridicule.' (JSA v.2, p.70)

29 JSA v.3, p.245

30 Isaacs, Travels, v.1, p.91

31 JSA v.1, p.12

32 Gray, p.129

33 Evidence of Henry Fynn, Bird v.1, p.122

34 JSA v.1, p.331

35 JSA v.1, p.287; other accounts of the first Pondo campaign are found in JSA v.2, p.272–4; and JSA v.3, p.217

4 THE MAKERS OF WONDERS

1 JSA v.1, p.291

2 JSA v.2, p.115

3 For the most comprehensive account of the border conflicts and Xhosa resistance see Noel Mostert's Frontiers

4 Fynn is generally a reliable source but his estimates of numbers are often on the high side. This appears to be one such example. See also notes 9 and 19

5 Stuart & Malcolm, p.73

6 Thompson, Travels p.172

7 Stuart & Malcolm, p.55–6

8 Thompson, Travels, p.174

9 Isaacs has been largely discredited as a source on the Zulu kingdom. Fynn's veracity has also been questioned in some quarters but the

publication as recently as 1992 of the papers of Charles Rawden Maclean, only the third white to leave memoirs of Shaka, echo Fynn in many respects and give his more detailed record the ring of overall authenticity despite certain problem areas, such as his account of Nandi's death

10 JSA v.3, p.228
11 JSA v.2, p.162; JSA v.3, p.26
12 Stuart & Malcolm, p.82
13 Gray, p.73
14 Stuart & Malcolm, p.84-5
15 Ibid, p.123-4
16 Ibid, p.126-7
17 Oral sources for this version include JSA v.1, p.8; v.1, p.57; v.1, p.311; v.2, p.22; v.2, p.166; v.2, p.81; and v.3, p.44
18 JSA v.1, p.30
19 Stuart & Malcolm, p.134-5. The earlier admonition about Fynn's tendency to exaggerate numbers should be born in mind.
20 Ibid, p.139

5 THE DEATH OF SHAKA

1 Hamilton, 'The Character and Objects of Chaka', p.18
2 Gray, p.71
3 *Cape Town Gazette & African Advertiser*, 4 June 1825. Quoted by Hamilton, p.12
4 JSA v.2, p.166
5 Stuart & Malcolm, p.142. The idea that Shaka was indeed concerned by the evidence of his aging has been ridiculed by some modern writers, such as Dan Wylie. However JSA v.2, p.251 substantiates Fynn
6 Gray, p.72
7 This account of the mission draws heavily on Robert's *The Zulu Kings*, and Hamilton's paper, 'The Character and Objects of Chaka'
8 Roberts, p.134
9 Ibid., p.139
10 Hamilton, 'The Character and Objects of Chaka', p.18
11 Stuart & Malcolm, p.157
12 JSA v.2, p.295
13 See, for example, JSA v.4, p.200; v.3, p.155
14 Stuart, 'Tshaka: His Life and Reign' – lecture, p.26, Stuart Papers, Killie Campbell Library
15 Evidence of Henry Fynn, Bird v.1, p.67
16 Fuze, p.59

6 THE QUIET ONE

1 JSA v.1, p.167
2 Ibid.
3 JSA v.1, p.6
4 Rycroft & Ngcobo, p.95
5 JSA v.1, p.318
6 Gardiner's *Narrative* contains the best description of Emgungundlovu by a European, but Lunguza better captures the atmosphere of the place in JSA v.1
7 JSA v.1, p.310
8 Stuart & Malcolm, p.164
9 JSA v.1, p.196
10 JSA v.1, p.6
11 JSA v.3, p.36
12 JSA v.3, p.89
13 JSA v.1, p.35
14 Stuart & Malcolm, p.239–243
15 Ibid., p.196
16 JSA v.1, p.58
17 An account of this little-known incident is found in JSA v.1, p.58–9
18 Kirby, p.169
19 see Liesegang, 'Dingane's attack on Lourenco Marques'

7 THE WORD AND THE GUN

1 Kotze, p.21
2 Ibid., p.31–3
3 The destruction of Philip's papers by fire in 1931 has hindered biographical study of this most important and interesting South African. See instead Macmillan's *Bantu, Boer and Briton*, which made use of Philip's papers before they were lost
4 Hedges' thesis illustrates how the trade at Delagoa Bay had advanced by this time
5 Gardiner, p.99
6 JSA v.1, p.308
7 JSA v.1, p.19
8 JSA v.1, p.313
9 JSA v.2, p.201–2
10 Gardiner, p.33–4
11 Stuart & Malcolm, p.240; Gardiner, p.161
12 Kotze, p.97
13 Ibid., p.122
14 Ibid., p.169
15 Ibid., p.156

16 Roberts, p.271
17 Owen diary, Bird, v.1, p.335
18 Roberts, p.279
19 Owen diary, Bird, v.1, p.346
20 JSA v.3, p.258
21 JSA v.3, p.257
22 Roberts, p.287
23 Owen diary, Bird, v.1, p.347
24 Ibid., p.380
25 JSA v.1, p.319
26 See Bird, v.1, p.370, 381, 455
27 Bird, v.1, p.102

8 THE BREAKING OF THE ROPE

 1 Owen diary, Bird v.1, p.354
 2 Kotze, p.241
 3 Bird, v.1, p.393
 4 Bird, v.1, p.435–6
 5 Bird, v.1, p.448
 6 JSA v.1, p.312
 7 Delegorgue, p.110
 8 Bird, v.1, p.517
 9 Bird, v.1, p.496
10 JSA v.2, p.201
11 JSA v.1, p.55
12 See 'Minutes of the Volksraad', Bird, v.1, p.536–544
13 Bird, v.1, p.535
14 Delegorgue, p.99
15 Ibid., p.114
16 Ibid., p.104
17 JSA v.4, p.191
18 Fuze, p.17
19 JSA v.1, p.111
20 JSA v.1, p.247
21 JSA v.1, p.113

9 A WHILE IN ELYSIUM

 1 Fuze, p.98
 2 Walter, p.218
 3 Gluckman, 'The Kingdom of the Zulu', *in African Political Systems*, p.36
 4 Webb, *A Zulu King Speaks*, p.84
 5 JSA v.1, p.31
 6 Delegorgue, p.106

7 JSA v.1, p.189
8 JSA v.4, p.90
9 A full list of Mpande's wives and his children by them is found in JSA v.3, p.103
10 See Berglund, *Zulu Thought-Patterns and Symbolism*
11 Berglund's is an exhaustive study of the Zulu spiritual life, but hard going for the casual reader. Although written more than forty years ago, Eileen Krige's *The Social System of the Zulus* and Bryant's *The Zulu People* remain the classic anthropological studies
12 Bird, v.2, p.146
13 Welsh, *The Roots of Segregation*, p.35
14 Shepstone is yet another major figure of the nineteenth century in South Africa badly in need of a modern biography. While his work has been analysed and dissected (see, for example, Welsh, *The Roots of Segregation*, and Etherington, 'The "Shepstone System"' in Duminy & Guest) the man remains an enigma
15 JSA v.1, p.216
16 Welsh, p.20
17 Morris, p.173
18 Welsh, p.33–5
19 Ibid., p.26

10 TWO BULLS, ONE PEN

1 JSA v.2, p.165
2 JSA v.1, p.49; v.2, p.243; v.4, p.199
3 JSA v.2, p.165
4 JSA v.4, p.77
5 JSA v.2, p.216; v.3, p.291; v.4, p.301; see also Fuze, p.61
6 JSA v.4, p.61
7 JSA v.3, p.292
8 JSA v.2, p.223
9 The best oral account of the battle is found in JSA v.2, p.241
10 JSA v.1, p.75
11 JSA v.4, p.166
12 See Janis, I. L. 'Group Identification under Conditions of Danger', *British Journal of Medical Psychology*, 36, p.227–238
13 For a comparative study of conflict in pre-literature societies, see also 'Warfare and the Anthropologists' in John Keegan's *History of Warfare*
14 JSA v.4, p.62
15 JSA v.4, p.140–1
16 JSA v.3, p.110
17 JSA v.2, p.190
18 Ibid.
19 Mzilikazi's firstborn, Nkulumane, had been killed as a suspected usurper, but after the Ndebele king's death in 1868 rumours gained

currency that the young prince was still alive, living in Natal. Astonishingly, Shepstone got so far as despatching an imposter named Kanda, who was in his employ, to the Ndebele capital to claim the succession. The attempt failed and another prince, Lobengula, was eventually installed

20 Rees, Colenso letters, p.42
21 Duminy & Ballard, *The Anglo-Zulu War*, p.19—20
22 Wallis, *The Northern Goldfields Diaries of Thomas Baines*, v.1, p.48
23 JSA v.3, p.202—3

11 A SOURCE OF PERPETUAL DANGER

1 Duminy & Ballard, p.43
2 Ballard, *The House of Shaka*, p.62—3
3 See Shepstone, 'Report of the Expedition to install Cetshwayo', in the Shepstone papers, Killie Campbell Library
4 Webb & Wright, *A Zulu King Speaks*, p.18
5 Shepstone, 'Report of the Expedition', p.46
6 Ibid., p.15
7 Ibid., p.65
8 Ibid.
9 JSA v.4, p.78; v.4, p.132
10 Ballard, 'The Historical Image of King Cetshwayo', *Natalia* magazine, December 1983, p.33
11 Guy, *The Heretic*, p.91
12 JSA v.1, p.259
13 Guy, *The Heretic*, p.133
14 Ibid., p.212
15 Ibid., p.259
16 Pakenham, *The Scramble for Africa*, p.58
17 Fuze, p.111
18 See 'Problems of Interpretation' by Colin Webb in Duminy & Ballard, p.2—11
19 Guy, *Destruction of the Zulu Kingdom*, p.46—7
20 Duminy & Ballard, p.41
21 Guy, *The Heretic*, p.256
22 Guy, *The Destruction of the Zulu Kingdom*, p.48
23 William Ngidi, Colenso's convert, also heard that the Zulus were likely to win the case: 'The Dutch are beaten, their paper has been lost – it has rotted away.' (Guy, *The Heretic*, p.261)
24 Etherington, *Preachers, Peasants and Politics*, p.75
25 Shepstone, 'Report of the Expedition', p.57
26 See Martin, S. J. R.: British Images of the Zulu, 1820—1879, Ph.D. thesis, Cambridge, 1982
27 Duminy & Ballard, p.63
28 Guy, *Destruction of the Zulu Kingdom*, p.49

29 JSA v.3, p.179
30 JSA v.1, p.167

12 END OF THE BEGINNING

1 Guy, *Destruction of the Zulu Kingdom*, p.50
2 Duminy & Ballard, p.62
3 Webb & Wright, *A Zulu King Speaks*, p.32
4 Accounts of the pre-war rituals are found in JSA v.3, p.296–300 and JSA v.1, p.124
5 JSA v.4, p.188
6 John Laband has carried out the most comprehensive study of the forces on either side. For the British, see *Field Guide to the War in Zululand*; for the Zulus see *Kingdom in Crisis*
7 Laband, *Fight Us in the Open*, p.6
8 The most detailed Zulu accounts of Cetshwayo's army are given by Mpatshana ka Sodondo and Mtshapi ka Noradu in vols 3 and 4 of the James Stuart Archive
9 Webb & Wright, *A Zulu King Speaks*, p.62
10 JSA v.3, p.307
11 JSA v.3, p.306
12 See evidence of Mpatshana and Mtshapi, note 8
13 JSA v.3, p.326
14 Fuze, p.113
15 JSA v.3, p.307
16 Laband & Thompson, p.143
17 JSA v.3, p.307; Laband, *Kingdom in Crisis*, p.85
18 Laband, *Fight Us in the Open*, p.17
19 Ibid.
20 JSA v.3, p.304
21 Webb, 'A Zulu Boy's Recollections of the Zulu War', *Natalia*, December 1978, p.11
22 Laband, *Fight Us in the Open*, p.18
23 For details of purification rituals, see JSA v.3, p.302 and p.318
24 Webb, 'A Zulu Boy's Recollections', p.13
25 Donald Morris's account of the Rorke's Drift engagement in *The Washing of the Spears* remains the best version

13 BEGINNING OF THE END

1 JSA v.3, p.320
2 Based on Laband's *Kingdom in Crisis* and *Field Guide*
3 Vijn, *Cetshwayo's Dutchman*, p.39; Laband, *Kingdom in Crisis*, p.149
4 Laband, *Fight Us in the Open*, p.35
5 Laband, *Kingdom in Crisis*, p.155–157

6 JSA v.3, p.314
7 Laband, *Fight Us in the Open*, p.35
8 Laband & Thompson, *Kingdom and Colony at War*, p.91
9 Ibid., p.94
10 Ibid., p.95
11 Vijn, p.40–1
12 Laband, *Kingdom in Crisis*, p.176
13 Morris, p.464, I have been unable to substantiate this story or take it any further
14 Vijn, p.47
15 Ibid.
16 Laband, *Kingdom in Crisis*, p.194
17 Ibid., p.195
18 Guy, *The Heretic*, p.268
19 Roberts, p.348, citing *Cambridge History of the British Empire* v.8, p.478
20 Laband, *Kingdon in Crisis*, p.196
21 JSA v.4, p.72–3; see also the account in Vijn p.51
22 JSA v.1, p.40; v.4, p.280
23 Morris, p.568
24 Laband, *Fight Us in the Open*, p.43

14 'A SATURNALIA OF WRONGDOING'

1 Guy, *Destruction of the Zulu Kingdom*, p.62
2 Brookes & Webb, p.145
3 Duminy & Ballard, p.138
4 Guy, *Destruction of the Zulu Kingdom*, p.87
5 JSA v.3, p.312
6 Nevertheless, he accepted the role of kinglet happily enough. See Sir Garnet Wolseley and John Dunn, *in* Duminy & Ballard p.120–142
7 Guy, *Destruction of the Zulu Kingdom*, p.80–1
8 Duminy & Ballard, p.129
9 Guy, *Destruction of the Zulu Kingdom*, p.125–131. See also Cetshwayo's letter to Sir Hercules Robinson in *A Zulu King Speaks*, p.45–70
10 Guy, *Destruction of the Zulu Kingdom*, p.126
11 Vijn, p.xiv
12 Webb, 'Great Britain and the Zulu People', *in* Thompson, *African Societies in Southern Africa*, p.311
13 Guy, *The Heretic*, p.298
14 Guy, *Destruction of the Zulu Kingdom*, p.114
15 Ibid., p.125
16 Ibid., p.130
17 Ibid., p.130
18 Ibid., p.129
19 Ibid., p.138
20 Morris, *Heaven's Command*, p.438–9

21 Guy, *Destruction of the Zulu Kingdom*, p.155
22 Ibid., p.154
23 Ibid., p.173
24 Ibid., p.193
25 Ibid., p.66
26 JSA v.1, p.259
27 JSA v.1, p.261
28 Guy, *The Heretic*, p.245
29 Guy, *Destruction of the Zulu Kingdom*, p.202–4
30 C. T. Binns's biography of Cetshwayo's son, Dinuzulu, has an appendix
    on this subject
31 JSA v.2, p.206
32 Webb, 'Great Britain and the Zulu People', p.317. Webb here analyses
    why Britain did not declare a protectorate over Zululand, as it did over,
    for example, Swaziland and Basutoland. At bottom, the visceral
    response of Derby – 'I don't want more niggers' – was probably as
    important as anything
33 Brookes & Webb, p.155

15 THE WANING OF THE PAST

 1 Early missionary activity and the rise of the *kholwa* is described in
    Etherington's *Preachers, Peasants and Politics in South-east Africa, 1835–80*
 2 For white attitudes, see Marks, *Reluctant Rebellion*, p.3–26
 3 Marks, *Reluctant Rebellion*, p.13
 4 JSA v.4, p.208
 5 See Van Onselen, 'The Small Matter of a Horse', *The Life of 'Nongoloza'
    Mathebula 1867–1948*
 6 JSA v.1, p.93
 7 JSA v.3, p.29. Another of Stuart's informants, Solomon Mabaso, offered
    a shrewd summary of industrial capitalism: 'A man is taught to take to
    clothing; this creates for him a certain standard of living up to which
    he, from fear of being ridiculed by others, strives to live. Due to the
    advent of Europeans there is this tendency to spend merely for the sake
    of being like others.' (JSA v.1, p.251)
 8 JSA v.1, p.216
 9 JSA v.1, p.243
10 JSA v.4, p.212
11 JSA v.3, p.155
12 Marks, *Reluctant Rebellion*, p.26
13 For Dinuzulu's life, see C. T. Binns's biography
14 Binns, p.119
15 Duminy & Guest, p.384–6. African marriages conducted under Natal's
    code for *lobola* halved over the three years up to 1899, despite a
    population increase
16 Binns, p.157

17 Duminy & Guest, p.221
18 Marks, *Reluctant Rebellion*, p.121
19 See Marks. James Stuart's account of the rebellion demonstrates that
   he was a better researcher than a writer. Marks's study, by comparison,
   is a model of modern scholarship
20 Marks, *Reluctant Rebellion*, p.208
21 Binns, p.279–81
22 At the outset of the disturbances, Dinuzulu wrote warning the
   authorities of hostility to the poll tax. 'If the government uses force and
   calls on the army, the country will be upset ... People are pained by
   this poll tax and even those who pay do not like it.' (Marks, *Reluctant
   Rebellion*, p.300)

16 CHRISTIANS AWAKE

1 Etherington, *Preachers, Peasants and Politics*, p.68
2 See Duminy & Guest, p.287–8; also Marks, *The Ambiguities of
   Dependence*, p.47
3 Vilakazi, *Zulu Transformations*, p.55
4 *Zulu Transformations*, p.143; see also Welsh, *The Roots of Segregation*,
   p.310
5 JSA v.4, p.14–15. This sceptic, Mqaukana ke Yenge, also told Stuart:
   'We do not understand how [God] communicted his will to the Europeans,
   for we do not see how paper could have come down from the sky'
6 JSA v.3, p.158
7 Welsh, p.71
8 *Preachers, Peasants and Politics*, p.137
9 Among many modern examples is the case of Annah Khanyile, a woman
   in her sixties, who was shot dead in the township of Kwamashu, near
   Durban, on 3 January 1990. Mrs Khanyile had antagonized two of her
   neighbours, who circulated stories that she kept a baboon in her shack, a
   sure sign that she was a *tagati*, or witch. She was paraded before a
   kangaroo court of teenage ANC 'comrades', one of whom, sixteen-year-
   old Dennis Vezi, pulled out a pistol and shot her. He was arrested but
   then freed on bail and absconded
10 Marks, *Reluctant Rebellion*, p.57
11 JSA v.1, p.216
12 Brookes & Webb, p.77
13 Marks, *Reluctant Rebellion*, p.58
14 Welsh, p.217
15 *Cape Illustrated Magazine*, November 1891, reprinted in *Natalia*
16 Pakenham, *The Boer War*, p.567
17 Ibid., p.572
18 Welsh, p.296
19 'The Early Press in Natal', *Natalia*, November 1986

20 See Vilakazi, Shembe, *The Revitalization of African Society*
21 *Zulu Transformations*, p.144

17 ACTIVISTS AND NATIONALISTS

1 Marks, 'Patriotism, Patriarchy and Purity', *in* Vail, p.222
2 Welsh, *The Rise of African Nationalism in South Africa*, p.34
3 Ngubane, *An African Explains Apartheid*, p.71
4 Holland, *The Struggle*, p.40
5 Ngubane, p.73
6 Welsh, p.35. *Nkosi Sikelel'i Afrika* was only adopted as the ANC anthem thirteen years later, in 1925. The first title of the organization known as the ANC was in fact the South African Native National Congress, later amended to African National Congress
7 Welsh, p.44
8 Davenport, *South Africa – A Modern History*, p.406–7
9 For the history of Asian migration see 'Natal's Indians' *in* Duminy & Guest, p.249–270
10 Welsh, p.213
11 Ibid.
12 'The Zulu's Appeal for Light and England's Duty' was a pamphlet by Dube, published in London in 1908, through which he tried to raise funds for Ohlange from philanthropic bodies. As Shula Marks has pointed out, its occasionally subservient tone needs to be seen as an attempt to achieve maximum impact on such groups as the Aborigines Protection Society
13 Swanson, *The Views of Mahlathi*, pxxv
14 Author's interview with Rowley Arenstein, Durban, 15.3.92
15 Bradford, *A Taste of Freedom*, p.92 & 104
16 Ibid., p.195–6
17 Marks, *The Ambiguities of Dependence in South Africa*, p.79
18 Swanson, p.68
19 See Cope, *The Zulu Petit Bourgeoisie* and *Zulu Nationalism in the 1920s*
20 Marks, *Patriotism, Patriarchy and Purity*, p.222. Asked once if he could reconcile the tribal system with progress, the *kholwa* Dube replied: 'Well, it is the only thing we have and I think if it were properly regulated, it would be the best.' (Ibid., p.221)
21 Bradford, p.98
22 Marks, *Patriotism, Patriarchy and Purity*, p.228
23 Cope, *Journal of South African Studies*, September 1990, p.440
24 Gluckman, *Analysis of a Social Situation*, p.35
25 Marks, *Ambiguities*, p.17–18
26 Ibid., p.36
27 Marks, *Patriotism, Patriarchy and Purity*, p.225
28 See, Gluckman, *Analysis*
29 Ibid.

18 'SEPARATENESS'

1 Lutuli, *Let My People Go*, p.170
2 Ibid., p.97
3 By the same token, Lembede espoused a policy of self-help, declaring 'no nation can free an oppressed group other than that group itself'. (Welsh, p.335)
4 Lodge, *Black Politics in South Africa since 1945*
5 See Jonathan Clegg, 'Bringing Back the Body', *in* Bonner, *Working Papers in South African Studies*, v.2. On the same subject, see John Argyle's paper, 'Faction fights, Ethnicity and Political Conflict' in Natal, presented at the University of Natal, September 1992.
6 Author's interview with Arnold Colenbrander, Eshowe, 10.12.91
7 Minnaar, *Conflict and Violence in Natal/KwaZulu*, p.31–34
8 See Clegg, 'Bringing Back the Body'
9 Webster, 'The 1949 Durban "Riots"' presents this episode in 'class' rather than 'ethnic' terms *in* Bonner, *Working Papers*
10 Lodge, p.61
11 Ibid., p.68
12 Ibid., p.115
13 Lutuli, p.46
14 Lodge, p.151
15 Lutuli, p.168
16 Lutuli, p.68 & 122. Lutuli could never bring himself to deny the monarch. 'The authority which he exerts by virtue of his place in the hearts of Zulus is great', he wrote
17 Lodge, p.73
18 *Cape Times*, 28.3.92
19 Meer, *Higher than Hope*, p.169
20 Karis & Gerhart, *From Protest to Challenge*, v.3, p.648
21 Ibid., *Document 65*
22 Author interview with Rowley Arenstein, Durban, 4.3.92
23 Lodge, p.202; see also Lutuli, p.208
24 Karis & Gerhart, v.3, p.649
25 Meer, p.169
26 Karis & Gerhart, v.3, p.799
27 Ibid.
28 Lutuli, p.186
29 Lutuli, p.206

19 BUTHELEZI AND INKATHA

1 Lutuli, p.179
2 Buthelezi won a standing ovation from the students on this occasion and returned to speak at Stellenbosch, a relatively liberal Afrikaans campus,

a number of times. Ten years later he addressed students at the markedly more right-wing Rand Afrikaans University. Increasingly, Buthelezi was to become the black leader with whom most Afrikaners felt they could do business

3 Author interview with Hermann Giliomee, Cape Town, 7.2.92

4 Author interview with Mangosuthu Buthelezi, Ulundi, 6.3.92

5 A good deal, mostly critical, has been written about Buthelezi's political use of Zulu history. Critics pointed to his encouragement of a personality cult, including his own *imbongi*, or praise-singer, and habit of referring to the Zulus' warrior past so as to intimidate opponents. At the same time, it needs to be noted that no research has proved anything false about Buthelezi's pride in the Zulu past. See also note 32.

6 Temkin, *Buthelezi*, p.96

7 Author interview with Arnold Colenbrander, Eshowe, 14.3.92. See also Temkin, *Buthelezi*, p.226-9; and Mzala, *Buthelezi*, p.90-1

8 Interview with Colenbrander, 14.3.92

9 Karis & Gerhart, *From Protest to Challenge*, v.5; publication forthcoming. Buthelezi made a similar request for Mandela's freedom at a meeting with the forbidding John Vorster in January 1975.

10 Author interview with Oscar Dhlomo, Durban, 9.3.92

11 He added: 'There is no Zulu freedom that is distinct from the black man's freedom in South Africa.' (Temkin, p.323-4)

12 In a report to an ANC conference in Zambia in 1985, Tambo acknowledged that Buthelezi had consulted with ANC leaders at each stage of his political career and that 'we agreed that [mass mobilization] would necessitate the formation of a mass democratic organisation . . . Inkatha originated from this agreement.' Tambo went on to say that Buthelezi had 'then built Inkatha as a personal power base far removed from the kind of organization we had visualized'.

13 Karis & Gerhart, v.5, forthcoming

14 *Frontline* magazine, September 1985

15 Inkatha naturally stood to benefit from the repeated assertions of association with the ANC, whose officials were infuriated by Buthelezi's patronising reference to 'the exiled wing' of the ANC

16 Karis & Gerhart, v.5, forthcoming

17 Interview with Colenbrander, 14.3.92

18 Mzala, p.124

19 *Independent on Sunday* magazine, 14.10.90

20 Karis & Gerhart, v.5, forthcoming

21 Interview with Arenstein, 15.3.92

22 Karis & Gerhart, vo.5, forthcoming

23 Interview with Dhlomo, 9.3.92

24 Karis & Gerhart, v.5, forthcoming

25 Shepherd Smith, *Buthelezi*, p.115

26 Author interview with Paulus Zulu, Durban, 5.3.92

27 See summary of inaugural meeting, Shepherd Smith, p.212

28 Shepherd Smith, p.210

NOTES

29 Author interview with Bishop Mogoba, Durban, 10.3.92
30 *Leadership* magazine; Author interview, Durban, 7.8.91
31 The so-called 'Inkathagate' revelations were made principally in the *Weekly Mail* newspaper. See especially, v.7, nos 28, 29, 49, and v.8, nos 2 & 4
32 Because of Buthelezi's open expression of his own Zuluness, even the terms 'tradition' and 'culture' became sticks with which to beat him. This would be less noteworthy were it not for the deferential way that the culture of indigenous peoples is usually treated by Western academics
33 Author interview with Harriet Ngubane, Cape Town, 10.2.92

BIBLIOGRAPHY

Killie Campbell Africana Library:
  H. C. Lugg papers
  Theophilus Shepstone papers
  James Stuart papers

PUBLISHED SOURCES

Ashe, W. A. & Wyatt Edgell, E. V.: *The Story of the Zulu Campaign* – London, 1880.

Ballard, Charles: *John Dunn, the White Chief of Zululand* – A. D. Donker, Johannesburg, 1985.

Ballard, Charles: *The House of Shaka* – Emoyeni Books, Durban 1988.

Berglund, Axel-Ivar: *Zulu Thought-Patterns and Symbolism* – C. Hurst & Co, London, 1989.

Binns, C. T.: *Dinuzulu, The Death of the House of Shaka* – Longmans, Green and Co, London, 1968.

Bird, John,: *The Annals of Natal, 1495–1845* – Reprint of the first edition by C. Struik, Cape Town, 1965.

Braatvedt, H. P.: *Roaming Zululand With a Native Commissioner* – Shuter & Shooter, Pietermaritzburg, 1949.

Bradford, Helen: *A Taste of Freedom, the ICU in Rural South Africa 1924–30* – Ravan, Johannesburg, 1988.

Brookes, E. H. & Webb, C. de B.: *A History of Natal* – Univeristy of Natal Press, 1987.

Bryant, A. T.: *Olden Times in Zululand and Natal* – Longmans, London, 1929.

Bryant, A. T.: *The Zulu People, as they were before the white man came* – Shuter & Shooter, Pietermaritzburg, 1967.

Buhrmann, M. Vera: *Living in Two Worlds* – Human & Rousseau, Cape Town, 1984.

Bulpin, T. V.: *Natal and the Zulu Country* – Books of Africa, Cape Town, 1966.

Burness, Donald (ed): *Shaka, King of the Zulus in African Literature* – Three Continents Press, Washington, 1976.

Clegg, Jonathan: '*Ukubuyia Isidumbu*' – 'Bringing Back the Body', *in* Bonner,

Philip. (ed): 'Working Papers in South African Studies', v.2 – Ravan, Johannesburg, 1981.

Cope, Jack & Krige, Uys: *The Penguin Book of South African Verse* – Penguin Books, Harmondsworth, 1968.

Curtin, Philip: *The Image of Africa* – University of Wisconsin Press, 1964.

Davenport, T. R. H.: *South Africa, A Modern History* – Macmillan, London, 1991.

De Kock, W. J. & Beyers, C. J. (eds): *Dictionary of South African Biography* (five volumes) – Human Sciences Resource Council, Pretoria, 1968–1987.

Delegorgue, Adulphe: *Travles in Southern Africa, Volume 1* – translated by Fleur Webb from the French, University of Natal Press, 1990.

Duminy, Andrew & Ballard, Charles (eds): *The Anglo-Zulu War, New Perspectives* – University of Natal Press, 1981.

Duminy, Andrew & Guest, Bill (eds): *Natal and Zululand, From Earliest Times to 1910* – University of Natal Press, 1989.

Du Plessis, J.: *A History of Christian Missions in South Africa* – Longmans, Green and Co, London, 1911.

Etherington, Norman: *Preachers, Peasants and Politics in South-east Africa, 1835–80,* 'African Christian communities in Natal, Pondoland and Zululand' – Royal Historical Society, London, 1978.

Etherington, Norman: *Rider Haggard* – Twayne Publishers, Boston, 1984.

Fage, J. D. & Oliver, Roland (eds): *Cambridge History of Africa, v.2* – Cambridge University Press, 1982.

Filter, H. and Bourquin, S.: *Paula Dlamini, Servant of Two Kings* – University of Natal Press, 1986.

Fuze, Magema M.: *The Black People, And Whence They Came* – University of Natal Press, 1986.

Gardiner, A. F.: *Narrative of a Journey to the Zoolu Country in South Africa* – Reprint of the 1836 edition by C. Struik, Cape Town 1966.

Gray, Stephen (ed.): *The Natal Papers of 'John Ross', Charles Rawden Maclean* – Universty of Natal Press, 1992.

Gluckman, Max: *Analysis of a Social Situation in Modern Zululand* – Manchester University Press, 1971.

Gluckman, Max: 'The Kingdom of the Zulu in South Africa', *in* Fortes, M. & Evans-Pritchard, E. E. (eds.): *African Political Systems,* Oxford University Press, 1940.

Guy, Jeff: *The Destruction of the Zulu Kingdom, the Civil War in Zululand, 1879–1884* – Longman, London, 1979.

Guy, Jeff: *The Heretic, the Life of John William Colenso 1814–1883* – Ravan, Johannesburg, 1983.

Holland, Heidi: *The Struggle, a History of the ANC* – Grafton, London, 1989.

Horowitz, Donald, L.: *A Democratic South Africa? Constitutional Engineering in a Divided Society* – Oxford University Press, 1991.

Isaacs, Nathaniel: *Travels and Adventure in Eastern Africa* – Reprint of 1836 edition by Van Riebeeck Society, Cape Town, 1936.

Karis, Thomas & Gerhart, Gail (eds.): *From Protest to Challenge, a Documentary*

History of African Politics in South Africa, vols 3 & 4 – Hoover Institution Press, Stanford, 1977.

Karis, Thomas & Gerhart, Gail (eds.): *From Protest to Challenge*, v.5 – forthcoming from Oxford University Press, 1995.

Keegan, John: *A History of Warfare* – Hutchinson, London, 1993.

Kirby, Percival: *Andrew Smith and Natal* – Van Riebeeck Society, Cape Town, 1955.

Kotze, D. J. (ed.): *Letters of the American Missionaries* – Van Riebeeck Society, Cape Town, 1950.

Krige, Eileen Jensen: *The Social System of the Zulus* – Seventh Impression, Shuter & Shooter, Pietermaritzburg, 1977.

Laband, John: *Kingdom in Crisis, the Zulu response to the British invasion of 1879* – University of Natal Press, 1992.

Laband, John: *Fight Us in the Open, the Anglo-Zulu war through Zulu eyes* – Shuter & Shooter, Pietermaritzburg, 1985.

Laband, John & Thompson, Paul: *Kingdom and Colony at War* – University of Natal Press, 1990.

Laband, John & Thompson, Paul: *Field Guide to the War in Zululand* – University of Natal, 1983.

Lodge, Tom: *Black Politics in South Africa since 1945* – Longman, London, 1983.

Luthuli, Albert: *Let My People Go* – Fontana, Glasgow, 1987.

Mackeurtan, Graham: *The Cradle Days of Natal* – Shuter & Shooter, Pietermaritzburg, 1948.

Macmillan, W. M.: *Bantu, Boer and Briton, the Making of the South African Native Problem* – Faber & Faber, London, 1929.

Mare, Gerhard, & Hamilton, Georgina: *An Appetite for Power, Buthelezi's Inkatha and the Politics of Loyal Resistance* – Rava, Johannesburg, 1987.

Marks, Shula: *Reluctant Rebellion, the 1906–9 Disturbances in Natal* – Clarendon Press, Oxford, 1970.

Marks, Shula: *The Ambiguities of Dependence in South Africa* – Ravan, Johannesburg, 1986.

Marks, Shula: 'The Traditions of the Natal "Nguni": a second look at the work of A. T. Bryant', *in* Thompson, L.: *African Societies in South Africa* – Heinemann, London, 1969.

Marks, Shula: 'Patriotism, Patriarchy and Purity: Natal and the Politics of Zulu Ethnic Consciousness', *in* Vail, Leroy (ed): *The Creation of Tribalism in Southern Africa* – James Currey, London, 1989.

Marks, Shula & Atmore, Anthony: 'The Problem of the Nguni', *in* Dalby, David (ed.): *Language and History in Africa* – Frank Cass, London, 1970.

Meer, Fatima: *Higher than Hope, the Authorised Biography of Nelson Mandela* – Penguin, London, 1990.

Minaar, A. de V.: *Conflict and Violence in Natal/KwaZulu, Historical Perspectives* – Human Scienes Research Council, Pretoria, 1991.

Mitford, Bertram: *Through the Zulu Country* – Kegan Paul, Trench & Co, London, 1883.

Morris, Donald R.: *The Washing of the Spears* – Sphere, London, 1990.

Morris, Jan: *Heaven's Command* – Penguin, London, 1979.

Mostert, Noel: *Frontiers* – Jonathan Cape, London, 1992.

Mzala: Gatsha Buthelezi, *Chief With a Double Agenda* – Zed Books, London, 1988.

Ngubane, Jordan: *An African Explains Apartheid* – Pall Mall Press, London, 1963.

Nyembezi, C. L. S.: *Zulu Proverbs* – Witwatersrand University Press, 1974.

Oliver, Roland: 'The Problem of the Bantu Expansion', *in* Fage, J. D. & Oliver, (eds): *Papers in African Prehistory* – Cambridge University Press, 1970.

Oliver, Roland & Fagan, Brian: 'Africa in the Iron Age' – Cambridge University Press, 1975.

Oliver, Roland & Crowder, Michael (eds): *The Cambridge Encyclopedia of Africa* – Cambridge University Press, 1981.

Omer-Copper, J. D.: *The Zulu Aftermath* – Longmans, London, 1966.

Pakenham, Thomas: *The Scramble for Africa* – Abacus, London, 1992.

Pakenham, Thomas: *The Boer War* – Jonathan Ball Publishers, Johannesburg, 1979.

Peires, J. B. (ed): *Before and After Shaka* – Rhodes University, Grahamstown, 1981.

Rasmussen, R. Kent: *Migrant Kingdom, Mzilikazi's Ndebele in South Africa* – Rex Collings, London, 1978.

Rees, Wyn (ed): *Colenso, letters from Natal* – Shuter & Shooter, Pietermaritzburg, 1958.

Ritter, E. A.: *Shaka Zulu* – Longmans, London, 1955.

Rive, Richard and Couzens, Tim: *Seme, the Founder of the ANC* – Skotaville, Johannesburg, 1991.

Roberts, Brian: *The Zulu Kings* – Book Club Edition, London, 1974.

Rycroft, D. K. and Ngcobo, A. B.: *The Praises of Dingana* – University of Natal Press, 1988.

Saunders, Christopher (ed): *Black Leaders in Southern African History* – Heinemann, London, 1979.

Schapera, I. (ed): *The Bantu-Speaking Tribes of South Africa* – Maskew Miller, Cape Town, 1937.

Selby, John: *Shaka's Heirs* – George Allen & Unwin, London, 1971.

Shepherd Smith, Jack: *Buthelezi* – Hans Strydom, Johannesburg, 1988.

Sparks, Allister: *The Mind of South Africa* – Mandarin, London, 1990.

Stuart, James & Malcolm, D. McK. (eds): *The Diary of Henry Francis Fynn* – Shuter & Shooter, Pietermaritzburg, 1950.

Summers, R. & Pagden, C. W.: *The Warriors* – Books of Africa, Cape Town, 1970.

Swanson, M. W. (ed.): *The Views of Mahlathi, Writings of A. W. G. Champion* – University of Natal Press, 1982.

Tabler, Edward C.: *Pioneers of Natal and south-eastern Africa* – A. A. Balkema, Cape Town, 1977.

Temkin, Ben: *Gatsha Buthelezi, Zulu Statesman* – Purnell and Sons, Cape Town, 1976.

Thompson, George: *Travels and Adventures in Southern Africa* – Reprint of 1827 edition by Van Riebeeck Society, Cape Town, 1967.

Trollope Anthony: *South Africa* – Reprint of 1878 edition by A. A. Balkema, Cape Town, 1973.

Van Onselen, Charles: *Studies in the Social and Economic History of the Witwatersrand 1886–1914*, v.1. New Babylon – Ravan, Johannesburg, 1982.

Van Onselen, Charles: *The Small Matter of a Horse, The Life of Nongoloza' Mathebula, 1867–1948* – Ravan, Johannesburg, 1984.

Vijn, Cornelius: *Cetshwayo's Dutchman, the Journal of a White Trader in Zululand During the British Invasion* – reprint of 1880 edition by Greenhill Books, London, 1988.

Vilakazi, Absolom: *Zulu Transformations* – Universty of Natal Press, 1962.

Vilakazi, Absolom (with Bongani Mthethwa and Mthembeni Mpanza): Shembe, *The Revitalization of African Society* – Skotaville Publishers, Johannesburg, 1986.

Walker, Eric A.: *A History of Southern Africa* – Longmans, Green and Co, London, 1957.

Wallis, J. P. R.: *Thomas Baines of King's Lynn, Explorer and Artist 1820–1875* – Jonathan Cape, London, 1941.

Wallis, J. P. R. (ed): *The Northern Goldfields Diaries of Thomas Baines* (three volumes) – Chatto & Windus, London, 1946.

Walshe, Peter: *The Rise of African Nationalism in South Africa, the ANC 1912–1952* – A. Donker, Johannesburg, 1987.

Walter, E. V.: *Terror and Resistance, a Study of Political Violence* – Oxford University Press, 1969.

Webb, C: 'Great Britain and the Zulu People 1879–1887', *in* Thompson, Leonard (ed): *'African Societies in Southern Africa'* – Heinemann, London, 1969.

Webb, C. de B & Wright (eds): *A Zulu King Speaks* – University of Natal Press, 1987.

Webb, C. de B. & Wright, John (eds): The James Stuart Archive of recorded oral evidence relating to the history of the Zulu and neighbouring peoples (four volumes) – University of Natal Press, 1979–1987.

Webster, Eddie: 'Durban "Riots"' *in* Bonner, P.: Working Papers in South African Studies – University of the Witwatersrand, 1977.

Welsh, D.: *The Roots of Segregation, native policy in Natal, 1845–1910* – Oxford University Press, 1971.

Wright, John: 'Politics, Ideology and the Invention of the "Nguni"', *in* Lodge, Tom (ed): *Resistance and Ideology in Settler Societies* – Ravan, Johannesburg, 1986.

THESES

Hedges, D. W.: Trade and Politics in Southern Mozambique and Zululand
in the 18th and 19th centuries – Ph.D. thesis, London, 1978.
Martin, S. J. R.: British Images of the Zulu, 1820–1879 – Ph.D. thesis,
Cambridge, 1982

ARTICLES AND PAPERS

Aitchison John: 'Interpreting Violence: the Struggle to Understand the Natal
Conflict' – paper presented at the Institute of Commonwealth Studies,
October 1990.
Argyle, John: 'Faction fights, Ethnicity and Political Conflict in Natal' –
paper presented at the University of Natal, September 1992.
Ballard, Charles: 'The Historical Image of King Cetshwayo' – *Natalia*
magazine, December 1983.
Cobbing, Julian: 'The Mfecane as Alibi: Thoughts on Dithakong and
Mbolompo' – *Journal of African History*, v.29, 1988.
Cobbing, Julian: 'A Tainted Well: the Objectives, Historical Fantasies, and
Working Methods of James Stuart, with Counter-Argument' – *Journal of
Natal and Zulu History*, XI, 1988.
Cope, Nicholas: 'The Zulu Petit Bourgeoisie and Zulu Nationalism in the
1920s' – *Journal of South African Studies*, September 1990.
Golan, Daphna: 'Inkatha and its Use of the Zulu Past' – *History in Africa*,
18, 1991.
Hamilton, Carolyn: 'The Character and Objects of Chaka' – paper presented
at the University of Cape Town, May 1991.
Hamilton, Carolyn: 'An Appetite for the Past: The Recreation of Shaka' –
South African Historical Journal, 22, 1990.
Hamilton, Carolyn: 'A Positional Gambit: "Shaka Zulu" and the Conflict in
South Africa' – *Radical History Review*, 44, 1989.
Hamilton, Carolyn & Wright, John: 'The Making of the AmaLala' – *South
African Historical Journal*, 22, 1990.
Liesegang, Gerhard: 'Dingane's Attack on Lourenco Marques in 1833' –
Journal of African History, X, 1969.
Lodge, Tom: 'Charters From the Past: The ANC and its Historiographical
Traditions' – *Radical History Review*.
Macmillan, Hugh: 'Max Gluckman, the Zulu Nation and the Common
Society' – paper presented at the University of Natal, September 1992.
Maphalala, Simon: 'The Black Man's Interpretation of South African
History' – paper presented at Stellenbosch University, October 1981.
Okoye, Felix: 'Dingane, a Reappraisal' – *Journal of African History*, X, 1969.
Webb, Colin (ed.): 'A Zulu Boy's Recollections of the Zulu War' – *Natalia*,
December 1978.

Wright, John: 'Political Mythology and the Making of Natal's *Mfecane'* – *Canadian Journal of African Studies*, v.23, 1989.

Wright, John: 'Pre-Shakan age-group formation among the north Nguni' – *Natalia*.

Wright, John: 'A. T. Bryant and "the Wars of Shaka"' – *History in Africa*, 18, 1991.

INDEX